Financial Inclusion, Regulation, Literacy, and Education in Central Asia and South Caucasus

Edited by
Peter J. Morgan and Yan Zhang

ASIAN DEVELOPMENT BANK INSTITUTE

© 2019 Asian Development Bank Institute

All rights reserved. First printed in 2019.

ISBN 9784899741053 (Print)
ISBN 9784899741060 (PDF)

The views in this publication do not necessarily reflect the views and policies of the Asian Development Bank Institute (ADBI), its Advisory Council, ADB's Board or Governors, or the governments of ADB members.

ADBI does not guarantee the accuracy of the data included in this publication and accepts no responsibility for any consequence of their use. ADBI uses proper ADB member names and abbreviations throughout and any variation or inaccuracy, including in citations and references, should be read as referring to the correct name.

By making any designation of or reference to a particular territory or geographic area, or by using the term "recognize," "country," or other geographical names in this publication, ADBI does not intend to make any judgments as to the legal or other status of any territory or area.

Users are restricted from reselling, redistributing, or creating derivative works without the express, written consent of ADBI.

ADB recognizes "China" as the People's Republic of China.

Note: In this publication, "$" refers to US dollars.

Asian Development Bank Institute
Kasumigaseki Building 8F
3-2-5, Kasumigaseki, Chiyoda-ku
Tokyo 100-6008, Japan
www.adbi.org

Contents

Tables and Figures	iv
List of Contributors	viii
Preface	x
Abbreviations	xiii

1. **Overview of Financial Inclusion, Regulation, Financial Literacy, and Education in Central Asia and South Caucasus**
   Peter Morgan, Yan Zhang, and Dossym Kydyrbayev — 1

2. **Armenia**
   Armen Nurbekyan and Naneh Hovanessian — 46

3. **Azerbaijan**
   Gubad Ibadoghlu — 85

4. **Georgia**
   Yaroslava Babych, Maya Grigolia, and Davit Keshelava — 126

5. **Kazakhstan**
   Kassymkhan Kapparov — 166

6. **Kyrgyz Republic**
   Savia Hasanova — 187

7. **Tajikistan**
   Roman Mogilevskii and Shokhboz Asadov — 225

8. **Uzbekistan**
   Muzaffarjon Ahunov — 257

Index — 287

Tables and Figures

Tables

1.1	Main Financial Inclusion Indicators for Central Asia and South Caucasus Countries	6
1.2	Elements of Financial Inclusion Strategies	14
1.3	Outstanding Loans by Type of Financial Institution, 2016	15
1.4	Regulatory Frameworks for Financial Inclusion in Central Asia and South Caucasus Economies	20
1.5	Strategies and Programs for Financial Inclusion	27
1.6	Financial Education Programs and Strategies	34
2.1	The Difference Between Universal Credit Organizations, Credit Unions, and Refinancing Credit Organizations	51
2.2	Financial Sector Participants	52
2.3	Global Findex Indicators for Armenia	55
2.4	Channels of Money Transfers	59
2.5	Accounts, Terminals, and Transactions	59
2.6	Difference in Prudential Measures Between Banks and Credit Organizations	63
2.7	Policies Promoting Financial Inclusion in Armenia	66
2.8	Assistance Programs for Small and Medium-Sized Enterprises	69
2.9	Results of Organisation for Economic Co-operation and Development Financial Literacy Survey	71
2.10	Quantitative Goals of the National Strategy for Financial Education of Armenia	74
2.11	Financial Literacy Projects	76
3.1	Summary Banking Sector Statistics	88
3.2	Summary Microfinance Sector Statistics	90
3.3	Account Penetration	91
3.4	Measures of Financial Inclusion and Development across Economies	92
3.5	The Structure of Loans to the Economy by Type of Credit Institution (End of Period)	95
3.6	Formal Saving and Formal Borrowing	96
3.7	Transactions through Interbank Payment Systems	100
3.8	Regional Comparison of Different Financial Literacy Scores	114
4.1	Select Financial Inclusion Indicators for Georgia, 2017	140
4.2	Enterprise Survey for Georgia, 2013	144
5.1	Overview of the Banking Sector in Kazakhstan	168
5.2	Number of Commercial Bank Branches by Region in Kazakhstan	169

5.3	Accounts in Formal Financial Institutions in Kazakhstan	172
5.4	Financial Inclusion Indicators in Kazakhstan	174
6.1	Status of Financial Inclusion	197
6.2	Selected Indicators of Financial Inclusion in the Kyrgyz Republic, Global Findex	197
6.3	Penetration of Bank Services	199
6.4	Index of Trust for Government Financial Institutions	204
6.5	Regulation of Financial Consumers' Rights	208
6.6	Coverage of State Support	214
6.7	Basic Results of the Survey on Financial Literacy	215
7.1	Financial Inclusion Indicators, 2017	234
7.2	Use of Mobile Payment Services	239
8.1	Banking Sector Deposits	259
8.2	Uzbekistan's Banking System Ownership and Concentration	259
8.3	Key Performance Indicators of Commercial Banks in Uzbekistan	261
8.4	Geographic Outreach of Financial Institutions in Uzbekistan	263
8.5	Banking Outreach and Use in the Regions of Uzbekistan	264
8.6	Credit Information Sharing	265
8.7	Bank Card, Internet, and Mobile Banking Use in Uzbekistan	267
8.8	Major Events in the Development of Electronic Payment Systems	267
8.9	Formal Account Ownership at a Financial Institution	268
8.10	Debit Card Ownership	269
8.11	Borrowing Behavior in Uzbekistan	270
8.12	Saving Behavior in Uzbekistan	270
8.13	Financial Inclusion Indicators for Small, Medium, and Large Enterprises in Uzbekistan	272
8.14	Major Reasons for Not Using Formal Financial Services and Reasons for Having No Bank Account	274
8.15	Top Reasons for Not Using Bank Loans/Lines of Credit	276
8.16	Who Makes the Decisions about the Savings, Investment, and Borrowing in Your Household?	281

Figures

1.1	Bank Branch Penetration per 100,000 Adults	8
1.2	Relation of per Capita Gross Domestic Product to Formal Account Penetration for Adults, 2017	9
1.3	Relationship between per Capita Gross Domestic Product and Loan Penetration for Adults, 2017	10
1.4	Share of Small Firms with a Bank Loan or Credit Line, 2013	10
1.5	Ratio of Life Insurance Premium Volume to Gross Domestic Product	11

1.6	Ratio of Non-Life Insurance Premium Volume to Gross Domestic Product	12
2.1	Asset Allocation in the Armenian Financial System (2016)	48
2.2	Credit and Deposits as a Percentage of GDP	49
2.3	Assets of the Banking Sector in Armenia	49
2.4	Assets of the Credit Organizations in Armenia	50
2.5	Assets of Insurance Companies in Armenia	51
2.6	Bank Branch Density in Armenia	53
2.7	ATM Density in Armenia	54
2.8	ATM Density for Rural and Urban Areas	54
2.9	Deposit Account Penetration per 1,000 Adults	55
2.10	Credit Penetration per 1,000 Adults	56
2.11	Number of Mortgage Loans per 1,000 Adults	56
2.12	Penetration of Banking Cards	57
2.13	Number of Insurance Contracts per 1,000 Adults	58
2.14	Access to Finance for Small and Medium-Sized Enterprises	60
2.15	Amount of Guaranteed Deposits in Armenia	65
3.1	Product and Service Offering Nonbank Credit Institutions	89
3.2	Sectoral Breakdown of Loans in 2016	95
3.3	Use of Banks, Microfinance Institutions, and Other Nonbank Credit Institutions by Income Quartile	97
3.4	Overview of Financial Product Awareness by Financial Institutions	115
4.1	Share of Financial Sector Assets Controlled by Different Financial Organizations in Georgia	128
4.2	Outstanding Deposits with Commercial Banks, (Total, Household, Small and Medium-Sized Enterprises)	130
4.3	Household Loans as a Share of Total Commercial Bank Loans	131
4.4	Domestic Credit to the Private Sector in the South Caucasus Countries	132
4.5	Branches of Commercial Banks per 100,000 Adults in the South Caucasus	138
4.6	Number of ATMs per 100,000 Adults in the South Caucasus Countries	139
4.7	Getting Credit—Distance from the Frontier in the South Caucasus Countries	141
4.8	Borrowers from Commercial Banks per 1,000 Adults	142
4.9	Household Debt Service—Principal Payments to Income Ratio	142
4.10	Market Real Interest Rates on Loans in National Currency, by Category	145
4.11	Attitudes toward Expenditure	155

4.12	Trust in the Banking System	156
4.13	Taking Care of Life in Retirement	157
6.1	Commercial Banks' Loans and Deposits	190
6.2	Structure of Credit Portfolio	192
6.3	Role of Microfinance Institutions	193
6.4	Use of Financial Products by Households	198
6.5	Development of Small and Medium-Sized Enterprises	201
6.6	Poverty and Remittances	202
6.7	What Would You Do if Your Income Suddenly Declined? % of Respondents' Answers	216
6.8	Scheme of the Program to Improve Financial Literacy	218
7.1	Gross Domestic Product Structure by Sector, 2016	226
7.2	Deposits	228
7.3	Loans	228
7.4	Loan Structure by Performing and Nonperforming Status, End of 2016	229
7.5	Number of Clients in Different Financial Institutions	230
7.6	Number of Banking Cards by System	231
7.7	Number and Volume of Transactions via Payment Cards	232
7.8	Development of Card Infrastructure	232
7.9	Banking and Microfinance Penetration Indicators	236
7.10	Currency Structure of Banking Accounts	236
7.11	Actual and Potential Use of Mobile Banking Services	240
7.12	Minimum Capital Requirements for Microfinance Organizations	244
8.1	Banking Sector Credit to Gross Domestic Product Ratio in Transition Economies in 2016	258
8.2	Domestic Credit and Gross Domestic Product per Capita	262
8.3	Weighted Average Interest Rates on Loans as of May 2018	276
8.4	Official and Black Market Exchange Rates (Sum/$)	278
8.5	Financially Literate Adult Population in Transition Economies	280

List of Contributors

Muzaffarjon Ahunov is an assistant professor at Endicott College of International Studies, Woosong University, Republic of Korea.

Shokhboz Asadov is a senior research fellow, Institute of Public Policy and Administration, University of Central Asia, Tajikistan.

Yaroslava Babych is an assistant professor of economics at the International School of Economics, Tbilisi State University (ISET), Georgia.

Maya Grigolia is an instructor of statistics at the College of Engineering and Technology, American University of the Middle East, Kuwait.

Savia Hasanova is an economic expert at the Public Association "Investment Round Table", Kyrgyz Republic.

Naneh Hovanessian is an economist at the Central Bank of Armenia, Yerevan.

Gubad Ibadoghlu is a senior policy analyst at the Economic Research Center, Baku, Azerbaijan.

Kassymkhan Kapparov is the managing partner at the Economics and Management Consulting Group, Kazakhstan.

Davit Keshelava is a researcher at the ISET Policy Institute (ISET-PI), Georgia.

Dossym Kydyrbayev is a managing partner at the Rakurs Consulting Group, Kazakhstan.

Roman Mogilevskii is an associate director and senior research fellow at the Institute of Public Policy and Administration, University of Central Asia, Kyrgyz Republic.

Peter J. Morgan is a senior consulting economist and vice chair of research at the Asian Development Bank Institute, Japan.

Armen Nurbekyan is head of the Economic Research Department, Central Bank of Armenia, Yerevan, Armenia.

Yan Zhang is a project consultant at the Asian Development Bank Institute, Japan.

Preface

Inclusive growth has recently become an important policy goal, and has been recognized as such in global forums such as the Group of Twenty. Governments, development institutions, and economists are promoting a broad agenda of inclusion in economic and social life, including universal access to education, health care, social security, clean water, and sanitation. Financial inclusion has also come to be viewed as an important part of this agenda for inclusion. This reflects the view that individuals, households, and firms cannot fully take advantage of available opportunities for economic and social development if they do not have adequate and appropriate access to financial products and services. Nonetheless, many economies in the Central Asia and South Caucasus (CASC) region still have relatively low rates of financial access, especially in rural areas.

Financial inclusion has come to refer to, not just any form of financial access, but access to financial products and services that is convenient, affordable (taking into account the relevant costs and risks), appropriate for the circumstances of the users, and accompanied by legal and supervisory safeguards, including consumer protection, deposit insurance, and regulatory and supervisory frameworks. Moreover, it is becoming increasingly recognized that consumers of financial products and services need to have adequate levels of financial literacy to make informed choices about important financial decisions. This is particularly important, because, as a result of pressure on fiscal resources and the aging of many populations, the responsibility for long-term financial planning is shifting increasingly from governments to households.

In general, the progress of financial inclusion and financial development in the economies in the CASC region has lagged behind that of other Asian economies, partly due to the disruptions and instabilities following the breakup of the Soviet Union in 1991. After gaining independence from the Soviet Union, many CASC countries have experienced similar economic circumstances. People lacked trust in financial institutions and were not ready to go through difficult procedures to use their services. Moreover, a number of financial crises challenged CASC countries and their banking sectors. The global financial crisis had a spillover effect on all seven CASC countries, and the subsequent fall in oil prices had negative shocks on the oil-exporting economies, leading to sharp currency devaluations. Policies aimed at promoting financial inclusion and financial literacy generally have not been pursued as actively in the CASC region as in other Asian regions.

This book focuses on the nexus of financial inclusion, financial regulation, financial literacy, and financial education in the seven CASC countries, that is, Armenia, Azerbaijan, Georgia, Kazakhstan, the Kyrgyz Republic, Tajikistan, and Uzbekistan. All of the chapters were written by country experts. The original papers were presented at a conference organized by the Asian Development Bank Institute in Almaty, Kazakhstan, on 26 October 2017. This book can be taken as a companion to ADBI's 2018 volume on *Financial Inclusion, Regulation and Education: Asian Perspectives,* edited by Naoyuki Yoshino and Peter Morgan.

By comparing country experiences in different areas, circumstances, and levels of income, the aim is to identify lessons regarding best practices and important innovations that would be useful for other countries. Such lessons include (i) the importance of crafting a national strategy that includes all major stakeholders; (ii) the need for a coordinated approach that includes financial education, consumer protection, and regulation and supervision to build trust as well as knowledge; (iii) the need to promote financial access in ways that are aligned with economic returns and with consistent regulation; (iv) the desirability of regulating microfinance entities "proportionately" in line with financial system risk; (v) the need to promote new delivery technologies and credit databases; and (vi) the need for national financial literacy data and financial education strategies.

Existing financial supervisory and regulatory frameworks have largely been shaped by the environment of traditional commercial banking, and this environment has not necessarily proved to be conducive for increasing financial inclusion. In many cases, efforts and policies to expand financial access have involved innovations in areas such as types of financial institutions (microfinance, crowd financing); borrowing regimes (mutual responsibility loans); service access (mini-branches); types of products (microcredit, microdeposits, microinsurance); delivery channels (mobile phone banking, e-banking, representative banking); and identity requirements (biometric identification). Such innovations often involve the adoption and adaptation of new technologies. Financial inclusion efforts must also address problems such as the lack of adequate financial data and of adequate collateral for lending.

All of these developments require that regulatory and supervisory frameworks be reviewed, extended, and adapted to cover them. New institutions also need to be developed, such as nationwide credit databases for households and small and medium-sized enterprises. Because trust is essential to encourage financial participation, consumer protection frameworks also need to be expanded to cover these developments.

Governments increasingly recognize the need to develop policies to promote financial education, but such efforts to date have tended to be fragmented and inadequate. Financial education efforts confront numerous hurdles, such as lack of literacy, including computer literacy, inadequate access in rural areas, lack of coordination among relevant institutions, and lack of basic data about the level of financial education. Separate programs need to be developed to target different groups, including schoolchildren of various ages, those in rural areas, women, the poor, and the elderly.

We wish to thank Rakurs Consulting Group of Kazakhstan for their able support, especially Dossym Kydyrbayev, Yukiko Ichikawa for excellent administrative support, Muriel Ordoñez and Kae Sugawara for coordinating the editing and production process, and Narxoz University in Almaty. We also thank the Kazakhstan Resident Mission of the Asian Development Bank for its support, especially Giovanni Capannelli.

Peter Morgan
Senior Consulting Economist and Co-Chair of Research
Asian Development Bank Institute

Yan Zhang
Project Consultant
Asian Development Bank Institute

Abbreviations

ABA	Azerbaijan Banks Association
ADB	Asian Development Bank
ADBI	Asian Development Bank Institute
ADIF	Azerbaijan Deposit Insurance Fund
AFI	Alliance for Financial Inclusion
AMFA	Azerbaijan Microfinance Association
AMFOT	Association of Microfinance Organizations of Tajikistan
ARUS	Armenian Remittances Unified System
ASEAN	Association of Southeast Asian Nations
AZN	Azerbaijani manat
BSE	Baku Stock Exchange
CASC	Central Asia and the South Caucasus
CBA	Central Bank of Armenia
CBAR	Central Bank of Azerbaijan Republic
CBU	Central Bank of Uzbekistan
CER	Centre for Economic Research
CGAP	Consultative Group to Assist the Poor
CIBT	Credit Information Bureau of Tajikistan
CIS	Commonwealth of Independent States
DIF	Deposit Insurance Fund
DNC	Development National Center
EBRD	European Bank for Reconstruction and Development
ECA	Eastern Europe and Central Asia
EDF	Entrepreneurship Development Fund
EIU	Economist Intelligence Unit
ENPF	Single Accumulative Pension Fund (*Edinyi Nakopitelnyi Pensionniy Fond*)
FAS	Financial Access Survey
FCB	Financial Capability Barometer
FCIS	Financial Capability and Inclusion Survey
FDI	foreign direct investment
FIMSA	Financial Markets Supervisory Authority
FSC	Financial Stability Council
FSM	Financial System Mediator
G20	Group of 20
GDP	gross domestic product
GNI	gross national income
GSE	Georgian Stock Exchange

IFC	International Finance Corporation
IMF	International Monetary Fund
INFE	International Network on Financial Education
IPO	initial public offering
IRP	International Risk Partnership
ISET-PI	International School of Economics at Tbilisi State University Policy Institute
KASE	Kazakhstan Stock Exchange
KDIF	Kazakhstan Deposit Insurance Fund
KPI	key performance indicator
MCF	microcredit fund
MCO	microcredit organization
MDO	microcredit deposit organization
MFI	microfinance institution
MFO	microfinance organization
MFU	Ministry of Finance of Uzbekistan
MTO	money-transfer operator
NBCI	nonbank credit institution
NBER	National Bureau of Economic Research
NBFI	nonbank financial institution
NBG	National Bank of Georgia
NBK	National Bank of Kazakhstan
NBKR	National Bank of the Kyrgyz Republic
NBT	National Bank of Tajikistan
NDS	National Development Strategy of Tajikistan 2030
NFES	National Fund for Entrepreneurship Support
NFLS	National Financial Literacy Strategy
NGO	nongovernment organization
NPL	nonperforming loan
NSC	National Statistical Committee
NSFE	National Strategy for Financial Education
NSO	National Statistics Office
OECD	Organisation for Economic Co-operation and Development
P2B	person-to-business
P2P	peer-to-peer
PFI	partner financial institution
POS	point-of-sale
PPP	purchasing power parity
PSP	payment service provider
Q	quarter
RKDF	Russian Kyrgyz Development Fund
SMEs	small and medium-sized enterprises
SOE	state-owned enterprise

SRM	strategic road map
TJS	Tajik somoni
UNDP	United Nations Development Programme
US	United States
USAID	United States Agency for International Development
WB	World Bank

1

Overview of Financial Inclusion, Regulation, Financial Literacy, and Education in Central Asia and South Caucasus

Peter J. Morgan, Yan Zhang, and Dossym Kydyrbayev

1.1 Introduction and Purpose of the Study[1]

Financial inclusion is increasingly receiving attention for its potential to contribute to economic and financial development while fostering more inclusive growth and greater income equality. In 2010, the Group of 20 (G20) leaders approved the Financial Inclusion Action Plan and established the Global Partnership for Financial Inclusion[2] to promote their financial access agenda. Likewise, the Asia-Pacific Economic Cooperation Finance Ministers' Process has a dedicated forum looking at financial inclusion issues,[3] and the implementation of the Association of Southeast Asian Nations (ASEAN) Framework on Equitable Economic Development has made the promotion of financial inclusion a key objective (ASEAN 2014). Development organizations have been responsive as well; for example, the Asian Development Bank (ADB) has approved 121 projects (amounting to $2.59 billion as of 2012) to support microfinance in Asia and the Pacific (ADB 2012). Many individual

---

[1] The chapters in this book were initially presented at a conference on "Financial Inclusion, Regulation, Literacy and Education in Central Asia and South Caucasus" at Narxoz University, Almaty, Kazakhstan on 26 October 2017.
[2] Global Partnership for Financial Inclusion. http://www.gpfi.org/ (accessed 15 October 2018).
[3] The annual forum was held most recently in Viet Nam in July 2017.

Asian economies have also adopted financial inclusion strategies as an important part of their overall strategy to achieve inclusive growth.

One key indicator of household access to finance is the percentage of adults who have an individual or joint account at a formal financial institution, such as a bank, credit union, cooperative, post office, or microfinance institution (MFI), or with a mobile money provider. According to the Global Findex database for 2017 (World Bank 2018), which is based on survey interviews, the worldwide average for this measure is 69%, and the total number of adults without accounts is about 1.7 billion; this represents a substantial improvement from 2.7 billion in 2011, but the figure is still high. The statistics for Asia show that much remains to be done to achieve access to finance, as East Asia, the Pacific, and South Asia combined account for over 40% of the world's unbanked adults, mainly in India and the People's Republic of China (Demirgüç-Kunt et al. 2018).

In terms of financial inclusion and development, the economies in Central Asia and the South Caucasus (CASC)—Armenia, Azerbaijan, Georgia, Kazakhstan, the Kyrgyz Republic, Tajikistan, and Uzbekistan—have generally lagged behind other Asian economies, partly due to the disruptions and instabilities that followed the breakup of the Soviet Union in 1991 (Yoshino and Morgan 2017). Since gaining independence from the Soviet Union, many CASC countries have experienced similar economic events. Their populations distrusted financial institutions, and they were unprepared to go through difficult procedures to avail themselves of the services offered by such institutions. Moreover, a number of financial crises have challenged the CASC countries and their banking sectors. The global financial crisis had a spillover effect on all seven CASC countries. In Tajikistan, the remittances of labor migrants fell from $3.7 billion in 2013 to $1.9 billion in 2016, leading to a major devaluation of the Tajik somoni. The fall in oil prices inflicted negative shocks on oil-exporting economies, leading to currency devaluations in Kazakhstan and Azerbaijan. Policies aimed at promoting financial inclusion and financial literacy generally have not been pursued as actively in this region as elsewhere in Asia.

The purpose of this study is to survey the experiences of the CASC economies to assess the factors—including financial literacy, financial education programs, and financial regulatory frameworks—affecting the ability of low-income households and small and medium-sized enterprises (SMEs) to access financial services; and to identify policies that can improve their financial access while maintaining financial stability. It also aims to identify successful experiences and lessons that can be adopted by other emerging economies.

1.2 Definitions of Financial Inclusion

Financial inclusion broadly refers to the degree of access of households and firms, especially poorer households and SMEs, to financial services. However, there are important variations in the usage and nuance of this term. The World Bank defined financial inclusion as "the proportion of individuals and firms that use financial services" (2014: 1), while ADB defined it as "ready access for households and firms to reasonably priced financial services" (2015: 71). Atkinson and Messy defined financial inclusion as:

> the process of promoting affordable, timely and adequate access to a wide range of regulated financial products and services and broadening their use by all segments of society through the implementation of tailored existing and innovative approaches including financial awareness and education with a view to promote financial well-being as well as economic and social inclusion (Atkinson and Messy 2013: 11).

The Alliance for Financial Inclusion (2010: 6) has "four commonly used lenses through which financial inclusion can be defined, in order of complexity: access...quality...usage... welfare". The Global Partnership for Financial Inclusion and the Consultative Group to Assist the Poor define financial inclusion as "...a state in which all working age adults, including those currently excluded by the financial system, have effective access to the following financial services provided by formal institutions: credit, savings (defined broadly to include current accounts), payments, and insurance." (GPFI and CGAP 2011: 8). Finally, Chakraborty (2011) defines financial inclusion as "the process of ensuring access to appropriate financial products and services needed by vulnerable groups such as weaker sections and low-income groups at an affordable cost in a fair and transparent manner by mainstream institutional players."

The World Bank definition focuses on the actual use of financial services, while the other definitions focus more on the potential ability to use such services. Moreover, "access" does not mean "any kind of access", but implies access at a reasonable cost and with accompanying safeguards, such as adequate regulation of firms supplying financial services, and laws and institutions for protecting consumers against inappropriate products, deceptive practices, and aggressive collection practices. Of course, it is difficult to define "reasonable cost" in cases where the amounts involved are small or information asymmetries exist. Therefore, a key question is the extent to which the government should subsidize such services or intervene in the market. This perspective also highlights the need for adequate financial education, as consumers cannot take proper advantage of access to financial services if they do not understand them properly.

Access to financial services has a multitude of dimensions reflecting the range of possible financial services, from payments and savings accounts to credit, insurance, pensions, and securities markets. Another important dimension is the actual usage of such products and services; for example, campaigns to increase the number of bank accounts fail if those accounts end up being rarely or never used.

Finally, the concept of financial inclusion also implies financial exclusion, also known as being "unbanked." Financial exclusion is defined as not using any financial services or products of formal financial institutions, including MFIs. However, it is important to distinguish between those who, for whatever reason, do not wish or need to use such services and products, and those who wish to use them but cannot do so due to insufficient funds, poor access, high costs, ignorance or lack of understanding, lack of trust, or identity requirements.

1.3 Rationale for Financial Inclusion

There are various arguments in favor of greater financial inclusion. As poor households are often severely cash-constrained, innovations that help them manage their cash more efficiently and allow them to smooth consumption can significantly impact their welfare. Relying on cash-based transactions involves many costs and risks; for example, many transactions entail carrying large amounts of cash, possibly over long distances, creating safety concerns. Furthermore, it has been found that the marginal return to capital in SMEs is large when capital is scarce, suggesting that SMEs could reap sizeable returns from greater financial access (Demirgüç-Kunt and Klapper 2013). This is particularly important in Asia, where SMEs contribute considerably to total employment and output.

Greater financial inclusion can also help reduce income inequality by raising the incomes of the poorest quintile (Beck, Demirgüç-Kunt, and Levine 2007). It may also contribute to financial stability by increasing the diversity (and thereby decreasing the risk) of bank assets, and by increasing the stable funding base of bank deposits (Khan 2011; Morgan and Pontines 2014). Greater financial access can also support government shifts toward cash transfer programs instead of wasteful subsidies, and the greater transparency associated with electronic funds transfers can help reduce corruption.

A growing body of evidence suggests that access to financial services can reduce poverty, raise incomes, and promote economic growth. However, the conclusions are, in some cases, still tenuous, as many earlier studies relied on macro data, which were subject to numerous issues such as endogeneity and missing variables (see Honohan 2004; Beck, Demirgüç-Kunt, and Levine 2007; World Bank 2008). There has also been a large volume of research on the impacts of microfinance (McKernan 2003; Pitt, Khandker, Chowdhury, and Millimet 2003; Kaboski and Townsend 2005), but the reliability of the results of many studies suffers from possible selection bias (Karlan and Morduch 2009). More reliable studies with randomized control trials or natural experiments are rare. Some found evidence that an increased number of bank branches reduced poverty and raised income and employment levels (Burgess and Pande 2005; Bruhn and Love 2013). In fact, in a recent survey of the literature on the subject, the World Bank concluded that

> Considerable evidence indicates that the poor benefit enormously from basic payments, savings, and insurance services. For firms, particularly the small and young ones that are subject to greater constraints, access to finance is associated with innovation, job creation, and growth. But dozens of microcredit experiments paint a mixed picture about the development benefits of microfinance projects targeted at particular groups in the population (World Bank 2014: 3).

In light of the substantial emphasis placed on microcredit in the literature, this assessment suggests caution in this area.

1.4 Status of Financial Inclusion for Individuals and Small and Medium-Sized Enterprises in Central Asia and the South Caucasus

Table 1.1 provides an overall picture of the status of financial inclusion in the CASC countries by listing several main indicators from the World Bank and International Monetary Fund (IMF) surveys related to financial inclusion. This shows that there is great variation in terms of the development of financial inclusion in the region, even though levels of financial inclusion are generally low. Secondly, levels of financial inclusion for individuals and firms are not necessarily at similar stages of development. For example, compared with the other CASC countries Armenia has the highest percentage of firms with bank loans, but comes

Table 1.1 Main Financial Inclusion Indicators for Central Asia and the South Caucasus Countries

		Armenia	Azerbaijan	Georgia	Kazakhstan	Kyrgyz Republic	Tajikistan	Uzbekistan
Branches of commercial banks per 100,000 adults[a]		23.1	10.7e	32.7	3.0	8.4	5.0d	36.1
ATMs (per 100,000 adults)[a]		61.1	32.7	74.3	74.0	31.2	9.1d	21.6
Share of adults with formal account (% aged 15+)[b]	All adults	47.8	28.6	61.2	58.7	39.9	47.0	37.1
	Women	40.9	27.7	63.6	60.3	38.9	42.1	36.0
	Adults belonging to the poorest 40%	34.4	18.1	46.1	48.8	35.7	38.5	29.7
	Young adults (% aged 15–24)	46.8	12.6	30.7	36.9	27.0	49.3	20.9
	Adults living in rural areas	46.8	20.2	55.1	56.7	39.1	46.3	34.4
Saved at a financial institution in the past year (% aged 15+)[b]		10.0	4.5	4.6	13.9	3.0	11.3	2.3
Borrowed from a financial institution in the past year (% aged 15+)[b]		28.5	13.1	23.7	20.0	9.4	14.7	2.1
Firms with a bank loan or line of credit (%)[c]		46.2	15.8	35.8	19.2	29.1	14.6	26.4
Small firms with a bank loan or line of credit (%)[c]		30.9	15.6	30.4	15.0	24.6	15.1	26.4
Firms using banks to finance investments (%)[c]		17.4	27.1	22.1	16.3	18.4	13.2	16.1
Firms using banks to finance working capital (%)[c]		39.2	17.6	27.6	13.0	23.3	19.2	13.1
Made digital payments in the past year (% aged 15+)[b]		39.8	12.9	29.6	38.2	28.6	40.3	33.6

continued on next page

Table 1.1 *continued*

	Armenia	Azerbaijan	Georgia	Kazakhstan	Kyrgyz Republic	Tajikistan	Uzbekistan
Mobile phone used to pay utility bills in the past year (% aged 15+)[b]	3.3	1.3	2.3	8.6	0.5	2.3	2.5
Mobile phone used to send a domestic remittance in the past year (% aged 15+)[b]	15.9	9.8	6.9	16.4	17.6	19.5	5.4

Sources: a International Monetary Fund, Financial Access Survey, 2016; b World Bank Global Findex Survey, 2017; c World Bank Global Financial Development Database, 2013; d National Bank of Tajikistan (2016); e 2015.

third (behind Georgia and Kazakhstan) in terms of the percentage of individual adults with formal accounts. Use of digital financial services such as e-money or mobile phones is generally low, but is increasing rapidly in several countries.

1.4.1 Banking Services

Banking Network

Figure 1.1 shows the penetration of bank branches in the seven CASC economies since 2004. Aside from Uzbekistan and Kazakhstan, the other five countries in this region have seen gradual increases in the level of bank penetration, although this remains very low in Azerbaijan, the Kyrgyz Republic, and Tajikistan. Overall, the number of bank branches has increased rapidly since 2004, especially in Georgia and Armenia; and in 2015 Armenia, Georgia, and Uzbekistan surpassed the world average of 20 branches per 100,000 adults. The declining trend in Kazakhstan and Uzbekistan reflects the very slow rate of increase in the number of branches relative to population growth.

The situation with the distribution of ATMs is somewhat different, with Armenia, Georgia, and Kazakhstan having significantly higher levels of penetration than the other four countries (Table 1.1). Moreover, ATM penetration has been growing relatively rapidly in all of the CASC economies, although in some cases from a very low base. The main issue is the extent to which the ATMs are concentrated in major cities instead of being distributed more evenly throughout the country. In Armenia, Georgia, and the Kyrgyz Republic, well over half of all ATMS are located in the three largest cities, while the share for Kazakhstan is about 30% (no breakdowns are available for Azerbaijan, Tajikistan, and Uzbekistan) (IMF 2018).

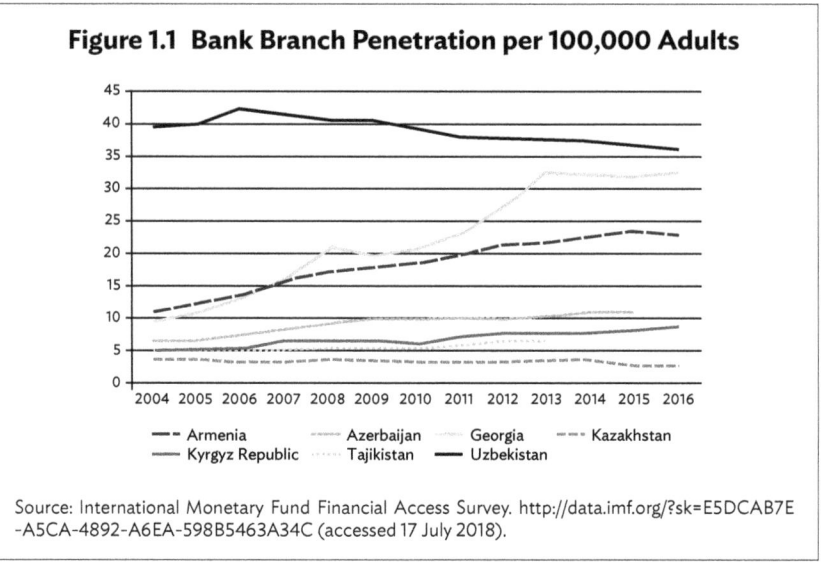

Figure 1.1 Bank Branch Penetration per 100,000 Adults

Source: International Monetary Fund Financial Access Survey. http://data.imf.org/?sk=E5DCAB7E-A5CA-4892-A6EA-598B5463A34C (accessed 17 July 2018).

Accounts

Using all Asian countries as the sample set, the financial access of households in terms of the percentage of adults with an account at a formal financial institution tends to rise along with per capita gross domestic product (GDP). Most CASC economies lie relatively close to the trend line, except for Azerbaijan, which falls far below this measure. However, there is still huge variation across countries in the CASC region (Figure 1.2), implying that other factors besides income (including overall financial development and regulatory, institutional, social, and geographic factors) play important roles. For example, Georgia has much higher deposit penetration than Uzbekistan or Armenia, even though the per capita income levels of these three countries are similar. Georgia, Tajikistan, and the Kyrgyz Republic lie modestly above the trend line, while the other CASC economies (especially Azerbaijan, Kazakhstan, and Uzbekistan) lie below it. Moreover, all the CASC economies except Georgia have penetration shares below 60%.

The fact that Azerbaijan has the lowest level of account penetration among adults (29%) despite having relatively high per capita income stands out as a puzzle. One possible reason for this is the country's very low level of bank branch penetration, which is much lower than in Armenia, Georgia, and Uzbekistan (see Figure 1.1). However, this cannot be the only explanation, as Kazakhstan, the Kyrgyz Republic, and

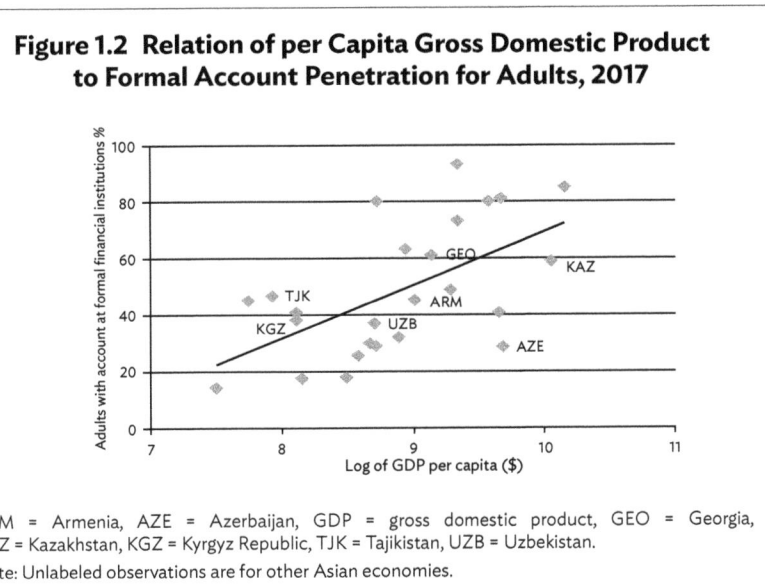

Figure 1.2 Relation of per Capita Gross Domestic Product to Formal Account Penetration for Adults, 2017

ARM = Armenia, AZE = Azerbaijan, GDP = gross domestic product, GEO = Georgia, KAZ = Kazakhstan, KGZ = Kyrgyz Republic, TJK = Tajikistan, UZB = Uzbekistan.
Note: Unlabeled observations are for other Asian economies.
Source: World Bank Global Findex Survey (2018). https://globalfindex.worldbank.org/#data_sec_focus (accessed 3 July 2018).

Tajikistan have even lower levels of bank branch penetration. Table 1.1 shows that Azerbaijan has by far the lowest level of account penetration in the region among the poorest 40% of the population, young adults, and the rural population. This points to a great disparity in account access among the population, suggesting that bank penetration in rural areas is very weak. Kazakhstan's low level of account penetration may reflect the high share of income from natural resources there.

Credit

Based on data from Asian countries, Figure 1.3 shows that the relationship between per capita GDP and the share of adults obtaining loans from formal financial institutions is positively sloped; however this relationship is weaker than that observed with accounts. Once again, large variations in the CASC region can be seen. In terms of borrowing rates, Kazakhstan, Azerbaijan, and the Kyrgyz Republic fall fairly close to the trend line, Armenia and Georgia are ranked much higher, and Uzbekistan is ranked especially low. Uzbekistan's ranking appears mainly to reflect cultural and religious factors; the 2017 Global Findex survey found that 30% of adults cite religious reasons for not using financial services.

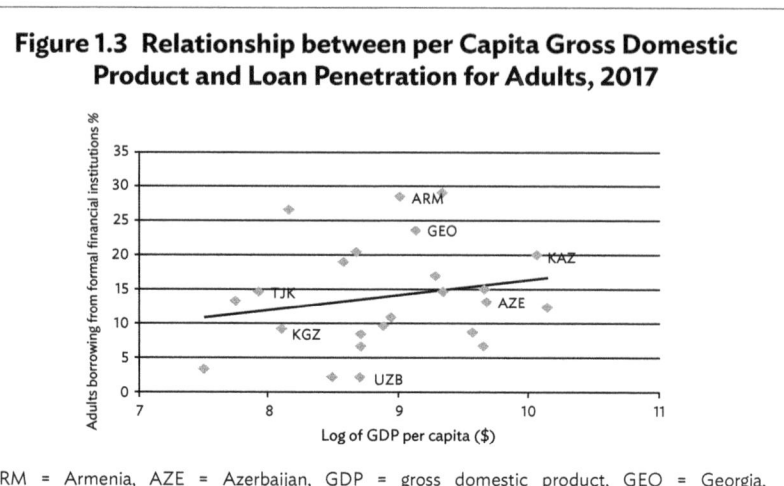

Figure 1.3 Relationship between per Capita Gross Domestic Product and Loan Penetration for Adults, 2017

ARM = Armenia, AZE = Azerbaijan, GDP = gross domestic product, GEO = Georgia, KAZ = Kazakhstan, KGZ = Kyrgyz Republic, TJK = Tajikistan, UZB = Uzbekistan.
Note: Unlabeled observations are for other Asian economies.
Source: World Bank Global Findex Survey (2016). https://globalfindex.worldbank.org/#data_sec_focus (accessed 3 July 2018).

Figure 1.4 shows a relatively flat but modestly positive overall relationship between per capita GDP and the share of small firms with a line of credit; however, once again, the CASC economies show a high degree of variation. Data are available for considerably fewer countries

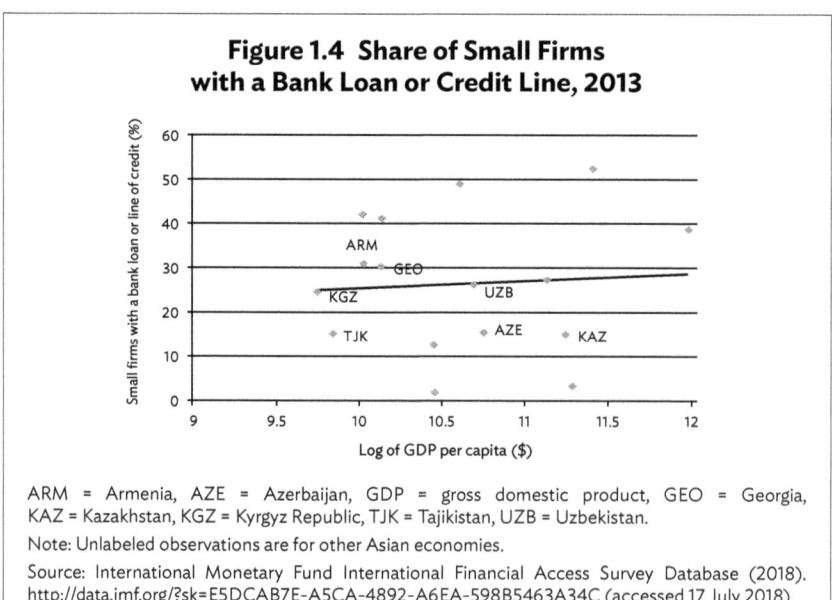

Figure 1.4 Share of Small Firms with a Bank Loan or Credit Line, 2013

ARM = Armenia, AZE = Azerbaijan, GDP = gross domestic product, GEO = Georgia, KAZ = Kazakhstan, KGZ = Kyrgyz Republic, TJK = Tajikistan, UZB = Uzbekistan.
Note: Unlabeled observations are for other Asian economies.
Source: International Monetary Fund International Financial Access Survey Database (2018). http://data.imf.org/?sk=E5DCAB7E-A5CA-4892-A6EA-598B5463A34C (accessed 17 July 2018).

than for household financial access. Borrowing rates for Azerbaijan, Kazakhstan, and Tajikistan are well below average, while the other four economies are close to the average. The low levels for Azerbaijan, Kazakhstan, and Tajikistan appear well correlated with the low levels of bank branch penetration shown in Figure 1.1.

1.4.2 Insurance

Use of insurance services remains very low in most of the countries in the CASC region. Most of the country studies find that their insurance markets are small and at a nascent stage. This is mainly due to a lack of information about most insurance products, a lack of trust in insurance companies, insufficient types of compulsory insurance, and a lack of control mechanisms for the sale of existing mandatory insurance products (see Ibadoghlu, Chapter 3). Figures 1.5 and 1.6 show the value of insurance premiums of life (Figure 1.5) and nonlife (Figure 1.6) companies relative to GDP. In the life insurance market, apart from some increases in Azerbaijan, Georgia, and Kazakhstan, the ratio of premiums to GDP is very low. Life insurance premiums are growing rapidly in Azerbaijan, but fell significantly from their near-term peak in Kazakhstan. The ratio in other economies is quite small, lower than 0.06% in all cases.

The nonlife insurance market is similarly small. The ratio for all countries is less than 0.6%, although Kazakhstan previously had ratios of more than 1%. The non-life premium to GDP ratio in Azerbaijan

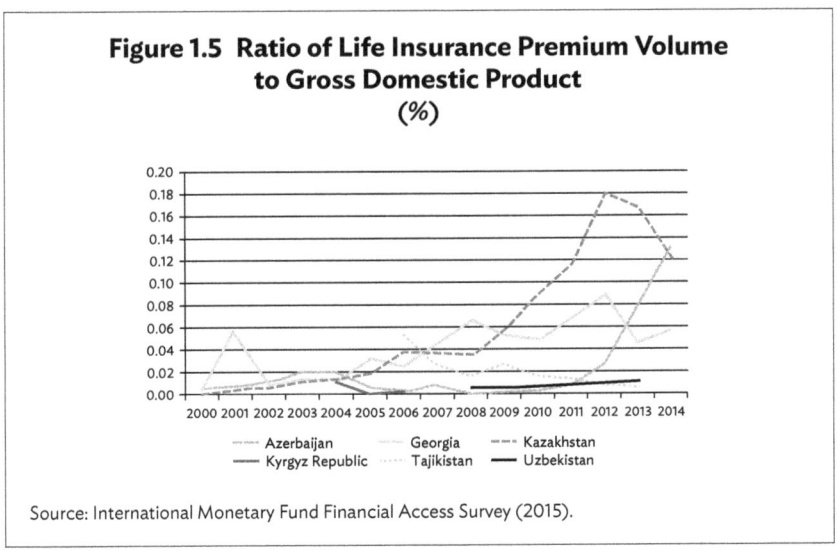

Figure 1.5 Ratio of Life Insurance Premium Volume to Gross Domestic Product (%)

Source: International Monetary Fund Financial Access Survey (2015).

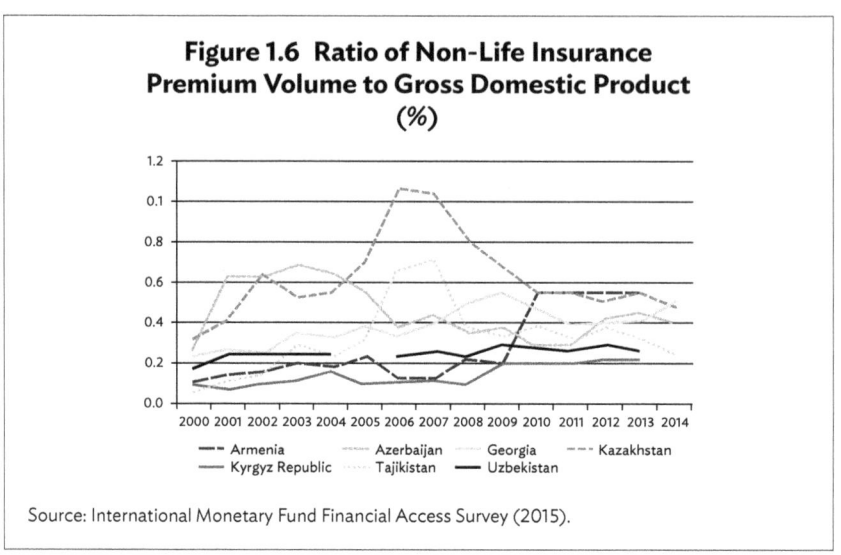

Figure 1.6 Ratio of Non-Life Insurance Premium Volume to Gross Domestic Product (%)

Source: International Monetary Fund Financial Access Survey (2015).

decreased after 2003, while those in Kazakhstan and Tajikistan decreased after 2007.

1.4.3 Pensions

In the CASC region, substantial efforts have been made to reform pension systems to ensure their long-term adequacy and sustainability. The defined-benefit, pay-as-you-go systems inherited from the Soviet era, that financed retirement benefits with contributions from current workers, have become unsustainable due to increased population aging in the CASC region (Schwarz and Arias 2014). Armenia, Kazakhstan, Tajikistan, and Uzbekistan have changed their systems to defined-contribution, funded pension plans, in which mandatory individual accounts are a common requirement (Social Security Administration and International Social Security Association 2015). The first country to initiate change in this area was Kazakhstan, which adopted a fully funded, defined-contribution pension scheme in the mid-1990s (see Kapparov, Chapter 5). Georgia replaced its pay-as-you-go system with a universal benefit social assistance program in 2013, and in 2014 Armenia introduced a new multi-pillar pension system for people born after 1 January 1974.

Workers' pension coverage is high in these former Soviet Union transition economies; however, this still mainly covers the formal labor sector, including the public sector. The lack of pension coverage for informal workers is a constraint on the social welfare system (see Ahunov, Chapter 8). In Armenia, Azerbaijan, and Kazakhstan, state-owned pension funds provide most or all of the pension coverage, and the market for private pension schemes is small. As of 2017, there were only three private pension schemes in Armenia, and none in Azerbaijan and Kazakhstan.

1.4.4 Remittances

Remittances are an important source of income for households in CASC economies as many workers migrate from these countries to Russia and other economies. For example, the size of remittances as a share of GDP is around 30% in the Kyrgyz Republic, 27% in Tajikistan, 13% in Armenia, 10.5%–12% in Georgia, and 2.7% in Azerbaijan. Due to the rapid growth of remittances, payment facilities and services have developed very quickly in this region. For example, remittances to Armenia originating from Russia are mostly transferred through formal channels since specialized banks provide low-cost money-transfer services in Commonwealth of Independent States countries (see Nurbekyan and Hovanessian, Chapter 2). Informal remittance channels also exist, especially if the migrant workers are engaged in occasional jobs. According to the 2015 World Bank Group Financial Capability Survey of Azerbaijan (World Bank 2016), about one person in 10 uses money-transfer operators, predominantly from poor and large households in urban areas. While 12% of the population currently has money-transfer products, more than one-third has used such products in the past, and three out of four persons know about services offered by money-transfer operators (see Ibadoghlu, Chapter 3).

1.4.5 Kinds of Financial Institution Involved

Inclusion-oriented financial institutions include MFIs, state-owned banks, post offices offering financial services, credit cooperatives, and international and community organizations. State-owned banks and governments often take the lead in initiating financial inclusion strategies and governing financial inclusion-related institutions. For example, the Government of Azerbaijan provides three different plans for SME financing. Other examples are the SME State Support Fund in Armenia, and the Nurly Zhol and People Initial Public Offering programs in Kazakhstan, although the latter are aimed chiefly at retail stock investors (see Table 1.2).

Table 1.2 Elements of Financial Inclusion Strategies

Country	Inclusive Financial Institutions	Subsidized Funding	Innovative Financial Products and Services	Innovative Delivery Technologies	Innovative Systems to Enhance Credit Access
Armenia	Banks, credit organizations, post offices	Small and Medium Entrepreneurship Development National Center of Armenia, government subsidies		e-Money, internet banking, mobile phone banking	Credit bureau
Azerbaijan	NBCIs, including Azerpost, credit unions, MFIs	Subsidized loans provided by National Fund for Support of Entrepreneurship, Mortgage Fund, Azerbaijani Investment Company, State Agency for Agricultural Credits	Various insurance products	Mobile banking, electronic payments through national payment terminals, such as e-Manat and Million	Credit Guarantee Fund of Azerbaijan, draft law for a free collateral registry prepared in consultation with the IFC
Georgia	Credit unions, MFIs		Supplementary pension-saving system, P2P lending, and crowdfunding	Digital banking enabling e-payments, receiving deposits, and transfers	Private credit bureau "CreditInfo Georgia", public credit database
Kazakhstan	The number of MFIs is increasing rapidly, but the level of loans remains small.	Interest rate subsidies and guaranteed loans	Microfinance	Electronic payments available with fairly wide usage	
Kyrgyz Republic	MFIs, credit unions	State mortgage companies providing subsidized rates for public employees and farmers	Microloans, collateral-free loans	Internet and mobile banking available but not widely used	Credit bureau, State Guarantee Fund, new law on warehouse receipts

continued on next page

Table 1.2 continued

Country	Inclusive Financial Institutions	Subsidized Funding	Innovative Financial Products and Services	Innovative Delivery Technologies	Innovative Systems to Enhance Credit Access
Tajikistan	MFIs, credit unions			Electronic payments and mobile banking available but not widely used	Credit guarantee fund, private credit guarantee facility
Uzbekistan	Banks, MFIs			Electronic payments, mobile banking, internet banking	Credit registries and public and private credit bureaus

IFC = International Finance Corporation, MFI = microfinance institution, NBCI = non-bank credit institution, P2P = peer-to-peer.
Sources: Chapters 2–8 in this volume.

Table 1.3 Outstanding Loans by Type of Financial Institution, 2016 (% of Gross Domestic Product)

Type of Institution	Armenia	Azerbaijan	Georgia	Kazakhstan	Kyrgyz Republic	Tajikistan	Uzbekistan
Commercial banks	41.8	44.2	55.1	30.4	20.4	15.1	26.4
Subtotal for SMEs	–	–	7.5	–	–	–	–
Credit unions and financial cooperatives	–	–	0.0	–	0.2	–	–
MFIs	–	<1.0	4.4	0.2	2.2	3.1	0.1
Other deposit takers	3.3	–	–	–	–	–	–
Other depository corporations	–	–	–	–	–	–	–
Other financial intermediaries	0.2	0.8	–	3.4	–	–	–
Total	45.3	44.9	59.5	34.0	22.8	18.2	26.5

– = not available, MFI = microfinance institution, SMEs = small and medium-sized enterprises.
Note: Data for Tajikistan are from the National Bank of Tajikistan. There is no separate category of MFIs in Armenia.
Sources: Authors' calculations. Data from the International Monetary Fund Financial Access Survey, 2016; gross domestic product data from the World Bank World Development Indicators Database; Azerbaijan MFI data from Ibadoghlu, Chapter 3.

Table 1.3 shows the breakdown of loans by type of financial institution as a percentage of GDP in the seven CASC economies. It shows that the lending landscape is clearly dominated by commercial banks and other depository institutions, mainly public sector banks.

Levels of development with respect to MFIs vary greatly. In Kazakhstan, the number of registered MFIs has grown very fast, from 136 at the beginning of 2017 to 160 in September 2017. In the first 6 months of 2017 the MFI loan portfolio increased by 30% to reach $0.4 billion, although this is still a tiny fraction of the total amount of SME and retail bank loans ($26 billion) (see Kapparov, Chapter 5). In Georgia, the number of registered microfinance organizations has increased dramatically, from two in 2004 to 81 in 2016, while MFIs' total assets as a share of GDP grew from 0.02% in 2006 to 8% in 2016. Similarly, MFI loans reached 4.4% of GDP in 2016, the highest in the region (see Babych, Grigolia, and Keshelava, Chapter 4). In the Kyrgyz Republic, the number of MFIs and credit unions reached a peak of 651 units, and loans amounted to 8% of GDP by 2011 (see Hasanova, Chapter 6). However, this share shrank to less than 3% of GDP by 2016 as a result of regulatory tightening and the conversion of some MFIs to bank status. In Tajikistan, MFIs account for 17.7% of all loans (perhaps the highest such measure in the region), reflecting in part the country's relatively low level of financial development. On the other hand, as highlighted by the World Bank (2016), the nonbank credit sector in Azerbaijan is underdeveloped and offers limited credit opportunities for SMEs, with total loans accounting for less than 1% of GDP (see Ibadoghlu, Chapter 3). Similarly, in Uzbekistan, MFI loans are limited, only accounting for 0.1% of GDP (see Ahunov, Chapter 8). There is no separate legal or regulatory definition of microfinance organizations in Armenia, but credit provided by credit organizations performing MFI activities rose from 0.3% of GDP in 2004 to 7.8% in 2016.

1.4.6 Inclusion-Related Financial Products and Services

To promote financial inclusion, governments and credit organizations provide various specialized and innovative products and services, including microproducts such as no-frills bank deposits, microcredit and microinsurance, agent banking, and microbranches. In Azerbaijan, agriculture-related financing products are provided, such as harvest insurance, index-based weather insurance, and index-based livestock mortality insurance. These products and services allow farm households to smooth fluctuations in household income due to seasonality and mitigate external risks associated with farming.

Most MFIs in the Kyrgyz Republic practice group lending. Over half (53%–71%) of MFIs' credit portfolios consist of group, collateral-free loans. Since women have restricted access to collateral, they have become the majority of MFI borrowers (70% during 2006–2016, on average). The accessibility of loans, simplified procedures of obtaining them, and branches in rural areas have made microfinance attractive to the low-income rural population. Relatively liberal laws have inspired the establishment of over 650 MFIs, and MFI loans accounted for almost half of the country's total credit portfolio in 2011 (see Hasanova, Chapter 6).

1.4.7 Innovative Delivery Technologies

Innovative delivery technologies, such as mobile phones, e-money, and internet banking, can also help bridge distances and save time. Digital banking services are developing very rapidly in the region, albeit from a very low base (Table 1.2). In Armenia in 2012, there were very few mobile phone, point-of-sale, and non-cash transactions; however, since then this activity has been growing exponentially, with the number of active mobile money accounts increasing by seven times from 2012 to 2016 (see Nurbekyan and Hovanessian, Chapter 2). Similarly, a national electronic payment system introduced in Azerbaijan has led to a large increase in utilization, and recent regulatory changes in Uzbekistan have created an upsurge in mobile phone banking (see Ahunov, Chapter 8).

In Georgia, the most commonly used technologies include internet banking, telephone banking, mobile banking, and text message banking. Georgians actively use electronic payments to pay public utilities and purchase goods (see Babych, Grigolia, and Keshelava, Chapter 4). According to a 2014 survey by the International Finance Corporation (IFC) in Tajikistan, very few types of banking services are currently available online, as the software used by banks and MFIs does not allow some operations to be implemented (see Mogilevskii and Asadov, Chapter 7). Nonetheless, several MFIs in Tajikistan have started using payment service provider terminals for loan repayment.

1.5 Barriers to Financial Inclusion

Barriers to financial inclusion can be classified as supply-side, demand-side, and institutional aspects. Supply-side barriers reflect limitations in the capacity or willingness of the financial sector to extend financial services to poorer households or SMEs. These can be further subdivided into three categories: market-driven factors, regulatory factors, and infrastructure limitations.

Market-driven factors include aspects such as relatively high maintenance costs associated with small deposits or loans, high costs associated with providing financial services in small towns in rural areas, a lack of credit data or usable collateral, and a lack of convenient access points. The provision of financial services in rural areas in particular can pose problems in countries with geographically difficult-to-reach rural areas, leading to a high cost of financial services. In Georgia, for example, the cost of providing services outside major cities is high, particularly for MFIs whose clients are mainly lower-income households. Six percentage points of the interest rate on household loans from MFIs can be attributed to operational cost requirements (see Babych, Grigolia, and Keshelava, Chapter 4).

The lack of credit data and reliable financial records also worsens the problem of information asymmetry, which discourages banks from lending to poorer households and SMEs. This leads to the expansion of the informal credit sector. In the Kyrgyz Republic, the shadow economy is estimated at 40% of GDP, and many entrepreneurs operate in the quasi-formal sector (see Hasanova, Chapter 6). The absence of transparent accounts and activities prevents entrepreneurs from accessing a sufficient level of finance, while persons receiving informal wages cannot prove their creditworthiness and must borrow from pawnshops or relatives.

Regulatory factors include capital adequacy and supervisory rules that may limit the attractiveness of small deposits, loans, or other financial products for financial institutions. Strict requirements regarding the opening of branches or ATMs may also restrict the attractiveness of doing so in remote areas. Although identification and other documentation requirements are important, both with respect to know-your-client requirements and the monitoring of possible money laundering and terrorist-financing activities, these can pose problems for poor households in countries that do not have universal individual identification systems. Regulatory requirements such as restrictions on foreign ownership and inspection requirements can also restrict the entry of MFIs. Regulatory requirements should be calibrated to be commensurate with the systemic financial risks posed by various financial institutions and the trade-off between financial stability and greater financial inclusion. In Tajikistan, for example, regulators tend to be slow to understand market evolution, and are therefore reluctant to experiment with new technology-based financial products (see Mogilevskii and Asadov, Chapter 7).

Infrastructure-related barriers include a lack of access to secure and reliable payments and settlement systems, limited availability of either fixed or mobile telephone communications, and limited availability of convenient transport to bank branches or ATMs. Numerous studies have identified a lack of convenient transport as an important barrier to financial access (see, for example, Tambunlertchai 2017). This makes it difficult to reach people living in rural and low-income areas, particularly in Kazakhstan, Armenia, and Tajikistan, where rural–urban disparities are large.

Demand-side factors include a lack of funds, lack of knowledge of financial products (i.e. financial literacy), and lack of trust. Lack of trust can be a significant problem when countries do not have well-functioning supervision or regulation of financial institutions, or programs of consumer protection that require adequate disclosure, regulation of collection procedures, and systems of dispute resolution. For example, in the Kyrgyz Republic, state institutions regulating the financial sector are widely distrusted, second only to police services (see Hasanova, Chapter 6). This lack of trust is partly associated with the collapse of the Soviet Union, which resulted in a widescale loss of household savings in Soviet-era banks. Although the Government of Armenia has begun to implement a promised compensation plan, the scars of this episode on the population remain (see Nurbekyan and Hovanessian, Chapter 2).

Lack of knowledge and low financial literacy are a general problem in this region. In particular, low financial awareness, limited knowledge, and a lack of positive attitudes toward finance are serious problems in Georgia, Kazakhstan, Armenia, and Azerbaijan. This is discussed further in Section 1.7.

Institutional barriers include inefficient bankruptcy laws and high collateral requirements due to weak credit assessment systems. For example, Azerbaijan's bankruptcy law does not function efficiently and is seldom used. Moreover, due to the absence of a collateral registry system for movable collateral (other than vehicles), most lenders require real estate as collateral for a significant portion of the loan value, and several only accept real estate collateral in practice (see Ibadoghlu, Chapter 3). In Uzbekistan, collateral requirements are particularly high, and firms name these as their third most important reason for avoiding formal finance.

1.6 Regulatory Frameworks

Table 1.4 summarizes the major features of regulations related to financial inclusion in the subject countries, including regulatory agencies, identification-related measures, regulation of MFIs, regulation of lending (mainly interest rate caps), and consumer protection.

Table 1.4 Regulatory Frameworks for Financial Inclusion in Central Asia and the South Caucasus Economies

Country	Regulatory Agencies	Identification-Related Measures	Regulation of MFIs	Lending Regulations	Consumer Protection
Armenia	Central Bank of Armenia is the only financial system regulatory authority	Electronic identification cards and social cards	Credit organizations cannot take deposits; subject to lower capital requirements and fewer restrictions than banks; no legal definition of MFIs	Interest rate caps; only licensed institutions can lend	The Center for Consumer Rights Protection and Financial Education within the Central Bank of Armenia; deposit insurance; Financial System Mediator
Azerbaijan	Financial Markets Supervisory Authority (banks and NBCIs, including MFIs); Ministry of Finance (insurance companies); Tax and Civil Code Authority (leasing companies)		Law on nonbank credit organizations (2010); lower capital requirements for NBCIs than for normal banks; no specific law on MFIs	Interest rate cap at 15%	Financial Market Supervisory Authority
Georgia	National Bank of Georgia (commercial banks and nonbank financial institutions, excluding pawnshops and online loan providers); State Insurance Supervision Service of Georgia (insurance companies and pension schemes)		Law on microfinance organizations: MFIs cannot take deposits but can borrow; pawnshops and online loans are regulated by the Civil Code of Georgia	Interest rate cap at 100%; total fee of loan must not exceed 150% of loan amount itself; limits on foreign currency loans	Reflected in lending regulations

continued on next page

Table 1.4 *continued*

Country	Regulatory Agencies	Identification-Related Measures	Regulation of MFIs	Lending Regulations	Consumer Protection
Kazakhstan	NBK (banks, insurers, pension funds, investment funds, credit bureaus, and securities markets). Based on the goals in the Concept for the Financial Sector Development of the Republic of Kazakhstan until 2030 (2030 Concept)		NBK Resolution No. 386 requires registration of MFIs	FinTech Association: voluntary threshold for MFIs of a maximum penalty for debtors of 300% of the principal balance	National law on consumer protection, but nothing specific on financial services; the NBK is tasked to establish call centers; Committee on Consumer Protection in Financial Services
Kyrgyz Republic	National Bank of the Kyrgyz Republic		Only credit unions and MFIs with a license can take deposits; Law on Microfinance Organizations (2002); higher requirements on capital; restrictions on multiple lending; introduction of maximum level of fines	Interest rate cap at 15% over weighted average interest rate; minimal collateral size; maximum ratio of credit payments to borrower's income	Deposit insurance for all banks; a number of legislative acts to protect financial consumers' rights
Tajikistan	NBT		Law on microfinance organizations (2012); the NBT's regulations on three types of microfinance organization; among MFIs, only microcredit deposit organizations can take deposits	Caps on foreign exchange, interest rates, and risks	NBT consumer protection division

continued on next page

Table 1.4 *continued*

Country	Regulatory Agencies	Identification-Related Measures	Regulation of MFIs	Lending Regulations	Consumer Protection
Uzbekistan	The CBU regulates both banks and MFIs		MFIs regulated by the CBU (law on banks and banking)	Liberalized access to foreign exchange for small businesses and private individuals	Law on protection of consumer rights

CBU = Central Bank of Uzbekistan, MFI = microfinance institution, NBCI = nonbank credit institution, NBK = National Bank of Kazakhstan, NBT = National Bank of Tajikistan.
Sources: Chapters 2–8 in this volume.

1.6.1 Institutions Responsible for Regulation

In all CASC countries except Azerbaijan, central banks have major responsibilities for regulating and supervising banks and other financial institutions. In Azerbaijan, the Financial Markets Supervisory Authority supervises banks and nonbank credit institutions (NBCIs, including MFIs) and takes responsibility for consumer protection, the Ministry of Finance supervises insurance companies, and the Tax and Civil Code Authority supervises leasing companies. In Armenia, the central bank is the single financial regulator. In Georgia, the central bank supervises all depository and lending institutions. In Kazakhstan, the central bank is responsible for the regulation and supervision of banks, insurers, pension funds, investment funds, credit bureaus, and securities markets. In the Kyrgyz Republic, the central bank is the main regulator of financial institutions in the country. In Tajikistan, the central bank oversees licensing, regulation, and supervision; and is authorized to issue normative acts for banks and MFIs, establish financial standards, impose sanctions and penalties, and request reports. In Uzbekistan, the central bank regulates both banks and MFIs.

Regulatory frameworks still have room for improvement. For example, in Tajikistan, supervision of financial institutions is still mainly compliance-based, with little focus on good governance and risk management. Regulation and supervision need to be strengthened to manage credit, market, operation, concentration, interest rate, and liquidity risks better, as well as to improve the corporate governance and internal control systems of financial institutions. The adoption of international financial reporting standards, more advanced risk assessment tools, stress testing, and crisis management tools are among the main measures that need to be introduced (see Mogilevskii and Asadov, Chapter 7).

1.6.2 Licensing Status of Microfinance Institutions

A consistent financial inclusion policy requires a coordinated regulatory approach. Compared with banks, MFIs typically have greater restrictions imposed on their activities. Therefore, they tend to be regulated separately from banks, which are typically supervised by the central bank or financial regulator, and are usually regulated more lightly than banks. This is particularly the case for Azerbaijan and Armenia. In Azerbaijan, the minimum required charter capital for registering an NBCI is only AZN300,000, whereas for banks the amount is AZN50 million. In Armenia, regulations for banks are much more stringent.

However, having a variety of lenders can spawn a multitude of regulatory frameworks, which can lead to inconsistencies and gaps. For example, in Azerbaijan, the Law on Non-Bank Credit Organizations (2010) defines the rules for the establishment, management, and regulation of NBCIs, with the aim of better meeting the demands of legal entities and individuals for financial resources and creating suitable conditions for access to financial services. The Law on Credit Unions (2000) determines the economic, legislative, and organizational bases for the establishment and operation of credit unions. Instead of defined "microfinance" laws, Azerbaijan has laws for NBCIs that permits them a greater number of activities, although expressly forbidding them from deposit-taking. In the Kyrgyz Republic, in response to the rapid growth of MFIs, the central bank has since 2010 strengthened its regulation of MFIs by raising capital requirements to reduce the number of non-working and small MFIs, restricting the amount permitted for multiple lending, and introducing fines.

Some countries bar some or all MFIs from taking deposits (Table 1.4). In Armenia, only banks can take deposits from natural and legal persons (Law on Microfinance Organizations 2002). In Azerbaijan, NBCIs are divided into two groups: those with the right to accept collateral deposits and those without that right. In Tajikistan, the legislation identifies three types of MFI: microcredit deposit organizations (MDOs), microcredit organizations, and microcredit funds. Of these three, only MDOs can offer deposit products. In Kazakhstan, MFIs need to obtain a banking license in order to take deposits. In the Kyrgyz Republic, only credit unions and MFIs with licenses can take deposits. In Tajikistan, MDOs are the only MFIs allowed to offer deposit products based on a license issued by the National Bank of Tajikistan. MFIs are not allowed to take deposits in Uzbekistan.

1.6.3 Risks Being Addressed by Regulation

Regulation on financial inclusion addresses several types of risk. The first is foreign currency risk. For example, in Georgia, loans of up to GEL100 thousand for individuals (not legal entities) may be issued only in national currency. Loans issued in the national currency but indexed or linked to a foreign currency are not considered national currency loans. This regulation aims to facilitate the de-dollarization of loans and further reduce foreign currency risks for borrowers (see Babych, Grigolia, and Keshelava, Chapter 4). Similarly, in Armenia, consumer credit can be extended only in local currency. In Tajikistan, capital requirements exist to control foreign exchange, interest rate, and other risks.

1.6.4 Consumer Protection

Consumer protection programs are seen as necessary supports for financial inclusion efforts, together with financial education and effective regulation and supervision of financial institutions. Consumer protection can help address the issue of trust as a demand-side barrier to financial inclusion. Consumer protection programs are at various stages of development in the CASC region.

Most countries in the region have issued laws to protect consumer rights (see Table 1.3). For example, in Uzbekistan, the State Committee on Privatization regulates consumer protection. In Kazakhstan, the national law on consumer protection covers consumer protection and access to safe and high-quality goods, but does not specifically address financial services. The situations in the Kyrgyz Republic and Georgia are similar.

Other institutions also help consumers protect their rights. In Armenia, the Center for Consumer Rights Protection and Financial Education within the Central Bank of Armenia (CBA) is responsible for consumer protection. Its responsibilities include creating a legal system to assure consumer protection, promoting programs on financial knowledge and education, and operating consumer services websites and hotlines. In Tajikistan, the central bank has a customer compliance department that tracks customer complaints and feedback on financial institutions' activities. In 2017, the Office of the President of Uzbekistan began receiving consumer complaints directly using hotlines and online channels (see Ahunov, Chapter 8).

In Azerbaijan, however, consumer protection seems less well-developed, and the country has no functioning out-of-court dispute resolution system. The Financial Markets Supervisory Authority, which has primary responsibility for protecting financial consumer rights, is still under development and has weak capacity (see Ibadoghlu, Chapter 3).

1.6.5 Deposit Insurance

Deposit insurance is widely implemented in the CASC region to protect bank depositors. Deposit guarantee funds have been established in several countries to provide guarantees up to a certain deposit amount.

Under the Deposit Guarantee Fund of Armenia, which was founded by the CBA as a non-commercial organization in 2005, the maximum amount covered by insurance is AMD10 million ($20,700) for local-currency deposits, and AMD5 million for foreign-currency deposits (see Nurbekyan and Hovanessian, Chapter 2). The Azerbaijan Deposit Insurance Fund founded in 2007 provides insurance for depositors only, not investors. In Georgia, the deposit insurance scheme launched on 1 January 2018 insures all bank deposits up to GEL5,000 ($2,066) (see Babych, Grigolia, and Keshelava, Chapter 4). In Kazakhstan, the Kazakhstan Deposit Insurance Fund provide guarantees for all retail deposits denominated in national currency up to T10 million ($30,000). This threshold incentivizes big depositors to split their deposits between several banks and accounts to guarantee their safety (see Kapparov, Chapter 5). The Deposit Protection Agency of the Kyrgyz Republic was established in 2011. In Tajikistan, the Deposit Insurance Fund was established in 2003, and its assets reached TJS260 million (6.3% of total deposits) by the end of 2016. The deposit amount covered by the fund in case of bankruptcy of a credit organization increased from TJS7,000 in 2003 to TJS14,000 in 2015 and TJS17,500 in 2017 (approximately $2,100). In Uzbekistan, all banks have been covered by explicit deposit insurance since 2002. A blanket guarantee on deposits was implemented under a Presidential decree in November 2008, and the statutory limit of 250 times the minimum wage was removed in October 2009 (Demirgüç-Kunt et al. 2018).

1.6.6 Fintech-related Regulation

New delivery technologies such as mobile phones and e-money hold promise for promoting financial inclusion, but need appropriate regulatory frameworks to achieve their potential while remaining consistent with financial stability and other regulatory requirements. In many cases, service providers are not banks, making it difficult to implement a consistent approach. In Armenia, there are no regulatory barriers for innovative technologies, such as telephone banking.

According to the 2017 Global Innovation Index survey, Azerbaijan ranked 82nd out of 127 countries, a relatively low rating. According to the 2016 FinTech Index Report, Azerbaijan is rated as having a relatively unstable political and regulatory environment, but a very supportive infrastructure and ecosystem for financial technology (see Ibadoghlu, Chapter 3).

1.7 Policies to Promote Financial Inclusion

1.7.1 National Strategy

Although the notion of financial inclusion is new to the CASC countries, it is becoming a major goal for their governments, which are beginning to include it along with financial education in their national strategies. Overall, the CASC countries have not implemented any systematic financial inclusion strategies or policies, and few targeted policies have been advanced. Most government efforts in this area have had only short-term effects.

Strategies are needed to set priorities and coordinate overall approaches to expanding financial inclusion. National-level strategies are most desirable, followed by those of the central bank, ministries, and/or financial regulatory bodies. Table 1.5 shows the range of approaches being taken in the CASC region. Of these countries, the Kyrgyz Republic and Azerbaijan have the most well-articulated financial inclusion strategies, and have incorporated them in their national economic planning strategies. Kazakhstan, Tajikistan, and Uzbekistan have long-standing policies backing their SME support programs, but no articulated national strategies for financial inclusion as such. In Armenia, some elements of a financial inclusion strategy are incorporated in the country's National Strategy for Financial Education.

Azerbaijan and the Kyrgyz Republic have included their policies for financial inclusion in their national development strategies. The Azerbaijan 2020 Vision highlights the role of entrepreneurship and SMEs in economic development, although it contains no specific strategies for financial inclusion. The Central Bank of Azerbaijan Republic (CBAR) developed the microfinance sector and financial inclusion strategy in consultation with all relevant departments, including Banking and Supervision, Credit Registry, Legal, Payments, Consumer Protection, Strategic Management, and Research. In the Kyrgyz Republic, the National Strategy for Sustainable Development 2013–2017 envisaged measures for SME development, improving access to long-term loans for women entrepreneurs, and a program for the development of women's entrepreneurship. In 2002, the Government of Armenia established the Small and Medium Entrepreneurship Development National Center Fund to provide state support to SMEs, including resources allocated from the state budget and technical and financial assistance.

Table 1.5 Strategies and Programs for Financial Inclusion

Country	National	Central Bank	Ministries/ Regulators	Private Sector
Armenia	SME State Support Programs implemented by the SME Development National Center Fund; pension reform in 2014	Various strategies and initiatives targeting different financial inclusion dimensions (e.g. financial infrastructure, system mediators, guarantor funds, and consumer rights protection)	Moveable Collateral Registry; agriculture insurance pilot program	
Azerbaijan	Azerbaijan 2020 Vision and other programs highlight the role of entrepreneurship and SMEs; Strategic Roadmap for Development of Financial Services in the Republic of Azerbaijan; no specific strategies for financial inclusion	Microfinance sector and financial inclusion strategy	SME subsidy programs under the Economy Ministry; Presidential Decree of 17 September 2017	Azerbaijan Microfinance Association
Georgia	No comprehensive national financial inclusion plan; SME development included in the Georgia 2020 Socio-Economic Development Program; SME Development Strategy of Georgia 2016–2020	National Bank of Georgia received a major grant from the IFC in 2014 to increase access		Several projects to improve financial inclusion with international funding, implemented by Credo Microfinance, FINCA Bank, and TBC Bank

continued on next page

Table 1.5 continued

Country	National	Central Bank	Ministries/Regulators	Private Sector
Kazakhstan	People's IPO program to increase investments and retail saving; unification of pension funds; 1 Trillion Tenge and Nurly Zhol programs in 2014–2017 to promote infrastructure and SME lending; DAMU Entrepreneurship Development Fund			
Kyrgyz Republic	Microfinance development strategies (2006–2010, 2011–2015) and other midterm programs; Law on State Support for SMEs			
Tajikistan		Signatory to Maya Declaration toward engaging 30% of the population in the formal financial sector, particularly through digital services		Several programs aimed at specific groups of beneficiaries
Uzbekistan			Credit Bureau, National Collateral Registry to support lending	Uzbek Association for Microfinance Institutions and Credit Unions

IFC = International Finance Corporation, IPO = initial public offering, SMEs = small and medium-sized enterprises.
Sources: Chapters 2–8 in this volume.

Nevertheless, there are gaps in the development programs and approaches in these countries. If the financial inclusion promotion programs are not implemented in a comprehensive and centralized way, the strategies may not yield significant results. In addition to common issues affecting the status of financial inclusion, each country faces specific problems affecting development, ranging from dependency on remittances to credit excesses in some of the more advanced countries. In Azerbaijan, overdue credit has become excessive, and there is a lack of policy to resolve this issue. There are also gaps in legislation, especially related to the protection of customers' financial rights.

1.7.2 Specific Strategies

Central banks, ministries, and other regulatory authorities have implemented various specific strategies and policies targeting different dimensions of financial inclusion. These include accessibility, electronic identification, innovative products and services, credit databases, credit guarantees, and subsidies. Some examples are described below.

Accessibility

Accessibility refers to all possible means, including ATMs and remote access channels, of enabling customers to select and use any financial service. Penetration depends heavily on the availability of financial and information and communication technology infrastructures in urban and rural areas, income levels, and education. Kazakhstan and Tajikistan have been very active in launching mobile banking, and mobile devices provide convenient product usage in any part of the country. However, in Tajikistan, only a few types of services are currently available by mobile phone.

Electronic Identification

Electronic means of identification are not well developed in the CASC region. The main example is the use of electronic identification cards and social cards in Armenia. These voluntary identification cards have a memory chip containing the data of the citizen (see Nurbekyan and Hovanessian, Chapter 2).

Innovative Products and Services

Enhancing financial inclusion requires a diverse range of financial products and services. Countries need to identify and design products and services appropriate for different target groups. The Kyrgyz Republic has implemented several programs, including the Concept for Stock and Bond Market Development until 2018 and the Concept for Insurance Market Development (2013–2017). However, these programs were unpopular because people were unused to investing in stocks and bonds. Tajikistan is one of the most remittance-dependent countries in the world. ADB, the European Bank for Reconstruction and Development, and the World Bank provide Tajik commercial banks and MFIs with low-cost financial resources, but these are insufficient to meet the high demand in Tajikistan's rural areas. Some international organizations have developed programs aimed at specific groups—for example, the European Bank for Reconstruction and Development provided $1 million to support female entrepreneurs through the Women in Business initiative.

Credit Databases

Information asymmetries, such as a lack of credit data, bankable collateral, and basic accounting information, often discourage financial institutions from lending to SMEs. Innovations to provide more information in this area, such as credit databases, credit guarantee systems, and rules to expand eligible collateral, can ease these asymmetries and increase financial institutions' willingness to lend. Financial education for SMEs can also encourage them to keep better records. Finally, the development of new investment vehicles, such as venture capital, specialized stock exchanges for SMEs and new firms, and hometown investment trusts, can expand SMEs' financing options.

Most CASC economies have been active in setting up credit bureaus and expanding and consolidating credit databases on households and SMEs; however, in most cases such efforts are still at an early stage, while efforts have not yet begun in other economies.

In Armenia, the ACRA Credit Reporting System was introduced in 2004 to gather and process credit-related data. In 2000, Uzbekistan created a credit bureau as part of its banking association; this became an independent unit in 2004. In 2012, a private credit bureau was established; it covered 27.8% of the adult population as of 2016 (see Ahunov, Chapter 8). In Azerbaijan, there is only one credit registry, but it does not meet the normal standards for credit bureaus. In Georgia, Creditinfo Georgia offers a variety of services to various clients, including commercial banks, MFIs, online lenders, leasing companies, and insurance companies. The information gathered includes the past and existing credit of individuals and firms, credit scores and ratings, factors affecting credit scores, changes in credit reports, and credit inquiries. It covers almost 96% of the adult population, higher than any country in the European Union. According to the World Bank Doing Business Project (2017), the Georgian credit bureau scores eight points out of eight on depth of consumer data. The bureau generates a credit report taking into account the most current information on the individual's (or firm's) characteristics, such as volume of liabilities, length of credit history, frequency of use of bank products, payment history, fulfilling commitments, and whether the individual or firm has overdue loans (see Babych, Grigolia, and Keshelava, Chapter 4).

The Kyrgyz Republic established a credit bureau in 2003. Its main function is to manage a database of borrowers and their credit history. Over 160 banks and nonbank financial institutions are partners of the credit bureau.

Two credit information bureaus provide services to credit organizations in Tajikistan: the Credit Information Bureau Tajikistan (CIBT) and the Bureau of Credit History Somonion. The CIBT cooperates with 17 banks and 56 MFIs, and holds information on 602,000 individuals and 25,000 firms, representing 887,000 credit transactions. The Bureau of Credit History Somonion covers five banks and 80 small MFIs, and holds information on 120,000 individuals and 8,500 firms, representing 332,000 credit transactions. Although both credit bureaus have their own clientele, they are not adequate, since the CIBT's scoring is unreliable and credit organizations do not use it. Secondly, not all financial institutions provide information on all their clients, and there are risks associated with these information gaps. Thirdly, the prices for CIBT services are high, possibly due to operational or technical support costs, as the CIBT rents its software. The National Bank of Tajikistan recently began collecting full datasets from credit organizations, and plans to establish a national registry wherein all necessary data from the entire sector will be stored; this registry is expected to provide information to market participants on a fee basis. The Credit Bureau was established in 2017, but has not yet completed state registration (see Mogilevskii and Asadov, Chapter 7).

Credit Guarantees and Subsidies

Credit guarantees can also ease access to finance for SMEs, although they encounter several problems, mainly moral hazard and high costs due to nonperforming loans. Guarantee funds act as mediators between borrowers and commercial banks to provide guarantees when a borrower lacks sufficient collateral.

Financial infrastructure development is also a key focus of the CBA. The Deposit Guarantee Fund and Moveable Collateral Registry are good examples of recently implemented initiatives. Armenia's SME Development National Center provides loan guarantees as one of its financial assistance measures for SMEs. On 15 September 2017, the President of Azerbaijan signed a decree on a number of measures to provide state support to entrepreneurs and help expand access to financial resources; these measures include the establishment of the Credit Guarantee Fund of Azerbaijan, which provides entrepreneurs with guarantees for manat loans taken out in authorized banks, and in some cases will also provide interest-rate subsidies. Following the 2008 financial crisis, Kazakhstan widened its schemes to help firms access financing through interest-rate subsidies and loan guarantees.

The Law on Guarantee Funds in the Kyrgyz Republic was passed in 2013, and there were six guarantee funds operating in four regions in 2016. During 2011–2015, loans to SMEs supported by guarantee funds amounted to Som190 million. In 2017, the Government of the Kyrgyz Republic established a public joint-stock company guarantee fund with capital supplied from the national budget (25%) and ADB (75%). The fund has representatives in every region, working with seven commercial banks and the Russian-Kyrgyz Development Fund. As of September 2017, the guarantee fund had issued 140 guarantees, 114 for SMEs and 51 for projects run by women (see Hasanova, Chapter 6).

The Credit Guarantee Fund of Tajikistan was established in 2014 to address financial institutions' strict collateral requirements. This fund provides credit guarantees to SMEs and technical assistance to Tajik partner financial institutions. Credit guarantees can also be offered in the form of investment guarantees rather than loan guarantees. Of the 23 largest microfinance investment funds, three offer investment guarantees on MFI or SME loan portfolios (see Mogilevskii and Asadov, Chapter 7).

1.8 Financial Literacy and Education

In the aftermath of the global financial crisis, financial literacy and financial education have received increasing attention. The crisis yielded sobering lessons, such as how the mis-selling of financial products directly contributed to the severity of the crisis, both in developed economies and in Asia. To a certain extent, this can be attributed to inadequate financial knowledge on the part of individual borrowers and investors.

Financial literacy has gained an important position on the policy agenda of many countries, and the importance of collecting informative, reliable data on financial literacy levels across the adult population has been widely recognized. At the Los Cabos Summit in 2012, G20 leaders endorsed the High-Level Principles on National Strategies for Financial Education developed by the Organisation for Economic Co-operation and Development (OECD) and International Network on Financial Education (INFE), thereby acknowledging the importance of coordinated policy approaches to financial education (G20 2012). At the same time, surveys consistently show that financial literacy is relatively low, even in advanced economies (OECD/INFE 2016). As individuals are increasingly required to manage their own retirement savings and pensions, mainly due to the trend of switching from defined-benefit to defined-contribution pension plans, the need for high levels of financial literacy is rising.

Lusardi and Mitchell (2014: 6) define financial literacy as "peoples' ability to process economic information and make informed decisions about financial planning, wealth accumulation, debt, and pensions." OECD/INFE (2016: 47) defines financial literacy as "[a] combination of awareness, knowledge, skill, attitude and behaviour necessary to make sound financial decisions and ultimately achieve individual financial wellbeing." Thus, this concept of financial literacy is multidimensional, reflecting not only knowledge but also skills, attitudes, and actual behavior.

Financial education can be viewed as a capacity-building process over an individual's lifetime, which results in improved financial literacy and wellbeing. Financial education is also necessary to prepare for old age. Financial education for SMEs is also important. Japan and Thailand have begun to collect SME databases; as a result, SMEs have started keeping their books, becoming more aware of their daily revenues and expenses in the process. Some SMEs have also started to think long-term. Therefore, collecting an SME database can be a good source of financial education for SMEs. At the same time, asset management has become vital for SMEs. SMEs must prepare pension contributions for their employees, leading to an accumulation of pension assets. Therefore, SMEs need to know how to manage their pension reserve assets.

1.8.1 Status of Financial Literacy

Mapping the current status of financial literacy (or financial capability) in Asia presents challenges to researchers and policymakers alike: this is a new area with limited data, the coverage of available surveys is relatively uneven, and methodologies and results are inconsistent. Only a limited number of Asian economies and target groups within them have been surveyed so far, and their results vary widely. Although there is some relationship between financial literacy and per capita income, rankings differ significantly across different studies. Greater coverage of target groups (e.g. students, seniors, SMEs, and the self-employed) is needed. It is desirable that international organizations, such as the OECD, World Bank, and ADB, sponsor surveys using the same kind of survey questionnaires and methodologies to establish a meaningful basis for international comparisons.

Surveys of financial literacy have been conducted in some CASC economies. For example, according to the 2010 OECD/INFE survey (Atkinson and Messy 2012) and 2014 Global Financial Literacy survey (Klapper, Lusardi, and Oudheusden 2015), Armenia scored in the lowest group of all countries based on a simple average of the three basic financial literacy dimensions utilized in the surveys.[4] According to a national survey in the Kyrgyz Republic, most of the population is passive and uninterested in obtaining information about financial markets, services, and products. According to the OECD/INFE International Survey of Adult Financial Literacy Competencies (OECD/INFE 2016), Georgia is among those countries where a high share of households have difficulty making ends meet; however, its average financial literacy score was slightly above average for its income level.

1.8.2 Financial Education Strategy

There are still many policy gaps in CASC economies in the areas of financial literacy and financial education. A variety of programs exist, as summarized in Table 1.6, which shows national strategies, the roles of central banks, regulators, and private programs, as well as the channels and coverage of such programs.

Table 1.6 Financial Education Programs and Strategies

Country	National	Central Bank	Other Regulators	Private Sector/ MDB	Coverage/ targets	Channels
Armenia	NSFE (since 2014)	One of the main stakeholders, the NSFE	Ministry of Education and Science, Ministry of Finance, Ministry of Labor and Social Affairs, Ministry of Territorial Administration and Development, National Institute of Education, and municipal authorities are stakeholders of the NSFE and its programs	Financial System Mediator, Armenian Deposit Guarantee Fund, Union of Banks, Union of Credit Organizations, Insurance Market Association, Consumer Rights Protection nongovernment organization, and the Armenian Motor Insurer's Bureau	Schoolchildren, students, the rural population, women, and individuals in teachable moments	School curriculum (Me and the World, Math, Algebra, Social Science); universities; workshops; training; competitions; games; and mass and social media

continued on next page

---

[4] Knowledge of interest, compound interest, and risk diversification.

Table 1.6 *continued*

Country	National	Central Bank	Other Regulators	Private Sector/ MDB	Coverage/ targets	Channels
Azerbaijan	National Financial Literacy Strategy (since 2016)	Financial Literacy Project 2010	Financial Literacy Project of the Ministry of Education	Azerbaijan Banks Association partnership with the CBAR, joint-training for commercial banks, and Azerbaijan Microfinance Association programs	Students, broad public, economic journalists, CBAR employees, and commercial bank employees	Awareness-raising programs, schools, seminars, and training
Georgia	National Strategy for Financial Education (since 2016)	The National Bank of Georgia is the leading authority in the National Strategy.		Stakeholders of the National Strategy	Youth, the rural population, the unemployed, and others in need	Training, awareness promotion campaigns, incorporation in school curricula (math and civil education), brochures, videos, and mass media
Kazakhstan	State Program for Enhancing the Investment Culture (2007–2011) (only for initial public offerings)	Program to improve the financial literacy of the population for 2016–2018; key performance indicators not directly linked to financial inclusion measures		Some financial education activities by commercial banks and microfinance institutions	Schoolchildren, students, and the general population	Mass media, school curriculum, meetings, public lectures, the National Bank of Kazakhstan's specialized website for financial inclusion, and other activities
Kyrgyz Republic	Program to Improve Financial Literacy 2016–2020	Key partner to the government's Financial Literacy Program		Several fragmented consultations, training, and books by financial institutions with limited coverage; and financial literacy programs by international organizations	Schoolchildren, youth, adults, and general citizens	New education curricula, training, consultation, media, and a specialized website for financial inclusion

continued on next page

Table 1.6 continued

Country	National	Central Bank	Other Regulators	Private Sector/ MDB	Coverage/ targets	Channels
Tajikistan	No comprehensive national financial education program	Expected: annual international financial literacy weeks, and the distribution of financial products booklets	Financial infrastructure development program initiated by the IFC 2015; activities by international donors in coordination with national agencies	Partnership with the IFC in the 2015 program, and other small-scale programs by credit organizations for branding purposes	Youth, students, teachers, and the wider citizenry	Workshop, training, mass media, social media, and booklet distribution
Uzbekistan	Plan developed in collaboration with Sparkassenstiftung pending ratification	Financial literacy program jointly held with the IFC, Association of Banks, and Chamber of Commerce (2017)		Financial literacy program by the National Association of Microfinance Institutions, and the Microfinance Centre	Small and medium-sized enterprise owners, general population, low-income groups	Training programs

CBAR = Central Bank of Azerbaijan, IFC = International Finance Corporation, MDB = multilateral development bank, NSFE = National Strategy for Financial Education.
Source: Chapters 2–8 in this volume.

In 2014, the Government of Armenia formally adopted its National Strategy for Financial Education, which is led by the CBA; and the Central Bank of Azerbaijan implemented its National Financial Literacy Strategy. In 2016, Georgia implemented its National Strategy for Financial Education with the goal of improving consumer wellbeing and consumer protection. In Kazakhstan, the 2014 Concept for the Financial Sector Development of the Republic of Kazakhstan until 2030 (2030 Concept) states that work to increase the level of financial education should be continuous and cover multiple aspects thereof; however, this has not yet been implemented. The Kyrgyz Republic adopted a program to improve financial literacy for 2016–2020, including the first centralized initiatives to provide financial education in the school curriculum. No national strategies for promoting financial literacy have yet been implemented in Tajikistan or Uzbekistan.

Institutions Involved

Both public and private institutions are involved in organizing financial literacy programs. Public institutions include the central banks, ministries of education, ministries of finance, international organizations (e.g. the World Bank and OECD), and schools. Private institutions include associations of banks and MFIs. In Armenia, the main stakeholders in the financial education program include the central bank, the Ministry of Education and Science, the Ministry of Labor and Social Issues, the Ministry of Territorial Administration, the Ministry of Finance, the National Institute of Education, and the municipality of Yerevan, as well as private and nongovernment organizations.[5] In Uzbekistan, the central bank, IFC, Association of Banks of Uzbekistan, and Chamber of Commerce of Uzbekistan implement programs on financial literacy. In Azerbaijan, the banks association established a Financial Literacy Council as a platform for discussing ideas, information, and experiences in this sector. In 2010, the CBAR and Azerbaijan Microfinance Association launched the Financial Literacy Project. In Kazakhstan, financial education is implemented by the National Bank of Kazakhstan and some commercial banks and MFIs. In the Kyrgyz Republic, although centralized financial education is relatively new, commercial banks and MFIs are also involved in financial education programs.

Target Groups and Programs

The fifth column of Table 1.5 summarizes the targets of financial literacy programs, including school students, the general population, youth, central bank and commercial bank employees, economic journalists, SME owners, the rural population, the unemployed working force, teachers, and low-income groups.

Types of Programs

Financial literacy programs are conducted via several different channels. The first is training and workshops. In 2016, the Rural Financial Education Project was implemented in certain regions of Armenia, including two-day workshops on personal finance management. Training and workshops are also being carried out in Azerbaijan, Georgia, the Kyrgyz Republic, Tajikistan, and Uzbekistan.

The second channel is social media. For example, the Financial Football project in Armenia, carried out jointly with Visa, is a tool for learning financial concepts. The project aims to strengthen the financial capabilities of the general public. Other examples are found in Georgia, Kazakhstan, the Kyrgyz Republic, and Tajikistan. Mass media tools such as videos are used to raise the awareness of the general population, especially youth and students.

---

[5] A list of all stakeholders can be found in Chapter 2.

The third channel is consultations, which private financial institutions usually provide to their clients. For example, in the Kyrgyz Republic, commercial banks and MFIs periodically inform their clients about financial products by providing consultations and trainings, and disseminating informational materials.

General Financial Education
Financial education has not yet been implemented in the general school curricula, but some CASC countries are now in the process of introducing it. For example, in the Kyrgyz Republic, a new curriculum for school education will be introduced to inculcate responsible financial behavior from a young age. Some related subjects will also be strengthened (see Hasanova, Chapter 6). From 2018, Armenia is planning to integrate financial education into school subjects, including Me and the World, mathematics, algebra, and social science. Similarly, Georgia is planning to integrate financial literacy topics into the national school curriculum (in mathematics and civil education classes). The pilot program, Schoolbank, is already in action, and the National Bank of Georgia is delivering training for pupils as well as training for teachers in 11 public schools.

1.9 Conclusions and the Way Forward

There are numerous arguments in favor of increasing financial inclusion, and a large body of evidence shows that increased financial inclusion can significantly reduce poverty and boost shared prosperity, but such efforts must be well-designed. Greater access to financial services by households can help smooth consumption, ease cash shortages, and increase savings for retirement and other needs, although the evidence on microfinance is less positive. Greater access for SMEs can allow them to take greater advantage of investment projects with potentially high returns and participate in international trade. Greater financial access may provide side benefits as well, such as greater financial stability and efficacy of monetary policy. Governments can also take advantage of greater financial access to rely more on cash transfer programs and reduce corruption and money laundering.

Nonetheless, there are numerous barriers to financial inclusion on both the supply and demand sides. On the supply side, the high costs of handling small deposits and loans in physically remote areas, together with information asymmetries and a lack of documentation and collateral, deter financial institutions from extending financial services to lower income households and SMEs. Regulatory restrictions on capital adequacy, identification requirements, and branch openings, as well as inadequate infrastructure for transport and payment systems, compound these problems. On the demand side, the chief barriers are a lack of cash, ignorance of financial products and services, and a lack of trust.

According to the most widely used measures, financial inclusion in the CASC economies on the whole falls slightly below the expected average relative to levels of per capita GDP. In terms of the percentage of adults with a formal account, Azerbaijan, Kazakhstan, and Uzbekistan rank significantly below the expected level, while the other five countries are fairly close to the general Asian trend. The low level of account penetration in Azerbaijan, which has relatively high per capita income, stands out as a puzzle. In terms of adult borrowing from a formal institution, levels are very high for Georgia and Armenia and very low for Uzbekistan. As Uzbekistan's low level partly reflects choices for religious reasons, the degree of involuntary financial access is probably less than indicated by the overall figure. Azerbaijan, Kazakhstan, and Tajikistan have relatively low levels of SME loans. Moreover, financial access can vary significantly between rural and urban areas, and between income or age groups. Although remittances play a large role in several CASC economies, banks do not typically target this market with specific products or services. Access to other financial products such as insurance is quite low.

Lack of trust in the financial sector remains a problem in the region, reflecting the legacy of financial and economic turmoil following the breakup of the former Soviet Union. This is especially true in Armenia and the Kyrgyz Republic. Inefficient bankruptcy laws and high collateral requirements due to weak credit assessment systems also present barriers to financial access. Corruption is also a significant problem in several countries, while widespread participation in the informal sector makes it difficult for workers and firms to provide data showing their creditworthiness.

The CASC economies notably lack strong financial inclusion strategies. The Kyrgyz Republic and Azerbaijan have the most well-articulated financial inclusion strategies, which are incorporated into their national economic planning strategies, but concrete impacts therefrom remain limited. A number of individual policies encourage SME finance, such as loan guarantee programs, credit databases, and subsidized loans, but there is no overall financial inclusion strategy. MFIs are growing rapidly in some economies, mainly Georgia and Kazakhstan, but have actually dwindled in the Kyrgyz Republic and are weakening in Azerbaijan in terms of asset quality. There is no separate category for MFIs in Armenia. Few specialized products or programs promote financial inclusion among poorer households, especially in rural regions (although Azerbaijan is an exception). Most CASC economies have some kind of credit bureau (Georgia's in particular is highly rated), and a number of economies also have credit guarantee programs. Mobile phone banking, e-money, internet banking, and other forms of financial technology are developing rapidly in the region (Tajikistan is an exception to this trend), albeit from a very low base.

All of the country chapter authors recommend developing and/or strengthening financial inclusion strategies where they do not currently exist or are insufficient. Such strategies should comprehensively involve public and private stakeholders, including all relevant ministries, the financial sector, and civil society institutions. They should also set clear goals and key performance indicators to measure progress toward achieving these goals. It is important to link the goal of financial inclusion to other overarching goals, such as inclusive and sustainable economic growth and financial and social development.

A comprehensive strategy for SMEs should be developed. Credit guarantee schemes should be introduced in countries where they are not already available, such as Azerbaijan, and credit databases and credit bureaus should be strengthened. Collateral registries should be adopted and expanded beyond physical property to facilitate SMEs' access to credit. Alternative sources of funding such as venture investment funds, business angels, peer-to-peer lending, and crowdfunding platforms should be encouraged. High interest rates remain an obstacle to borrowing in several countries, and the factors behind such rates should be investigated to identify possible policy interventions, without undermining the need to price risk appropriately. For example, insufficient competition in the banking sector can push up interest rates in some countries, and increased competition among financial service providers needs to be encouraged to bring down prices and promote innovation.

State support programs for financial institutions aimed at increasing coverage and the level of access to financial services for households in remote districts should be provided. For example, an adequate infrastructure to support financial operations and transactions in rural areas could be created in post offices. Since postal services enjoy the trust of the rural population, post offices could be an important financial access point for households in rural areas. Promoting a shift from cash to digital payments can also be consistent with a financial inclusion strategy.

Insurance services have been under-utilized in some countries. Where lacking, compulsory third-party motor liability insurance can be a big leap forward, and there are similarly significant opportunities in health and agriculture insurance. Mandatory health insurance provides another potential avenue to provide access to health insurance besides employer health plans; this can eliminate adverse selection and increase the quality of health services due to increased competition.

Financial inclusion policies need to be supported by adequate information. Countries should increase the frequency of surveys about lending, borrowing, and the savings behavior and practices of households and SMEs. Collecting such information should be a priority goal of national statistical agencies.

In general, financial regulation in the CASC economies is relatively consistent, with the central bank typically having oversight of all lending institutions. However, some shortcomings persist; for example, in Tajikistan, supervision of financial institutions is still mainly compliance-based, with little focus on good governance and risk management. Also, the regulators there tend to be slow to understand market evolution, leading to a reluctance to experiment with new technology-based financial products. The adoption of international financial reporting standards, more advanced risk assessment tools, stress testing, and crisis management tools are some of the primary measures that should be introduced.

It is also necessary to strengthen the governance of regulators, including greater independence and transparency to increase public trust in the financial system. Transparency and proper information disclosure by commercial banks and MFIs should be improved as well. Regulatory issues related to the participation of mobile network operators in innovative financial services must be resolved, and regulatory "sandboxes" should be created to test innovative financial products and services. Finally, improving macroeconomic policy management can help increase trust in the financial system by reducing the volatility of inflation, interest rates, and the exchange rate, thereby reducing the incentive for dollarization.

Consumer protection efforts in CASC economies are generally rudimentary, with few specific rules covering consumer finance, and mainly consist of interest-rate caps on loans. One exception to this rule is Armenia, where the central bank's responsibilities include creating a legal system to assure consumer protection, promote programs on financial knowledge and education, and operate consumer services websites and hotlines. Consumer protection policies should be expanded to cover misleading advertising, excessive collection practices, and dispute handling and resolution processes; and consumer hotlines should be established where they do not exist.

Financial literacy levels in CASC economies are generally low, although actual survey evidence remains incomplete. More national financial literacy surveys using consistent and internationally comparable methodologies are needed in the region.

Among the CASC economies, Armenia, Azerbaijan, Georgia, and the Kyrgyz Republic are the most advanced in the area of financial education, as they have already established national financial education strategies. The Kyrgyz Republic is notable for having developed a financial education program for schools, although it has not yet been implemented. So far, Kazakhstan, Tajikistan, and Uzbekistan do not have such programs.

All country chapter authors also recommend strengthening financial education strategies and programs. Effective national strategies for financial education contain four key elements: (i) coordination among major stakeholders, including regulatory authorities, the education ministry, educational institutions, financial institutions, and civil society institutions; (ii) an emphasis on customer orientation and addressing both demand- and supply-side gaps; (iii) a combination of broad-based functional interventions, such as in school curricula, and targeted programs for vulnerable groups according to the availability of resources; and (iv) the adoption of a long-term timeline with flexibility to respond to changing needs.

Programs for financial education should include its introduction into the school curriculum at various levels, as well as programs for specific target groups such as SME entrepreneurs, including separate programs for women entrepreneurs, farmers, migrants, women, the poor, the disabled, pensioners, and other vulnerable groups. Financial education programs can involve financial service providers, industry associations, nongovernment organizations, mass media, higher education institutions, municipalities, and financial consultants. Key issues to be addressed include managing borrowing costs prudently and developing long-term savings goals.

Monitoring and evaluating national financial education strategies is vital to build experience and encourage program adaptation. If appropriate incentives are provided, think tanks and universities can help with monitoring and evaluating efforts. Since government support programs will be insufficient to maintain adequate financing, the private sector, such as life insurance firms, must supply long-term financial products suitable for self-protection. Long-term asset allocation by households can support the necessary infrastructure and other investments where long-term finance is required.

References

Alliance for Financial Inclusion. 2010. *Financial Inclusion Measurement for Regulators: Survey Design and Implementation.* Bangkok: Alliance for Financial Inclusion.

Asian Development Bank (ADB). 2012. *Technical Assistance for Improving Financial Inclusion in Asia and the Pacific.* Manila: ADB.

ADB. 2015. *Asian Development Outlook 2015: Financing Asia's Future Growth.* Manila: ADB.

Association of Southeast Asian Nations. 2014. *The ASEAN Framework for Equitable Economic Development.* Jakarta: Association of Southeast Asian Nations. http://www.asean.org/news/item/the-asean-framework-for-equitable-economic-development (accessed 2 February 2016).

Atkinson, A., and F. Messy. 2012. Measuring Financial Literacy: Results of the OECD/International Network on Financial Education (INFE) Pilot Study. Organisation for Economic Co-operation and Development (OECD) Working Paper on Finance, Insurance and Private Pensions 15. Paris: OECD Publishing.

Atkinson, A., and F. Messy. 2013. Promoting Financial Inclusion through Financial Education: OECD/INFE Evidence, Policies and Practice. OECD Working Paper on Finance, Insurance and Private Pensions 34. Paris: OECD Publishing.

Beck, T., A. Demirgüç-Kunt, and R. Levine. 2007. Finance, Inequality, and Poverty: Cross-Country Evidence. *Journal of Economic Growth* 12(1): 27–49.

Bruhn, M., and I. Love. 2013. The Economic Impact of Expanding Access to Finance in Mexico. In *Banking the World: Empirical Foundations of Financial Inclusion*, edited by R. Cull, A. Demirgüç-Kunt, and J. Morduch, 137–156. Cambridge, MA: Massachusetts Institute of Technology Press.

Burgess, R., and R. Pande. 2005. Do Rural Banks Matter? Evidence from the Indian Social Banking Experiment. *American Economic Review* 95(3): 780–795.

Chakraborty, K. C. 2011. Financial Inclusion: A Road India Needs to Travel. Speech. Mumbai: Reserve Bank of India. https://rbi.org.in/scripts/BS_SpeechesView.aspx?Id=607 (accessed 13 December 2015).

Consultative Group to Assist the Poor. 2004. Interest Rate Ceilings and Microfinance: The Story So Far. Occasional Paper 9. Washington, DC: Consultative Group to Assist the Poor.

Demirgüç-Kunt, A., and L. Klapper. 2013. Measuring Financial Inclusion: Explaining Variation across and within Countries. *Brookings Papers on Economic Activity* Spring: 279–321.

Demirgüç-Kunt, A., L. Klapper, D. Singer, S. Ansar, and J. Hess. 2018. *The Global Findex Database 2017: Measuring Financial Inclusion and the Fintech Revolution.* Washington, DC: World Bank.

Global Partnership for Financial Inclusion. 2018. Washington, DC: Global Partnership for Financial Inclusion. http://www.gpfi.org (accessed 9 September 2018).

Global Partnership for Financial Inclusion (GPFI) and Consultative Group to Assist the Poor (CGAP). 2011. *Global Standard-Setting Bodies and Financial Inclusion for the Poor: Toward Proportionate Standards and Guidance.* Washington, DC: Global Partnership for Financial Inclusion. Available at: http://www.gpfi.org/publications/global-standard-setting-bodies-and-financial-inclusion (accessed 21 January 2019).

Group of Twenty (G20). 2012. G20 Leaders Declaration. Los Cabos, Mexico, 19 June. http://www.g20.utoronto.ca/2012/2012-0619-loscabos.html (accessed 1 December 2016).

Honohan, P. 2004. Financial Development, Growth and Poverty: How Close Are the Links? World Bank Policy Research Working Paper 3203. Washington, DC: World Bank. https://www.adb.org/publications/financial-inclusion-financial-literacy-and-financial-education-azerbaijan.

International Finance Corporation. 2014. *Money Flow Mobile Money Market Survey.* Washington, DC: International Finance Corporation.

International Monetary Fund. 2018. *International Financial Access Survey (FAS).* Washington, DC: International Monetary Fund. http://data.imf.org/?sk=E5DCAB7E-A5CA-4892-A6EA-598B5463A34C (accessed 29 May 2018).

Kaboski, J., and R. Townsend. 2005. Policies and Impact: An Analysis of Village-Level Microfinance Institutions. *Journal of the European Economic Association* 3(1): 1–50.

Karlan, D., and J. Morduch. 2009. Access to Finance, in *Handbook of Development Economics, Vol. 5*, edited by D. Rodrik and M. Rosenzweig. Amsterdam: Elsevier.

Khan, H. R. 2011. Financial Inclusion and Financial Stability: Are They Two Sides of the Same Coin? Address given at BANCON 2011. Chennai, 4–6 November.

Klapper, L., A. Lusardi, and P. van Oudheusden. 2015. *Financial Literacy Around the World. Insight from the Standard & Poor's Ratings Services Global Financial Literacy Survey.* http://gflec.org/wp-content/uploads/2015/11/Finlit_paper_16_F2_singles.pdf

Lusardi, A., and O. Mitchell. 2014. The Economic Importance of Financial Literacy: Theory and Evidence. *Journal of Economic Literature* 52(1): 5–44. http://dx.doi.org/10.1257/jel.52.1.5 (accessed 12 December 2016).

McKernan, S. 2003. The Impact of Microcredit Programs on Self-Employment Profits: Do Noncredit Program Aspects Matter? *Review of Economics and Statistics* 84(1): 93–115.

Morgan, P., and V. Pontines. 2014. Financial Stability and Financial Inclusion. Asian Development Bank Institute (ADBI) Working Paper 488. Tokyo: ADBI.

National Bank of the Republic of Kazakhstan. 2016. *Report of the National Bank of the Republic of Kazakhstan for 2015*. Almaty: National Bank of the Republic of Kazakhstan.

OECD/INFE. 2016. *OECD/INFE International Survey of Adult Financial Literacy Competencies*. Paris: OECD.

Pitt, M., S. Khandker, O. Chowdhury, and D. Millimet. 2003. Credit Programs for the Poor and the Health Status of Children in Rural Bangladesh. *International Economic Review* 44(1): 8–118.

Schwarz, A. M., and O. S. Arias 2014. *The Inverting Pyramid: Pension Systems Facing Demographic Challenges in Europe and Central Asia*. Washington, DC: World Bank.

Social Security Administration and International Social Security Association. 2015. *Social Security Programs throughout the World: Asia and the Pacific, 2014*.

Tambunlertchai, K. 2017. Thailand. In N. Yoshino and P. Morgan, eds. *Financial Inclusion, Regulation and Education: Asian Perspectives*. Tokyo, Japan: Asian Development Bank Institute.

World Bank. 2008. *Finance for All? Policies and Pitfalls in Expanding Access*. Washington, DC: World Bank.

World Bank. 2014. *Global Financial Development Report: Financial Inclusion*. Washington, DC: World Bank.

World Bank. 2016. *Enhancing Financial Capability and Inclusion in Azerbaijan*. Washington, DC: World Bank. http://documents.worldbank.org/curated/en/880631470853969754/pdf/107748-WP-P125462-PUBLIC-10-8-2016-12-5-10-Azerbaijan EnhancingFinancial CapabilityandInclusionFINAL.pdf.

World Bank. 2017. *Doing Business Project*. Washington, DC: World Bank. http://www.doingbusiness.org/data/exploretopics/getting-credit (accessed 4 April 2017).

World Bank. 2018. *Global Findex Survey*. Washington, DC: World Bank. http://www.worldbank.org/en/ programs/globalfindex (accessed 3 July 2018).

Yoshino, N., and P. Morgan, eds. 2017. *Financial Inclusion, Regulation and Education: Asian Perspectives*. Tokyo: Asian Development Bank Institute.

2
Armenia

Armen Nurbekyan and Naneh Hovanessian

2.1 Introduction

Financial inclusion is steadily climbing the priority lists of international development agencies and policy makers. It is considered a key enabler of poverty reduction and inclusive growth. In 2017, the World Bank Group announced its Universal Financial Access 2020 initiative. In the same year, Group of 20 (G20) finance ministers and central bank governors committed to advancing financial inclusion worldwide.[1]

While there are clear opportunities to be seized, financial inclusion may come with costs when not accompanied by sound regulatory and supervisory frameworks (Sahay et al. 2015). There is, however, no question that high-quality financial infrastructure enhances both financial stability and financial inclusion. This has been the focus of financial inclusion policies in Armenia.

Financial inclusion in Armenia has advanced significantly during the last decade. For example, the credit to gross domestic product (GDP) ratio has increased by around five times since 2006, reaching approximately 48% in 2016. Similarly, the ratio of bank deposits to GDP increased from 10% in 2006 to around 41% in 2016. Other quantitative indicators such as bank branch, credit, and deposit penetration have increased exponentially as well. However, the growth potential of the insurance sector remains largely untapped. The main driver of the insurance sector was the introduction of third-party motor liability insurance in 2011. The introduction of pension reform in 2014 replaced the pay-as-you-go system with the multi-pillar one. This flagship reform makes it possible to generate long-term savings in Armenia and significantly contributes to financial inclusion by building trust in the financial system.

---

[1] http://www.gpfi.org/news/baden-baden-g20-communiqu-commits-advance-financial-inclusion

The financial system in Armenia is bank-based, and the Central Bank of Armenia (CBA) is its single regulator. The CBA is also responsible for the protection of consumer rights and market conduct in the financial system. Broad-based banking reforms, which were implemented at the end of the 1990s and the beginning of the 2000s, cleaned up the banking sector and laid the foundation for future development. The two big shocks in the last decade, the global financial crisis and the Russian Federation currency crisis in 2014, tested the resilience of the financial sector. The financial sector has successfully weathered these shocks without undermining trust in the system.

The CBA is responsible for advancing financial inclusion and financial literacy in Armenia. Policies promoting financial inclusion in Armenia have focused on building high-quality financial infrastructure on the one hand, and building trust in the financial system through financial education and consumer protection on the other. Important milestones of financial infrastructure development include the creation of a credit bureau, the Armenian Card payment system, a financial mediator, a deposit guarantee fund, compulsory third-party motor liability insurance, pension reform, and the first venture capital firm.[2] On the demand side, CBA policies focus on consumer enhancement aimed at the design and oversight of an appropriate legal framework, the effective resolution of consumer complaints, and increased financial literacy among consumers. In 2014, the CBA spearheaded the National Strategy for Financial Education (NSFE) with the goal of increasing financial literacy. The NSFE targets specific quantitative indicators, which will be assessed every 5 years using the Financial Capability Barometer (FCB) developed jointly by the Alliance of Financial Inclusion (AFI) and the CBA.

Despite the fact that the NSFE includes some quantitative targets for financial inclusion,[3] policies aimed at increasing financial inclusion in Armenia do not generally target specific indicators; the CBA's national strategy of 2015–2017 focused on the development of financial system regulations, supervision, and financial infrastructure.

The absence of high-quality financial inclusion data is a major constraint for policy makers. Despite the efforts of the CBA to collect accurate data, the absence of consistently collected financial inclusion data, especially in the small and medium-sized enterprise (SME) sector, makes it difficult to identify obstacles to financial inclusion and tailor policies to address them.

---

[2] Unlike the other milestones, the first venture capital firm was not created by the CBA; it is mentioned to illustrate an important development in the financial infrastructure.

[3] For example, the NSFE has quantitative targets for the share of adults with banking cards and accounts.

Barriers to financial inclusion in rural and urban areas are different. On the supply side, physical infrastructure is one of the main issues in rural areas, while the main obstacles on the demand side are financial illiteracy, lower incomes, and a lack of trust in the financial system. Another significant barrier to financial inclusion is the large share held by the informal sector, which creates high monitoring costs for financial institutions and leads to higher loan rates. As a result, the informal sector increases lending costs in the economy and hinders the financial inclusion of firms.

2.2 Overview of the Armenian Financial System

Armenia's financial system is dominated by banks, which account for 88% of the system's total assets (followed by credit organizations with 8.7%) (Figure 2.1). There are no separate legal or regulatory definitions of microfinance institutions. Credit organizations cover microfinance activities in Armenia and are regulated by the CBA. Insurance companies account for only 1% of total assets.

After the banking sector reforms at the end of the 1990s and beginning of the 2000s, the sector began to develop rapidly, bringing foreign capital and prominent global banks to Armenia. In 2005, a single framework of risk-based supervision was introduced, and has remained at the core of supervisory and regulatory activities. The share of foreign capital in the statutory capital was 62% in 2016. The banking sector

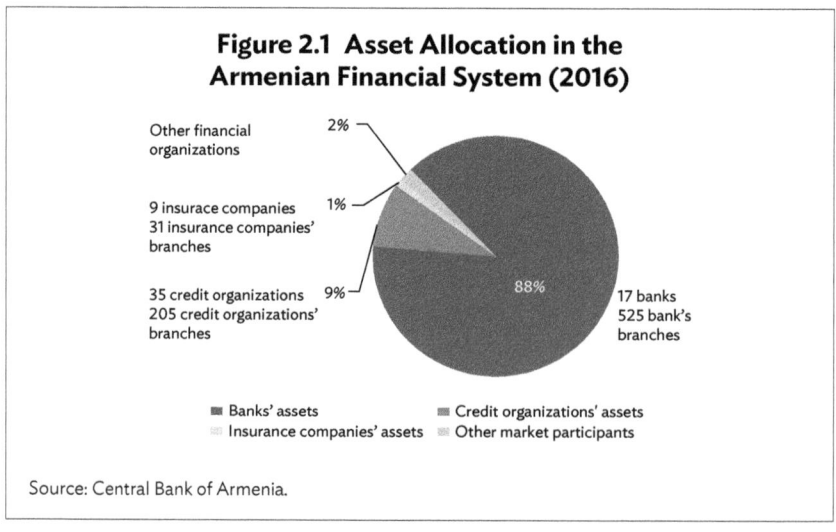

Figure 2.1 Asset Allocation in the Armenian Financial System (2016)

Source: Central Bank of Armenia.

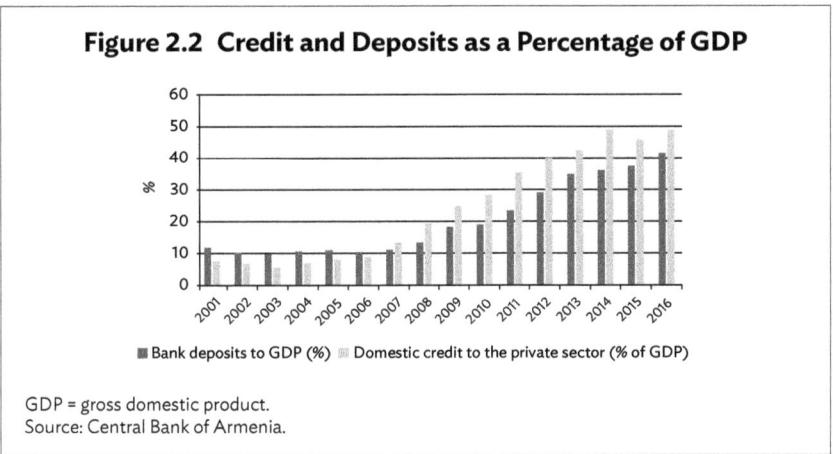

Figure 2.2 Credit and Deposits as a Percentage of GDP

GDP = gross domestic product.
Source: Central Bank of Armenia.

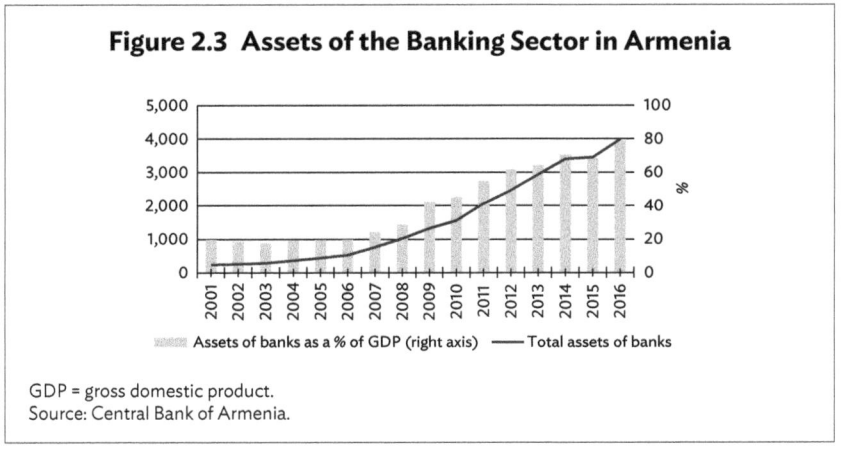

Figure 2.3 Assets of the Banking Sector in Armenia

GDP = gross domestic product.
Source: Central Bank of Armenia.

includes no state banks. In 2010, the Pan-Armenian Development Bank was established with the aim of providing long-term financing to export-oriented private enterprises to fund their investment projects. The statutory capital of the bank was AMD7.5 billion, with the CBA being the only shareholder. The bank was transformed into an investment fund in 2017.

The financial system has experienced rapid growth since the global financial crisis. Figure 2.2 shows the evolution of credit and deposits as a ratio of GDP: the ratio of bank deposits to GDP increased from 10% in 2006 to around 40% in 2016, while the credit-to-GDP ratio increased from less than 10% in 2006 to about 50% in 2016.

Banking sector assets increased from AMD0.5 trillion in 2006 to AMD4.0 trillion in 2016. During the same period, banks' assets-to-GDP ratio quadrupled, reaching 80% in 2016 (Figure 2.3). This asset-side growth was driven by deposit growth of 658%, as well as funding from international financial institutions (IFIs) and international donors.

Credit organizations underwent a similar development. Assets of credit organizations increased from AMD21 billion in 2006 to AMD391 billion in 2016 (Figure 2.4). The assets-to-GDP ratio reached 7.77% in 2016 from 0.78% in 2006. As of December 2017, there were 35 credit organizations in Armenia, including 31 universal credit organizations, 3 refinancing credit organizations, and 1 credit union. Credit unions and universal credit organizations extend loans, while refinancing credit organizations refinance the loans of banks and credit organizations. Table 2.1 shows the main differences between the regulatory requirements for different types of credit organizations. Both the number and branch coverage of credit organizations have increased rapidly: from 2006 to 2017 the number of credit organizations more than doubled to 35, and the number of branches increased from 2 to 205.

The insurance market is small, accounting for only 1% of financial sector assets as of the end of 2016. Although the assets-to-GDP ratio of insurance companies almost tripled during the last decade, it remains quite low at around 0.9% (Figure 2.5). The main driver of growth in

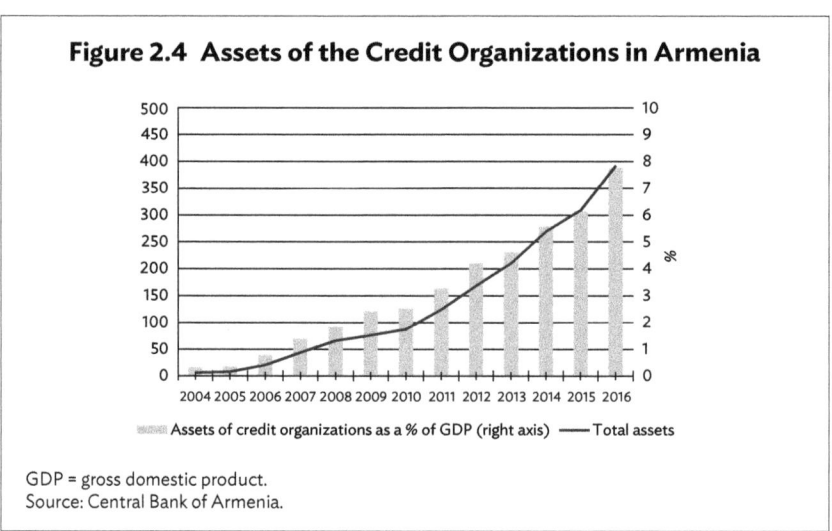

Figure 2.4 Assets of the Credit Organizations in Armenia

GDP = gross domestic product.
Source: Central Bank of Armenia.

Table 2.1 The Difference Between Universal Credit Organizations, Credit Unions, and Refinancing Credit Organizations

Refinancing Credit Organization	Universal Credit Organization	Credit Union
• Capital requirement: AMD4,000 million • Maximum exposure to single largest borrower: 30% of capital • Capital adequacy ratio: 10%	• Capital requirement: AMD150 million • Maximum exposure to single largest borrower: 20% of capital • Capital adequacy ratio: 10%	• Capital requirement: AMD50 million • Maximum exposure to single largest borrower: 25% of capital • Capital adequacy ratio: 6%

Source: Authors.

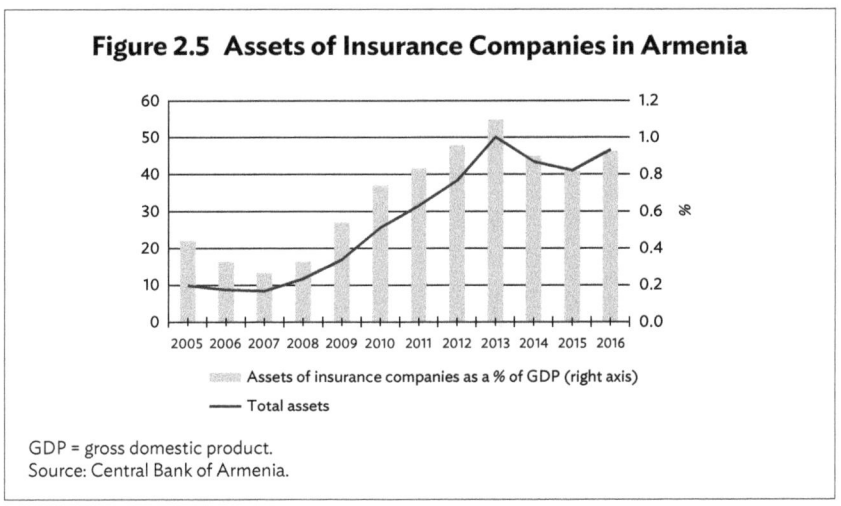

Figure 2.5 Assets of Insurance Companies in Armenia

GDP = gross domestic product.
Source: Central Bank of Armenia.

the sector has been the introduction in 2011 of compulsory third-party motor liability insurance in Armenia.

Table 2.2 contains the complete list of market participants. Two facts are worth mentioning. First, in 2014 the CBA increased minimum capital requirements for banks from AMD5 billion to AMD30 billion (effective in 2017), triggering mergers in the banking sector. As a result, the number of commercial banks decreased from 20 to 17 in 2017. The number of branches, however, has increased. Second, the last row of the table shows the emergence of pension funds after 2013 when the pension reform changed the pay-as-you-go system to the multi-pillar one.

Table 2.2 Financial Sector Participants

Year	2006	2008	2010	2012	2014	2016	2017
Commercial banks/ branch offices	20/299	21/380	20/405	20/479	20/509	18/526	17/526
Credit organizations/ branch offices[a]	17/2	23/48	32/66	32/114	32/149	34/169	35/208
Insurance companies/ insurance brokers	15/6	11/5	11/5	7/3	7/2	7/3	7/3
Pawnshops	64	70	128	143	142	146	116
Exchange offices/currency dealers	288/7	238/1	254/2	238/0	241/1	215/1	183/1
Money transfer companies/ organizations engaged in processing and clearing of payment instruments and payment documents	3/1	11/7	9/6	7/4	7/4	7/4	6/5
Securities market participants/ investment service providers/ investment fund managers/ pension funds	2/20/0/0	2/10/0/0	2/8/0/0	2/9/0/0	2/8/4/8	2/8/3/8	2/9/3/8

[a] Number of branch offices does not include headquarters.
Source: Central Bank of Armenia.

2.3 Status of Financial Inclusion for Individuals and Small and Medium-Sized Enterprises

The wide range of financial inclusion definitions illustrates its multiple dimensions.[4] We chose three dimensions to measure financial inclusion: outreach, usage, and quality of financial services (Amidžić, Massara, and

---

[4] See Yoshino and Morgan 2016 for a discussion of financial inclusion definitions.

Mialou 2014). The numbers of bank branches and ATMs per land mass and 1,000 adult inhabitants cover the outreach dimension. The numbers of deposit accounts with commercial banks, banking cards per 1,000 adults, and loan accounts by economic activity are the main indicators describing the usage dimension. The quality dimension, described by factors such as legal framework and financial literacy level, is discussed in the following sections. We use data from the International Monetary Fund's financial access survey, the World Bank's Global Findex database, the Accounting and Corporate Regulatory Authority credit bureau, and the CBA.

Figure 2.6 illustrates the evolution of the number of bank branches since 2004. In 2004, there were around 11 bank branches per 100,000 adults in Armenia, well below the world average of around 18. Branch penetration in Armenia has been increasing rapidly since then, and surpassed the world average in 2011. In 2017, the number of bank branches per 100,000 adults in Armenia was 23.1 compared to the world average of 18.4. The number of bank branches per 1,000 square kilometers increased from 9 in 2004 to 19 in 2017.

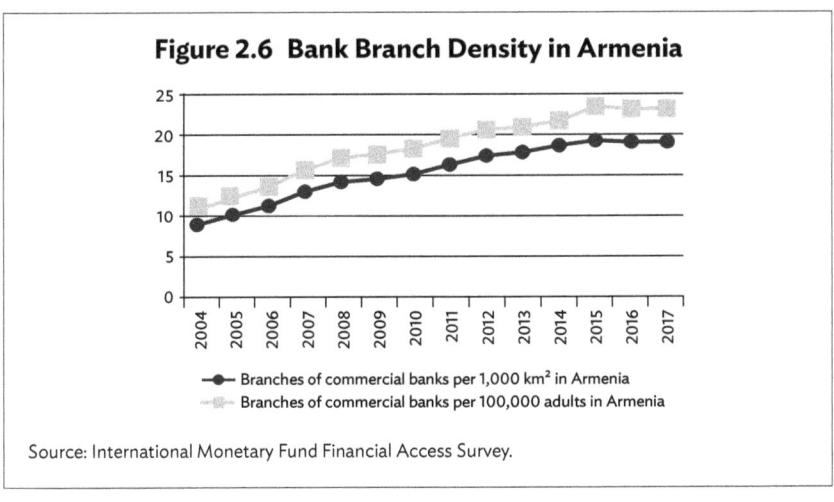

Figure 2.6 Bank Branch Density in Armenia

— Branches of commercial banks per 1,000 km² in Armenia
— Branches of commercial banks per 100,000 adults in Armenia

Source: International Monetary Fund Financial Access Survey.

Figure 2.7 shows the impressive growth of ATM penetration in Armenia. The number of ATMs per 100,000 adults increased from 3 in 2004 to 63.7 in 2017, above the world average of 55.7. During the same period, the number of ATMs per 1,000 square kilometers increased from 2.5 to 52.4. The distribution of ATMs, not surprisingly, is uneven between rural and urban areas: there were 109 ATMs per 100,000 adults in urban areas compared to 8.5 in rural areas (Figure 2.8). Unfortunately,

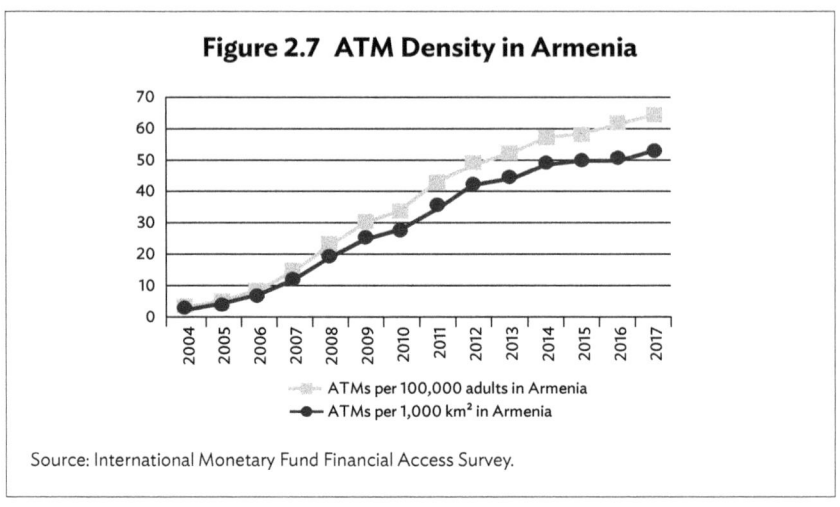

Figure 2.7 ATM Density in Armenia

Source: International Monetary Fund Financial Access Survey.

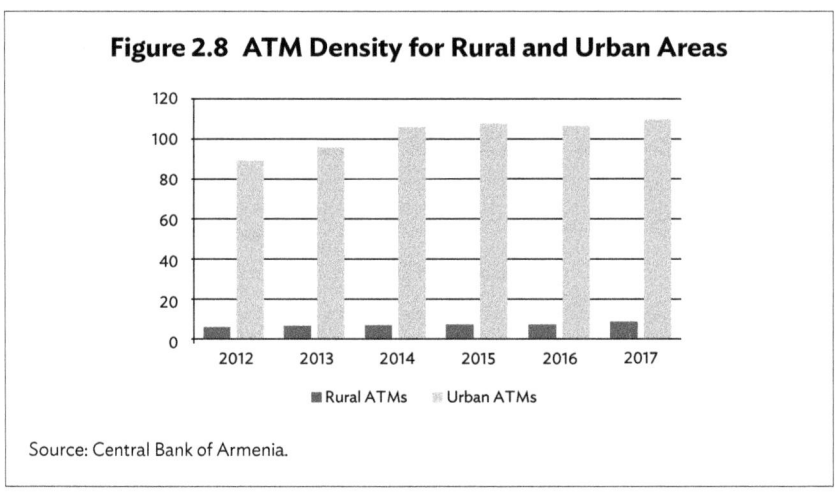

Figure 2.8 ATM Density for Rural and Urban Areas

Source: Central Bank of Armenia.

no consistent cross-country data on ATMs in rural and urban areas are available for comparison.[5]

We next turn to the usage dimension. The World Bank Global Findex database 2017 provides a summary of some of the main usage indicators: the number of banking accounts, formal savings, and formal borrowing. In 2017, 48% of the adult population had accounts with formal financial institutions, 10% saved with a formal institution, and 29% borrowed

---

[5] Barua, Kathuria, and Malik 2017 present a similar pattern for India.

Table 2.3 Global Findex Indicators for Armenia

Indicator	2011	2014	2017
Account (% aged 15+)	17.5	17.7	47.8
Account at a financial institution, rural (% aged 15+)	15.4	15.2	45.2
Account at a financial institution, income, poorest 40% (% aged 15+)	15.0	11.1	33.7
Account at a financial institution, female (% aged 15+)	18.1	14.3	39.4
Borrowed any money in the past year (% aged 15+)	–	48.0	55.3
Borrowed from a financial institution (% aged 15+)	18.9	19.9	28.5
Borrowed from a financial institution, rural (% aged 15+)	21.6	22.7	27.6
Saved any money in the past year (% aged 15+)	10.5	21.0	31.3
Saved any money in the past year, rural (% aged 15+)	9.2	14.3	35.1
Saved at a financial institution (% aged 15+)	0.8	1.6	10.0
Saved at a financial institution, rural (% aged 15+)	0.3	1.0	13.1

Source: World Bank, Global Findex (accessed 10 October 2018).

from formal institutions. Account penetration was 39% for women and 34% for the poorest 40% of the population. We see a substantial increase in all of the financial inclusion indicators from 2014 to 2017.

Figure 2.9 shows the first component of the usage dimension: deposit account penetration. According to the International Monetary Fund Financial Access Survey, the number of deposit accounts per 1,000 adults increased from 215 in 2004 to 1,583 in 2017.

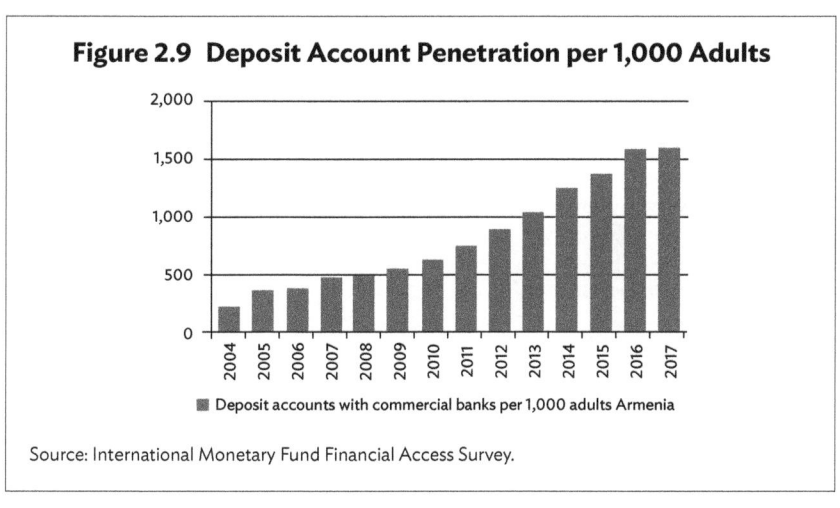

Figure 2.9 Deposit Account Penetration per 1,000 Adults

Source: International Monetary Fund Financial Access Survey.

We use data from the Accounting and Corporate Regulatory Authority Credit Bureau to construct the credit penetration indicator. The number of outstanding credits per 1,000 adults has been growing steadily, from 515 in 2012 to 900 in 2016 (Figure 2.10). The share of agricultural loans remained stable at around 12% of the total credits for the last 5 years. Furthermore, around 40% of outstanding agricultural loans during these 5 years were originated by credit organizations. Due to their extensive presence and branch availability in rural areas, credit organizations hold a disproportionately high share of agricultural loans.

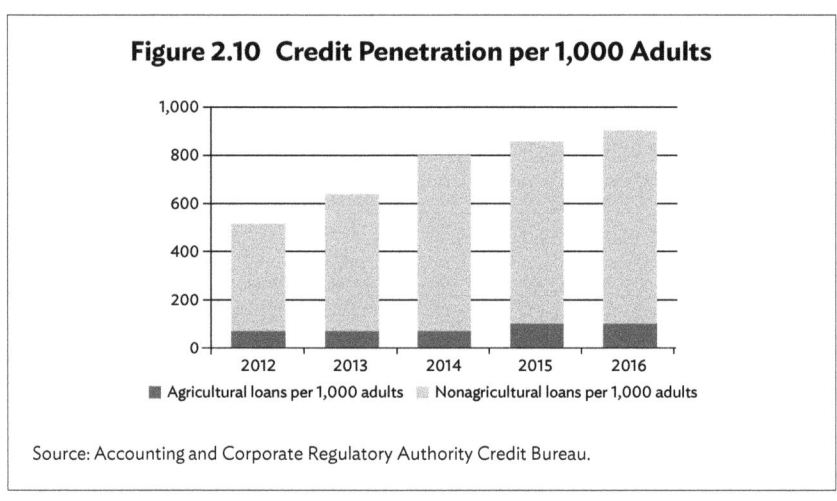

Figure 2.10 Credit Penetration per 1,000 Adults

Source: Accounting and Corporate Regulatory Authority Credit Bureau.

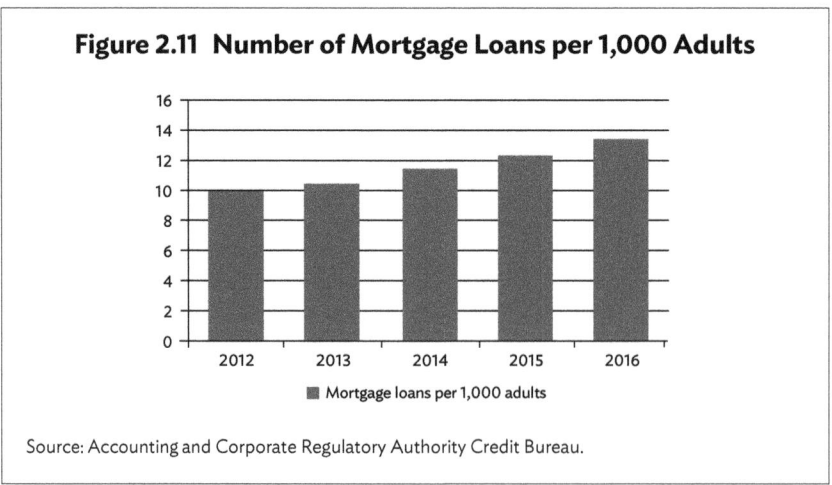

Figure 2.11 Number of Mortgage Loans per 1,000 Adults

Source: Accounting and Corporate Regulatory Authority Credit Bureau.

During the last 5 years, consumer loans represented around 82% of all outstanding loans, on average. During the same period, the number of outstanding mortgage loans per 1,000 adults increased from 10 to around 14 (Figure 2.11). The Russian Federation crisis in 2014 did not have a visible impact on credit penetration.

Another indicator of usage of financial services, the number of banking cards per 1,000 adults, increased from 91 in 2007 to 610 in 2016 (Figure 2.12).

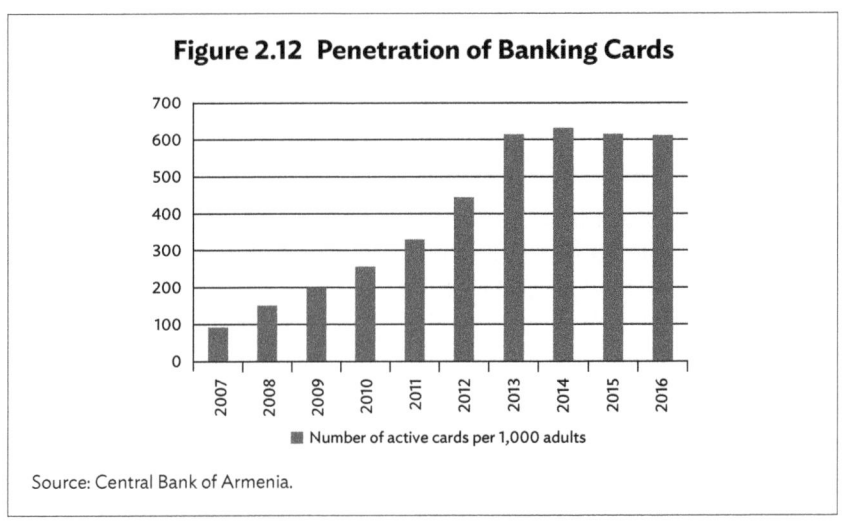

Figure 2.12 Penetration of Banking Cards

Source: Central Bank of Armenia.

The number of insurance contracts signed during the year shows the development of the insurance sector and closely resembles the dynamics of insurance-sector assets presented earlier. The development of the insurance sector has mostly relied on the 2011 reform of compulsory third-party motor liability insurance. Indeed, the number of insurance contracts per 1,000 adults spiked in 2011 and 2012 after the reform, and has since flattened (Figure 2.13). It increased from 25 in 2010 to around 300 in 2016.

Remittances are an important source of income for Armenian households. In 2016, the volume of remittances received from abroad was $1,330 million, accounting for around 13% of GDP. According to a household survey conducted by the CBA, in 2008 over one-third of households were receiving remittances and nearly one-third of senders remitted to more than one household. Unfortunately, more up-to-date

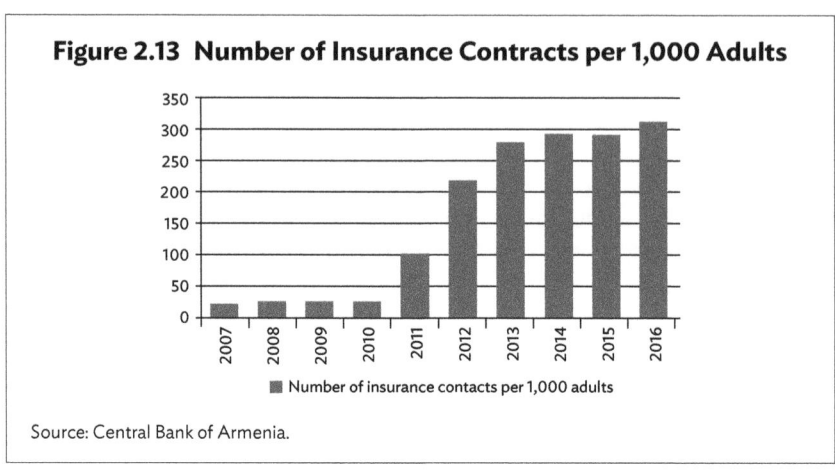

Figure 2.13 Number of Insurance Contracts per 1,000 Adults

Source: Central Bank of Armenia.

survey data are not available. For a better understanding of the underlying mechanisms, Table 2.4 lists the formal and informal remittance transfer channels. Remittances originating from the Russian Federation are mostly transferred through formal channels because specialized banks provide low-cost money transfer services in Commonwealth of Independent States countries (Roberts and Banaian 2005). For example, postal service operator HayPost launched its money transfer system in 2005 with transaction fees of 2% for individuals and 4% for legal entities. The transaction time is 5–30 minutes. HayPost provides such services in all villages. In 2016, the postal service partnered with one of the largest money-transfer companies in the world, Ria Money Transfer, to provide money-transfer services. Currently, there are a number of money-transfer services in Armenia with relatively low transfer fees and wide geographical availability. Both physical availability and reasonable pricing of financial services matter. In the case of remittances, the combination of the two delivers sizable welfare gains for the rural population, which is highly dependent on remittance income, through financial inclusion.

Technology has also played a role in the development of the financial system in Armenia. Although mobile and internet banking transactions represent only a small proportion of all transactions, usage of these services has been rising rapidly. Quantities and volumes of mobile, point-of-sale, and noncash transactions have been growing exponentially since 2012 (Table 2.5). For example, the number of active mobile money accounts increased seven times from 2012 to 2016. The number and values of mobile transactions followed a similar pattern.

Table 2.4 Channels of Money Transfers

Formal Channels	Informal Channels
Bank transfers	Carried by oneself
Dedicated money transfer operators: Western Union, MoneyGram, etc.	Carried by friends, relatives
	Courier services
	Hawala-type services[a]

[a] Transfer by money brokers.
Source: United States Agency for International Development remittances in Armenia.

Table 2.5 Accounts, Terminals, and Transactions

	2012	2013	2014	2015	2016
Number of registered mobile money accounts	55,309	100,402	251,684	276,311	344,143
Number of active mobile money accounts	5,383	5,419	10,884	15,906	35,511
Value of mobile money transactions (during the reference year) in AMD million	904	2,187	1,915	2,871	6,649
Number of mobile money transactions (during the reference year)	217,544	663,642	492,284	706,569	1,702,579
Number of POS terminals	6,674	6,834	6,954	6,414	6,971
POS transactions	16,329,438	20,919,815	29,927,927	32,553,561	33,782,030
Non-cash transactions[a]	17,614,390	22,417,247	32,063,807	35,128,498	37,318,298

POS = point-of-sale.
a Noncash transactions include noncash transactions with ATMs, noncash transactions with payment cards, POS noncash transactions, and e-commerce.
Source: Central Bank of Armenia.

In 2016, there were around 70,000 SMEs, including 58,000 micro and small, and 10,000 medium-sized enterprises. This sector employed 302,001 people, around 68% of the total number of employed persons. SMEs comprise around 98% of all registered enterprises.

The Organisation for Economic Co-operation and Development (OECD) SME policy index for Armenia in 2016 was 3.53 (from 0 to 5), above the average of the countries in the region (Figure 2.14). The index takes into account the legal and regulatory framework, bank financing, nonbank financing, venture capital, and financial literacy level for SMEs. According to the survey, around 32% of firms were discouraged from taking loans, the most commonly cited reasons being complex procedures and high interest rates. The World Bank financial development data indicate that in 2013 46.2% of firms had bank loans or lines of credit. On the other hand, the 2013 enterprise survey indicated that 25.9% of firms identified access to finance as a major constraint. Only 17.4% of firms used bank loans for their investment. The 9.5% of the total investments are financed by banks. At the same time, financial institutions struggled with a lack of transparency in the real sector, which significantly increases monitoring costs. The data availability issue for the SME sector remains a major obstacle to assessing the level of financial inclusion in the sector and designing policies to improve its access to finance. This is undoubtedly one of the areas in which improvement can yield sizable gains for policy makers.

Both outreach and usage indicators of financial inclusion have been steadily increasing during the last decade in Armenia. In many

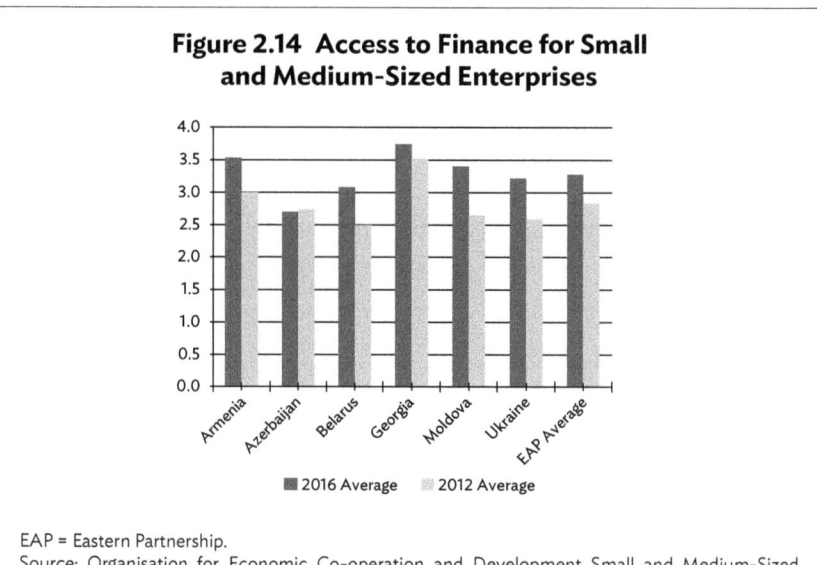

Figure 2.14 Access to Finance for Small and Medium-Sized Enterprises

EAP = Eastern Partnership.
Source: Organisation for Economic Co-operation and Development Small and Medium-Sized Enterprises Policy Index.

cases, Armenia scores better than the world average, having started far below it a decade ago. Although data on rural and urban distribution are scarce, the available data indicate that positive trends may mask uneven developments between rural and urban areas. While the dynamics are undoubtedly positive, any assessment of the current state of financial inclusion in Armenia in comparison with its peers must be well thought through. For example, it is necessary to control carefully for factors such as income and geography.

2.4 Barriers to Financial Inclusion

Barriers to financial inclusion are divided into supply- and demand-side issues. Supply-side barriers in turn comprise three subgroups: market-driven factors, regulatory factors, and infrastructure limitations (Yoshino and Morgan 2017).

As discussed earlier, bank branches and ATMs are unevenly distributed between rural and urban areas. One of the main reasons for this uneven distribution is the lower level of economic activity in rural areas. Another reason is the higher cost of providing financial services in villages due to the large number of small villages and the resulting absence of economy of scale. As a result, the lack of convenient access points in rural areas is a constraint that increases the costs of financial services for the rural population.

Regulatory factors have not been identified as supply-side barriers. The minimum capital adequacy ratio is 12% for banks and 10% for universal credit organizations. The actual average capital adequacy ratio of 20% for the financial system indicates that the capital adequacy requirement is not a binding constraint for banks and credit organizations and hence is not likely to impede financial inclusion. The regulation does not differentiate based on the size of loans and deposits, and there are no regulatory barriers for innovative technologies, such as telephone banking.

Of the infrastructure factors, the main barrier is the limited availability of transportation in rural areas to access bank branches or ATMs. Given the lack of ATMs and bank branches in rural areas, the underdevelopment of basic infrastructure such as roads and transportation is a serious limitation.

Demand-side barriers are divided into three subgroups: lack of funds, lack of knowledge, and lack of trust (Yoshino and Morgan 2017). The 30% poverty rate is undeniably a demand-side barrier to financial inclusion. Lack of knowledge about financial products and services has also been indicated as a barrier. According to the 2015 Global Financial Literacy survey (Klapper, Lusardi, and Van Oudheusden 2015), only

18% of Armenian residents are financially literate.[6] The 2012 World Bank Financial Capability survey indicated that 61.7% of respondents trust the banking system, and 30.0% abstain from account ownership due to this lack of trust. The lack of trust is partly associated with the collapse of the former Soviet Union, as a result of which households lost their savings in Soviet banks. Although the Government of Armenia has begun to implement the promised compensation plan, the scarring effect of this episode persists today.

Supply-side barriers exist for insurance as well. Although the compulsory third-party motor liability insurance policy provided a boost for insurance companies, there are still significant untapped opportunities in health and agricultural insurance. Health insurance services are currently underutilized due to information asymmetry and adverse selection. Currently, individuals mainly access health insurance through employers. Mandatory health insurance is a clear opportunity to provide access to health insurance as it will eliminate adverse selection and increase the quality of health services due to increased competition. High-quality e-health infrastructure must be developed to support health insurance and decrease the severity of asymmetric information. Agricultural insurance is also under-researched and underutilized. Compared to credit for agricultural purposes, agricultural insurance has the potential to provide higher returns from financial inclusion, especially for small farms, which are subject to serious financial stress after weather shocks. Several initiatives have been announced in this area, but have not yet been implemented.

2.5 Regulatory Framework

2.5.1 Regulatory Agencies

The CBA is the sole financial system regulatory authority. In 2005, a single framework for risk-based financial regulation and supervision was introduced. The CBA was given the authority to regulate and supervise the activities of all participants in the financial system. Consequently, the CBA is also responsible for the licensing of banks, credit organizations, and insurance companies, among others. There is no separate legal or regulatory definition of microfinance organizations in Armenia. All activities of banks and credit organizations are governed by the Constitution of the Republic of Armenia, the Civil Code of the Republic

---

[6] The survey was conducted by Standard & Poor's jointly with Gallup, the World Bank, and the Global Financial Literacy Excellence Center at George Washington University.

of Armenia, other laws of the Republic of Armenia, international agreements of the Republic of Armenia, and, when prescribed by law, legal normative acts of the Central Bank of the Republic of Armenia. The Law of the Republic of Armenia on Bankruptcy of Banks, Credit Organizations, and Insurance Companies governs the insolvency and bankruptcy procedures of these institutions. These regulations cover the risks posed by unlicensed organizations and individuals by stating that no person shall engage in activities prescribed by the law on credit organizations without a proper license and, if not observed, a legal liability shall be imposed thereon by the Legislation of the Republic of Armenia. Thus, the previously mentioned regulation eliminates the legal risk of unlicensed and informal institutions providing credit.

2.5.2 Banks and Credit Organizations

Banks in Armenia are licensed by the CBA. Credit organizations mainly consist of refinancing and universal credit organizations. The law on credit organizations, however, defines several types of credit organizations: credit unions, savings unions, leasing companies, factoring companies, universal credit organizations, and refinancing credit organizations. Only banks can take deposits from natural and legal persons. Accordingly, the regulations for banks are much more stringent. Table 2.6 illustrates the difference in prudential measures between banks and credit organizations. In line with the principles of risk-based financial regulations, credit organizations are subject to significantly fewer prudential measures.

Table 2.6 Difference in Prudential Measures Between Banks and Credit Organizations

Banks	Universal Credit Organizations*
• Capital requirement: AMD30 billion • Minimum capital adequacy ratio: 12% • Maximum risk on a single borrower: 20% • Maximum risk on major borrowers: 500% • Maximum risk on one related party: 5% • Maximum risk on all related parties: 20% • Minimum ratio of highly liquid assets to total assets (all currencies): 15% • Reserve requirement: 18% • Maximum ratio of foreign currency open position to total capital: 10% • Minimum ratio of banks' highly liquid assets to demand liabilities: 60%	• Capital requirement: AMD150 million • Minimum capital adequacy ratio: 10% • Maximum risk on a single borrower: 25%

Note: *The prudential measures of other types of credit organizations are discussed in Table 2.1.
Source: Banking Activity Regulation (Regulation n.2), Credit Organization's Regulation (Regulation n. 14).

2.5.3 Other Regulatory Measures

In addition to regulating banks and credit organizations, the CBA adapts measures to make the financial system more inclusive and accessible for the public.

Protection of Consumer Rights
The Center for Consumer Rights Protection and Financial Education within the CBA is responsible for the regulation and supervision of market conduct in the financial system and financial education policies. Its responsibilities include the creation and amendment of necessary legislation to ensure consumer rights protection, the creation and improvement of business conduct codes for financial institutions, the implementation of programs to raise financial knowledge and awareness among consumers, the development and improvement of financial education tools, the development and administration of a special web page, ABCFinance, designed for financial-sector consumers, as well as a financial products comparative website, FinInfo, and the operation of a hotline.[7]

Deposit Guarantee Fund
The Deposit Guarantee Fund of Armenia is a noncommercial organization founded by the CBA in accordance with the Law on the Guarantee of Remuneration of Bank Deposits of Physical Persons in 2005. The maximum amount subject to remuneration of guaranteed deposits is AMD10 million ($20,700). The maximum amount of foreign-currency deposits subject to remuneration is AMD5 million. The maximum amount was doubled in 2016 (Figure 2.15). The fund covers the deposits of physical persons and individual entrepreneurs.

Financial System Mediator
Another important infrastructure element is the Financial System Mediator (FSM) office, which was founded by the CBA and has been functioning since 2009. The goals of the FSM are the protection of consumer rights and interests in the financial market; fast, effective, and free-of-charge review and handling of client claims; and the enhancement of public confidence in the financial sector. During 2016, 4,735 complaints were received, including 4,118 complaints related to the financial sector; of these, 2,989 were eligible under the law for review by the FSM. Some 40% of all claims were settled in favor of the

---

[7] ABCFinance. www.abcfinance.am (accessed); FinInfo. www.fininfo.am (accessed October 2018).

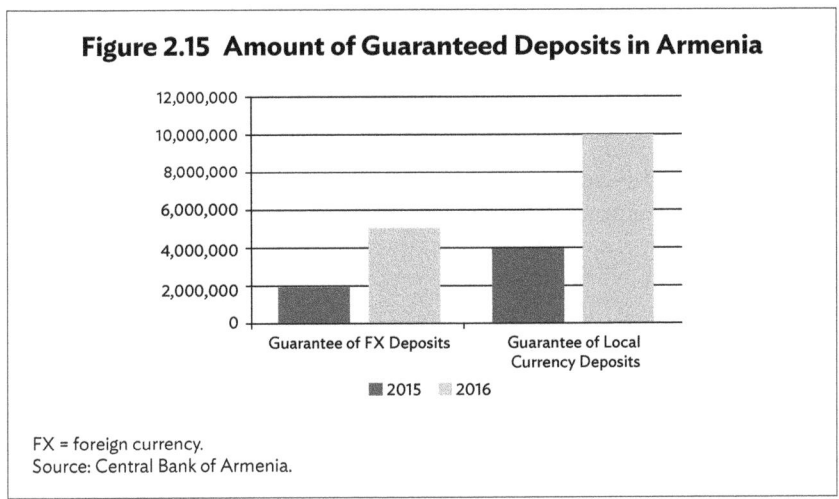

Figure 2.15 Amount of Guaranteed Deposits in Armenia

FX = foreign currency.
Source: Central Bank of Armenia.

clients, and 29.8% were partially settled. In monetary terms, clients received a total of $395,150 in compensation as a result of the FSM's work. This figure does not cover settlements involving nonmonetary reimbursements, such as when clients sought claims to change the terms of a loan contract or reclassify an overdue loan in favor of the client. The largest compensation in 2016 was $16,752.

Compulsory Insurance

In 2010, the CBA introduced compulsory third-party motor liability insurance to manage the risks of car accidents effectively. As a result, the financial assets and liabilities of insurance companies increased sizably, and the number of registered insurance agents increased from 65 in 2008 to 5,524 at the end of 2011.

Guarantor Protection Measures

In August 2017, the CBA introduced guarantor protection measures. The new measures have two implications: increased guarantor knowledge about responsibilities in cases of borrower default, and access to loan repayment information.

2.6 Policies to Promote Financial Inclusion

CBA policies to promote financial inclusion are aimed at synergies between financial stability and inclusion. Focusing on synergies between financial inclusion and stability means targeting actions that do not move the financial system along the financial development–stability frontier, but rather shift the frontier. In practice, this means that the CBA is focused on high-quality financial infrastructure; financial infrastructure improves development-stability trade-offs, as it addresses market failures in the system. Table 2.7 illustrates the wide array of policies dealing with market failures impeding financial inclusion.

There is no national financial inclusion strategy with quantitative targets. However, the NSFE sets a specific target of 30% by 2019 for "inclusion in the formal financial system." A national financial inclusion strategy would help bring together the wide range of stakeholders and define quantitative targets.

Table 2.7 Policies Promoting Financial Inclusion in Armenia

Policy	Date of Introduction	Function
ACRA Credit Reporting	2004	Data gathering and processing
Armenian Card	2000	Armenian payment and settlement system
Financial System Mediator	2009	Protection of consumers' rights and the solving of disputes between financial institutions and consumers
Deposit Guarantee Fund	2005	Guarantee of remuneration of bank deposits of physical persons
Moveable Collateral Registry	2015	Online collateral registry for moveable assets
Armenian Remittances Unified System	–	Single money transfer system
Idram, Mobidram	2004	Providing e-money services
Consumer Rights Protection	2007	See subsection 2.5.3.1
SME Development National Center	2002	Supporting the SME sector
Consumer Loans General Fact Sheet	2014	General information about loan options
Pension Reform	2014	Multi-pillar pension system
Mandatory Insurance	2010	Compulsory third-party motor liability insurance
Home for Youth	–	Mortgage loans for young people
Guarantor Protection Measures	2017	Raising awareness of guarantor responsibilities

continued on next page

Table 2.7 continued

Policy	Date of Introduction	Function
Mandatory Health Insurance	2017	A pilot program on mandatory health insurance
Venture Capital	2013	Providing funding, expertise, and networks to promising technology-driven startups
Agriculture Insurance Program	2018	Launching a pilot agricultural insurance program
Identification Cards	2014	Documents certifying citizens' identity

ACRA = Accounting and Corporate Regulatory Authority, SMEs = small and medium-sized enterprises.
Source: Authors.

2.6.1 Market Infrastructure

Accounting and Corporate Regulatory Authority Credit Reporting

Accounting and Corporate Regulatory Authority Credit Reporting Closed Joint Stock Company (CJSC), the first private credit bureau in Armenia, was founded by the CBA in 2004. The primary objective of credit bureau operations is data gathering from banks, credit organizations, and utility and insurance companies; and the processing, timely updating, and safeguarding of information, while preserving the necessary confidentiality. Credit reporting contributes to financial inclusion, as it eliminates the information asymmetry between lenders and borrowers that could result in inefficiently low credit. Centralized access to credit information also diminishes the information monopoly that a creditor has over its borrowers, leading to better and healthier competition between creditors.

Armenian Card

The Armenian Card was also established by the CBA with the goal of establishing and developing a trusted payment system that would allow cardholders to transact with low fees. It allows banks to issue and acquire Armenian Card, Mastercard, Visa, and other payment cards. Settlements in the system are implemented according to the principle of multilateral netting, while the final settlement is done via correspondent accounts of participant banks with the CBA.

Moveable Collateral Registry

The Moveable Collateral Registry is an online registration platform for moveable assets that operates under the authority of the Ministry of Justice. Established in 2015, this institution helps to overcome information asymmetry, enabling creditors to enquire whether a moveable property has been previously collateralized for another credit.

Pension Reform

The pension reform, employed on January 2014, introduced a mandatory multi-pillar system instead of Armenia's previous pay-as-you-go system. According to the new system, employees under the age of 40 were required to contribute part of their income, matched with the government contribution to private pension funds until retirement age. Contributions of individuals with salaries less than AMD500,000 were 5% of their wage matched by another 5% from the government; contributions were capped at AMD25,000 for salaries higher than AMD500,000. Due to initial public backlash, the first stage of the reform included only individuals newly entering the labor market, government employees, and volunteers. Starting in July 2018, the reform was fully implemented to include all employed individuals. The government contribution, however, increased from 5% of the salary to 7.5%, while individual contributions decreased to 2.5%. According to government announcements, the contribution rates will go back to 5% when the new tax reform decreasing the income tax rates will be implemented. The reform aims at replacing the pay-as-you-go system with a system that will provide meaningful pensions, while ensuring long-term budget sustainability. As a positive side effect, the reform also intends to make available long-term local funding, promote a savings culture, and contribute to capital deepening in Armenia.

Armenian Remittances Unified System

The CBA intends to introduce the Armenian Remittances Unified System (ARUS), which will connect all financial institutions. The ARUS will be a multifunctional tool for providing retail customers with financial services, such as account-to-account transfers, credit card-to-credit card transfers, and cash-based transfers, as well as combinations of these. The design and implementation of this system was discussed in the CBA national strategy for 2015–2017, but it is still in the testing stage. The ARUS will
   (i) be a retail payment system with free competition, which will ensure affordable and high-quality services;
   (ii) exclude the risk of any money-transfer provider occupying a dominant and dictating position;

(iii) increase security and efficiency;
(iv) decrease the costs of transactions; and
(v) decrease the effect of foreign payment systems' insolvency on Armenia's financial system; and
(vi) increase the confidence of the society in the financial system.[8]

2.6.2 Targeted Policies

Small and Medium-Sized Enterprises Development National Center

In 2016, 98% of businesses in Armenia were SMEs with a 68% employment share. The government established the Small and Medium Entrepreneurship Development National Center Fund (SME DNC) in 2002. The SME DNC is authorized to provide state support to SMEs through the implementation of annual SME state support programs with resources allocated from the state budget. This fund also gives technical and financial assistance to SMEs operating in the country. In 2016, $319,220 was dedicated to the SME DNC from the state budget. Table 2.8 summarizes the DNC's activities.

Table 2.8 Assistance Programs for Small and Medium-Sized Enterprises

Technical Assistance	Financial Assistance
• Information and consulting on all aspects of doing business in Armenia • Promotion and branding of local products • Sales promotion • Export promotion • Startup support • Supporting the realization of new technology and innovation	• Provision of loan guarantees • Equity financing • Startup support • Partial subsidizing of credit interest rates

Source: Small and Medium Entrepreneurship Development National Center of Armenia.

Home for Youth

The mission of the Home for Youth Refinancing Credit Organization Closed Joint Stock Company (CJSC) is to provide mortgages with

---

[8] CBA press release (25 July 2016), providing information on the Armenian Remittances Unified System.

favorable conditions for young families.[9] Within the framework of the program, a mortgage loan is provided for at least 10 years with a maximum interest rate of 10.5%. The government subsidizes part of interest payments (2% in the case of real estate in Yerevan; 4% in other regions).

Mandatory Health Insurance

On 1 September 2017, as a government-approved pilot program, a new procedure came into force for the provision of medical services within the social package for state employees. At this stage of the program it has 80,000–100,000 beneficiaries. The new procedure allocates the state package to state employees through insurance companies. If implemented successfully, it will include 612,000 socially disadvantaged citizens in the next stage. The final aim is the implementation of universal mandatory health insurance.

Agriculture Insurance Program

In 2018, the Armenian Ministry of Agriculture launched a pilot agricultural insurance program, which was included in the 2018–2020 budget plan.

Identification Cards

In 2014, voluntary identification cards with memory chips containing each citizen's data were introduced in Armenia. These provide citizens with an e-signature that they can use to carry out their tax obligations online, and in banks, among other uses.

2.7 Financial Education and Financial Literacy

2.7.1 Status of Financial Literacy

Armenia has a lot of room to increase the financial literacy of its population. However, the low overall level of financial literacy masks a sizable heterogeneity among social, economic, and demographic backgrounds. The underlying reasons are also quite different. For example, people's attitude towards saving is the most important factor dragging down the overall level of financial literacy in Armenia, whereas financial knowledge and behavior are generally rated much higher. The heterogeneity of financial literacy levels, both in terms of population

---

[9] According to the Home for Youth project, a young family is a family in which the sum of the ages of the spouses does not exceed 65.

background and underlying financial literacy dimensions, has important implications for the design and implementation of financial education policies. This calls for targeted financial education policies aimed at the most vulnerable groups.

We used the 2010 OECD International Network for Financial Education (INFE) (Atkinson and Messy 2012), the 2014 Global Financial Literacy survey (Klapper, Lusardi, and Van Oudheusden 2015), and the 2014 FCB survey 2014 (Ambadar and Boletawa 2014) to assess the status of financial literacy in Armenia.

In 2010, the OECD INFE conducted a pilot study in 14 countries to assess the financial literacy of people across countries and various sociodemographic backgrounds.[10] The survey covered three dimensions: financial knowledge; behavior; and attitude towards various aspects of financial literacy including budgeting, financial planning, and financial product choice (Atkinson and Messy 2012). Armenia scored in the lowest group along with Poland and South Africa on the basis of a simple average of the three financial literacy dimensions used in the survey (see Table 2.9). Armenia's low overall score was the result of a very low score in the attitude dimension. According to the survey, 46% of those surveyed scored highly on knowledge questions, 41% did well

Table 2.9 Results of Organisation for Economic Co-operation and Development Financial Literacy Survey (%)

Country	High Knowledge Score	High Behavior Score	High Attitude Score
South Africa	33	43	54
Norway	40	59	57
Peru	41	60	71
Albania	45	36	69
Armenia	46	41	11
Poland	49	43	27
Malaysia	51	67	63
United Kingdom	53	51	49

continued on next page

---

[10] The countries that participated in the study were Albania, Armenia, the British Virgin Islands, the Czech Republic, Estonia, Germany, Hungary, Ireland, Malaysia, Norway, Peru, Poland, South Africa, and the United Kingdom.

Table 2.9 continued

Country	High Knowledge Score	High Behavior Score	High Attitude Score
British Virgin Islands	57	71	67
Czech Republic	57	48	62
Ireland	60	57	49
Germany	58	67	63
Estonia	67	21	46
Hungary	69	38	69

Source: Atkinson, A. and F. Messy. 2012. Measuring Financial Literacy: Results of the OECD/ International Network on Financial Education (INFE) Pilot Study. Organisation of Economic Co-operation and Development Working Papers on Finance, Insurance and Private Pensions, No. 15. Paris: OECD Publishing.

on financial behavior questions, and only 11% had a positive attitude towards long-term saving. In contrast, Poland had the second lowest score, 27%, in the attitude dimension, and Estonia had the third lowest with 46%. Armenia's position in the financial knowledge and behavior dimensions was close to the average for the studied countries.

The sociodemographic background for the OECD INFE survey included gender, age, income, education level, and attitude towards risk. In Armenia, the female population on average had lower financial knowledge and behavior results, but scored similarly in terms of attitude. The proportion of females with a high level of financial knowledge was 41%, compared to 51% of males. For financial behavior, the results were 38% for females and 43% for males, respectively. The distribution of scores across age groups revealed an interesting pattern observed only in Armenia. The survey found that levels of financial literacy decrease significantly with age. Financial literacy in the low-income group is lower than in the average- and high-income groups. There is, however, no sizable difference between the financial literacy levels of average- and high-income groups. A similar pattern is observed in terms of education levels, that is, financial literacy levels increase with the education level.

The results of the Global Financial Literacy survey conducted by Standard & Poor's in 2014 are similar to the OECD INFE conclusions. Armenia has quite a low level of financial literacy, with only 18% of adults being financially literate. According to the survey, 36% of respondents reported taking out another loan to cover old ones, and only 6% of the respondents saved with a financial institution, although 64% mentioned that they saved for unexpected events.

The latest nationwide financial literacy survey in Armenia, the FCB survey, was conducted in 2014 by the CBA with support of the AFI. The survey was conducted with 1,536 individuals and consisted of 118 questions on seven topics: understanding financial and macroeconomic concepts; efficient management of a personal budget; saving and long-term planning; efficient debt management; information collection, comparison, and decision-making; protection of personal rights; and fraud. Respondents scored much higher on knowledge questions than on behavioral questions; for example, 65% of respondents scored highly on the questions on effective management of a personal budget, but only 10% scored highly on the behavior dimension of the same category. Logistic regression analysis (Mkhitaryan forthcoming) showed that, on average, financial knowledge is positively associated with behavior. Moreover, in line with the OECD INFE survey results, the urban population behaves better financially and is likely to have a more positive attitude towards formal financial institutions, while employment increases the probability of better financial behavior.

The nationwide surveys indicate that the level of financial literacy in Armenia needs substantial improvement. Attitudes towards long-term saving and trust in formal institutions are the main negative factors behind the low level of financial literacy. A more granular analysis suggests that the financial literacy levels of different socioeconomic and demographic groups vary significantly. On average, the female population has a marginally lower level of financial literacy. Higher age, unemployment, and lower education levels tend to be negatively associated with financial literacy levels. The rural population has a lower level of financial literacy than the urban population. Therefore, financial education projects targeted towards specific groups can be particularly useful tools for increasing financial literacy in Armenia.

2.7.2 Financial Education Strategy

Financial education in Armenia is organized around the NSFE and the National Steering Committee, which elaborated and has been implementing the NSFE. The steering committee has been led by the CBA and the Ministry of Education and Science (for the part associated with schools). The government formally adopted the NSFE in 2014. The NSFE's mission is to increase the level of financial literacy in Armenia, which will contribute to increased financial stability, financial inclusion, and welfare for the people of Armenia. According to the NSFE, its main goal is to create and develop an institutional framework that will lead to higher financial literacy levels in Armenia. More precisely, it targets (i) the formation of an institutional body responsible for the NSFE;

(ii) the inclusion of financial literacy in schools; (iii) the creation of infrastructure for enhancing financial literacy for adults; and (iv) the establishment of processes that will make it possible to coordinate, monitor, and evaluate the effectiveness of financial literacy projects. The NSFE's quantitative goals are presented in Table 2.10.

Table 2.10 Quantitative Goals of the National Strategy for Financial Education of Armenia[1] (%)

% of Adults		2012	2019	2024	2029	2034
1. Financial literacy		–	30	50	60	75
	1.1. Effectively managing personal and family budgets	14	30	50	75	90
	1.2. Saving for the long term	14	30	50	75	90
	1.3. Effectively managing debt	47	60	70	80	90
	1.4. Comparing different options before using financial products	1–12	30	50	75	90
	1.5. Assigning importance to professional advice	8	30	50	70	80
	1.6. Actively defending their personal rights	9	30	50	75	90
	1.7. Having a positive attitude towards personal financial management	–	30	50	75	90
2. Inclusion in the formal financial system		–	30	50	75	90
	2.1. Having bank deposits	6	30	50	75	90
	2.2. Share of adults with debt having credit from a formal financial institution	14	30	60	80	90
	2.3. Having a bank account or banking card	25–40	50	65	75	90

continued on next page

Table 2.10 *continued*

% of Adults	2012	2019	2024	2029	2034
2.4. Using insurance products	–	30	50	60	70
2.5. Percent of employed persons actively managing pension accounts	–	30	50	75	90

[a] Amended based on 2014 FCB survey data.
Source: National Strategy for Financial Education in Armenia.

The NSFE specifies quantitative targets for financial literacy as well as financial inclusion in Armenia. Targets are set for every 5 years starting from 2014 (the year of the NSFE's adoption), and these will be evaluated based on the FCB. The logic of the FCB (discussed in the previous section) is based on the quantitative targets of the NSFE since this is the main tool for assessing the strategy's effectiveness. An FCB survey will be conducted every 5 years. The 2012 numbers are based on the World Bank's Diagnostic Review of Consumer Protection and Financial Literacy conducted in 2012 and are approximations. The quantitative targets were amended based on the 2014 FCB results. The amendment will be reflected in the reviewed NSFE, which is expected to come out in 2019–2020.

The main stakeholders of the NSFE include the CBA, Ministry of Education and Science, Ministry of Labor and Social Issues, Ministry of Territorial Administration, Ministry of Finance, National Institute of Education, and Yerevan Municipality. Apart from the public institutions, NSFE stakeholders also include private, financial, and nongovernment organizations (NGOs), such as the FSM, the Armenian Deposit Guarantee Fund, the Union of Banks, the Union of Credit Organizations, the Insurance Market Association, the Consumer Rights Protection NGO, and the Armenian Motor Insurer's Bureau. These stakeholders are organized under the NSFE steering committee, enabling effective public–private partnership. The CBA also collaborates closely with international organizations, such as the AFI, the OECD, the World Bank, the INFE, the Consultative Group to Assist the Poor (CGAP), GRID Impact, Child and Youth Finance International, and the Savings Banks Foundation for International Cooperation.

The NSFE has a 5-year timeframe, and the coordinating body meets at least once every quarter.[11] It comprises two working groups: financial education in schools and financial education after school.

---

[11] See the OECD INFE Policy Handbook (2015) for more details on the NSFE.

Table 2.11 provides a summary of CBA initiatives and activities in the framework of building financial capacity and raising public awareness.

Based on an agreement with the Ministry of Education and Science of Armenia, financial education will be integrated into school curricula from 2018. Since 2016, the NSFE working subgroups have been developing educational standards and programs for the following four subjects: "Me and the World," mathematics, algebra, and social studies.

The content of financial literacy projects is based on the Financial Competency Matrix covering seven thematic areas of personal finance

Table 2.11 Financial Literacy Projects

Project	Target Audience	Delivery Method	Delivering Organization	Evaluation
Financial Education in Schools	Schoolchildren	Obligatory integration into school curricula	CBA CRP&FE, Ministry of Education and other public institutions	Survey, focus groups, RCT
Financial Education in Rural Areas	Rural population	Workshop	CBA CRP&FE, Ministry of Education, Ministry of Territorial Administration	RCT, Survey
My Finance Month	General public with a strong focus on youth, women	Workshops, seminars, club discussions, anti-cafe meetings, excursions, games, competitions, etc.	CBA CRP&FE, and other public and private organizations	Surveys
Finmarzum	Women	Workshop	CBA CRP&FE and American University of Armenia	Surveys
Global Money Week World Savings Day Project CITIZEN Campus of Mediation Brain Ring	Children and youth	Competitions, debates, expositions, games, fairs, passive channels (posters, brochures, leaflets, etc.)	CBA CRP&FE and other public and private organizations	Surveys

continued on next page

Table 2.11 *continued*

Project	Target Audience	Delivery Method	Delivering Organization	Evaluation
www.abcfinance.am, and social media	General public	Web page, Facebook, Twitter, YouTube, Instagram, etc. Educational articles, vocabulary, calculators, financial games, etc.	CBA CRP&FE	Focus groups, Google Analytics, Facebook Insights, YouTube Insights, Twitter Insights, AWStats
Shopping around www.fininfo.am	Financial product buyers	Online tool comparing financial products	CBA CRP&FE	Google Analytics
Digital and mass media	General public	Newsarmenia.am (Wallet blog), Iravunk weekly, television show (Brainiest), television informational videos	CBA CRP&FE, AMI Novosti Armenii news agency, Iravunk newspaper, Armenia television company	Post by report, monitoring
Educational materials	General public	Budgeting brochure, financial advice from experts, Savings Game, Budgeting Game, "Finance otherwise" card game, Financial Football, Money puzzle, etc.	CBA CRP&FE and other public and private organizations	Focus groups, surveys

CBA = Central Bank of Armenia, CRP&FE = consumers' right protection and financial education, RCT = randomized controlled trial.
Source: Central Bank of Armenia.

management: economic impact, budget management, savings and long-term planning, debt management, shopping around, personal rights protection, financial fraud, and scams.

The Financial Education in Rural Areas Project is a part of the NSFE. The special program for regions of Armenia was launched in 2016 and included 2-day workshops on personal finance management.

During 2016 a total of 11 seminar instructors from six regions underwent training and received trainer's qualification certificates, which allowed them to conduct seminars in 50 rural communities.

Parallel to this, another project has been implemented for rural communities based on behaviorally informed research and design methodologies that leverage a human-centered design process. In cooperation with the CGAP and GRID Impact, the CBA is developing various financial education interventions in different categories (e.g. seasonality, farming, planning and budgeting, a normalized culture of debt, comparison-shopping, and savings) targeting a direct impact on financially responsible behavior. Currently discussions are taking place of these interventions to be piloted in 2019.

The Financial Education in Schools project was initiated in 2014. In November 2016, financial education topics were integrated into four subjects—mathematics, "Me and the World," algebra, social science—for all primary, secondary, and high schools. The pilot of the project was launched in September 2017 and the results were summarized in June 2018. The nationwide integration of financial education components into school curricula started in 2018 in 350 schools and will cover all schools within 3 years.

"My Finance Month," a financial education umbrella initiative, takes place every year under the framework of the NSFE. The main goal of the program, which is carried out in collaboration with more than 35 public and private institutions, is to highlight the importance of effective management of personal finance. My Finance Month hosts over 25 small educational projects targeting all groups of the general public. The program aims to help create a clear understanding of finance and financial services in particular.

Besides these initiatives, the Consumers' Right Protection and Financial Education Center is actively engaged in collaborative projects with partner institutions to ensure the continuous implementation of financial education projects throughout the year (Table 2.11).

2.7.3 Effectiveness of the Financial Education Strategy

The main tool for assessing the NSFE's effectiveness is the FCB, which will allow systematic diagnostics to be carried out. The first FCB survey was conducted in 2014, with the next planned after the end of the 5-year NSFE timeframe. Until now, assessment of the policies has been carried out for only a few projects. Given the large number of financial education initiatives, the assessment of project effectiveness and its clear documentation should be prioritized.

The Rural Financial Education Project conducted in 2016 as a part of the NSFE is the first large-scale project to be assessed systematically. In December 2016, 100 villages were randomly selected to form treatment and control groups, each consisting of 50 villages. After the groups were selected, 2-day financial education classroom workshops were conducted in the treatment group. Pre- and post-treatment surveys were conducted to assess the effectiveness of the treatment. The post-treatment survey was conducted upon completion of the classroom workshops. The results of a logistic regression analysis (Kacarevic, Hovanessian, Mkrtchyan, and Nurbekyan 2018) suggest significant short-term effects of the treatments on knowledge. A follow-up post-treatment survey will be conducted to assess longer-term impacts.

The effectiveness of financial education policies is hard to evaluate. While it is relatively straightforward to measure improvement in knowledge as a result of interventions, measuring actual behavior is complex. The CBA, jointly with the CGAP and GRID Impact, is currently designing a new financial literacy project in rural areas that emphasizes behavioral aspects of learning rather than solely concentrating on traditional classroom methods of learning. Designing an assessment of effectiveness is one of the main challenges, and is an integral part of the project.

2.8 Conclusions and Policy Recommendations

Financial inclusion and development have steadily advanced in Armenia during the last decade. The credit-to-GDP ratio of the total financial system increased from 8.8% in 2006 to 48.9% in 2016. Banks' assets-to-GDP ratio quadrupled during this period, reaching 80% in 2016. Quantitative indicators such as bank branch, credit, and deposit penetration have increased exponentially. However, these positive developments may mask the uneven distribution of improvements between rural and urban areas. For example, in 2017 there were 109 ATMs per 100,000 adults in urban areas compared to eight in rural areas.

The main supply-side barriers are the high cost of providing financial services in rural areas and inadequate basic physical infrastructure, such as transportation, in rural areas. The gap between rural and urban areas is largely addressed by credit organizations, which have a greater presence in rural areas than banks. The number of credit organization branches accounts for 25% of financial service providers' branches (banks and credit organizations only), while holding only around 8% of assets. On the demand side, the main barriers are poverty and a low level of financial literacy. Other major impediments are the low level of trust in formal financial institutions, particularly in rural areas, and a negative attitude towards saving. According to the OECD INFE survey conducted in 2010, only 11% of respondents had a positive attitude towards long-term saving (Atkinson and Messy 2012).

Armenia's comprehensive NSFE encompasses multiple stakeholders, including NGOs, and includes specific quantitative targets. The FCB survey was introduced in 2014 to support the national strategy and measure its effectiveness every 5 years (synchronized with the NSFE timeframe). The strategy also plans to enhance financial education in schools through the pilot project that began in September 2017. Multiple projects have been and are being implemented in the area of financial education; consequently, systematic evaluation and coordination of these projects are crucial.

Policies promoting financial inclusion in Armenia have focused on building high-quality financial infrastructure. The credit bureau, Armenian Card payment system, FSM, deposit guarantee fund, compulsory third-party motor liability insurance, and the first venture capital firm are important parts of this infrastructure. Both financial infrastructure and consumer enhancement through financial education and consumer protection exploit the synergies between financial stability and financial inclusion.

The presence of trade-offs between financial inclusion and stability means that high-quality data are indispensable for policy makers. Data gaps, especially for the SME sector, are currently among the main barriers for policy makers. The new design of the CBA credit registry, which will include more granular information, is an important step. The design and systematic collection of financial inclusion data are needed to inform policy.

Innovative technologies should be used to address the physical infrastructure gaps in rural areas. The presence of postal services in all villages is likely an opportunity to seize. Importantly, postal services enjoy the trust of the rural population. Thus, postal services can become an access point for households in rural areas.

Unlike credit, insurance services have been underutilized. Although compulsory third-party motor liability insurance was a big leap forward, significant opportunities remain in health and agricultural insurance. Currently, a large share of the population lacks access to health insurance, and individuals access health insurance mainly through employers. Mandatory health insurance is a clear opportunity to provide access to health insurance as it will eliminate adverse selection and increase the quality of health services through increased competition. High-quality e-health infrastructure is necessary to support health insurance and decrease the severity of asymmetric information.

To further increase financial inclusion the following recommendations are proposed:
  (i) Address data gaps through the design and systematic collection of financial inclusion surveys. Build data infrastructure for easy access to SME financial inclusion data.
  (ii) Create a national strategy for financial inclusion with quantitative targets, or clarify whether it is envisioned as part of the NSFE;
  (iii) Use innovative technologies to address physical infrastructure gaps;
  (iv) Exploit the presence of and high level of trust in postal services in rural areas by making postal services convenient access points;
  (v) Consider the largely untapped potential in the insurance market;
  (vi) Implement health insurance programs, such as mandatory health insurance, along with high-quality e-health infrastructure, which will make it possible to reduce information asymmetry in the health insurance market and will provide a boost for the insurance sector;
  (vii) Explore cost-efficient opportunities for agricultural insurance, which can provide more benefits from financial inclusion when compared with credit, especially for small farmers.
  (viii) Systematically evaluate and document the effectiveness of the large number of financial education initiatives.
  (ix) Design targeted interventions for financial education for the most vulnerable groups (survey data show that the rural population and the unemployed perform worst in terms of financial literacy).

References

Ambadar, D., and E. Boletawa. 2014. *Financial Capability Barometer, Financial Inclusion in Armenia: The Financial Capability Assessment Project (FCAP)*. Kuala Lumpur: Alliance for Financial Inclusion.

Amidžić, G., A. Massara, and A. Mialou. 2014. Assessing Countries' Financial Inclusion Standing—A New Composite Index. International Monetary Fund (IMF) Working Paper 14/36. Washington, DC: IMF.

Atkinson, A., and F. Messy. 2012. Measuring Financial Literacy: Results of the OECD/ International Network on Financial Education (INFE) Pilot Study. Organisation of Economic Co-operation and Development (OECD) Working Paper on Finance, Insurance and Private Pensions 15. Paris: OECD Publishing.

Barua, A., R. Kathuria, and N. Malik. 2016. The Status of Financial Inclusion, Regulation, and Education in India. Asian Development Bank Institute (ADBI) Working Paper 568. Tokyo: ADBI.

Beck, T., A. Demirgüç-Kunt, and R. Levine. 2007. Finance, Inequality, and Poverty: Cross-Country Evidence. *Journal of Economic Growth* 12(1): 27–49.

Beck, T. 2015. Microfinance—A Critical Literature Survey. Institute of Economic Growth Working Paper 2015/4. Delhi: Institute of Economic Growth.

Buera, F. J., J. P. Kaboski, and Y. Shin. 2012. The Macroeconomics of Microfinance. National Bureau of Economic Research (NBER) Working Paper 17905. Cambridge, MA: NBER.

Buera, F. J., J. P. Kaboski, and Y. Shin. 2016. Taking Stock of the Evidence on Micro-Financial Interventions. NBER Working Paper 22674. Cambridge, MA: NBER.

Demirgüç-Kunt, A., and L. Klapper. 2013. Measuring Financial Inclusion: Explaining Variation Across and Within Countries. *Brookings Papers on Economic Activity* Spring: 279–321.

Demirgüç-Kunt, A., L. Klapper, D. Singer, and P. van Oudheusden. 2015. The Global Findex Database 2014: Measuring Financial Inclusion Around the World. World Bank Policy Research Working Paper 7255. Washington, DC: World Bank.

Dabla-Norris, E., Y. Ji, R. M. Townsend, and D. Filiz Unsal. 2015. Distinguishing Constraints on Financial Inclusion and Their Impact on GDP, TFP, and Inequality. NBER Working Paper 20821. Cambridge, MA: NBER.

Global Partnership for Financial Inclusion (GPFI). 2017. Baden-Baden G20 Communiqué Commits to Advance Financial Inclusion. GPFI

News Release, 27 March. http://www.gpfi.org/news/baden-baden-g20-communiqu-commits-advance-financial-inclusion

Han, R., and M. Melecky. 2013. Financial Inclusion for Stability: Access to Bank Deposits and the Deposit Growth during the Global Financial Crisis. Munich Personal RePEc Archive Paper 45157. Munich: University Library of Munich.

Han, R., and M. Melecky. 2016. *Risks and Returns: Managing Financial Trade-Offs for Inclusive Growth in Europe and Central Asia.* December. Washington, DC: The World Bank.

Kaboski, J., and R. Townsend. 2005. Policies and Impact: An Analysis of Village-Level Microfinance Institutions. *Journal of the European Economic Association* 3(1): 1–50.

Kacarevic, S., N. Hovanessian, A. Mkrtchyan, and A. Nurbekyan. 2018. *The Effectiveness of Short-Term Financial Education Workshops in Rural Areas: The Case of Armenia.* Kuala Lumpur: Alliance of Financial Inclusion.

Klapper, L., A. Lusardi, and P. van Oudheusden. 2015. Financial Literacy Around the World. Standard & Poor's Ratings Services Global Financial Literacy Survey. http://media.mhfi.com/documents/2015-Finlit_paper_17_F3_SINGLES.Pdf.

Mehrotra, A., and J. Yetman. 2015. Financial Inclusion—Issues for Central Banks. *Bank for International Settlements Quarterly Review* March: 83–96.

Mkhitaryan, A. (forthcoming). Does Knowledge Imply Behavior? Central Bank of Armenia Working Paper.

Morgan, P., and V. Pontines. 2015. Financial Stability and Financial Inclusion. ADBI Working Paper 488. Tokyo: ADBI.

OECD. 2013. *Financial Literacy and Inclusion: Results of OECD/INFE Survey across Countries and by Gender.* Russian Trust Fund. Paris: OECD.

OECD. 2015. *OECD /INFE Policy Handbook National Strategies for Financial Education.* Paris: OECD. http://www.oecd.org/g20/topics/employment-and-social-policy/National-Strategies-Financial-Education-Policy-Handbook.pdf.

OECD, European Union, European Bank for Reconstruction and Development, European Training Foundation. 2015. *SME Policy Index: Eastern Partner Countries 2016: Assessing the Implementation of the Small Business Act for Europe.* Paris: OECD.

Roberts, B., and K. Banaian. 2005. Remittances in Armenia: Size, impacts, and measures to enhance their contribution to development. Report prepared for the US Agency for International Development, Yerevan, 148.

Sahay, R., et al. 2015. Rethinking Financial Deepening: Stability and Growth in Emerging Markets. IMF Staff Discussion Note 15/08, May. Washington, DC: IMF.

World Bank. 2012. *Armenia: Diagnostic Review of Consumer Protection and Financial Literacy, Volume 2. Comparison with Good Practices.* Washington, DC: World Bank. https://openknowledge.worldbank.org/handle/10986/13225.

Yoshino, N., and P. Morgan. 2016. *Financial Inclusion, Regulation, and Education.* Tokyo: ADBI.

3
Azerbaijan

Gubad Ibadoghlu

3.1 Introduction

Over the last decade, the economy of Azerbaijan experienced rapid growth, peaking at 35% in 2006, thanks to the increasing export of oil products on favorable terms. The financial system has benefited from the Government of Azerbaijan's investment of oil revenues in the non-oil economy, as well as the rapid expansion of higher margin retail and microlending. However, after oil production peaked in 2011–2013, oil prices began to fall continuously, leading to a slowdown in oil production and economic growth in 2014; this caused the Azerbaijan manat to be devalued by 34% in February 2015 and by 48% in December 2015. The drop in oil prices and weaker macroeconomic fundamentals against a backdrop of negative external shocks have led to the devaluation of the national currency and erosion of public trust in the financial sector. During the last 3 years, some financial institutions have ceased operations and are now in the process of leaving the sector. During the same period, 15 banks (2 in 2015, 11 in 2016, and 2 in 2017) had their licenses revoked due to their inability to meet capital requirements.

The Azerbaijani financial sector is facing a variety of challenges in the wake of the national currency devaluations. Over the last 2 years, the consistently observed double-digit inflation rate along with declining oil revenues and industrial output have had a profoundly adverse effect on the financial sector.

Therefore, restoring financial stability, renewing consumer and investor confidence, reducing dollarization, and mobilizing higher savings in manats are the top priorities of Azerbaijani policy makers. The authorities are increasingly discussing the issues of consumer and depositor protection, responsible lending, and access to finance. The consumer protection, financial inclusion, and financial literacy agenda is increasingly crucial for Azerbaijan in the light of the latest market developments and the need to enhance financial stability and restore public and investor trust. Consumer protection and financial capability are becoming essential elements of the financial sector stabilization and development agenda in Azerbaijan.

3.2 Overview of the Financial System

The financial sector in Azerbaijan is dominated by banks, with the nonbanking sector continuing to offer limited opportunities. In 2015, banks held 88% of the total assets of the financial system, nonbank credit organizations held 9.7%, and insurance companies held 2.3%. The nonbanking financial sector, particularly the microfinance sector, is underdeveloped but is an essential source of finance for small and medium-sized enterprises (SMEs).

Banks and nonbank credit institutions (NBCIs) participating in the Azerbaijani financial market experienced positive development until the national currency devaluation and played a significant role as sources of financial services for individuals and SMEs.

In Azerbaijan, the primary sources of financial services for individuals and SMEs are divided into two groups: the banking sector and nonbank credit organizations.

3.2.1   Banking Sector

Of the 30 banks currently in operation in Azerbaijan, only two are state banks. The government announced the privatization of the International Bank of Azerbaijan in 2018. There are 15 foreign capital banks, including a number of local branches of foreign banks. The government lifted all restrictions on foreign capital in the sector in 2005, but large foreign banks have yet to penetrate the market.

For comparison, 43 banks were operating in Azerbaijan at the end of 2015, down from 46 at the end of 2008 and from 200 banks at the end of 1996. During 2008–2017, just one new bank opened (in 2010), while 15 closed. Although the number of intermediaries decreased, the total number of bank branches has increased since 2008 (although a decline occurred in 2012), and overall bank assets increased (in local currency terms) from the end of 2008 to 2016.

According to the Financial Markets Supervision Authority of the Republic of Azerbaijan, the assets of the Azerbaijani banking sector had reached AZN27,921.0 million by 31 December 2017,[1] 11.2% less

---

[1]   Bank sektorunun icmal göstəriciləri, 31 dekabr 2017-ci il tarixinə Azərbaycan Respublikasının Maliyyə Bazarlarına Nəzarət Palatası, Bakı-2018.

than at the end of 2016. The credit portfolio of banks decreased by 28.5% in 2017 compared to the same period in 2016. Since the decline, the credit portfolio of banks has faced the problem of excess liquidity. According to Zakir Nuriyev, president of the Association of Banks of Azerbaijan, "currently, the banking sector has liquidity of AZN4 billion, and therefore there is no need to raise funds from abroad. Shortly, the auction mechanism between banks will be involved and liquid funds distributed among the market participants. Solving liquidity problems created an opportunity to lower loan interest."[2]

At present, most banks offer short-term trade financing, long-term project financing, mortgage products, and other banking products. The overall lack of medium- to long-term capital is a constraint on the financing of private business in Azerbaijan. The credit supply is far too small to provide a suitable environment for the development of SMEs in the country. In fact, most SMEs have insufficient access to affordable credit lines given collateral requirements and loan terms, among other things. Long-term trade and project financing are in their infancy.

According to the Economist Intelligence Unit (EIU) (2017a) the banking sector is uncompetitive, fragmented, and poorly developed, and suffers from poor corporate governance. Lending as a share of gross domestic product (GDP) is low, and the banking sector plays only a marginal intermediation role in the economy. State and elite influence over the sector is high. Lending is overwhelmingly focused on Baku, the capital, and is largely directed toward established medium-sized and large enterprises. EIU experts claim that the outlook for the banking sector in the near term is poor. Low oil prices will keep the economy in recession this year, resulting in a fall in demand for credit and deterioration in asset quality. A large share of loans is denominated in foreign currency and is now nonperforming following the two devaluations of the manat in 2015. Dollarization of the economy is high, exposing the banking sector to ongoing exchange rate risks. The EIU expects further consolidation of the sector in the coming 2 years. There remains a risk that the manat will depreciate or fluctuate further, putting the financial sector under added strain.

According to the Fitch ratings, the outlook for Azerbaijan's banking sector is still negative due to continued asset quality pressures (AMFA 2016). The banking system remains quite small relative to the size of the economy. Even with high assets and the growth of loans and deposits in Azerbaijani banks over the last few years, total banking assets were about 52.4% of GDP, with loans accounting for about 27.4% and deposits

---

[2] Zakir Nuriyev, Bank sektorunda 4 mlrd. manat məbləğində likvidlik yaranıb, Banko.az saytı, 06-10-2017.

by individuals only 12.4% at the end of 2016—a much lower ratio than the 35%–60% characteristic of advanced transitional economies in Central and Southeastern Europe.

To provide a general picture, key banking sector indicators are presented in Table 3.1.

Table 3.1 Summary Banking Sector Statistics

No.	Banking Sector	2005	2010	2015	2016
1	Number of banks	44	45	43	32
2	Number of state-owned banks	2	1	2	2
3	Number of private banks	42	44	41	30
4	Assets (AZN million)	2,252.0	13,290.8	34,906.0	31,439.5
5	Assets in GDP (%)	17.9	31.3	64.2	52.4
6	Gross capital	388.3	1,897.1	3,654.0	1,908.8
7	Gross capital in GDP (%)	3.1	4.5	6.7	3.2
8	Total credits (AZN million)	1,441.0	9,163.4	21,730.4	16,444.6
9	Total credits in GDP (%)	11.5	21.7	39.9	27.4
10	Total credit portfolio of nonbank finance institutions (AZN million)	39.6	191.6	578.4	473.4
11	Total loans in national currency (AZN million)	542.9	5,865.3	10,994.5	8,663.2
12	Total loans in foreign currency (AZN million)	898.1	3,298.1	10,735.9	7,781.4
13	Loans to households (AZN million)	389.2	2,700.8	8,383.6	5,858.7
14	Total deposits (AZN million)	1,368.7	7,625.8	23,431.4	22,091.0
15	Deposits in national currency (AZN million)	280.2	3,205.3	4,301.7	5,459.0
16	Deposits in foreign currency (AZN million)	1,088.5	4,420.5	19,129.7	16,632.0
17	Dollarization of deposits (%)	79.5	58.0	81.6	75.3
18	Deposits of households (AZN million)	494.5	3,029.8	9,473.9	7,432.1
19	Deposits of financial organizations (AZN million)	–	2,177	6,358.8	4,509.5
20	Deposits of nonfinancial organizations (AZN million)	874.2	2,419	7,630.4	2,256.3
21	Foreign debt of banking sector (AZN million)	158.2	2,470.4	8,204.5	7,224.8

Source: Central Bank of Azerbaijan Republic, Statistics bulletin, December 2016.

3.2.2 Nonbank Credit Institutions

Microfinance first started in the middle of the 1990s with the participation of international nongovernment organizations (NGOs), and the sector has grown steadily over time. However, double devaluations have affected not only the banking sector but also nonbank credit organizations. As a result of these devaluations and due to the cancellation of the licenses of 13 NBCIs, the number of NBCIs and other participants in financial markets has decreased during the last 2 years. At the end of 2016, there were 144 NBCIs in the country, including nonbank credit organizations (47) and credit unions (97). For comparison, 157 NBCİs (48 nonbank credit organizations and 109 credit unions) were operating in Azerbaijan at the end of 2015. In the same period, a weakening in the quality of the portfolio reduced the number of customers and assets, resulting in losses for NBCIs.

Even so, microfinance has not yet reached its potential. This has been strongly highlighted by the World Bank (2013): "The non-bank credit sector is underdeveloped and offers limited opportunities for Azerbaijani SMEs." The combined microfinance loan portfolio is still only about 1% of GDP, despite considerable demand for microfinance services. Sector concentration is high, with the two largest providers of microfinance, Access Bank and FINCA, together accounting for 46% of the market. According to Suleyman Kalashov, chairman of the Azerbaijan Microfinance Association (AMFA) (2018), "customers of microfinance institutions have sharply declined in the past 3 years; the microfinance institutions had 600,000 customers in 2015. Customers

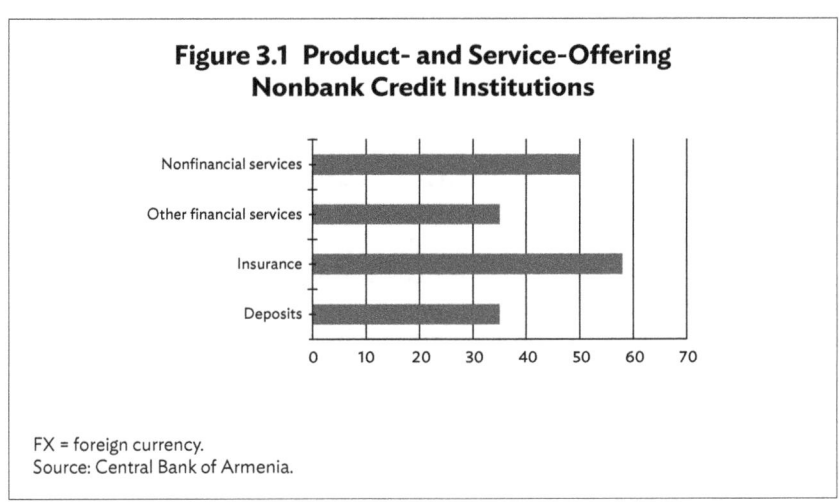

Figure 3.1 Product- and Service-Offering Nonbank Credit Institutions

FX = foreign currency.
Source: Central Bank of Armenia.

fell to 298,000 in 2016 and 118,000 in the first 9 months of 2017. Besides, the microfinance institutions' loan portfolio amounted to $348 million in 2015, and $80.1 million in the equivalent period of 2017."

He noted that microfinance organizations issue loans at 40% per year, but only solving liquidity problems would create an opportunity to lower loan interest.

Initially, the products offered for microfinance were mainly micro, small, and medium-sized business loans and agriculture. However, as more and more institutions entered the market, they began to diversify their product range to include consumer loans, loans for travel or medical purposes, education loans, emergency loans, and other specialized loans. NBCIs are not allowed to take deposits. Thus, NBCIs offer only loan products while banks also offer mobile banking and express loans along with their deposit products.

To provide a general picture, key indicators of the nonbanking sector are presented in Table 3.2.

Table 3.2 Summary Microfinance Sector Statistics

Number	Microfinance Sector	2015	2016
1	Number of microfinance institutions	157	144
2	Number of nonbank credit organizations	48	47
3	Number of credit unions	109	97
	Number of customers	600,000	298,000
4	Assets (AZN million)	614	3,897.7*

* The sharp increase in assets is due to the International Bank's purification of toxic assets of AZN3 billion by Aqrarkredit, a stock credit organization.
Source: MIX Market, Factsheet for Azerbaijan, Dec 2017.

3.3 Status of Financial Inclusion for Individuals and Small and Medium-Sized Enterprises

One of the major factors preventing the development of SMEs is inadequate access to financial resources. It is worth highlighting that an evaluation of the enabling business environment carried out by different international agencies in the country has shown that entrepreneurship subjects are finding it difficult to attract the required financial resources.

The statistical data provided by the World Bank and State Statistical Committee in Azerbaijan do not disclose the process related to the distribution of allocated credit investments for entrepreneurship by the size of enterprises. Nevertheless, it is worth emphasizing several factors that contribute to SMEs' poor access to credit resources based on analysis and surveys.

Azerbaijan was ranked 38th out of 55 countries for overall financial inclusion under Microscope 2014 (EIU 2014). Of the seven states covered in the report on Eastern Europe and Central Asia, Azerbaijan ranked 5th. In Eastern Europe and Central Asia three of the countries included in 2014—Armenia, Azerbaijan, and Georgia—have been dropped from the index, while the Russian Federation was added in 2015.

According to the 2014 World Bank Global Financial Inclusion (Global Findex) Database (Demirguc-Kunt et al), almost 30% of adults have accounts at a formal financial institution, and the operating environment in Azerbaijan is reasonably conducive to financial inclusion. The 2014 Global Findex Database shows that the level of financial inclusion in Azerbaijan is higher than in Armenia and lower than in Georgia (Table 3.3). The penetration rate in Azerbaijan is well below some transition countries and the European Union.

Table 3.3 Account Penetration

	Account (% aged 15+)				
	All Adults	Women	Adults Belonging to the Poorest 40%	Young Adults (% aged 15–24)	Adults Living in Rural Areas
Azerbaijan	29.2	25.9	26.9	10.0	30.1
Armenia	17.7	14.7	10.9	10.4	15.5
Georgia	39.7	39.8	28.6	9.9	40.1
Europe and Central Asia	51.4	47.4	44.2	35.6	34.7

Source: World Bank. The Global Findex Database, 2014.

The results analyzed in the framework of the Financial Capability and Inclusion Survey Report (World Bank 2016a) prove that the level of financial inclusion in Azerbaijan rose from about 15% in 2011 to 29% in 2014 (2014 Global Findex Database) and 36% in 2015 (Financial Capabilities Survey in Azerbaijan 2015).[3] When investments, private

---

[3] Data on formal account ownership are drawn from the 2015 Financial Capabilities Survey (Azerbaijan).

pensions, and insurance products were included as formal financial products, the survey found that 47.2% of Azerbaijani adults use some formal financial product. According to the Financial Capability and Inclusion Survey (FCIS), there is a strong correlation between income level and financial inclusion. In fact, the gap in financial inclusion between the richest and the poorest quartiles is 22.9%, corresponding to nearly half of that of the richest quartile. Adults who are out of the labor force were found to be 6% less financially included than the average employed adult. Household size is correlated with financial inclusion; however, there is only a 3.1% average difference between the smallest and the largest households. There is only a small difference in financial inclusion between genders overall, but an in-depth analysis suggests that levels of financial inclusion are lower among younger women than among younger men, providing a backdrop to women's lower economic participation. When the sample is broken down into age groups, a marked difference in inclusion appears in favor of younger male respondents in Azerbaijan (financial inclusion is 5.2% higher for men aged 18–20). Inclusion tends to be more or less gender-neutral between the ages of 21 and 55, after which it reverses in favor of women (financial inclusion is 5.7% higher for women aged 56 and older). This pattern suggests degradation in the younger generation of women compared to their elders.

According to the 2015 Financial Capabilities Survey, around 36% of surveyed adults in Azerbaijan report owning an account at a formal financial institution (bank, microfinance institution [MFI], or e-money agent), a commonly used metric for international comparison. Compared to the averages of other upper middle-income economies, Azerbaijan is behind in terms of financial inclusion, number of commercial bank

Table 3.4 Measures of Financial Inclusion and Development across Economies

	ATMs (per 100,000 adults)	Commercial Bank Branches (per 100,000 adults)	Firms Using Banks to Finance Investment (% of firms)
Azerbaijan	32.72	10.7	27.1
Armenia	61.14	22.0	17.4
Georgia	74.31	27.0	22.0
Europe and Central Asia	59.99	22.3	24.3

Source: Data on formal account ownership are drawn from Demirguc-Kunt et al (2014) and World Bank (2015).

branches, and domestic credit provided by the financial sector (see Tables 3.3 and 3.4).

The total number of bank branches per 100,000 inhabitants in Azerbaijan is about 10.7, much lower than in Armenia (22.0) and Georgia (27.0). In terms of the number of ATMs per 100,000 adults, Azerbaijan falls behind its neighbors as well as the regional average. Due to the decline in the number of ATMs and population increase in the past year, the number of ATMs per 100,000 people increased from 20.5 in 2010 to 28.0 in 2015. For comparison, the world average in 2015 was almost 600 ATMs per 100,000 adults. This indicator is 50% better than the relevant index for Azerbaijan. The same trend was observed in the number of point-of-sale (POS) terminals in 2016. According to the Central Bank of Azerbaijan Republic (CBAR), most ATMs and POS terminals are in the capital city. In 2016, 53.87% of ATMs and 56.4% of POS terminals were functioning in Baku, although, according to official figures, only a quarter of Azerbaijanis live in Baku.

According to the World Bank's Financial Capability and Inclusion Survey, Azerbaijan 2015, regional differences in financial inclusion do exist; however, they remain small to moderate. Ganja-Qazakh has the highest level at 38.3% (5.2% above the national average), and Shaki-Zaqatala has the lowest level at 32.3% (11.3% below the national average). The next highest levels are in Daglig-Shirvan (3.5% above the national average) and Absheron-Baku (1.1% above the national average).

3.3.1 Accounts

In Azerbaijan, bank accounts are the most commonly used financial product. According to the FCIS report, only about one-third of the population have a bank account; however, almost everybody, whether men or women, urban or rural, rich or poor, know about the services offered by banks. The most notable difference is that 44% of rich people have bank accounts compared to 27% of the poor, a difference of about 17%. In general, 34% of the population currently have a formal bank account, 84% claim to have used banks in the past, and 98% know about services offered by banks. Usage of bank accounts varies moderately between regions, with a 9% spread between the highest and lowest usage of bank accounts. There is a positive connection between levels of wealth at the regional level (as measured by income per capita) and the holding of bank accounts. However, there is a strong negative correlation between historical and current holding of bank accounts. In fact, regions with a high usage of bank services in the past tend to have the lowest present holding of bank accounts and vice versa. This suggests that many past users of bank services were dissatisfied and decided to revert to other mechanisms.

According to the latest data, in 2017 there were 5,352,456 bank customers and 15,161,312 accounts. Compared with 2016, the total number of customers declined by 6.35%, the number of individual bank customers fell by 5.78%, and the number of unique customers engaged in entrepreneurial activity fell by 4.71%. Bank customers as a legal entity declined sharply from 36% in 2016 compared to the equivalent period of 2015.

At the beginning of 2017, bank customers accounted for 54.6% of the total population and 71.2% of the population older than 15.

In 2016, there were more closed customer accounts than there were bank customers. This can be explained by the fact that most individual customers kept one of their many previous bank accounts. In the same period, credit accounts declined by 26.1% and deposit accounts fell by 17.83%. This negative trend can be explained mainly by the increase in credit risk and the depreciation of deposits with the national currency.

3.3.2 Credit

After the devaluation of the manat, commercial banks changed their lending policy, refused to give loans in manat, and increased the number of loans in dollars, thereby reducing the number of citizens who went to banks. Azerbaijani banks offer costly lending terms (usually 10%–15%, but occasionally higher) in dollar-denominated loans with a maximum 2-year term. Many Azerbaijani firms cannot afford such loans and turn to private sources (i.e. personal deals) for finance. According to the CBAR, before the devaluation in 2015, the average lending rate of the banks in Azerbaijan amounted to 13.6% in local currency, compared to 13.81% in 2014. After devaluation at the end of 2015, the average interest rate was 13.76% in the national currency and 13.74% in foreign currency. There was a small difference between manat and dollar loans in 2015, but the difference began to increase gradually after devaluation. Thus, at the beginning of 2017, the average interest rate was 12.05% in the national currency and 8.60% in foreign currency. Nevertheless, due to high risk and a double-digits inflation rate, loan interest rates increased again in 2017, and the difference between currencies decreased as a result. Due to high inflation rates and economic uncertainty, banks find it disadvantageous to provide long-term loans or grace-period loans, which are important for new businesses. As a rule, access to credit is on the banks' terms, which include interest rates, securitization of credit, and period of borrowing. Such conditions are unfavorable for SMEs to take out bank loans and involve relatively high maintenance costs associated with small deposits or loans.

Table 3.5 The Structure of Loans to the Economy by Type of Credit Institution (End of Period)

Year	Total Loans	State Banks		Private Banks		Nonbank Institutions	
		In AZN	%	In AZN	%	In AZN	%
2005	1,441.0	748.3	51.9	653.1	45.3	39.6	2.7
2010	9,163.4	3,901.9	42.6	5,069.9	55.3	191.6	2.1
2015	21,730.4	7,289.3	33.6	13,875.2	63.8	566.0	2.6
2016	16,444.6	5,749.2	35.0	10,222.0	62.2	473.4	2.9

Source: Central Bank of Azerbaijan Republic, Statistics Bulletin, December 2016.

According to the CBAR, average deposits and interest rates are going down; nevertheless, loan interest rates are high, especially in foreign currency. As for the loan interest rate in the national currency, it is currently less than the inflation rate in the same period.

As you can see from Table 3.5, the total loan portfolio of banks and nonbank institutions decreased by 24.3% at the end of 2016 compared to 2015. As a result of the structural change, the share of nonbank institutions in the total credit portfolio increased by 0.7%; however, input from nonbank institutions remains low.

The sectoral breakdown of loans in 2016 is presented in Figure 3.2.

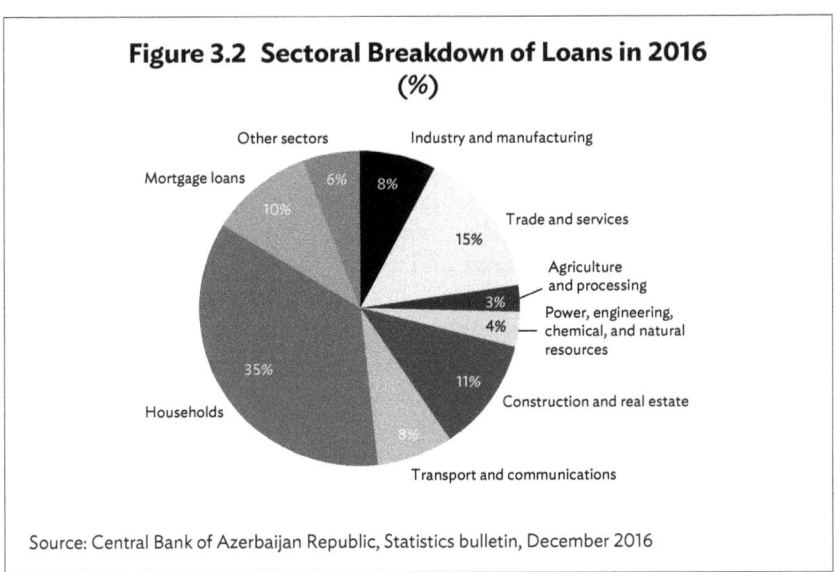

Figure 3.2 Sectoral Breakdown of Loans in 2016 (%)

Source: Central Bank of Azerbaijan Republic, Statistics bulletin, December 2016

Table 3.6 Formal Saving and Formal Borrowing

	Formal Saving (% Aged 15+)	Formal Borrowing (% Aged 15+)	Domestic Credit Provided by Financial Sector (% of GDP)
Azerbaijan	5	19	33.7
Armenia	2	20	47.2
Georgia	1	14	45.3
All upper-middle income	32	10	
Europe and Central Asia	8	12	69.1

GDP = gross domestic product.
Source: Data on formal account ownership are from Demirguc-Kunt et al (2014) and World Bank (2015).

As you can see from Figure 3.2, 45% of credits were invested in the industry and manufacturing, and trade and services sectors in 2016.

According to the 2014 Findex survey, 19% of the population in Azerbaijan used bank credit, and those over the age of 15 in Azerbaijan used formal borrowing at a higher rate than in Georgia, but less than in Armenia. Domestic credit provided by the financial sector accounted for 33.7% of GDP, almost half the regional average (Table 3.6).

According to the Financial Capabilities Survey in Azerbaijan 2015, about 4% more people utilize bank credit in urban than in rural areas. About 3% more people in Baku have credit cards than in the rest of the country. The urban population uses formal credit (16%) and credit cards (9%) more than their rural peers (12% and 7%, respectively). Many people living in Baku use credit cards; in fact, 12% of Baku inhabitants hold credit cards compared to 8% nationally. On the other hand, most bank account holders (about 22%) own a debit card, which are utilized more by rich people (32%) than by poor people (18%).

As for transactions with debit and credit cards, trend analyses of financial transactions with debit and credit cards show that, although the number of social and salary cards has increased, the number of total payment cards has declined in recent years. In terms of the structure of the cards, the number of salary and social cards accounted for 76.35% of all cards functioning in the last year. At least a quarter of bank cards in Azerbaijan are used for mandatory payments. At the same time, it is noteworthy that only 11.82% of the current cards are credit cards, and these decreased in number by 37.5% from 2015 to 2016.

The decline in the number of credit cards can be explained by the closing of 11 banks in the past 2 years, as well as the increased credit risk

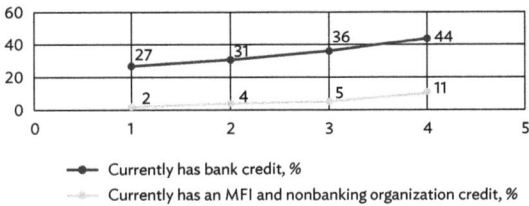

Figure 3.3 Use of Banks, Microfinance Institutions, and Other Nonbank Credit Institutions by Income Quartile

MFI = microfinance institution.
Source: World Bank (2015).

management and reduced public trust in banks. Another factor is that individual bank customers preferred to avoid risk by closing their card accounts during the crisis period due to low financial literacy.

According to the 2015 World Bank's Financial Capability Survey, Azerbaijan, approximately half of the population does not borrow money, preferring to use informal credit instead. Furthermore, 11% more poor people than rich have informal credit and 6% more rich than poor have formal credit. As can be seen, 14.51% of the population has no credit whatsoever. Informal credit is the most popular borrowing method, having a 15% lead over formal credit. There is little difference between men and women in borrowing statistics overall. Nevertheless, there are socioeconomic and demographic variations worth mentioning. Of informal credit, 27% is found among the poor and 20% among the rich. These findings seem to confirm the argument that poor people are more likely to work independently or informally in the private sector than their rich counterparts, and as such are less likely to obtain bank credit.

Banks are not interested in allocating financial resources to regions. Besides observing a decline in the flow of credit investments from the capital to other regions, annual interest rates on credit are also skyrocketing. One of the financial problems faced by SMEs operating in the regions is high interest rates and barriers to accessing long-term credit. Entrepreneurs who took part in the survey of the Qabus Research and Consulting Company have highlighted this problem especially.

3.3.3 Insurance

Azerbaijan's insurance market is currently at the very beginning of the development process. Despite the fact that insurance market and the potential of the country's economy are higher, the insurance market has been experiencing a decline in recent years. Various objective reasons for this include the lack of information on the majority of insurance products, a lack of trust in insurance companies, insufficient types of compulsory insurance, and a lack of control mechanisms for the sale of existing mandatory insurance products.

According to the experience of developing countries with stable economies, insurance premiums should account for at least 2% of GDP. This figure is low in Azerbaijan, at just 0.73% in 2016 (up from 0.68% in 2015). Non-life insurance overwhelmingly dominates the take-up in insurance premiums. Tax incentives for life insurance schemes are currently limited to just 3 years, thereby reducing their attractiveness.

Insurance is still nascent in Azerbaijan, and the sector remains small, although the government has begun to support its development by strengthening the environment and introducing mandatory insurance. Unfortunately, the total number of insurance companies declined from 71 in 1995 to 29 in 2003. By 2012, the sector comprised 29 insurance companies, 1 reinsurer, 7 brokers, about 200 agents, and the Association of Azerbaijani Insurers. Total assets accounted for less than 1% of GDP. The industry is moderately concentrated, with the 10 leading insurers accounting for 75% of premiums in 2012. Many insurance companies are linked with banks; however, most insurance companies focus on specific products, such as medical, motor, real estate, and life insurance.

According to the World Bank's Financial Capability Survey, Azerbaijan 2015, approximately half of the population has used an insurance product in the past, but fewer than one of 10 persons (and only 3% of rural inhabitants) currently have an insurance policy. This suggests a strong need for improvement. Furthermore, 30% of the population is unaware of services offered by insurance companies. Usage of insurance products tends to increase with household size; however, there is a notable difference between urban and rural areas. In fact, four times more urban than rural people currently have an insurance policy. This is rather astonishing, especially for agriculture in rural areas where there are few buyers of harvest insurance that would smooth fluctuations in household income due to seasonality. Usage of insurance varies significantly between regions, and there is a correlation between the usage of such services and regional wealth. According to the 2015 Financial Capabilities Survey, the spread between the highest and lowest usage of insurance services is more than 10%. It is notable that the largest users of insurance products are based in Absheron-Baku and Daglig-Shirvan, the two wealthiest regions in Azerbaijan.

In summary, sector segmentation is high and competition limited, which has a negative impact on quality and product cost.

3.3.4 Pensions

At the beginning of 2018, there were 1,320,400 pensioners in Azerbaijan (13.5% of the total population). Azerbaijan has a universal pension system. In 2001, the state pension was converted from a pay-as-you-go legacy system inherited from the Soviet era to a defined contribution system. This pension reform concept lays the groundwork for a privately funded pension system. The Law on Nonstate Pension Funds is prepared but has not yet been passed as the government is concerned that the financial markets are not yet adequately developed. Private pensions do not exist. The current average retirement pension is $120 per month. The International Bank of Azerbaijan and Kapital Bank are the only banks authorized to provide pension services. There is no existing private pension fund in Azerbaijan.

3.3.5 Remittances

In recent decades, permanent and temporary labor migration has gained remarkable significance in all Commonwealth of Independent States countries. While some states, such as Armenia, Azerbaijan, Moldova, Tajikistan, and Uzbekistan, are predominantly labor-exporting regions, the Russian Federation is an immigration as well as an emigration country. According to unofficial data, around 2 million legal and illegal Azerbaijani workers are employed in the Russian Federation. Citizens from Azerbaijan can enter the Russian Federation without a visa, but they have to register with the local authorities to be eligible for a work permit. The majority of foreign workers from Azerbaijan in the Russian Federation are men, and they predominantly work in construction, services, trade, and agriculture. Connected to labor migration, the receipt of remittances (outflow) decreased between 2010 and 2016 (Table 3.7). Additionally, it should be emphasized that official statistics on payments most likely underestimate the actual inflow of these resources to a considerable extent.

Although the CBAR approved the Guidelines on Cashless Settlements and Money Remittances in the Republic of Azerbaijan on 17 September 2013,[4] so far, many migrants have transferred money outside the official channels, especially if they perform irregular work.

According to the World Bank's Financial Capability Survey, when receiving remittances from abroad, about one person in 10 uses

---

[4] Central Bank of Azerbaijan Republic, Guidelines on Cashless Settlements and Money Remittances in the Republic of Azerbaijan on 17 September 2013.

Table 3.7 Transactions through Interbank Payment Systems

	Remittance system					
	Inflow			Outflow		
Year	Number of Transactions (AZN'000)	Amount of Transactions (AZN'000)	Amount per Transaction (AZN'000)	Number of Transactions (AZN'000)	Amount of Transactions (AZN million)	Amount per Transaction (AZN'000)
2010	153.0	89.0	581.7	46.0	42.6	926.1
2015	215.8	130.4	604.6	116.9	76.5	654.4
2016	223.2	151.8	680.1	94.5	55.3	585.2

Source: Central Bank of Azerbaijan Republic, Statistics Bulletin, December 2016.

money transfer operators (MTOs), predominantly from poor and large households in urban areas (especially Baku). Some 12% of the population currently have money transfer products, and more than one-third have used such products in the past. Furthermore, three out of four persons know about services offered by MTOs. Such services were found to be utilized by 30% of people in urban areas (especially Baku), by 33% of people from poor households, and by about 20% of people living in the largest households. These facts support the notion that poor people receive more financial support from family and friends. In fact, 37% of poor households declare this kind of support as a source of household income, while only 15% of the richest households affirm the same. MTO usage is linked to the remittance trend in Azerbaijan. Azerbaijan is one of the top remittance-sending countries (25th worldwide and eighth among middle-income economies). Such remittances represent about 2.7% of GDP ($2.0 billion) (World Bank 2016b).

3.3.6 Securities

According to the World Bank's Financial Capability Survey, more than one in three persons have used brokerage house products in the past, and a very small fraction of people (whether male or female, urban or rural, rich or poor) currently have investments, which may highlight the lack of trust or interest in such products. Of the overall population, 49% know about the services offered by brokerage houses and 36% have utilized investment products in the past. However, only 0.3% of persons currently hold an investment, perhaps due to bad performance. Rich people seem to know more about such products (57%) by a factor of 1.24, and 45% use these products versus 33% of poor people (a difference of

12%). These results may be associated with the fact that the brokerage industry is concentrated in Baku. In fact, there is only one authorized stock exchange in Azerbaijan, the Baku Stock Exchange (BSE). Furthermore, there are very few participants in the securities market, which comprises 12 brokerage companies, 13 dealers, 3 securities managers, 1 clearinghouse, 2 registrars, and 1 depository. The first equity transactions at the BSE were recorded in 2001. The corporate bonds market started in 2004. There were 651 joint stock companies registered in the stock market (OECD 2015). Entities applying for membership must meet the conditions set under the internal procedures of the BSE. The eligibility of an applicant is assessed and decided by the Internal Membership Committee. Exchange membership is granted on the applicant's eligibility and conformity to the requirements. According to the BSE Membership Rules,[5] entities who apply for membership should be a joint stock company. Therefore, SMEs cannot be listed on the stock market.

Although small, Azerbaijan's securities markets do contribute to capital mobilization. The basic institutional framework for securities markets has been in place for more than a decade. The authorities are now strengthening it under the State Program for the Development of Securities Markets for 2011–2020 with World Bank support, alongside measures to strengthen the legal and regulatory framework.

3.3.7 Kinds of Financial Institutions Involved

Some other institutions are involved in this process, such as postal institutions and pawnshops. According to the Financial Market Supervisory Authority (FIMSA), there are 63 postal institution branches and 1,111 post offices of mail institutions with financial services. There are 1,200 pawnshops.

3.4 Barriers to Financial Inclusion

3.4.1 Supply-Side Barriers

Reduced number of banks and NBCIs and their branches. During the last 3 years, the CBAR and FIMSA withdrew the licenses of 15 banks and 13 NBCIs. According to the FIMSA report, due to the crisis in the financial market, as of 31 December 2017 there were 506 bank branches

---

[5]   Baku Stock Exchange "CJSC, Membership Rules approved by Board of Directors Protocol No. 08 "30" December 2015

operating in Azerbaijan (63 fewer than at the end of 2016), and 142 bank offices (11 fewer than at the end of 2016). Meanwhile, the number of bank employees had decreased from 16,947 at the end of 2016 to 16,161. This means that there is not enough capacity to extend financial services to poorer households or SMEs.

High interest rates on credit are major factors preventing SMEs from accessing credit resources. The high interest rates on credit in the country are acknowledged at both the official level and by entrepreneurs. Of the respondents who participated in the survey conducted by the Qabus Research and Consulting Company to determine SMEs' level of access to credit, 38% indicated that they did not access credit organizations due to high interest rates. Moreover, 81% of the entrepreneurs who took part in this survey suggested lowering interest rates to increase access to credit funds. Additionally, 85% of them reported annual average interest rates of credit of more than 20%. According to 87.4% of entrepreneurs, when interest rates exceed 15% the environment is unfavorable for business.

Problems related to securing credit. Azerbaijani legislation does not have a guarantee of credit mechanism for SME subjects. The same applies to both the insurance of risks concerning SME credit and guarantee of collateral security from this category. In other words, collateral is required to access National Fund for Entrepreneurship Support credit just like other credit, in which case all responsibility falls on the shoulders of the entrepreneurship subjects.

Lack of credit guarantee institutions. One of the main reasons for refusal of commercial lending is the demand for credit guarantee requirements. An in-depth analysis shows that banks prefer real estate as collateral to secure credit. The fact that approximately 60% of entrepreneurs conduct their businesses on leased premises means that they can only use their living accommodation as collateral, which does not satisfy the banks. Also, because SME operations are often not transparent due to their not keeping financial records, the banks cannot evaluate companies' operations, which in turn limits banks' ability to assess creditworthiness and possible loan issuance.

Limited availability and quality of credit data. The target market for these NBCIs includes small farmers, trade and service SMEs, and individual enterprises, which mostly produce consumer goods; thus, the target group for these microcredit institutions mainly includes SMEs of various sorts. Not having accurate credit information on borrowers causes microcredit organizations to introduce tougher requirements (e.g. higher interest rates, shorter terms) to mitigate risk. Registry information does not offer a detailed analysis of the client.

Poor and base types of financial products and services. SMEs and households have limited access to the modern variety of financial services. There are not enough new players in financial markets, such as venture investment funds, business angels, and crowdfunding platforms and campaigns; and no access to alternative financial instruments like guarantees, bills, and factoring.

3.4.2 Demand-Side Barriers

Poor mutual understanding between banks and SMEs. All in-depth interviews with the entrepreneurs demonstrated that they had an imperfect knowledge and understanding of the services and information that banks offer. This corresponds to the lack of full and adequate information that banks have on their clients. Business people who have never applied for credit often complain about the terms and conditions offered by banks that they have learned by word of mouth rather than through direct experience with banks. Banks do not actively conduct information campaigns targeting SMEs and entrepreneurs that are insufficiently informed about the services they offer. In many respects, the attractiveness of any bank service often stems from advertisements and campaigns aimed at promoting the service.

Lower financial awareness. A lack of financial literacy regarding management, procedures, and instruments in an environment with complicated application procedures for bank loans and high financing costs (e.g. interest rates and transaction costs) creates a substantial disadvantage for SMEs. The increased incidence of parallel borrowing and overindebtedness coupled with the massive dollarization or withdrawal of savings from banks indicates the need for increased financial literacy and education to reach a healthier and more stable microfinance sector through client-focused activities (along with other bank-level measures for internal pro-client campaigns, rescheduling, and new risk management or hedging, among others) and education for long-term saving and investment opportunities.

Lost client trust. Decreasing long-term savings, investments, and need for banking services affect the reputation of the banking sector in the market and are negatively expressed by a worsening client repayment culture.

3.4.3 Institutional Aspects

The most significant institutional constraint noted by banks is the absence of a collateral registry system for movable collateral (other than vehicles). As a result, collateral requirements tend to be somewhat strict in Azerbaijan. Most lenders require that real estate collateral covers a significant portion of the loan value, and several only accept real estate collateral in practice. A draft law for a free collateral registry was prepared in consultation with the International Finance Corporation. There are a few other constraints, although they are less critical than the collateral registry issue. The public credit bureau, which is managed by the CBA, does not include information from public utilities, mobile phone companies, and other providers who would be relevant for assessing credit risk and avoiding overindebtedness. There is currently an effort underway to start Azerbaijan's first private bureau, which may help to resolve this issue. Other constraints are the considerable length of time that it takes to determine bankruptcy (1.5 years on average) and low average recovery rates ($0.396 on the dollar, according to the World Bank's Doing Business Report [2017]), which discourage lending, particularly to higher risk applicants such as startup companies.

3.4.4 Bankruptcy Law

Azerbaijan's Bankruptcy Law, which does not function efficiently and is rarely used, continues to be a hindrance to economic development, as do the country's weak credit-reporting institutions. Under this law, which applies only to legal entities and entrepreneurs, not individuals, bankruptcy proceedings may be started by either a debtor facing insolvency or any creditor. In general, the legislation focuses on liquidation procedures. For example, a court-approved "rehabilitation plan" may not exceed 2 years.

According to the World Bank's Doing Business 2017: Equal Opportunity for All, Azerbaijan ranks 86th out of 189 countries for ease of "resolving insolvency".

3.4.5 Land Registry

Registration of land and property takes place at the State Committee on Property Issues of the Republic of Azerbaijan. In accordance with the Resolution of the Cabinet of Ministers of the Republic of Azerbaijan No. 266 (dated 31 July 2014), the electronic service on "receipt of applications and documents for issuance of technical documents (passport and plan) regarding real estate registered in the state registry of real estate at the discretion of the owner" has been added to the list of electronic services provided by the State Registry Service of Real Estate.

On 18 November 2014, the Collegium of the State Committee on Property Issues approved the administrative regulation on the receipt of applications and documents for the issue of technical documents (passport and plan) regarding real estate registered in the state registry of real estate at the discretion of the owner. With these materials, it has become possible to apply for technical documents (passport and plan) via an online procedure.

3.5 Regulatory Framework

The regulatory framework is conducive to the development of the banking sector, and the state has provided adequate, timely support to banks in past times of stress. Banking regulations are mostly in line with international standards, with no unusually burdensome requirements.

The CBAR, formerly known as the National Bank of Azerbaijan, was the central regulatory body until the creation of the FIMSA in early 2016. The CBAR continued its policy of ensuring financial sector stability and sustainability in 2015 and undertook some policy actions to that end. New capital adequacy requirements came into force in January 2015, and all banks were either able to comply or given additional time to do so. The largest banks, which hold 85% of all banking assets, already met the new requirements. The FIMSA is likely to continue similar policies to ensure financial sector stability. The CBAR now focuses on monetary policy and exchange rate stability.

As you can see from the activities mentioned above, the CBAR is the primary regulator implementing licensing, supervising, enforcement, and reporting requirements for all banks and NBCIs. The Law on Banks (2004) defines the principles, rules, and standards of organization, internal management, and regulation of activities and liquidation of banks. The purpose of aligning the legal framework of the banking system with international standards is to increase the role of banking services in the economy, enforce the protection of bank depositors and creditors, and maintain the stable and safe performance of the banking system.

The Ministry of Finance regulates insurance companies. Leasing companies are controlled by the Tax and Civil Code Authority of Azerbaijan. The CBAR does not regulate retail shops and informal sector financial service providers like pawnshops, moneylenders, and lotteries (informal savings mechanisms).

The Azerbaijan microfinance sector is served by a diverse set of financial service providers, including regulated and nonregulated entities. The CBAR regulates banks and nonbank credit organizations. NBCIs include institutions that offer microfinance as well as credit unions. The NBCI category also comprises Azerpost, foreign exchange providers, consumer finance companies, and payment and money transfer service providers.

All financial institutions report performance statistics to the CBAR and online Centralized Credit Registry. Additionally, 38 members of the AMFA report to association on a monthly basis through a MATRIX report covering 10 indicators.

The CBAR licensed exchanges in the country; however, after the devaluation of the manat by 50% in December 2015, the CBAR issued a decree on 13 January 2016 waiving the license of all transactions in the nation. Therefore, exchanging currency can currently only be done in banks.

Pawn businesses also play a part in meeting poor people's urgent need for cash. Opening a Lombard business in Azerbaijan does not require a license, and they are not regulated. They register as a limited liability company at the respective regional department of the Ministry of Taxes, and their reporting requirements are similar to those of any limited liability company operating in the country.

3.5.1 Licensing and Status of Microfinance Institutions

Registration, licensing, and regulation of financial institutions are managed by the CBAR. According to the legislation, the required charter capital is AZN300,000 for registering an NBCI and AZN50 million for registering a bank.

The Law on Nonbank Credit Organization (2010) defines the rules on the establishment, management, and regulation of NBCIs with the aim of better meeting the demand of legal entities and individuals in Azerbaijan for financial resources and creating suitable conditions for access to financial services. The Law on Credit Unions (2000) determines the economic, legislative, and organizational basis for the establishment and operation of credit unions.

Azerbaijan has laws for NBCIs instead of defined "microfinance" laws and allows a greater number of permitted activities, although NBCIs are expressly forbidden from taking deposits. In Azerbaijan, NBCIs are divided into two groups—those with the right to accept collateral deposits and those without that right. NBCIs that receive a license to provide loans can also undertake the following activities: (i) purchasing and selling liabilities (factoring, forfeiting); (ii) leasing;

(iii) registering of notes; (iv) provision of guarantees; (v) provision of services or insurance agents; and (vi) provision of consulting services on financial, technical, and management issues to borrowers and collective borrowers. Azerbaijan is also the only country in Central Asia where insurance agent services are on the list of permissible activities. The NBCI law does not provide for foreign exchange operations.

3.5.2 Scope of Supervision and Regulation, Including Provisions for Maintaining Financial Stability

The Financial Stability Council (FSC) was established to maintain macroeconomic and financial stability in the country at the decree of the President of the Republic of Azerbaijan on 15 July 2016. The FSC helps to achieve systemized coordination of activities aimed at ensuring macroeconomic and financial stability. The FSC mobilizes all resources to enable a more accurate determination of the macro-framework, and to ensure that fiscal and financial policies supplement each other.

3.5.3 Consumer Protection, Including Disclosure and Interest Rate Caps

Consumer protection is becoming an important element of the financial sector stabilization and development agenda in Azerbaijan. The drop in oil prices and weaker macroeconomic fundamentals against a backdrop of negative external shocks have led to the devaluation of the national currency and erosion of public trust in the financial sector. Restoring financial stability, renewing public and investor confidence, and mobilizing higher savings to finance growth are the top priorities of Azerbaijan policy makers. The authorities are increasingly discussing the issues of consumer and depositor protection, responsible lending, and access to finance.

Another important finding of the World Bank's Financial Capability Survey is that 12% of the respondents experienced conflicts with financial service providers, the majority of whom did not try to resolve the conflicts they encountered. Fewer than 20% of Azerbaijani adults who encountered a dispute took action to try to resolve it. Interestingly, twice as many of those who did not experience a conflict (40%) stated that if they were to face one they would try to resolve it.

With regard to actions taken in the event of a dispute, those who experienced conflict with their financial service provider hardly ever sought help from internal complaints-handling systems and legal courts. The most common actions taken to try to resolve disputes were submitting a claim to the appropriate government authority (57%) and stopping use of the services before the contract expired (36%). Only around one in five (19%) reportedly submitted a grievance to the company that sold the product, while around 7% approached the legal courts.

In general, the main causes of inertia are related to either perceived power imbalances between financial service providers and their clients, or a lack of trust in, or awareness of, respective government authorities that can be approached in the event of a dispute. More than two-thirds of those who did not take any action to resolve a dispute reported that the main reason for their inertia was that they perceived financial institutions as being too powerful. Slightly fewer (61%) indicated that they thought that government authorities did not work properly, followed by 52% who were not aware of any government agencies they could approach for help. Slightly more than one-third of those who did not try to solve a conflict mentioned that they did not take any action because they thought the law does not adequately protect consumers. Only 3% of those who did not take any action to resolve a dispute declared that they were too shy to redress the dispute.

Official guidelines from the Central Bank of Azerbaijan dated December 2013 on "Dealing with the Appeals of Financial Service Consumers" provide clear guidance on how to build an effective system of responding to and processing complaints, suggestions, and any other appeals from clients.

3.5.4 Deposit Insurance

The Azerbaijan Deposit Insurance Fund (ADIF) was founded on 12 August 2007, after the law on deposit insurance was adopted by the Parliament of the Republic of Azerbaijan. The deposit insurance scheme was established to prevent the loss of money deposited by individuals and to ensure the sustainability and development of the financial and banking system whenever banks and local branch offices of foreign banks become insolvent. Since 24 February 2015, deposits with an annual interest rate of 12% and less have been protected, and in the case of an insurance event preserved deposits are compensated to a maximum of AZN30,000. The original cap of AZN6,000 was recently raised to AZN30,000 to prevent bank runs in connection with the deepening global economic crisis. Starting on 2 March 2016, deposits were accepted by the fund's member banks with an annual interest rate of 3% in foreign currency and 15% in the national currency, and fully insured for 3 years. According to the rule of law "on deposit insurance," interest on deposits shall be paid in the amount accrued by the date of the insurance event (ADIF 2019).

After the revoking of the licenses of 13 banks between 2012–2017 by the FIMSA, as of 1 January 2019, AZN 824,3 million (99.2% of the total compensation obligation) was reimbursed to depositors protected by the ADIF. The ADIF only provides insurance for depositors, not for investors.

3.5.5 Fintech-Related Regulation and Receptivity to Financial Innovation

According to the Global Innovation Index 2017 (WIPO 2017), Azerbaijan ranked 82nd of 127 countries. According to the 2016 FinTech Index results (ING 2016), in terms of demand versus country risk, Azerbaijan is on the list of lower fintech needs that meet a relatively unstable political environment. In the unit of fintech index results, in terms of demand versus supply, Azerbaijan is on the list of countries where more moderate fintech needs meet a supportive fintech environment. In the group of fintech index results, in terms of infrastructure versus ecosystem, Azerbaijan includes easy implementers, while good support meets a favorable business environment. The 2016 FinTech Index report shows that fintech-related regulation is weak, but that its potential is high due to good infrastructure.

After 2013, digital financial services started to be integrated into banks' operations and then gradually integrated by the large NBCIs. Mobile banking is also a part of most bank services that are being developed and expanded by and within the financial institutions. Payments are available through national payment terminals, such as eManat and Million.

3.6 Policies to Promote Financial Inclusion

3.6.1 Contents of National Strategy

On 6 December 2016, the President of the Republic of Azerbaijan approved strategic road maps (SRMs) on national economic perspectives and 11 sectors. The SRM for the prospects of Azerbaijan's national economy covers the short-, medium-, and long-term horizon and comprises the economic development concept and action plan for 2016–2020, the long-term outlook by 2025, and the target outlook for the period after 2025. According to the SRM, Azerbaijan will develop a competitive environment enabling equal access to the technologies, markets, and finance of the fourth industrial revolution. One of the 11 SRMs covers the development of financial services in Azerbaijan.

The SRM for the development of financial services contains the following strategic targets:
(i) Establish a financial system comprising dynamic and sound institutions.
(ii) Develop the financial markets.
(iii) Strengthen the infrastructure.
(iv) Improve regulation and control mechanisms.
(v) Improve financial literacy.

3.6.2 Level of Policy, National or Otherwise

Although the level of access of SMEs and households in Azerbaijan to financial services is indicated as one of the problems both within conducted surveys and published research in this direction, neither the government nor the CBAR has a specific policy in this field.

3.6.3 Institutions Involved

The main institutions involved in policies to promote financial inclusion are the Center for Analysis of Economic Reforms and Communication, which was established on 20 April 2016; and the FIMSA, which was established on 3 February 2016. The objective of the Center for Analysis of Economic Reforms and Communication is to develop proposals for the realization of economic reforms based on analytical data by conducting analyses and research at the macro- and microeconomic levels to ensure the country's sustainable economic development, as well as to prepare mid- and long-term forecasts, provide government authorities and agencies with the same, and organize the promotion of Azerbaijan's achievements in various sectors of the economy. The mandate of the FIMSA is financial market regulation and supervision to ensure financial sustainability and protection of the rights of investors and consumers.

3.6.4 Specific Strategies

There is no specific strategy for MFIs and banks.

3.6.5 Credit Databases

Currently, there is only one credit registry, and it does not meet the typical credit bureau standards. Some limitations prevent the credit registry from expanding into a proper credit bureau; for example, the registry information is closed to NBFIs. Currently, 144 NBCIs operate in Azerbaijan. Their target market includes small farmers, trade and service SMEs, and individual enterprises, which mostly produce consumer goods; that is, the target group for these microcredit institutions mainly includes SMEs of various sorts. A lack of accurate credit information on borrowers causes microcredit organizations to introduce more stringent requirements (e.g. higher interest rates, shorter terms) to mitigate risk. Moreover, registry information does not offer a detailed analysis of the client.

Unlike the registry, a credit bureau processes the information received, that is, it generalizes, classifies, and sells clients' credit reports (histories) to the banks. The registry services include only a small portion of the bureau's possibilities.

3.6.6 Credit Guarantees and Subsidies

In 2014, the government took a step toward the establishment of a legal framework for secured transactions (this is yet to be completed). Credit guarantee schemes with private sector participation are underdeveloped in Azerbaijan. Letters of credit, trade insurance, leasing, and factoring are also limited by both supply and demand factors. At the same time, stronger legal frameworks are required to create an enabling environment for venture capital activities.

As for state subsidies for SME development, the government provides three different plans for SME support. The largest is the Azerbaijani Investment Company, which invests in companies by taking equity stakes of at least $1 million and providing venture capital. The National Fund for Support of Entrepreneurship provides highly subsidized loans (up to $3.2 million in value) to SMEs. Finally, the Mortgage Fund also provides highly subsidized credit for a particular purpose. All three funds rely heavily on state oil revenues and issue debt at below-market rates.

3.6.7 Assessment of Effectiveness, Gaps, and Issues

Technological factors, which are considered an essential element of ensuring access to finance, are underdeveloped in the country. According to the research findings, supply problems in the field of access to financial resources are more difficult to deal with than problems with demand quality. A number of these issues originate from an economic policy carried out by the government as well as the monetary credit and exchange rate policy implemented through the CBAR. Despite a surplus across banks due to restrictions imposed over credit investments in the economy and increased risks, it is impossible to improve their financial and technical base and infrastructure at the expense of additional resources. The main reason for this is that it increases expenditure and worsens the economic status of banks. It should be noted that overdue credits are overabundant, and there is a lack of policy to resolve this issue and conduct expert discussions. Despite high expectations for both the CBAR and FIMSA to find a solution to this problem, neither can carry out an adequate policy to settle the existing issue in the new period. Similarly, existing deficiencies and gaps in the current legislation are limiting in terms of finding a fair solution to this problem in the courts.

Notwithstanding the decrease in credit interest rates, they are creating substantial expenses for SMEs and households, considering the current conditions. It is worth highlighting that costs accrued as a result of a difference between the pre-devaluation exchange rate and the rates on credit, including high interest rates, are paralyzing the business activities of SMEs and households. Thus, an absence of centralized and specific policy in this sphere is aggravating the relationships of banks and NBCIs with their customers. This results in cases being taken to court. Consequently, a reliable customer database is disappearing, and trust and confidence in banks are dropping.

Despite a presidential order on the activities of credit guarantee foundations, problems regarding the access of individuals lacking collateral and property to credit remain, given that an order implementation process has not yet been launched.

It should also be underlined that the attitude of Azerbaijan's Parliament toward changes in the legislation in this area is not good enough. Additionally, the current gaps related to the protection of the financial rights of customers are making it challenging to win court cases. Furthermore, the absence of specialized public unions and customer financial protection bureaus is leaving customers legally and publicly unguarded. This requires the revision of current rules and procedures, but no changes have been made in recent years. It should be noted that the decline in modernization and innovation within the economy does not go unnoticed within financial markets. Moreover, both SMEs and households that are actors in financial markets benefit from innovative products, and banks cannot reduce their expenses by applying innovations in this direction. Additionally, difficulties related to the creation of a credit database and ensuring its access as a centralized resource remain, particularly for NBCIs.

Even though the adoption of the SRM on access to financial services is commended, there has been no significant achievement in its execution. Moreover, the tasks set before the CBAR and FIMSA with the aim of efficiently carrying out the responsibilities outlined in the

SRM are progressing slowly, and decisions regarding implementation are being delayed. Although there are some definite changes regarding access to financial markets on a national level in Azerbaijan, targets for a particular policy at the micro level have not yet been identified.

3.7 Financial Education and Financial Literacy[6]

3.7.1 Status of Financial Literacy

Financial capability and education are an important priority for the CBAR as they help to empower people to become effective partners of these institutions as productive economic agents, and improve people's lives. To this end, the CBAR developed a national financial literacy strategy (NFLS) and a financial education website. Since 2010, the CBAR has launched and incorporated, under its mission plan, the Financial Literacy Project with five main objectives: "(a) make customers economically and financially more educated and skillful, (b) educate parents through children, (c) make changes to the financial behavior of people, (d) inspire corporate social responsibility, and (e) mitigate risks."

Given all these factors, the CBAR launched the Financial Literacy Project in 2010 under its mission plan. One of the key goals of this project is the promotion of financial and economic literacy as a public value.

3.7.2 Survey Results

The only Financial Literacy Survey conducted within the Financial Services Development Project was supported by the CBAR, the World Bank, and Swiss State Secretariat for Economic Affairs by AMFA in 2009. AMFA evaluated the current and starting situation in the field of financial literacy through surveying respondents in 2009; however, it could not repeat this evaluation to measure progress. An analysis of the starting situation has proved that NGOs should work intensively with state agencies in this direction with the aim of filling existing gaps.

To support the authorities in Azerbaijan in their efforts to advance financial capability, the World Bank has implemented a nationally

---

[6] According to the OECD Guidance Note on the Development and Implementation of National Strategies on Financial Education and of Financial Education Programmes, the terms "financial education" and "financial literacy" have different emphases, although, in practice, the terms tend to be used interchangeably: "financial education" refers to the provision of training, information, and advice to help people to manage their finances; and "financial literacy" refers to a person's knowledge, understanding, skills, and (sometimes) confidence to manage their finances.

representative financial capability survey of the adult population in Azerbaijan. This survey constitutes a key diagnostic tool that will inform the development of a detailed implementation action plan for the NFLS. Moreover, it will help the authorities set quantifiable and concrete targets, and assess the effectiveness of future financial capability by enhancing programs.

The Azerbaijani authorities, with the support of the World Bank, have conducted this financial capability survey, which will provide a detailed baseline for strategies regarding financial inclusion and literacy.

According to the World Bank Financial Capability Survey, Azerbaijan 2015, knowledge of basic financial concepts is a significant challenge in Azerbaijan mirrored by the fact that, on average, Azerbaijani adults were able to answer 3.9 out of 7 financial capability-related questions correctly. Azerbaijani adults are most comfortable with performing simple financial calculations (90%), identifying better bargains (79%), and understanding the concept of inflation (67%). However, they were found to be less familiar with risk diversification (19%) and lacked the numeracy skills needed to calculate simple and compound interest (46%). An international comparison of 21 countries confirms that Azerbaijanis' financial knowledge and awareness are within the norm in general. In fact, respondents in Azerbaijan ranked 9th for inflation, 10th for simple division, and 19th for simple interest.

An international comparison of some countries confirms that Azerbaijanis' financial knowledge and awareness are within the norm in general, except for interest rate calculation. Table 3.8 shows, for Azerbaijan and Armenia, the proportion of adults with a good grasp of basic financial concepts.

As far as the average number of financial products known is concerned, respondents were familiar with products provided by 5.8 out of 8 different types of providers. The survey participants were found to be well aware of the financial products offered by the main financial institutions, except brokerage houses.

Product awareness reached 98% for banks, 89% for other NBCIs, 74% for MFIs and MTOs, 68% for insurance companies, 64% for e-money

Table 3.8 Regional Comparison of Different Financial Literacy Scores

Country	Year	Inflation	Simple Interest	Compound Interest	Simple Division
Azerbaijan	2015	67	35	46	90
Armenia	2010	83	53	18	86

Source: World Bank (2015).

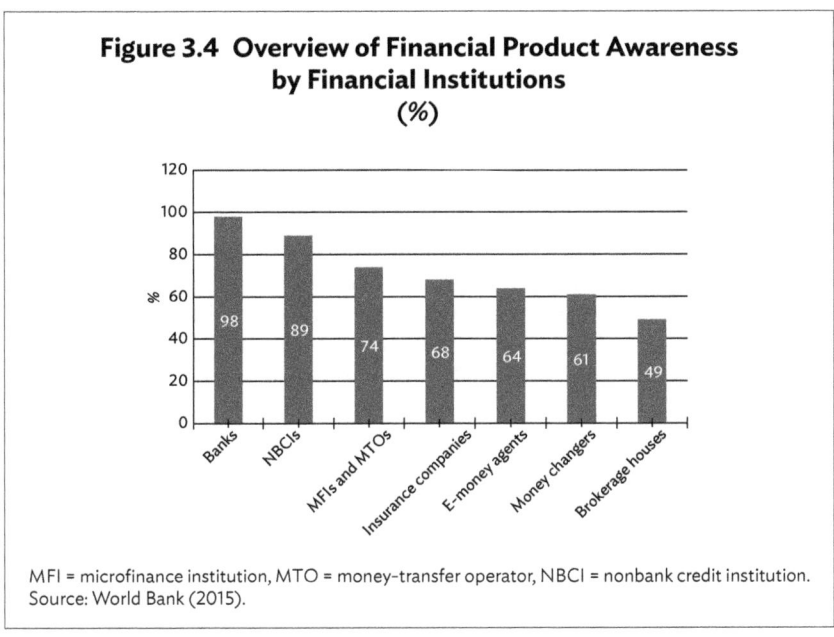

Figure 3.4 Overview of Financial Product Awareness by Financial Institutions (%)

MFI = microfinance institution, MTO = money-transfer operator, NBCI = nonbank credit institution.
Source: World Bank (2015).

agents, and 61% for money changers, but only 49% for brokerage houses. This is most likely due to the fact that the capital market in Azerbaijan is currently in a nascent stage.

Respondents who are the most familiar with financial products offered by financial providers tend to have a higher income and be more than 54 years old.

Azerbaijani adults showed relative strengths in using information and advice, and in choosing financial products; also, to a certain degree, they tend to be far-sighted and think about the future. Respondents scored highest in using information and advice for making an important financial decision (75%), choosing financial products (59%), and being far-sighted (54%). On the other hand, such respondents scored lowest in making provisions for old-age expenses (21%), saving and not overspending (25%), and controlled budgeting (35%).

A comparison to respondents in 14 countries confirms that Azerbaijani adults are mastering the task of choosing financial products but struggle to translate their far-sightedness into proper long-term action. Azerbaijan is ranked third out of 14 in choosing financial products but, given the difficulties that respondents faced in understanding simple and compound interest, it may be questioned whether people always end up selecting those products that best meet their needs. Moreover, the international comparison reveals that, although Azerbaijani adults are ranked sixth out of 14 regarding their propensity to think about the future, they are at the back of the pack in the area of budgeting and in making provisions for old-age expenses. This finding is especially concerning, given its implications for people's long-term well-being.

There is no clear evidence of a correlation between socioeconomic characteristics and financial behavior scores, suggesting that many people struggle with sound financial decision-making. While urban residents achieved better scores than their rural peers in some financial capability areas, including their propensity to use information and advice, and to save and refrain from overspending, they were worse off regarding their ability to control their budgets and achievement orientation. Furthermore, the richest people fared better than the lowest income segments in controlling their budgets and demonstrated higher levels of achievement orientation. However, compared to the lowest income earners, people living on the highest incomes lack the propensity to think about the future and to use information and advice when making a financial decision.

3.7.3 Institutions Involved (Both Public and Private)

One of the main institutions, the Financial Literacy Council, was established on 7 March 2017 as an initiative of the Azerbaijan Banks Association. Aimed at general discussion and coordination of planned activities related to financial literacy, the Financial Literacy Council will be developed under the Azerbaijan Banks Association, and will include top managers (members of boards of directors) among its members. Members will determine the main directions of the council's activities with the participation of the Azerbaijan Bank Education Center. The council will serve as a platform for the discussion of ideas, information, and experiences in this sector.

AMFA encourages its members to offer nonfinancial services (for example, financial literacy education), and provides capacity-building assistance for these activities. Currently, 33% of members provide financial literacy and entrepreneurship development training.

There are initiatives aimed at increasing the financial literacy of the population by both the CBAR and AMFA as a local association, with some initiatives being supported by the foreign development and investment agencies. The CBAR launched the Financial Literacy Project in 2010 under its mission plan. The Development Department of the Center for Research and Development implements these activities on behalf of the CBAR. The Center for Research and Development of the CBAR held training for commercial banks jointly with the PricewaterhouseCoopers Academy.

The Center for Research and Development of the CBAR has become a member of the International Network on Financial Education. Currently, the network is represented by more than 135 state agencies, mainly central banks, from 74 countries. Azerbaijan is the third country in the Commonwealth of Independent States to join the network actively, which is represented by such leading countries as the United States, Canada, Germany, and France.

Partners of the Development Department on Financial Literacy include the Azerbaijan Library Confederation, the Organization for Economic Cooperation and Development, the International Federation of Library Associations, the American Resource Center, the Germany International Cooperation Society, PricewaterhouseCoopers, the World Bank, the German Savings Banks Fund for International Cooperation, and the Ministry of Education.

3.7.4 Target Groups and Programs

The key target audience of the Financial Literacy Project is high school students, the broader public, economic journalists, CBAR employees, commercial bank employees, and students majoring in banking.

3.7.5 Types of Programs

The Development Department's various activities to date include a study of international practice, communication with donor organizations, educational events for high school students and journalists, meetings with high school students jointly with the Ministry of Education, elaboration of curriculum recommendations, a series of "banks to schools, students to banks" events, the Economic Football interactive game held jointly with Visa and the Ministry of Taxes, and the International Savings Day at the end of the previous year.

Future financial literacy activities include enhancement of the socioeconomic growth of the country, support for the development of the Azerbaijani banking system, raising economic and financial awareness in the country, promoting financial literacy as a public value, and changes to people's behavior. The harmonized action plan includes conducting population surveys to evaluate financial literacy, elaborating the financial literacy strategy, improving financial and economic education in high schools, preparing optional programs for four- to eight-year high school students on raising financial awareness and skills, and holding a series of "banks to schools, students to banks"

http://responsiblefinance.worldbank.org/~/media/GIAWB/FL/Documents/Publications/National-Strategies-for-Financial-Education.pdfevents.

3.7.6 General Financial Education

Azerbaijan's population was targeted to promote financial inclusion through financial education. Under the European Bank for Reconstruction and Development support, a financial literacy training program was extended to 160,000 people in Azerbaijan, Armenia, the Kyrgyz Republic, Georgia, Moldova, and Tajikistan between 2011 and 2013. This initiative targeted the recipients of remittances, which make up 45% of GDP in the Commonwealth of International States countries. Nearly 27,500 new bank accounts were opened as a result of this program, and the equivalent of more than $25 million was brought into formal financial institutions (EBRD website).

The European Union-funded project called "Building Female Professionals and Promoting Women Entrepreneurship Development in Rural Regions of Azerbaijan" (MFC 2014) was managed together with AMFA. The results of the project serve as a successful model for addressing the issue of female participation in microfinance and, more generally, women's employment in rural areas.

Additionally, the CBAR developed a NFLS and a financial education website.

3.7.7 Debt Management Programs

Since the double devaluation, there have been deteriorating debt problems in Azerbaijan. Overdue credit accounted for 13.83% of the total credit for 1 January 2018. Nevertheless, there is no systematic and centralized program for solving overdue credit problems and helping creditors to manage finance better.

3.7.8 Assessment of Effectiveness

AMFA evaluated the current and starting situation in the field of financial literacy through surveying respondents in 2009; however, it was unable to repeat this survey to measure progress. An analysis of the starting situation has proved that NGOs should work intensively with state agencies in this direction with the aim of filling existing gaps. Nevertheless, the controversial changes made to legislation regulating the activities of foreign donors in Azerbaijan starting from 2014 have weakened their operations and negatively affected the funding of programs in this direction. In particular, these changes have caused a reduction in the programs of AMFA.

3.8 Conclusions and Recommendations

3.8.1 Conclusions

The financial sector is small, banking penetration rates are low, and the transmission mechanism between the cost of CBAR lending and the money supply is weak. Dollarization of the economy remains high, and oil prices will continue to play a dominant role in shaping inflation expectations, the exchange rate, and the money supply. Confidence in the manat is likely to remain low following the devaluation of the currency in December 2015 and the depreciation in the second half of 2016. There is also a risk of further currency volatility if oil prices fall again, which could prompt further CBAR interventions.

MFIs are weakening in terms of the quality of their portfolio and the declining number of their customers and assets, and are facing losses as a result. Financial education and literacy are not satisfactory, neither in a quantitative nor in a qualitative context. The scope of these programs is small and nonsystematic, and is not continuous.

3.8.2 Recommendations

Recommendations are presented in four categories: the financial market, financial inclusion, financial literacy, and consumer protection.

Financial Market
(i) **The financial sector of Azerbaijan must liberalize.** Despite the financial market and the relatively open legal framework for foreign investment, government rules and regulations can complicate entry to market. Therefore, the liberalization of the foreign investment policy should be part of a broader deregulation of the financial sector. In particular, the insurance market must be completely open to foreign investors. Foreign companies may enter the market without barriers. Azerbaijani insurance companies can compete with foreign companies in the domestic market. Azerbaijan should reaffirm its commitment on services to accede to the World Trade Organization and to enact all possible measures to intensify the process.

(ii) **The legal base of regulation of the financial markets must be improved.** Completing key pieces of legislation (e.g. on facilitating the establishment of a private credit bureau, a movable collateral registry, and legal reforms regarding secured transactions) would fill the gaps in the country's financial structure.

(iii) **The structural reforms in the financial sector must be accelerated.** The policy on consolidation of bank capital should be pursued along with the privatization of the International Bank of Azerbaijan with the participation of foreign investors through an open and competitive investment contest.

(iv) **Innovation support in financial markets must be promoted.** Innovative approaches, including the establishment of a credit guarantee scheme and improvements to current schemes, could encourage banks to lend to SMEs.

(v) **A reliable credit database must be established.** Credit risks should be managed more effectively through the creation of a single and centralized data system of responsible and reliable customers. The government must intensify its efforts to increase the level of detail and quality of loan statistics, and improve the accessibility of the data (e.g. by publishing regular updates on the websites of the national statistical offices) due to the functioning of the credit bureau.

Financial Inclusion

(i) **Develop a national strategy for financial inclusion and promote the provision of financial services.** This policy should be geared toward specific customer needs, including through digital financial services (e.g. mobile financial services).

(ii) **Improve access for rural and other urban populations to financial services.** Competition among institutions and organizations providing financial services should be increased, their service network upgraded, and service fees decreased. In particular, state support programs for financial institutions aimed at increasing coverage and the level of access to financial services in remote districts should be provided. In addition to this, an infrastructure that meets minimum standards and enables financial operations and transactions to be carried out should be created in post offices.

(iii) **Enrich types of products and services.** Financial products and services offered to customers should be enriched through new actors and tools from the financial market. Access to financial services for SMEs and households should be increased through new financial market players (e.g. venture investment funds, business angels, and crowdfunding platforms and campaigns) and alternative financial instruments (e.g. guarantees, mortgages, bills, leasing, and factoring).

(iv) **Directions for NBCIs' services should be expanded.** Relevant amendments should be made to the current legislation of NBCIs that will allow them to realize payment or remittance and business counseling services.

(v) **Increase the range of financial services in rural and other urban areas.** The infrastructure in rural and remote regions should be developed for SMEs and households regarding access to consumer, business, and mortgage loans; bank deposit accounts; insurance; current bank accounts; fiber-optic internet; mobile banking; local and foreign money remittance; and other financial services in those areas.

(vi) **Encourage the use of payment cards.** To ensure broad use of payment cards in the purchase of goods and services, large-scale awareness-raising campaigns on the capacity of cards should be carried out, opportunities for the use of payment cards should be created in more places, the normal function of ATMs should be ensured, and the quality of internet services should be increased. Studies show that ATMs often contain no money and there are not enough of them in other urban and rural areas.

Financial Literacy

(i) **Create a detailed implementation action plan to accompany the NFLS.** The action plan should address the key challenges identified through this survey and should outline (a) a concrete and self-explanatory description of the actions to be implemented; (b) the entity (or entities) responsible for its execution (in the case of actions involving multiple stakeholders, a primary implementing entity is identified); (c) the timeframe for the implementation of said action; and (d) the priority of executing said action (high, medium, or low).

(ii) **Develop a monitoring and evaluation framework to measure progress in the implementation of the NFLS.** The goal of the monitoring and evaluation framework is to outline a robust monitoring and evaluation system for the NFLS that extends beyond a simple list of national-level impact indicators to include program-level intermediate indicators, a theory of

change, coordination details, and an emphasis on evaluation and improvements in data collection.
(iii) **Develop a targeted policy on increasing financial literacy in the specific area.** Financial literacy should be targeted at a population of rural and remote areas. Women, the poor, the disabled, pensioners, and other vulnerable groups should be given attention first. It is reasonable to involve financial service providers, line associations, NGOs, mass media, higher education institutions that fit the economic–financial profile, municipalities, and financial consultants in the process of increasing financial literacy.
(iv) **Strengthen awareness-raising activities.** Mass media should be actively involved in awareness-raising events and a wide range of programs should be used, including text messages and mobile phone applications, to enhance financial knowledge and change attitudes and financial behaviors.
(v) **Integrate financial capability content in the school curriculum.** Basic economic and financial concepts, simple accounting calculations (calculations of the interest rate on credit and deposits), financial services, and mode of use and management of a family budget should be taught from **an early age**.
(vi) **Increase the confidence of the population in financial organizations.** Control over confusing and/or deceptive advertisements in the mass media should be improved and relevant issues regulated.
(vii) **Stimulate a general education campaign on products and services offered by banks.** The credit portfolio does not correspond to the institutional trend of lending institutions in Azerbaijan. Moreover, the study points to a profound lack of mutual understanding and information sharing between the banks and the intended clients, (i.e. a poor marketing strategy). This is a partial underlying cause of the low lending rate.

Consumer Protection

(i) **A reliable system protecting the credit and financial rights of customers should be created.** Therefore, relevant changes should be made to the current legislation in this direction and the effectiveness of both state and nonstate institutions' functioning in this area should be increased. Along with this, opportunities regarding the protection of rights of customers should be increased through courts and non-court institutions.

(ii) **Establish a clear mandate of the financial regulator in the area of financial consumer protection, enforcement, and redress.** Expand the content of the National Financial Education website to include other financial services in addition to banking products and establish special sections with information on consumers' rights and complaint-handling mechanisms.
(iii) **Establish an independent alternative dispute resolution mechanism.** Enforce full compliance of financial institutions with consumer protection requirements including information disclosure, fair advertising, and complaint handling and redress; and promote sound business practices by using adequate market conduct supervisory tools, including mystery shopping.

References

Azerbaijan Deposit Insurance Fund (ADIF). 2019. Press Release on Compensation Liability to the Provided Professional Banks on the Insurance Event. January.

Ayyagari, M., and T. Beck. 2015. *Financial Inclusion in Asia: An Overview.* Asian Development Bank (ADB) Economics Working Paper 449. Manila: ADB.

Azerbaijan Microfinance Association (AMFA). 2016. *Social Performance Management in the Azerbaijani Microfinance Sector.* Baku: AMFA. http://en.apa.az/azerbaijan-economy/finance-news/amfa-microfinance-institutions-see-sharp-decline-in-clients.html

Central Bank of the Republic of Azerbaijan. 2009. *Final Report. Results of the Financial Literacy Survey.* Baku: Central Bank of the Republic of Azerbaijan.

Conrad, J.F. 2012. *Azerbaijan: Financial Sector Assessment.* ADB Central and West Asia Working Paper 3, December. Manila: ADB.

Demirguc-Kunt, A., L. Klapper, D. Singer, and P. Van Oudheusden. 2014. *The Global Findex Database 2014. Measuring Financial Inclusion around the World.* World Bank Policy Research Working Paper 7255. Washington, DC: World Bank.

Economist Intelligence Unit (EIU). 2014. *Global Microscope 2014. The Enabling Environment for Financial Inclusion.* London: EIU.

Economist Intelligence Unit (EIU). 2017a. *Industry Report, Financial Services, Azerbaijan, 3rd Quarter.* Baku: Economist Intelligence Unit. www.eiu.com/financialservices

Economist Intelligence Unit (EIU). 2017b. *Country Risk Service December 2017.* Baku: Economist Intelligence Unit. www.eiu.com.

European Bank for Reconstruction and Development (EBRD). *Financial Inclusion.* http://www.ebrd.com/what-we-do/financial-inclusion.html.

ING. 2016. *FinTech Index Report 2016.* https://www.slideshare.net/ING/fintech-index-report-2016

Klapper, L., A. Lusardi, and P. van Oudheusden. 2016. *Financial Literacy around the World.* Washington, DC: World Bank.

Guliyev, A. 2017. Quarterly Factsheet. Promotion Financial Inclusion through Data and Insight. www.themix.org.

Hajiyeva, J. 2016. *RIF Regulation Mapping: Azerbaijan.* March. Baku: AMFA.

Microfinance Centre (MFC). 2014. Financial Education in Azerbaijan. http://mfc.org.pl/financial-education-in-azerbaijan-read-the-case-study/

Organisation for Economic Co-operation (OECD). 2015. *Global Forum on Transparency and Exchange of Information for Tax Purposes Peer Reviews: Azerbaijan 2015, Phase 1: Legal and Regulatory Framework.* Paris: OECD.

Organisation for Economic Co-operation and Development (OECD)/ International Network on Financial Education (INFE). 2015. *National Strategies for Financial Education: OECD/INFE Policy Handbook.* Paris: OECD/INFE.

Strategic Roadmap on Development of Financial Services in the Republic of Azerbaijan approved by the Decree of the President of the Republic of Azerbaijan dated 6 December 2016.

World Bank. 2013. *Azerbaijan Economic Diversification and Growth, Access to Finance: Measure to Ease a Binding Constraint.* Report No. 89360. Washington, DC: World Bank.

World Bank. 2014. *Guidance Note on the Development and Implementation of National Strategies on Financial Education and Financial Education Programmes.* Washington, DC: World Bank.

World Bank. 2015. *The Little Data Book on Financial Inclusion.* Washington, DC: World Bank.

World Bank. 2016a. *Enhancing Financial Capability and Inclusion in Azerbaijan. A Demand-side Assessment.* Washington, DC: World Bank.

World Bank. 2016b. *Migration and Remittances Fact Book 2016.* Washington, DC: World Bank.

World Bank. 2017. *Doing Business 2017: Equal Opportunity for All.* Washington, DC: World Bank.

World Intellectual Property Organization (WIPO). 2017. *The Global Innovation Index 2107. Innovation Feeding the World.* Geneva: WIPO.

4
Georgia

Yaroslava Babych, Maya Grigolia, and Davit Keshelava

4.1 Introduction

Financial inclusion, broadly defined as the access of households and firms (low-income households and small and medium-sized enterprises [SMEs] in particular) to financial services (Yoshino and Morgan 2016), has become one of the most important issues in modern development discourse. While cross-country studies can offer a bird's-eye view of the general patterns that are common across countries, each developing country has its unique set of problems related to the financial inclusion of vulnerable households and SMEs. In this respect Georgia offers an interesting case study.

Georgia is a country with 3.7 million inhabitants (National Statistics Office [NSO] 2017) situated in the South Caucasus and bordering the Russian Federation, Turkey, Azerbaijan, and Armenia. After gaining independence in 1991, the country experienced the deepest economic collapse among the transition economies, exacerbated by several wars and refugee crises. Following the Rose Revolution of 2003, the country's economy, and its financial system in particular have undergone deep structural transformations, increasingly attracting foreign capital participation.[1]

The National Bank of Georgia (NBG) managed to establish and maintain a rather strong micro- and macro-prudential regulatory system, slowly restoring trust in commercial banks.[2] The structural transformation of the banking system implied consolidation, reducing

---

[1] In 1995, just three out of 211 banks were foreign-controlled, while in 2016 the vast majority (11 out of 19 commercial banks) had 50% or more foreign capital participation.

[2] While the NBG tightly controlled commercial banks, nonbank financial institutions were much less regulated until recently. The details of the regulatory environment are discussed in Section 4.6.

the number of players on the market.³ At the same time, the number of people serviced by commercial banks was rising continuously as well.⁴ In this respect, Georgia's indicators outperformed the average for Europe and Central Asian (ECA) countries (excluding high-income countries).

Despite impressive progress in financial access across several dimensions, Georgia's poverty rate remains one of the highest in the region.⁵ Various surveys, including the quarterly Business Confidence Index run by the ISET Policy Institute (ISET-PI), also indicate that access to finance remains one of the biggest obstacles to doing business for SMEs. Yet, it remains unclear whether the poorest Georgians and small businesses remain underserved by the financial system, and what the obstacles to greater financial inclusion for these groups are. One possibility is that access to finance is impeded by low household incomes and low profitability of small businesses. In this regard, the question is whether policy makers have access to medium-term solutions to this problem, and whether greater financial literacy levels could improve the situation for poorer households and small firms.

This chapter provides an overview of the current financial sector situation in Georgia, and investigates the obstacles to financial inclusion based on an analysis of the available statistical data, the most recent studies and reports on the subject, and the results of the most recent surveys.

4.2 Overview of the Georgian Financial System

4.2.1 Sources of Financial Services for Individuals and Small and Medium-Sized Enterprises

In the last 27 years, the Georgian financial system has undergone substantial structural changes. The level of financial access for individuals and SMEs has also changed quite dramatically.

---

3   The number of banks operating in Georgia declined from 211 in 1995 to just 19 in 2016, with the two largest banks currently controlling 60% of the total assets of the banking system.

4   For example, the number of borrowers from commercial banks per 1,000 adults grew from 32 in 2004 to 680 in 2015, and the number of commercial bank branches per 100,000 adults rose from 9.3 to 31.9 during the same period.

5   Poverty rates have been dropping substantially in recent years (World Bank, World Development indicators). Despite this, the country's poverty rate (having an income of less than $3.10 per day) substantially exceeds the corresponding rates in the wider region (25.27% of the population in Georgia, versus 6.24% in Europe and Central Asia [ECA] countries) and even those of neighboring countries, such as Armenia, where the rate is 14.62%.

Despite the fact that between 1996 and 2017 the number of banks in the country decreased from 174 to just 16, access to banking services via bank service points (branches) more than tripled, from 242 branches in 1996 to 826 in 2016. The number of registered microfinance organizations (MFOs) increased drastically from 2 in 2004 to 81 in 2016. Unfortunately, until 2013 the NBG gathered no data on non-regulated financial lending institutions, such as pawnshops. The first survey of pawnshops in 2013 accounted for 1,307 organizations around the country (NSO 2013).

As of 2016–2017, financial services in Georgia were provided by 16 banks, 11 nonbank depository corporations (e.g. credit unions), 14 insurance corporations (of which 2 are private pension schemes), 81 MFOs, 1,307 pawnshops (NSO 2013), the Georgian Stock Exchange (GSE), 6 brokerage companies (securities dealers), 124 money remittances units, and 1,200 active foreign exchange bureaus. The overall size of the financial sector in Georgia has grown quite impressively. In 2000 total assets of financial corporations accounted for 31.8% of gross domestic product (GDP), and in 2016 this share was already 127.4% of GDP. The most rapid growth spurt occurred between 2005 and 2007, when total financial sector assets grew 2.4 times in absolute terms, increasing from 38.5% to 63.0% of GDP. Since the growth spurt, financial sector assets have grown at a steady pace of 17% per year on average.[6] In particular, the total assets of MFOs as a share of GDP grew from 0.02% to 8.03% in just 10 years (2006–2016).

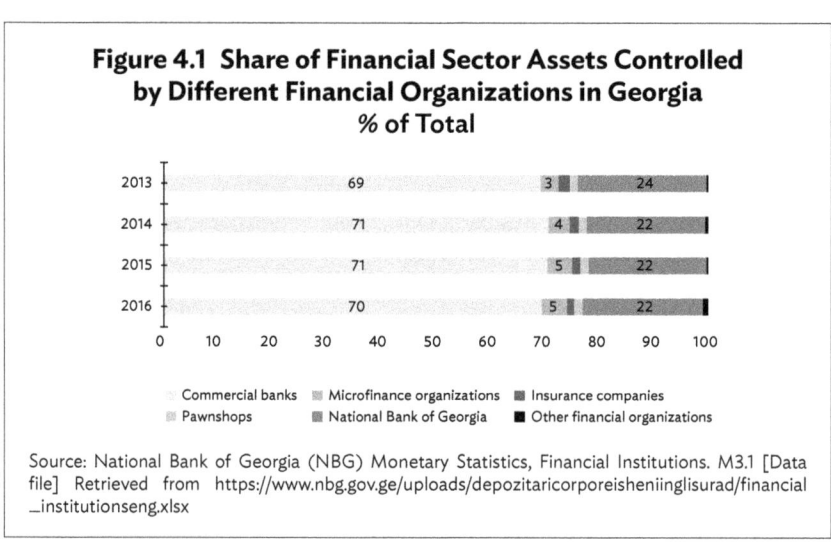

Figure 4.1 Share of Financial Sector Assets Controlled by Different Financial Organizations in Georgia
% of Total

Source: National Bank of Georgia (NBG) Monetary Statistics, Financial Institutions. M3.1 [Data file] Retrieved from https://www.nbg.gov.ge/uploads/depozitaricorporeisheniinglisurad/financial_institutionseng.xlsx

---

[6] Excluding the year of the financial crisis, 2009.

Despite the impressive growth in the microfinance sector in recent years, the financial system remains largely dominated by commercial banks, which account for 70% of the financial sector's total assets (NBG 2016). Other financial corporations, like insurance companies, MFOs, and pawnshops account for about 8% of total financial sector assets. Of these, 80% are controlled by MFOs.

4.2.2 Deposits

The market for deposits in the country is also dominated by commercial banks. Nonbank depository institutions such as credit unions account for a tiny proportion (0.0326%) of the total deposits in the economy. The value of total deposits in commercial banks (in both domestic and foreign currencies) amounted to GEL18.7 billion ($7.75 billion) by the end of the third quarter (Q) of 2017, while the same variable for nonbank depository institutions amounted to only GEL6.1 million ($2.5 million).

Other financial institutions, such as MFOs, are barred by law from taking deposits. However, they are allowed to enter into loan agreements with private individuals and firms. Such loan agreements typically offer significantly higher interest rates on both foreign and domestic currency than regular bank deposits.[7]

In the last 12 years, the number of commercial bank deposit accounts per 1,000 adults has been growing steadily; while the number of household deposit accounts per 1,000 adults quintupled from 366 in 2005 to 1,798 in 2016. The indicators of access to deposit accounts have shown improvement over the years, but more so for households than for SMEs.

As these figures indicate, outstanding deposits of SMEs with commercial banks as a share of GDP have remained flat at 3.1%–3.7% for the last 8 years, while household deposits grew impressively from 6.02% to 21.28%. While it is difficult to pinpoint the exact reason for this phenomenon, low financial literacy may play a role here. Another concern is that remaining in the "shadow" of mainstream economic activity is still the preferred way of doing business for SMEs.

---

[7] Since July 2017, MFOs can only enter into such loan agreements with customers if the amount of funds loaned exceeds GEL100,000 or the equivalent in United States dollars. This regulation helped move large amounts of de facto deposits from microfinances to commercial banks. For microfinances, it means that they will increasingly rely on commercial bank loans for liquidity.

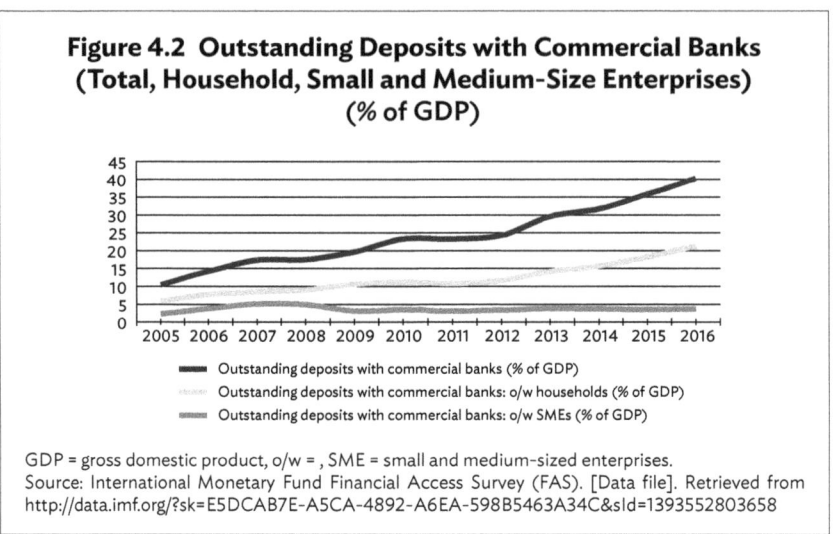

Figure 4.2 Outstanding Deposits with Commercial Banks (Total, Household, Small and Medium-Size Enterprises) (% of GDP)

GDP = gross domestic product, o/w = , SME = small and medium-sized enterprises.
Source: International Monetary Fund Financial Access Survey (FAS). [Data file]. Retrieved from http://data.imf.org/?sk=E5DCAB7E-A5CA-4892-A6EA-598B5463A34C&sId=1393552803658

4.2.3 Lending

Commercial banks in Georgia also dominate the market in terms of the total amount of loans issued. The amount of loans granted by banks to nongovernment, non-financial sector entities and households is roughly 13 times the amount of loans granted by MFOs.[8] Overall, MFOs lent GEL1.4 billion as of the end of 2016 (equivalent to $0.59 billion[9]), while the commercial banks' total non-financial sector loans amounted to GEL18.9 billion ($8.0 billion). In absolute terms, banks dominated the market in lending to households. By the end of 2016, the MFOs' loan portfolio was about GEL1.4 billion (the vast majority of these loans are to households and small business clients), while commercial banks' household lending was GEL8.9 billion ($3.76 billion).

In relative terms, commercial banks' loans to households comprise just above 50% of their total loan portfolio. In contrast, the MFOs' portfolio consists almost entirely of household and small business lending.

---

[8] For example, at the end of 2016 the total loans of the commercial banking sector amounted to GEL18.9 billion, while the loans of microfinance institutions amounted to GEL1.4 billion.

[9] Lari amounts converted to dollars at the average annual exchange rate for the corresponding year.

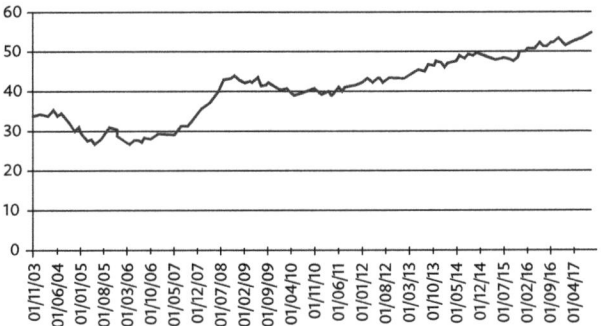

Figure 4.3 Household Loans as a Share of Total Commercial Bank Loans (%)

Source: Author's calculations, National Bank of Georgia. Loans to the National Economy, L3.10.1 [Data file] Retrieved from https://www.nbg.gov.ge/uploads/loansinglisurad/loans_structure_l3.10.1eng.xlsx

The figures on microlending presented here do not include pawnshops. The NBG periodically surveys pawnshops,[10] allowing us to judge the relative size of the pawnshop lending market. For example, in the 2013 survey pawnshops had GEL310 million ($186 million) in outstanding loans, whereas microcredit institutions in 2013 had about twice that amount—GEL620 million ($373 million).

According to the 2017 data, Georgia had the fastest growing and highest amount of domestic credit to the private sector as a share of GDP in the South Caucasus. The country has been ahead of both Armenia and Azerbaijan since 2015. Private credit expanded to 62% of GDP in 2016 (Figure 4.4)[11].

To a large extent, the growth in credit reflects borrowing by households. In particular, household debt has been rising since 2005; it slowed in 2009 but picked up again in 2011 (following roughly the same pattern as the expansion of household loans depicted in Figure 4.3). Overall, the household debt to GDP ratio has risen from 2.2% in 2001 to 30% in 2016.

---

[10] The pawnshop survey is scheduled to be repeated in 2017–2018.

[11] The pace of credit growth was curbed slightly in 2017 from 62% to 58.5%, Source: International Monetary Fund International Financial Statistics (FSA), 2018

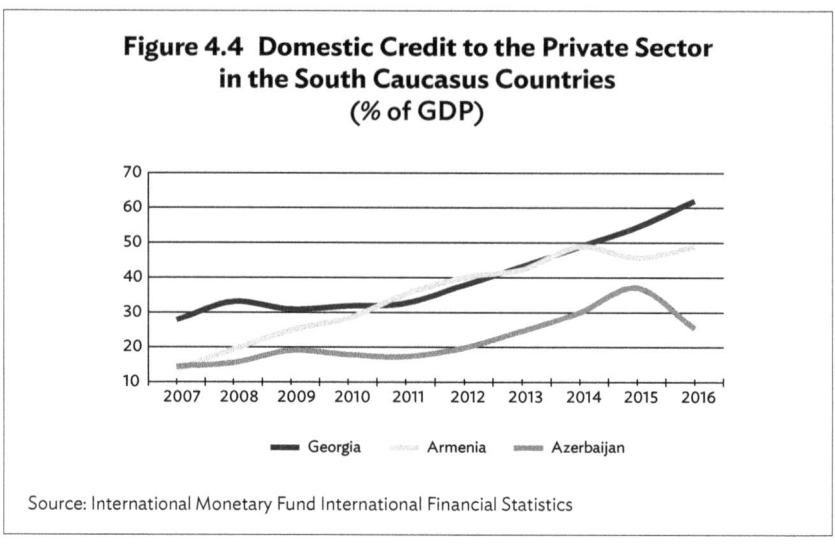

Figure 4.4 Domestic Credit to the Private Sector in the South Caucasus Countries (% of GDP)

Source: International Monetary Fund International Financial Statistics

4.2.4 Insurance

The market for insurance in Georgia is still quite small. The share of assets held by insurance companies is small, both relative to the size of the economy and the size of the financial system. For example, both in 2016 and in 2017, the gross earned market premium was just 1.086% of GDP. Health insurance holds the largest market share (49.7% of the total gross written insurance premiums), followed by road transport insurance (16.0%), and property insurance (15.7%).

4.2.5 Pensions Services

In Georgia, the size of the market for private pension schemes is very small. All citizens above 60 years old (female) and 65 years old (male) receive a government pension of GEL160, which currently constitutes about 17% of the average wage in the country.

Despite the low income replacement rate of the current government pension, private pension schemes are not very popular, primarily due to the low incomes and low savings rates of households.[12] In 2017,

---

[12] The rate of savings for old age is particularly low in Georgia. According to Financial Inclusion Indicators for 2014, in Georgia only 0.9% of the adult population saved for old age, compared to 12.5% in lower middle-income countries, and 11.7% in ECA developing countries.

there were three private pension schemes in Georgia with 22,507 participants. By the end of Q2 of 2017, the combined pension reserves of these companies were GEL24 million, constituting only 0.07% of GDP in 2016.

Currently in Georgia, a supplementary (Pillar II) pension savings system (with matching government and employer contributions) is seen as a way to improve the adequacy of the current pension scheme and stimulate long-term saving behavior. The draft law of the system is ready and is planned to come into force from Q3 2018. Due to the low capacity for saving from labor income and high risks associated with political distortions and investments in the long run, questions regarding the risks and challenges related to this reform remain open.

4.2.6 Capital Markets

Georgia has only one organized security market, the GSE, which was founded in 1999. The stated market capitalization as of 3 January 2018 was $1.286 billion (around 8.5% of GDP in 2017), while daily turnover in January 2018 amounted to $11,185.[13]

The GSE operates two listed tiers (A and B) and an "admitted" tier. Companies must satisfy special requirements to be listed in Tier A or Tier B. As of 8 January 2018, there were only three companies in Tier A (the European Bank for Reconstruction and Development [EBRD], Silknet, and the Bank of Georgia (BGEO); six securities on Tier B (the Georgian Leasing Company, M2 Real Estate, Nikora Trade, Nikora, Liberty Bank, and Teliani Valley); and 97 securities on the "admitted" tier. Only a few Georgian companies are listed on international stock exchanges. For example, as of March 2017, the equities of several Georgian companies like the BGEO,[14] TBC Bank Group, and Georgian Healthcare Group, were actively traded on the London Stock Exchange.[15]

According to recent literature assessing the development of capital markets,[16] the Georgian equity market remains underdeveloped. There are several reasons for this. First, company owners are unwilling to give up their stakes and seek other sources of finance. Second, the

---

[13] Georgian Stock Exchange. http://www.gse.ge/en/about-gse.

[14] It is worth mentioning that the BGEO was divided into two independent companies: Bank of Georgia Group (commercial bank) and BGEO Investment. Both of these companies will be listed on the London Stock Exchange.

[15] All three companies are listed in a premium equity listing category.

[16] For example, ADB (2015), Ministry of Economy and Sustainable Development of Georgia, Ministry of Finance of Georgia and NBG (2016), USAID (2014).

cost of equity remains high. Third, equities are considered to be much riskier investment opportunities for banks, retail clients, or other investors.

Despite the fact that the bond market should be relatively more attractive for firms and investors, as the cost of debt is lower than the cost of equity, bonds are still not the main source of finance in Georgia. For instance, there were only six bond issuers in 2015; this number increased slightly to eight in 2016. Some bonds (including those issued by resident legal entities in local currency) can be used by commercial banks as collateral for receiving refinance loans[17] from the NBG.

The main legislative acts that regulate activities in the capital market are the Law of Georgia on Entrepreneurs (1994) and Law of Georgia on the Security Market (1998). Recently, Georgia prepared and approved a capital market development strategy and introduced new standards on (i) independent board members and audit committee, (ii) disclosure requirements for related party transactions and management compensation, and (iii) the protection of minority investors. Furthermore, the Government of Georgia is planning to improve corporate governance standards by making the publishing of annual reports[18] based on the International Financial Reporting Standards mandatory for Georgian companies (Paresishvili 2017).

4.2.7 Remittances

Remittances constitute an important part of Georgian national income. Studies estimate that about 1 million people benefit from remittance transfers from abroad (EBRD 2007). In recent years, the amount of remittance transfers fluctuated between 12.0% and 10.5% of the country's GDP (NBG). This number is much higher than the Europe and Central Asian (ECA) countries' average of 1.4%.[19] In 2016, Georgia ranked 29th of countries worldwide in terms of remittance transfers as a share of GDP (World Bank 2018a). Remittances play a crucial role in alleviating poverty among the most vulnerable households and in supplementing overall income and savings, and their potential role in the country's financial system therefore is very significant. Yet, according to data from

---

[17] This represents one of the main instruments for commercial banks to manage liquidity.

[18] This new initiative will come into force step-by-step; it began with large and medium-sized entities in 2018 and will apply to small and micro businesses in 2019.

[19] The ECA countries group refers to Europe and Central Asia, excluding high-income countries.

the 2007 EBRD survey, only 1% of remittance recipients had a savings account in a bank, and about 11% of recipients had no bank account at all (despite the fact that 81% of the recipients had a "positive view" of banks in Georgia) (EBRD 2007).

Most remittance transfers were sent and received via money-transfer operators (MTOs) (25.0% of senders and 35.6% of recipients). The shares of remittance transfers sent or received via MTOs is about twice as high in Georgia as in other lower middle-income countries or the ECA region. According to the NBG, there are currently 106 registered remittance money-transfer units in Georgia.

In 2014, about 22.1% of adult Georgians received money from abroad. Of these recipients, only 10% received transfers via financial institutions, while more than one-third of recipients (35.6%) used an MTO. This may reflect the fact that a vast majority of remittances come from the Russian Federation; thus, official financial ties with Georgia are much weaker (and more expensive) for political reasons.

4.2.8 Technologies Driving Financial Sector Development

Georgia's financial sector technologies are now in the active growth stage. The following range of financial technologies is available to the general population and SMEs in the country: debit and credit cards, e-money accounts, mobile banking and mobile money accounts, e-wallets and mobile wallets, ATMs, point-of-sale (POS) terminals, payment service provider (PSP) terminals, and electronic signature services. These systems are used for making payments, receiving deposits, and transfers (including remittance transfers and salaries).

Some of the most commonly used technologies are distance banking services, which include internet banking, telephone banking, mobile banking, and text message banking. Today, seven commercial banks have licenses for internet acquiring from international payment systems and serve their clients successfully (NBG 2018).[20] According to recent data from the Global Payment Systems Survey, the number of debit cards in circulation tripled in the last 5 years (from 2.5 million in 2010 to 7.3 million in 2015). As of December 2017, there were 8.3 million debit cards and 0.8 million credit cards issued in Georgia. Georgians actively use electronic payments to pay public utilities and purchase goods.[21]

---

[20] Electronic systems work with internationally recognized security technologies, with three levels of card authentication (3D Secure).

[21] These goods are mainly purchased from Amazon, Alibaba, AliExpress, and eBay.

Despite the significant progress made in recent years, according to the Global Payments Systems Survey (World Bank 2016), the usage of financial technologies in Georgia is currently well below the regional average (a detailed description and analysis is provided in Section 4.2.9). For example, according to the Financial Inclusion Survey of the World Bank, in 2014, 39.7% of Georgian adults owned a debit card, more than 10 percentage points lower than in the rest of the ECA.

Interviews with the representatives of financial institutions (commercial banks and microfinance institutions [MFIs]) confirm these findings. Financial executives in Georgia point to the low usage of financial technologies, such as ATMs, mobile banking, and e-banking. One of the reasons for this (although usage is improving rapidly) is the relatively low internet usage in the country—only 50.0% of the population were reportedly internet users in 2016, versus 62.0% in Armenia, 78.2% in Azerbaijan, and 63.7% in ECA developing countries. Also, as mentioned previously, a very low percentage of Georgian youth are using banking services. However, as more and more young people enter the job market, the number of financial technology users is increasing, underlying the positive trend in usage.

The low usage of financial technologies increases the cost of doing business for banks. Personnel expenses and fixed assets and inventory expenses as a share of total expenses in the Georgian banking system have not changed much in the last 15 years, amounting to 24% for personnel expenses and 5% for fixed assets and inventory expenses in 2017.

4.2.9 Peer-to-Peer Lending and Crowdfunding and Cryptocurrencies

In Georgia, new financial technologies include peer-to-peer (P2P) lending platforms (one of the most popular is Mintos), which work with various loan originators in Georgia. Unfortunately, as mentioned earlier, there is a conspicuous lack of reliable data on the size of this market. Based on incomplete data obtained from the website of the P2P platform, the effective annual percentage rate charged to borrowers by loan originators can vary from 24% to 236%. Interest rates offered to P2P investors range from 15.8% to 11.4%. The amount of loans originated by these companies since their founding range from €45 million to €203 million.[22] Such operations are typically outside the regulatory reach of

---

[22] Information on loan originators from Georgia retrieved from the Mintos website (https://www.mintos.com/en/loan-originators/).

the NBG. Online lenders are governed by the Civil Code of Georgia, which was recently updated to prohibit predatory lending.[23]

Similar to P2P lending, crowdfunding could potentially provide small investors with access to investment opportunities by raising funds from a large number of individuals or investors through online web-based platforms. However, this type of non-traditional funding is associated with a number of risks (e.g. fraud, asymmetric information, and the short-term nature of investments). Currently, there is very little reliable data available on crowdfunding opportunities for small enterprises in Georgia, and the market for crowdfunding is largely underdeveloped. Thus, crowdfunding remains outside the regulatory realm of the NBG. However, the government has already announced legislative amendments that will make it easier to finance investment projects using crowdfunding platforms.

The worldwide cryptocurrency boom reached Georgia quite early. The country managed to become a leader in mining cryptocurrencies due to cheap electricity, a liberal legislative system, and government-awarded privileges. According to a Global Cryptocurrency Benchmarking Study carried out by the Cambridge Center for Alternative Finance, in 2017 Georgia was in second place globally in terms of energy consumption for mining cryptocurrencies. Cryptocurrencies are not specifically regulated in Georgia, although they have gained such popularity in the country that the NBG issued a special statement warning citizens about the risks associated with cryptocurrencies. In this statement, the NBG clearly indicated that cryptocurrencies are not a legal means of payment in Georgia, and there is no agency that protects citizens against risks (Abashidz 2018). However, regulators have welcomed the use of blockchain technologies. In 2017, the government even began using blockchain technology to store land registration data for the Georgian Public Registry.[24] Furthermore, the Georgian Ministry of Justice plans to introduce blockchain for business registration.

Improving financial technologies and access to them is one of the most important challenges for the Georgian financial system. Higher demand for internet banking and other distance banking services will reduce the operational costs of commercial banks, reduce interest rates, and improve access to finance for individuals and firms through regulated financial institutions.

---

[23] See Section 4.5 for a more detailed description of the relevant changes to the Civil Code of Georgia.

[24] In partnership with Bitfury, the world's leading bitcoin mining company that owned 15% of total bitcoin generation in 2016.

4.3 Status of Financial Inclusion for Individuals and Small and Medium-Sized Enterprises

Different studies on financial inclusion, cross-country studies in particular, use a wide variety of indicators to measure financial inclusion. The choice of indicators suitable for cross-country analysis mostly depends on data availability. The set of indicators typically used in the financial access literature can be grouped into the following categories: (i) access indicators (e.g. the number of ATMs, bank branches per 1,000 adults, and PSP branches); (ii) outreach indicators (such as geographical and demographic penetration of financial services); (iii) usage indicators (e.g. the number of debit and credit accounts, and the volume of deposits and lending to SMEs and households); and (iv) quality indicators (disclosure requirements, dispute resolution, and cost of usage).

In this section, we will identify and summarize the status of the main trends in financial inclusion for both individuals and SMEs in Georgia, and put these trends in a wider regional context.

4.3.1 Access Indicators

Access to ATMs, Banks, and Payment Services

Figures 4.5 and 4.6 compare the number of commercial bank branches and ATMs per 100,000 adults in the South Caucasus. Among the South Caucasus countries, Georgia is clearly leading in terms of access to commercial bank branches, and number of ATMs per 100,000 adults.

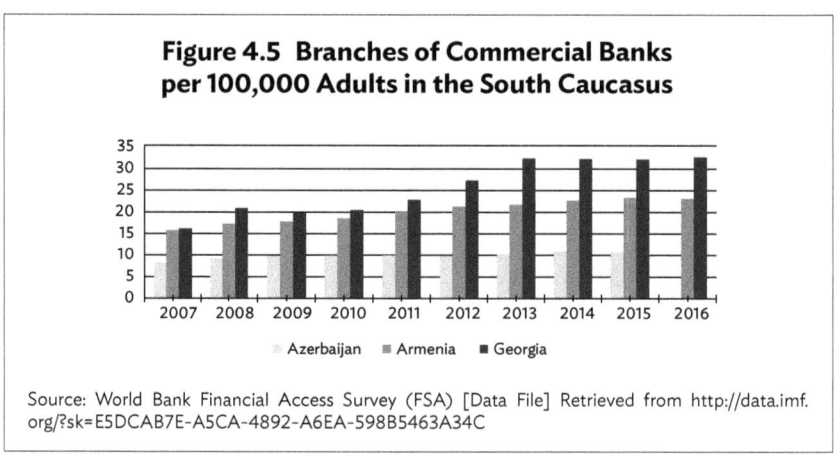

Figure 4.5 Branches of Commercial Banks per 100,000 Adults in the South Caucasus

Source: World Bank Financial Access Survey (FSA) [Data File] Retrieved from http://data.imf.org/?sk=E5DCAB7E-A5CA-4892-A6EA-598B5463A34C

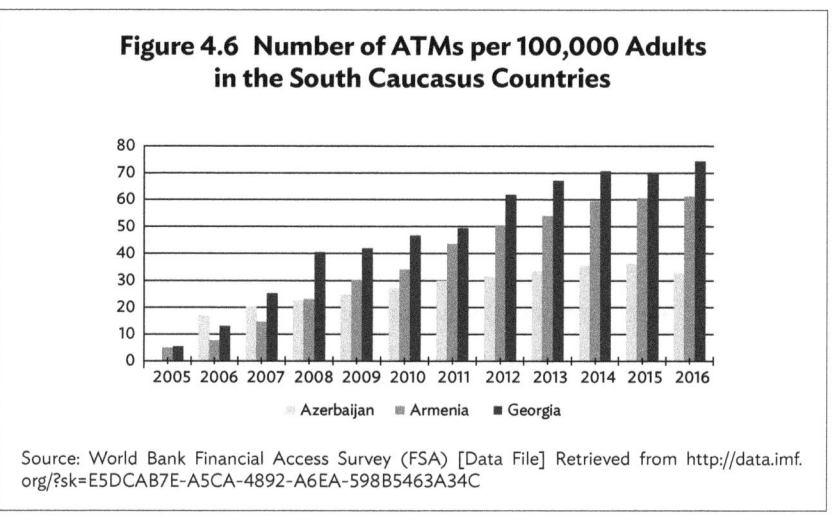

Figure 4.6 Number of ATMs per 100,000 Adults in the South Caucasus Countries

Source: World Bank Financial Access Survey (FSA) [Data File] Retrieved from http://data.imf.org/?sk=E5DCAB7E-A5CA-4892-A6EA-598B5463A34C

Other indicators of financial access have also been evolving quite rapidly. For example, over the last 5 years the number of POS terminals has tripled, while the number of PSP branches has also increased quite dramatically, from 641 to 1,769.

Geographic and Demographic Outreach

One of the first indicators of geographic outreach in financial services is the number of bank branches and ATMs available outside the major cities of Tbilisi, Batumi, and Kutaisi. The data show a clear improvement in the absolute number of ATMs and bank branches available outside these three cities; from 2005 to 2016 the number of ATMs grew from just 31 to 674, while that of bank branches grew from 141 to 427. Yet, a significant share of the Georgian population outside these cities remains underserved. According to the latest (2014) census figures, 36.5% of the Georgian population lives in the three largest cities, where the bulk of access to financial services is concentrated. This is illustrated by the simple fact that in 2016 the three largest cities contained about 70% of the country's ATMs, a much higher percentage than the share of the country's population living in these cities. The share of ATMs in the three largest cities was even higher in 2005, reaching 83% of the total. Similarly, the three largest cities contain about 56% of the bank branches, despite only containing about 36.5% of the population.

4.3.2 Usage Indicators

Deposit or Savings Accounts

Table 4.1 below provides a snapshot of the deposit and/or savings account access status for the adult population in Georgia in 2017, in comparison with the ECA region and lower middle-income countries.

Table 4.1 Select Financial Inclusion Indicators for Georgia, 2017

Financial Inclusion Indicators (2017)	Georgia	Europe and Central Asia (Excluding High-Income Countries)	All Lower Middle-Income Countries
Accounts (% aged 15+)	61.2	65.3	57.8
All adults	63.6	62.5	53.0
Adults belonging to the poorest 40%	46.1	56.3	50.7
Young adults (% aged 15–24)	30.7	50.1	49.4
Adults living in rural areas	55.1	61.7	57.6

Source: World Bank Global Financial Inclusion Surveyhttps://globalfindex.worldbank.org/sites/globalfindex/files/databank/Global%20Findex%20Database.xlsx

The most striking feature of financial inclusion in Georgia is the low percentage of young adults with deposit or savings accounts in 2017 (30.7%, compared to 50.1% in the ECA region, a difference of almost 20 percentage points). Nevertheless, the current situation represents a dramatic improvement from 2014, when only 9.9% of young adults in Georgia had a deposit or a savings account. This result is likely driven first by the low rate of economic activity among young people (57.6% of those aged 20–24 were economically active in 2016) and high rate of unemployment in this cohort (30% in 2016). Secondly, a lack of economic independence leads to a lack of financial inclusion among young people.

As the data in Table 4.1 indicate, adults belonging to the poorest 40% of the population are also underserved compared to the ECA average, as well as the indicator for lower middle-income economies. On the other hand, the share of women with deposit or savings accounts in Georgia is about 63.6%. This number is higher than in other low middle-income countries (53.0% of the population), and also higher (by about one percentage point) than in the ECA region.

Credit Usage Indicators

In terms of access to credit, Georgia is one of the countries with the greatest ease of access in the South Caucasus (Figure 4.7).[25]

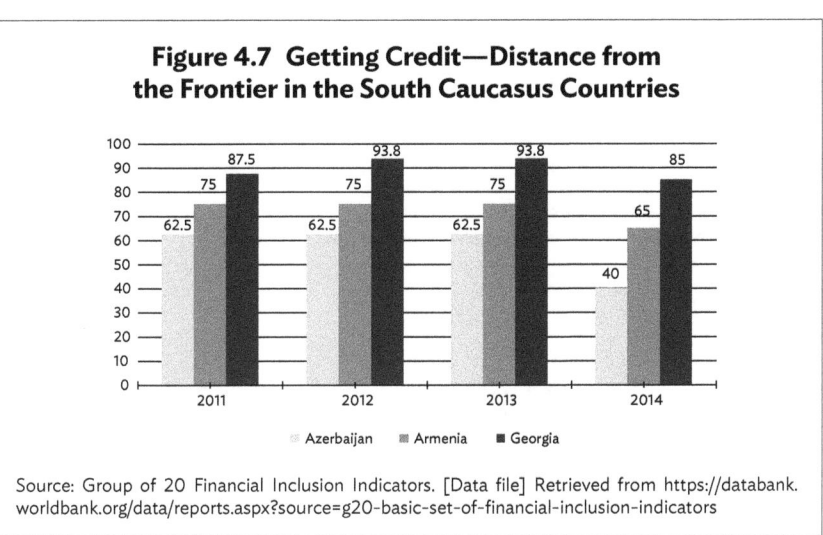

Figure 4.7 Getting Credit—Distance from the Frontier in the South Caucasus Countries

Source: Group of 20 Financial Inclusion Indicators. [Data file] Retrieved from https://databank.worldbank.org/data/reports.aspx?source=g20-basic-set-of-financial-inclusion-indicators

Georgia is ahead of Azerbaijan and some Central Asian countries in terms of the number of borrowers from commercial banks per 1,000 adults (Figure 4.8). Yet, in recent years the indebtedness of households (measured by principal payments to income ratio) has grown rapidly. In 2015, the debt service to income ratio reached 12.8%. This figure

---

[25] According to the Group of 20 Financial Inclusion Indicators, the Getting Credit indicator measures "the strength of credit reporting systems and the effectiveness of collateral and bankruptcy laws in facilitating lending. Measured as 'distance to frontier'... This measure shows the distance of each economy to the WBG [World Bank Group] Doing Business 'frontier,' which represents the best performance observed on each of the indicators across all economies in the sample since 2005.... An economy's distance to frontier is reflected on a scale from 0 to 100, where 0 represents the lowest performance and 100 represents the frontier. For example, a score of 75 in DB [Database] 2015 means an economy was 25 percentage points away from the frontier constructed from the best performances across all economies and across time." Global Partnership for Financial Inclusion. G20 Financial Inclusion Indicators. http://datatopics.worldbank.org/g20fidata/home#void (accessed January 2018).

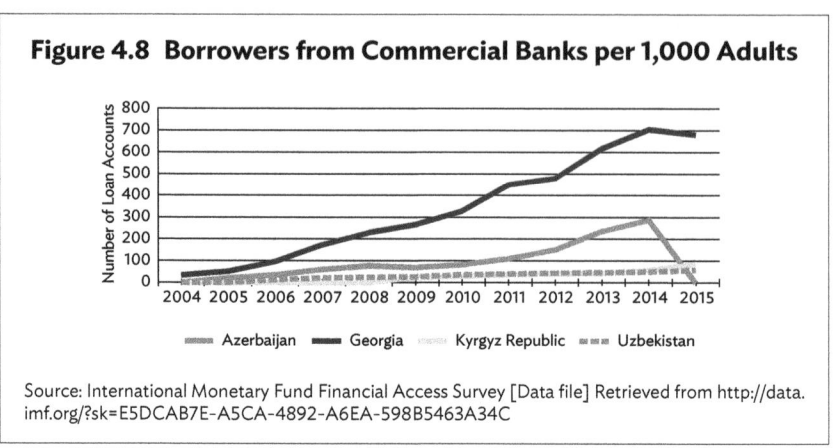

Figure 4.8 Borrowers from Commercial Banks per 1,000 Adults

Source: International Monetary Fund Financial Access Survey [Data file] Retrieved from http://data.imf.org/?sk=E5DCAB7E-A5CA-4892-A6EA-598B5463A34C

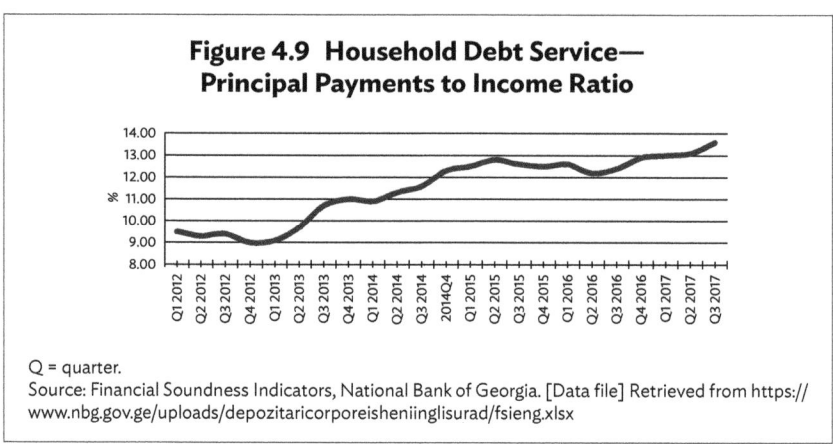

Figure 4.9 Household Debt Service—Principal Payments to Income Ratio

Q = quarter.
Source: Financial Soundness Indicators, National Bank of Georgia. [Data file] Retrieved from https://www.nbg.gov.ge/uploads/depozitaricorporeisheniinglisurad/fsieng.xlsx

started declining in 2015–2016[26] only to increase again following another round of lari depreciation reaching a record high of 13.6% in Q3 2017 (Figure 4.9).

In addition, the amount of real estate and movable property repossessed by microfinance firms increased very sharply in 2013 and then again in 2015; overall the total has increased by more than 6.5 times, from GEL2.5 million in Q1 2013 to GEL16.7 million in Q3 2017. The rapid increase in defaults was most likely due to the fact that most of these

---

[26] Most likely, the decline was caused by the fact that fewer households qualified for loans from banks in that period.

loans were denominated in United States dollars, creating currency mismatch problems for indebted households.

Despite the fact that household finance indicators showed clear signs of stress, especially after Q1 2015, nonperforming loans (NPLs) as a share of the total loans of commercial banks remained quite low and stable. Between Q1 2015 and Q2 2017, the NPL share was just 3.3% on average, based on the International Monetary Fund methodology; based on the more conservative NBG methodology for tracking NPLs, this figure was 7.6%. This discrepancy suggests that financially vulnerable groups of the population remain outside the realm of bank lending.

Thus, in Georgia the rapid growth in consumer credit has prompted concerns about the sustainability of credit expansion. Georgia's main financial concern was not so much about access to credit, but about making sure that borrowers were protected and making informed decisions. Since then, the government and the NBG have called for stronger consumer protection measures, pushed for rapid de-dollarization of small and medium-sized loans and stepped up efforts to promote financial literacy. Sections 4.5 and 4.6 examine these issues in greater detail.

4.3.3 Financial Inclusion of Small and Medium-Sized Enterprises

As mentioned earlier, while the financial access indicators for households were growing rapidly, the indicators for SMEs stayed largely the same. According to the World Bank Enterprise Survey 2013, 20.4% of SMEs identified finance as a major constraint (in the ECA region, this figure for SMEs was 16.4%).

In 2016, outstanding loans to SMEs accounted for only 7.5% of GDP, while outstanding loans to households accounted for 26% of GDP. The share of SMEs with a bank loan or line of credit constituted 30.3% of firms, the same as in the ECA region and 2 percentage points higher than the world average.

This indicates that, while receiving a loan may not be a problem per se for SMEs in Georgia (as compared to the ECA region and other countries), securing the desired amount of funding may be problematic. From Table 4.2 one can see, for example, that only 7.2% of SMEs reported their recent loan application as rejected, while this figure is much higher in the ECA countries (14.6%).

Finally, an important indicator of financial access for both households and firms is the cost of funds; in Georgia's case, the cost of funds is largely determined by interest rates on loans charged by

Table 4.2 Enterprise Survey for Georgia, 2013

Indicators, Enterprise Survey, 2013	Georgia All Firms	Georgia Small Firms^a	Europe and Central Asia Small Firms	All Countries Small Firms
Percentage of firms with a bank loan or line of credit	35.8	30.3	32.7	26.2
Proportion of loans requiring collateral (%)	95.6	97.9	75.7	76.8
Value of collateral needed for a loan (% of the loan amount)	223.3	232.0	197.9	216.0
Percentage of firms whose recent loan application was rejected	4.6	7.2	14.6	14.8
Percentage of firms using banks to finance investments	22.0	15.3	22.3	23.2
Percentage of firms identifying access to finance as a major constraint	18.3	20.4	16.4	26.6

Source: Georgia (2013), World Bank Group. [Data file] Retrieved from http://www.enterprisesurveys.org/data/exploreeconomies/2013/georgia#2

different financial institutions. Figure 4.10 indicates that real interest rates on loans have been on a declining trajectory since 2012.[27] Real interest rates went up again briefly in 2015 following the regional crisis and devaluation of the lari, then started falling again from September 2016, when the currency value stabilized.

From January 2017 a new law has prohibited the issue of loans in foreign currency for loan amounts below GEL100,000 (this was part of the de-dollarization campaign by the NBG and the government). Since most banks and MFOs raise funds in dollars, the cost of financing lari loans has increased. According to interviews with bank and MFI executives, the cost of hedging the currency risk on a lari loan increased from 3%–4% to over 10%. Part of these cost increases could be passed on to consumers in the form of higher interest rates, although some financial institutions have opted to keep lending interest rates at about

---

[27] The prominent dip and a sharp rise in real interest rates during the years after the financial crisis of 2008–2009 was largely driven by the behavior of the inflation rate, which fell in September 2009 and rose sharply again until May 2011.

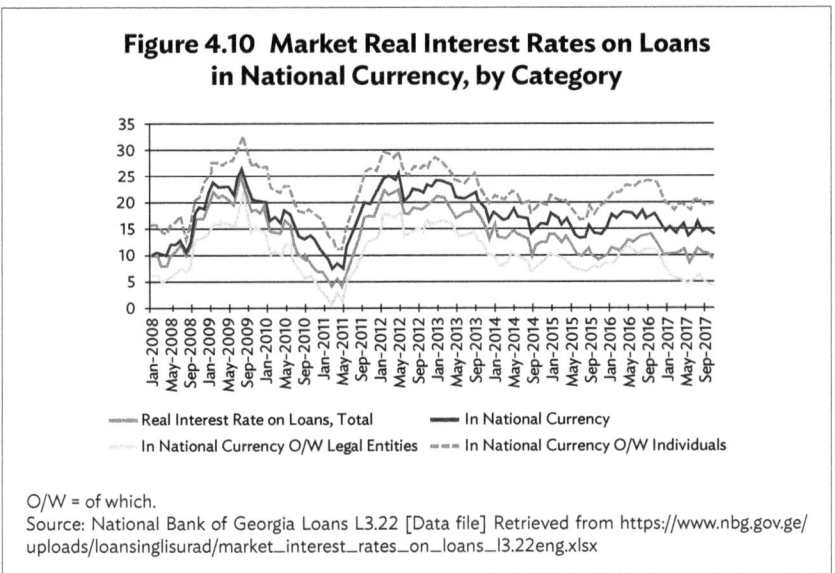

Figure 4.10 Market Real Interest Rates on Loans in National Currency, by Category

— Real Interest Rate on Loans, Total — In National Currency
In National Currency O/W Legal Entities --- In National Currency O/W Individuals

O/W = of which.
Source: National Bank of Georgia Loans L3.22 [Data file] Retrieved from https://www.nbg.gov.ge/uploads/loansinglisurad/market_interest_rates_on_loans_l3.22eng.xlsx

the same level to avoid raising the risk of their customer pool. Interest rates on loans in foreign currency, on the contrary, decreased.

4.3.4 Summary

To summarize the results of this section, Georgia has been making rapid improvement on a number of financial inclusion indicators, especially access to payment systems, new financial technologies, number of savings and deposit accounts, and credit to households. For households, the main concern is not so much access to credit, but rather low levels of income, low levels of savings, provision for retirement, and low levels of financial literacy.

SMEs in Georgia report problems with access to finance. According to the data, access to deposit and savings accounts is high for SMEs, but in fact SMEs save very little. Moreover, while the number of SMEs with loans and lines of credit from the bank is reasonable (on par with global and regional averages), SMEs may be credit-constrained in the sense that the amount of funds they can secure from banks is seen as insufficient for the development of the business. Interviews with commercial bank and MFI executives point largely in the same direction—many SMEs would like to borrow more than their financial situation allows.

4.4 Barriers to Financial Inclusion

4.4.1 Supply-Side Barriers

Supply-side barriers to financial inclusion refer to factors that limit the ability of financial institutions to extend deposit, savings, and/or credit to households and businesses. Among them, the literature distinguishes between market-driven, regulatory, and infrastructure-related barriers.

The main markers of market-driven barriers to financial inclusion identified in the literature include:
  (i) relatively high maintenance costs of small deposits and loans;
  (ii) high costs of providing financial services in small towns and rural areas (e.g. transport-related problems);
  (iii) information asymmetry on the market (lack of credit data about the clients and/or lack of usable collateral); and
  (iv) a lack of convenient access points to financial services.

The markers for regulatory barriers include:
  (i) strict requirements for opening branches and ATMs;
  (ii) strict identification requirements, which can limit access for poor households; and
  (iii) restrictions on foreign ownership, which may restrict the entry of financial institutions, including MFIs.

Infrastructure barriers include:
  (i) the lack of a reliable payments and settlements system;
  (ii) limited availability of phone access (either fixed or mobile phones);
  (iii) a lack of convenient transport to ATMs; and
  (iv) the lack of a reliable internet connection.

From the data presented in the previous section, small towns and rural areas in Georgia may indeed be underserved in terms of access to financial infrastructure, such as ATMs, and bank branches. Georgia is behind the ECA average in terms of access by rural and, particularly, poor households to financial services, such as deposit accounts.[28] The

---

[28] Table 4.1 indicates that 46.1% of adults belonging to the poorest 40% of the population have deposit accounts, about 5 percentage points lower than in other lower middle-income countries, and 10 percentage points lower than in the ECA region. About 55% of adults in rural areas are served with deposit accounts (close to 7 percentage points lower than in the ECA region), but the percentage of the rural population served is about the same in other lower middle-income countries.

existing data, unfortunately, do not provide a clear answer as to the drivers behind these low financial inclusion figures.

We conducted a series of interviews with the executives of large commercial banks and MFIs in Georgia to better assess the issue of supply-side barriers. According to these interviews, the cost of servicing small loans and deposit accounts is not the main obstacle to financial inclusion. The costs of providing services outside major cities and servicing the lower income population may indeed be higher, especially for MFIs that mainly serve households, including lower income households. For MFIs, about 6 percentage points of the interest rate on household loans are due to operational cost requirements. Thus, operational costs are estimated to account for about 25% of the total cost of credit. This includes the need to maintain and train staff; for example, one of the large MFIs with a loan portfolio of GEL150 million maintains 50 branches around the country and a staff of around 800 employees.

Information asymmetry is less of a problem for MFIs, who adhere to a relationship-based banking model. Even commercial banks in Georgia have largely avoided this problem thanks to the credit database maintained and shared among the financial institutions. Subscribers to the database can see whether a particular physical person or a company has ever defaulted, the number of defaults, and the size of defaults. The presence of a customer's name in the database is not an automatic reason to disqualify a loan application, and financial institutions look at the pattern of defaults or amount of defaults to assess the client's creditworthiness.[29]

Transport and access to financial services is not a major problem, considering that large MFIs and the commercial banks oriented on servicing small deposits and loans (e.g. Liberty Bank, which services government-provided pension plans for the elderly) have already established extensive networks outside the major cities, relying on so-called mobile branches to reach their client base. The regulatory barriers to access in Georgia are probably the least problematic, as there are no strict requirements on operating branches and ATMs, and no restrictions on foreign ownership for financial institutions (which could limit the amount of foreign funds entering the market). Banks cite the current regulations on identification requirements as one of the problems for increasing financial access. According to regulations, opening a bank account requires the physical presence of a customer (business or household client) in the branch to sign the required

---

[29] See Section 4.5 for more information on CreditInfo, the private credit bureau in Georgia.

documents. Although e-signature technology is available, it cannot be used at present to open a deposit account.

Infrastructure barriers, such as a poor internet connection, lack of a phone (mobile or landline) network, and transport are not a major concern for the financial institutions. The number of mobile subscriptions in Georgia is quite high (129 per 100 persons in 2016), higher than in other countries of the South Caucasus and higher than the ECA regional average (125 per 100 persons). Internet coverage is available throughout the country, although internet usage in Georgia is not as widespread as mobile phone usage. According to World Bank data, in 2016, only 59.2% of the population in Georgia use the internet, compared to 62.4% in the ECA region, 64.3% in Armenia, and 78.2% in Azerbaijan[30].

Although the use of mobile or internet banking is not widespread, usage is rapidly improving, suggesting that there is large potential for including a larger share of the population in financial services.

4.4.2 Demand-Side Barriers

Demand-side barriers to financial inclusion consist of all factors that might limit the demand of households for financial services. The major factors include but are not limited to the following:
 (i) low income levels among the population;
 (ii) lack of knowledge (low levels of financial literacy);
 (iii) lack of trust in financial institutions; and
 (iv) institutional aspects, such as bankruptcy laws and assessment of creditworthiness.

The demand-side barriers to financial inclusion are very prominent in Georgia, with low income levels among the population as the most important. One piece of evidence in this regard is the high share of the population that lives on less than $3.10 per day (28.1%, on average during 2005–2015, and 17.1% in 2016 (World Bank 2018b). Such high poverty rates are not common in other countries in the region. Armenia, for example, has a comparable GDP per capita,[31] but the share of the

---

[30] World Bank, International Telecommunication Union, World Telecommunication/ICT Development Report and database (2017). Individuals Using the Internet, % of population [Data file] Retrieved from https://data.worldbank.org/indicator/IT.NET.USER.ZS?locations=GE-AZ-AM-7E

[31] According to the World Bank, the PPP adjusted GDP per capita in 2016 was $8,832 in Armenia, and $10,004 in Georgia Source: World Bank Open Data (2018). GDP per capita, PPP (current international $), [Data file] Retrieved from https://data.worldbank.org/indicator/NY.GDP.PCAP.PP.CD?locations=AM-GE

population living on less than $3.10 per day was 18.5% on average during 2005–2015, and only 14.1% in 2016.

Several surveys (ACT 2011, EBRD 2007, ISET-PI/TBC 2016, OECD/INFE 2016) touching upon the saving behavior of Georgian households reveal that only a small share of the population manages to save money in some form (the estimates range from as low as 16% in 2011 to 37.9% in 2016). In addition, the Organization for Economic Co-operation and Development International Network on Financial Education (OECD/INFE) survey revealed that 61% of Georgians were unable to make ends meet at least once in the last 12 months, and 45% resorted to borrowing. The 2011 Savings Behavior Survey, which distinguished between rural, urban, and Tbilisi respondents, showed that the percentage of households that currently had savings was lower in villages (12%) than the overall average (16%) (ACT Research 2011). The same survey revealed that people with a monthly family income of GEL700 (about $424 at the time) were three times as likely to save money than people with an income below that level.

Another serious barrier is low financial literacy, which is discussed in more detail in Section 4.6. Lack of trust in the financial system is not a big problem in Georgia. The country enjoys high levels of public trust in banks, as confirmed in several surveys. For example, according to the ISET-PI/TBC survey of financial literacy, 79% of the surveyed population unconditionally trust the banks with their money, while 85% of the population would not entrust their money to other financial institutions (e.g. credit unions or microfinance institutions). This result is corroborated by evidence from the World Gallup Poll (2013), which showed that 62% of Georgian respondents reported having confidence in the banks. In fact, Georgia ranked fifth among European countries for trust in banks.

One survey result that stands apart from these findings is the 2015 Caucasus Research Resource Center poll, the Caucasus Barometer. One of the survey questions asked "how much [do] you trust or distrust Georgian banks?" As many as 34% of respondents fully or somewhat distrusted Georgian banks. The reasons for this result are discussed in more detail in section 4.6.

Institutional aspects, such as adequate bankruptcy laws and assessment of creditworthiness, do not feature very prominently and are largely overshadowed by the other factors, such as low incomes and low financial literacy levels. Interviews conducted with MFOs in the course of this study suggested that microfinance institutions do not automatically exclude people from borrowing on the basis of low credit scores, and tend to look at the entire credit history and current circumstances of the household before making a decision on lending.

4.5 Regulatory Framework and Financial Inclusion

4.5.1 Regulatory Framework and Policies to Promote Financial Inclusion for Small and Medium-Sized Enterprises and Households

Currently in Georgia there is no official document outlining the country's financial inclusion strategy. Greater financial access to SMEs, however, is a stated priority for the government in several strategic documents, such as the Georgia 2020 Socio-Economic Development Program (Government of Georgia 2016a), and the SME Development Strategy of Georgia 2016–2020 (Government of Georgia 2016b). According to the SME development strategy document, improving access to finance for SMEs will be achieved via the following policy actions:
  (i) improving financial literacy among SMEs,
  (ii) training to help SMEs conduct financial reporting and meet the International Financial Reporting Standards requirements,
  (iii) increasing knowledge of fundraising among SMEs,
  (iv) attracting SME-oriented private equity funds to Georgia via existing programs like "Produce in Georgia",
  (v) enhancing existing schemes of SME financing via commercial banks and MFIs, and
  (vi) improving SME financing through grants.

Currently, the government program specifically aimed at SMEs is the Micro and Small Business Support Project of Enterprise Georgia,[32] which offers financial assistance to startups as well as expanding companies in the form of grants of GEL5,000–GEL15,000. The project began in 2016, and has so far supported 5,313 entrepreneurs with an average grant of GEL7,276 per project.[33]

---

[32] Enterprise Georgia is a government agency established under the Ministry of Economy and Sustainable Development. It is mandated to facilitate private sector (and in particular SME) development through a variety of financial and technical support mechanisms, as well as export support.

[33] A different program, "Produce in Georgia," which aims to provide enterprises with financial, technical, and infrastructural support covers SMEs only partially. The requirements of the program apply mostly to medium-sized and large companies. The program has three main components: (i) access to finance (cofinancing the loan interest and supporting it with secondary collateral), (ii) technical support (supporting the enterprise with training and consultations), and (iii) infrastructure (the transfer of state property to the beneficiary for GEL1).

The same agencies are implementing different projects on a smaller scale and with specific objectives. For example, Enterprise Georgia is supervising a separate project for the promotion of hospitality. The Agriculture Projects Management Agency is involved in agricultural insurance, garden development, and other agriculture-related programs.[34] In addition, Georgia's Innovation and Technology Agency is implementing financing programs for startups in the field of commercialization of innovative projects; so far it has supported six startups. All of these programs partially cover SMEs in certain sectors, but unfortunately do not act as a holistic mechanism for supporting a wide variety of SMEs in the country.

As far as financial access of households is concerned, Georgia has a comprehensive financial education strategy developed by the NBG (2016b). The strategy is described in more detail in Section 4.6. The country, however, does not have any government-managed debt relief programs to help alleviate existing debt burden.

Deposit Insurance

A deposit insurance scheme was launched in Georgia on 1 January 2018. Under this scheme, all bank deposits in Georgia are insured up to GEL5,000 ($2,066 equivalent) (Deposit Insurance Agency of Georgia 2017).[35] The economic literature suggests that explicit deposit insurance might increase depositors' confidence and prevent bank runs. However, the deposit insurance scheme also gives commercial banks incentive to undertake unnecessary risks (the "moral hazard" problem) and increase lending and borrowing spreads (Carapella and di Giorgio 2003).

The direct effect of the newly introduced deposit insurance on financial stability is likely to be quite limited, as Georgia already has a successful regulatory framework[36] that has proven to be resilient toward large negative shocks on the financial market.[37] The large commercial banks that currently dominate the financial market already enjoy implicit deposit insurance.[38] However, the newly introduced deposit insurance may have an effect on people with lower levels of financial literacy. For them, a deposit insurance

---

[34] Agricultural Projects Management Agency.
[35] Converted using the exchange rate in Q3 2017.
[36] Based on the most recent Basel III regulatory framework.
[37] The case in point here is the regional crisis of 2014–2015, which saw a sharp depreciation of regional currencies; however, the Georgian banking system remained stable.
[38] Since the two largest commercial banks in Georgia account for the majority (60%) of total financial sector assets, the likelihood of a bailout in the event of a banking crisis is quite strong.

scheme may deliver a much clearer guarantee of trustworthiness than any refinement of the regulatory framework (such as the introduction of Basel III).

Credit Data

In the early years of transition (through 2005), Georgia had neither a private nor a public credit bureau that would assess the creditworthiness of individuals and legal entities. In 2005, CreditInfo Georgia was created as a joint venture between CreditInfo International and three large commercial banks: Procredit Bank, TBC Bank, and BGEO (International Risk Partnership 2017). By February 2017, the CreditInfo Georgia database was providing information about more than 2.5 million individuals (88.6% of the adult population[39]) and 70,000 companies (Society and Banks 2017). Coverage increased to 95.7% of the adult population in 2017. This is higher than the same measure for countries in the European Union in 2017 (54.2%) and ECA developing countries (40.6%).

4.5.2 Structure of Regulatory Framework

In Georgia, basic relationships between lenders and borrowers are regulated by the Civil Code of Georgia, while the main institution responsible for supervising the financial sector in the framework of financial stability is the NBG.[40] One of the main responsibilities (and targets) of the NBG is to contribute to the stable functioning of the financial sector. Therefore, the NBG has been granted full authority to supervise the activities of commercial banks and nonbank financial institutions, such as credit unions, MFOs, securities registrars, brokerage companies (excluding insurance brokers), and Georgia Stock Exchange (GSE). The NBG is also authorized to regulate money transfer agents and foreign exchange bureaus to prevent the legalization of illicit income and circulation of forged money.[41]

The Organic Law of Georgia on the NBG also defines the notion of a qualified credit institution as a legal person (excluding commercial banks) that satisfies at least one of the following criteria:

---

[39] World Bank database on private credit bureau coverage (% of adults).

[40] The functions and responsibilities of the NBG as a supervisor are defined in Articles 95 and 96 of the Constitution of Georgia; Organic Law of Georgia on the National Bank of Georgia; and other laws, regulations, orders, and rules.

[41] Organic Law of Georgia on the National Bank of Georgia (2009, No 1676-IIS).

(i) The legal person attracts funds from more than 400 people.
(ii) The amount of funds attracted exceeds GEL5 million ($2.07 million).

The supervision of insurance companies and pension schemes is conducted by a separate agency, the State Insurance Supervision Service of Georgia.[42] Other financial institutions, including pawnshops and online loan providers are outside the supervision of the NBG and are regulated only by the Civil Code of Georgia.

4.5.3 New Regulations Affecting Consumer Protection and Access to Finance

At the end of 2016, Parliament approved the law on an amendment to the Civil Code of Georgia. The government introduced the following additional regulations related to lender liabilities, interest rates on loans, and restrictions on attracting new funds:

(i) Effective annual interest rate of the loan shall not exceed 100%, including the extension of the loan term. This regulation (interest rate cap) aims to protect borrowers from excessively high interest rates (mainly charged by online loan providers).
(ii) The total amount of any fees related to the loan provision, any cost of the loan agreement, penalties imposed on each day for any violation of the loan agreement, and any form of financial sanctions shall not exceed the annual 150% of the residual amount of the loan principal of the loan provided according to the agreement.
(iii) Loans up to GEL100,000 for individuals (not legal entities) shall be issued only in national currency. Loans in the national currency but indexed or linked to a foreign currency shall not be considered national currency loans. This regulation aims to facilitate the de-dollarization of loans and further reduce foreign currency risks for borrowers.

Efforts to impose interest rate caps and de-dollarize lending aimed at protecting consumers became a political issue after a series of lari devaluations in 2013–2016. The unintended consequences of these regulations could be the higher cost of hedging instruments for banks

---

[42] The State Insurance Supervision Service of Georgia was established as a separate legal entity of public law in March 2013. This entity was previously a department of the NBG.

and MFIs, higher domestic currency interest rates for households, and, consequently, less affordable loans for households. On the other hand, lending in foreign currency for legal entities, such as SMEs, could become cheaper. This would be particularly advantageous for export-oriented SMEs.

4.6 Financial Education and Financial Literacy in Georgia: What Do We Know?

Financial literacy is seen by many stakeholders (commercial banks, MFIs, the NBG) as the key to improving the financial wellbeing of households in Georgia. Since several waves of lari devaluation hit borrowers in 2013–2016, the government has been pushing for tougher consumer protection and sweeping de-dollarization measures, while the NBG has been advocating the improvement of financial literacy levels among the general population.

As part of the effort to establish a baseline for financial literacy outreach in the country, a number of studies and surveys have been undertaken. These include (i) the financial literacy survey conducted by the ISET-PI together with the TBC bank and TNS[43] (ISET-PI and TBC Bank 2016); (ii) the financial literacy study conducted by the NBG (NBG 2016a); and (iii) the OECD INFE International Survey of Adult Financial Literacy Competencies (OECD/INFE 2016). The main results of these surveys are summarized below.

4.6.1 Financial Literacy

International School of Economics at Tbilisi State University Policy Institute TBC Survey

In this survey, a nationally representative sample of 1,000 persons were interviewed in 2016. The literacy questions assessed knowledge about simple and compounded interest rates, inflation, financial risks, and effective interest rates (fees and commissions attributed to credits and installments). One of the surprising findings was that only 5.8% of the surveyed population answered all four questions correctly; 42% of the population's knowledge fell in the moderate range (two or three correct answers), while the remaining 52% exhibited low levels of financial literacy (one or no correct answers).

The country survey indicated strong regional disparities in financial literacy, particularly between the capital city and other areas

---

[43] TNS refers to Market Intelligence Caucasus, http://tns-global.ge/

of the country. This likely mirrors differences in access to finance. The Georgian survey found that financial literacy is significantly higher in the capital, Tbilisi, where 81% of the population with high financial literacy levels reside.

Although it is difficult to say whether lack of financial literacy is an obstacle to greater financial access or vice versa, in general, people with lower educational attainment were less likely to answer questions correctly. Of those respondents with all correct answers, 78% held a university or equivalent diploma. Respondents with only a primary and secondary education were more likely to report the "do not know" option. Yet, despite the low levels of financial literacy revealed in the survey, only 14% of the population admitted a lack of knowledge in finances.

4.6.2 Financial Attitudes and Behavior

Recording expenditures is not used as a tool to control finances, and only 8.3% of the population conduct detailed recording of expenditures.

The population of Georgia tends to be disciplined in tax obligations, and 86% of the respondents reply that they do not delay tax payments. They are also very cautious about buying new things, and 68% state that they think and analyze to see if they can afford the purchase before they buy. The reason for this pattern of cautious behavior is likely to be low levels of income, rather than high levels of financial literacy.

According to the survey, trust in the banking system in Georgia is one of the highest in the region and even in the European Union; 79% of the surveyed population trust the banks unconditionally, while 85% of the population do not entrust their money to other financial institutions,

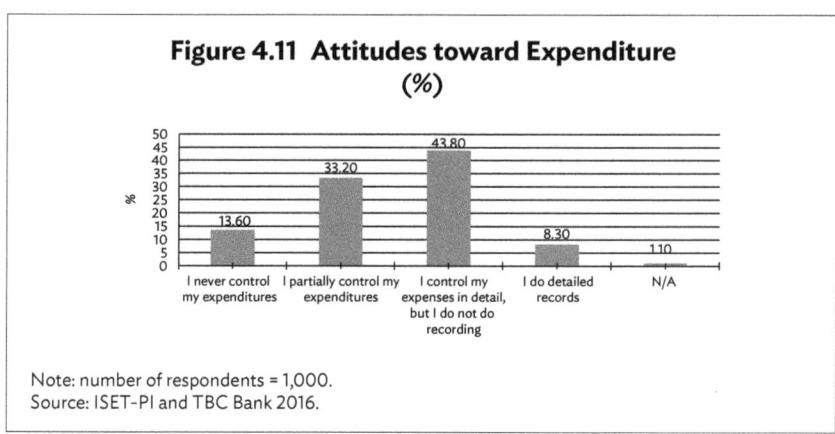

Figure 4.11 Attitudes toward Expenditure (%)

Note: number of respondents = 1,000.
Source: ISET-PI and TBC Bank 2016.

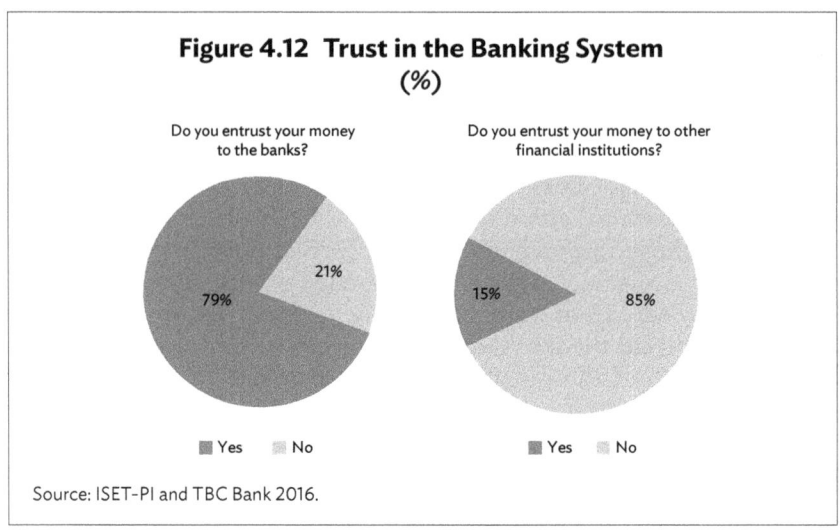

Figure 4.12 Trust in the Banking System (%)

Source: ISET-PI and TBC Bank 2016.

such as microfinance institutions and credit unions. The conservative regulation of the banking system by the NBG has led to a stable and credible banking system, while the non-regulated part of the financial sector is seen as unreliable in the eyes of the population. This result should be treated with caution, however. As mentioned before, trust in the banking system greatly depends on the question that is being asked. For example, if a question is asked about trust in the banking system in general, the percentage of positive responses is lower (CRRC 2015). This may be because people do not trust banks to provide them with fair lending terms, although they may trust them with deposits.

Despite the high credibility of the regulated part of the financial market, long-term financial planning and bank saving are not common among respondents. Only 12.4% of respondents are saving for retirement purposes; 14.3% of the population will be totally dependent on the basic state pension, which is at about the minimum subsistence level in Georgia; and 25.1% hope to have a job during their retirement.

Several findings in the survey indicate that, together with low levels of financial literacy, low income remains one of the main obstacles to more sophisticated financial inclusion among the population. Only 35% of the respondents managed to save during 2015, while 57% took out a loan during the same period. Among those who managed to save, 30% made a deposit saving, while 44% kept their cash outside the bank. Cash savings were most likely intended for very short-term goals or purposes, not long-term planning for the future.

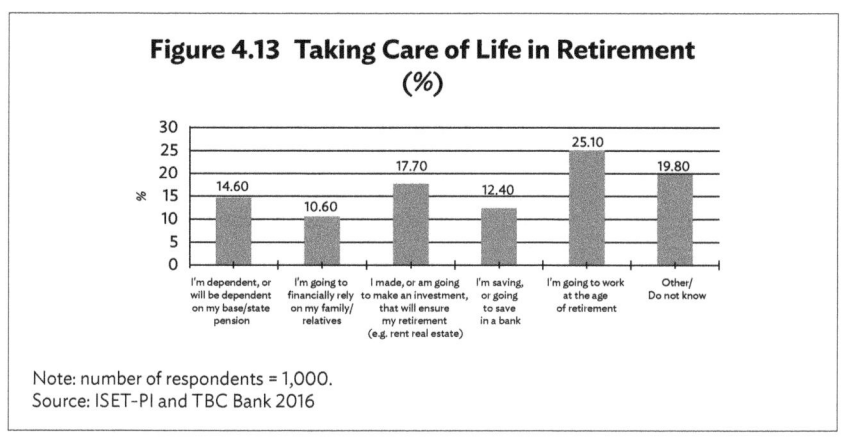

Figure 4.13 Taking Care of Life in Retirement (%)

Note: number of respondents = 1,000.
Source: ISET-PI and TBC Bank 2016

According to the OECD INFE International Survey of Adult Financial Literacy Competencies (OECD/INFE 2016), Georgia is among the countries where families have trouble making ends meet. In comparison, countries where a significant share of the population were unable to make ends meet at least once in the last 12 months were as follows: Thailand (64%), Georgia (61%), Belarus (57%), Albania (54%), and Turkey (50%). Furthermore, at least four in 10 respondents resorted to borrowing to make ends meet in Thailand (45%), Georgia (45%), Turkey (42%), Albania (41%), and Belarus (41%). This indicates a high level of financial fragility in these countries, possibly due to low and/or fluctuating incomes.

Another important aspect of financial literacy is familiarity with financial products. Even though the use of financial products in Georgia is not low, a significant share of the population does not understand the intricacies of various financial products. According to the study and survey conducted by the NBG in 2016 (NBG 2016a), people tend not to shop around for best offers on financial products, and take the first available deal that is offered to them.

The NBG survey further characterized the segments of population in Georgia according to their financial attitudes and behavior. According to the survey, only 11.7% of the population can be characterized as *business minded*, that is, distributing monthly income, making at least small savings, and setting long-term financial goals. The financial literacy score was the highest (65.6 out of 100) in this segment of the population. *Financially responsible* people (who demonstrate practical financial behavior, meet financial responsibilities, and maintain close control of their finances, among other things) comprise just over one-third (34.3%)

of the population and have the second highest financial literacy score (63 out of 100). Unfortunately, the remainder of the population (54%) can be characterized as either *financially fearful* (characterized by poor financial capabilities, fear toward financial affairs) (21.6%), *burdened by debt* (hardly make ends meet, deeply in debt) (16%), *enjoy spending* (live for today only, focus on short-term goals) (11%), or *shopaholics* (make spontaneous financial decisions) (5%). People in these categories had the lowest financial literacy scores ranging from 57.7% (*burdened by debt*) to 49.2% (*enjoy spending*).

As these surveys show, Georgia has a long way to go to reach the level of the OECD average in financial literacy, behavior, and attitudes. To this end, the NBG developed the National Strategy for Financial Education in Georgia (NBG 2016b), which was implemented in 2016. In the following section, we will summarize the main points of the strategy.

4.6.3 Financial Education Strategy of Georgia

In addition to the goal of improving the overall financial wellbeing of the Georgian population, the strategy's aim is to protect consumers' rights. The following are three strategic focus points to help achieve the goals of financial education.

(i) Raise awareness of the benefits of financial education, by enhancing awareness of the importance of financial education in society, and stimulating a greater demand for and use of financial education initiatives.

Enhance coordination and collaboration among stakeholders, by optimizing resources for achieving synergy, extending the impact and reach of education initiatives, and sharing experience and good practice.

(ii) Extend opportunities to learn, by encouraging lifelong learning of financial matters from an early age, and making financial education initiatives available through diversified venues, settings, and languages.

To coordinate this effort, the NBG established a steering committee composed of different types of stakeholders including financial institutions (banks and MFIs), universities, civil society organizations, and government entities for the implementation of the strategy. The committee's goals are to evaluate existing and future programs, raise initiatives, and provide advisory, financial, and technical assistance.

The strategy identified the following high-need, vulnerable segments: (i) the younger generation (pupils and students); (ii) the unemployed;

(iii) people employed in large companies and organizations;[44] (iv) the rural population; and (v) people facing special life events (such as the birth of a child, a wedding, or a university education).

The guidelines for activities under the strategy for 2017–2019 have been drafted, but are not yet enforced. These activities include training, awareness-raising campaigns, and communication using various channels. The integration of financial literacy topics in the national curriculum in schools (in math classes and in civil education classes) has been planned. The pilot of the program SchoolBank is already in action, and the NBG is training pupils and teachers in 11 public schools.

4.7 Conclusions and Recommendations

4.7.1 Main Takeaways from the Study

Adequate Access, but Low Usage of Financial Services in Georgia

On a number of financial inclusion indicators, Georgia is outperforming the ECA developing countries cohort (in particular in terms of access indicators, such as the number of ATMs, bank branches, and POS terminals). Yet, in terms of usage of financial products and technologies, Georgia is still very much behind its peer group of countries. Strikingly, the percentage of young adults with deposit or savings accounts is very low (9.9%) compared to the ECA regional average (50.1%). This result is likely driven by the low rate of economic activity among young people and a high rate of unemployment in this cohort. The lack of economic independence leads to a lack of financial inclusion among young people. The same factors are likely to be responsible for the low usage of financial technologies, such as internet and mobile banking. Once the current youth cohort becomes integrated into the economic life of the country, usage of modern financial technologies is expected to increase.

Poor Households Remain Underserved

Despite rapidly growing indicators of access to financial services (such as deposits and credit), a significant cohort of the population remains underserved. This concerns mainly the poor and to some extent

---

[44] Arguably, these people are not financially vulnerable, but are easy to target with financial education programs at a low cost.

rural populations. Only 46% of poor adults have a deposit or savings account, as opposed to 61% of adults overall. The rural population has adequate (country average) indicators of usage, but is much more likely to be engaged in low-income subsistence agriculture, less likely to have accumulated savings, and have lower financial literacy scores. In addition, rural inhabitants dominate the segment of the population that can be described as financially fearful, according to the NBG financial literacy survey.

Access to Credit has been Growing Rapidly for Households, but not Small and Medium-Sized Enterprises

Indicators of financial access among SMEs have remained largely the same since 2012. At the same time, credit to households, in particular credit secured by real estate, has been expanding rapidly in the past few years. Indebtedness of households has been growing rapidly as well. While the ratio of NPLs to total loans in commercial banks remained stable, the data from microfinances are different—the value of repossessed property increased sharply around the time of the lari devaluation (NBG Statistics website). This suggests that financial strain was experienced mostly by households who did not, for various reasons, qualify for a loan from a commercial bank. In addition, credit score distribution data from the country's only credit bureau, which covers 88.6% of the adult population, indicates that the distribution is skewed toward the high-risk category. There are notably more MFI clients in the E3, the sub-prime segment, than bank clients (International Risk Partnership 2017), as banks have much stricter requirements for giving credit. As rapid growth in consumer credit prompted concerns about the sustainability of credit expansion, the government and NBG called for stronger consumer protection measures, pushed for rapid de-dollarization of small and medium-sized loans, and stepped up efforts to promote financial literacy.

Financial Literacy Levels Can Be Described as Inadequate for the Given Level of Financial Sector Development

In Georgia, the financial sector has been developing and growing quite rapidly. Yet, various financial literacy indicators show that the majority of the population is only familiar with basic financial concepts, like simple interest, inflation, and risk and return. Slightly more complicated questions about calculating a simple interest on a deposit or detecting the effect of compounding remain challenging. There is evidence that Georgians choose financial products without "shopping around," and are, in many cases, unaware of various financial products available to them.

Low Levels of Financial Literacy in Conjunction with Low Incomes are Among the Main Obstacles to Greater Financial Inclusion

Financial literacy and financial inclusion go hand in hand. People with higher levels of financial literacy tend to save more, are more aware of various financial products, and are more responsible borrowers. The data analyzed for the purposes of this study point to the conclusion that financial literacy is correlated with income and education levels. While there may be a causal relationship in the direction from financial literacy to income level (as financial literacy may proxy ability), one can imagine reverse causation as well, that is, low income levels may be partly responsible for low levels of financial inclusion and thus lead indirectly to lower levels of financial literacy.

4.7.2 Recommendations

The analysis of various financial inclusion indicators and financial sector policies in Georgia leads us to conclude that the country's problems with financial inclusion of the poor, young, and rural populations stem from low income levels as well as low levels of financial literacy.

As the Georgian authorities navigate different policy options to improve financial inclusion for households and SMEs, they must keep in mind that financial literacy, general education, and income levels are interrelated concepts, and it is not possible to fully address one aspect of the problem (e.g. financial literacy) without simultaneously addressing the issues related to general education and the lack of stable incomes.

The government needs to develop a comprehensive national strategy for financial inclusion of the population (currently lacking) that will address different aspects of this problem, including consumer protection, education, employment opportunities, and, last but not least, financial literacy. In particular, promoting employment among youth could go a long way toward encouraging their financial integration and more responsible financial behavior in the future.

Greater financial access for SMEs remains a challenge. SMEs face a "chicken and egg" problem, in which they find it hard to grow without greater access to finance, while banks are reluctant to lend in excess of what the financial situation of these firms currently allows. The solution to this problem could be to experiment with different approaches, which do not necessarily imply interest rate subsidies or collateral pledges. Education programs and training for SME entrepreneurs may be a way to solve the problem of low financial reporting standards as well as other structural problems plaguing the SME sector.

As far as regulatory issues are concerned, the recent steps by the government to promote consumer protection, de-dollarize the economy, and increase the level of financial literacy are adequate and timely. However, policy makers need to be cautious about changes that can affect both consumers and providers of financial services. As financial inclusion is driven by both demand and supply factors, efforts to de-dollarize lending to households can also increase the cost of hedging instruments for banks and MFIs, increase domestic currency interest rates, and, consequently, lead to fewer affordable loans for households.

Finally, policy makers need to stay vigilant and informed about the new financial technologies that appear on the market that can potentially affect vulnerable population groups. In this respect, the recent changes to the Civil Code to keep effective interest rates capped were an adequate response to rapidly growing predatory lending practices. Yet, policy makers need to develop the means to keep an eye on various segments of the financial market, not just commercial banks or MFIs, to detect problems before they arise. One of the instruments employed could be more frequent surveys on the lending, borrowing, and savings behavior and practices of households and SMEs.

References

Abashidze, Z. 2018. Cryptocurrency Boom in Georgia – Money 'Out of Thin Air' for Citizens and Business Tycoons. *JAM News*. https://jam-news.net/cryptocurrency-boom-in-georgia-money-out-of-thin-air-for-citizens-and-business-tycoons/

ACT Research. 2011. Savings Behavior Assessment Survey in Georgia. Tbilisi: ACT Research.

Asian Development Bank (ADB). 2015. *The Georgian Capital Market– Diagnostic Study and Recommendations*. Tbilisi: ADB.

Carapella, F., and G. di Giorgio. 2003. Deposit Insurance, Institutions and Bank Interest Rates. Columbia University Discussion Paper series. New York: Columbia University Academic Commons. https://doi.org/10.7916/D8K64W87.

Caucasus Research Resource Center (CRRC). 2015. *Caucasus Barometer 2015. Georgia*. http://caucasusbarometer.org/en/cb2015ge/TRUBANK/.

Deposit Insurance Agency of Georgia. 2017. Who Is Insured? http://diagency.ge/en/who%20is%20insured. (accessed 26January 2019).

European Bank for Reconstruction and Development. 2007. *Georgian National Public Opinion Survey on Remittances*. London: European Bank for Reconstruction and Development. http://www.ebrd.com/downloads/sector/etc/surge.pdf.

Government of Georgia. 2016a. *Social-Economic Development Strategy for Georgia 2020*. Tbilisi: Government of Georgia. http://www.mrdi.gov.ge/sites/default/files/social-economic_development_strategy_of_georgia_georgia_2020.pdf.

Government of Georgia. 2016b. *SME Development Strategy for Georgia 2016–2020*. Tbilisi: Government of Georgia. 2http://www.economy.ge/uploads/files/2017/ek_politika/eng_sme_development_strategy.pdf.

International Risk Partnership. 2017. *Review of CreditInfo Georgia and the Georgian Economy*. Tbilisi: International Risk Partnership.

International School of Economics at Tbilisi State University Policy Institute and TBC Bank. 2016. *Financial Literacy Survey in Georgia* (available only in Georgian). http://iset-pi.ge/index.php/en/private-sector-projects/completed-projects/1360-financial-consciousness-research-in-georgia-geo.

Ministry of Economy and Sustainable Development of Georgia; Ministry of Finance of Georgia; National Bank of Georgia (NBG). 2016. *Capital Market Development Strategy*. Tbilisi: Ministry of Economy and Sustainable Development of Georgia.

National Bank of Georgia (NBG). European Fund for Southeast Europe. (EFSE). 2016a. *Financial Literacy and Financial Inclusion Survey*. Tbilisi: NBG.

NBG. 2016b. *National Strategy for Financial Education in Georgia*. Tbilisi: NBG. http://nbg.gov.ge/cp/uploads/stategy/FinLit_Strategy_ENG.pdf.

NBG Statistics. 2018a. Assets and Liabilities of Micro Financial Organizations. [Data file] Retrieved from https://www.nbg.gov.ge/index.php?m=304.

NBG Statistics. 2018b. Balance of Payments. [Data file] Retrieved from https://www.nbg.gov.ge/uploads/banalceofpayments/bopbpm6eng.xlsx

NBG. 2018. List of Registered Payment Service Providers at NBG. [Data file] Retrieved from https://www.nbg.gov.ge/uploads/sagadaxdo/rtgs/2018/list_of_providers_eng.xlsx

National Statistics Office of Georgia. 2013. *Pawnshop Survey*. Tbilisi: National Statistics Office of Georgia.

National Statistics Office of Georgia (Geostat). 2017. *Population Statistics 2017*. Tbilisi: National Statistics Office of Georgia http://www.geostat.ge/index.php?action=page&p_id=152&lang=eng. (accessed 26 January 2019).

Organisation for Economic Co-operation and Development (OECD)/International Network on Financial Education(INFE). 2016. International Survey of Adult Financial Literacy Competencies. Paris: OECD/INFE. https://www.oecd.org/daf/fin/financial-education/OECD-INFE-International-Survey-of-Adult-Financial-Literacy-Competencies.pdf

Paresishvili, G. 2017. *Georgian Capital Market Development*. Tbilisi: Georgia Stock Exchange. https://www.saras.gov.ge/Content/files/GSE-Capital-Market-Development-FINAL-ENG-19.06.17.pdf.

Society and Banks. 2017. *Role of the Credit Bureaus in Development of the Financial Sector of Georgia*. Tbilisi: Society and Banks.

United States Agency for International Development Caucasus; Economic Policy Research Center (USAID). 2014. *Regulatory Impact Assessment Georgian Law on Securities Market Final*. Tbilisi: United States Agency for International Development Caucasus.

World Bank. 2016. *Global Payment Systems Survey (GPSS)*. http://www.worldbank.org/en/topic/financialinclusion/brief/gpss

World Bank. 2018a. *Migration and Remittances – Recent Developments and Outlooks*. Migration and Development Brief 30.

World Bank. 2018b. World Bank Open Data. Poverty Headcount Ratio at $3.10 a day (2011 PPP) (% of population). https://data.worldbank.org/indicator/SI.POV.LMIC?locations=AM-GE

World Gallup Poll. 2013. News 10 May. European Countries Lead the World in Distrust of Banks http://news.gallup.com/poll/162602/european-countries-lead-world-distrust-banks.aspx. Accessed on January 26, 2019

Yoshino, N., and P. Morgan. 2016. Overview of Financial Inclusion, Regulation and Education. ADB Institute Working Paper 591, Tokyo: ADB Institute.

5

Kazakhstan

Kassymkhan Kapparov

5.1 Introduction

Kazakhstan is a middle-income country, with an economy that experienced booming growth in oil exports in the 2000s and early 2010s. Some of the outcomes of its rapid economic growth was the development of the financial sector and improvements in the areas of financial inclusion and financial literacy. However, serious problems remain in terms of both supply and demand for financial services. These problems have not fully been addressed in the agenda of the Government of Kazakhstan so far, and they remain among the barriers to more dynamic and inclusive economic growth.

Financial inclusion is becoming a goal for more governments and central banks around the world. National strategies are being designed with the help of international organizations and are being implemented in coordination with a wide range of governmental agencies. Most of these strategies include financial education as one of the pillars for ensuring higher financial inclusion. Research has shown that there is a strong correlation between financial literacy and financial inclusion. People who are aware of at least five financial products tend to have higher levels of financial literacy than those who are less aware (Atkinson and Messy 2013).

Effective financial inclusion policies and the role of financial education should take into account best practices from other countries, but also be based on good understanding of local specifics and the dynamics of social life. Low levels of financial literacy are most likely to be considered a major barrier to financial inclusion (Gardeva and Rhyne 2011). Hence, one of the tools for achieving higher and safer financial inclusion should be financial education. It is important to note that the ultimate goal of a financial inclusion strategy should not solely be hitting numeric targets or the share of the population actively using financial services, but rather the share of the population using these services responsibly to improve their life conditions in the long term.

Ensuring financial inclusion is an ongoing process that takes a long time and is difficult to implement completely. Diagnostics of the current situation should preside over the drafting of a national strategy for financial inclusion. It is important to ensure that the drafting of a national strategy is discussed widely by all key stakeholders, including policy makers from various governmental agencies directly and indirectly involved in its implementation, regional and local municipalities, financial service providers, the business community, civil society, and nongovernment organizations (NGOs). It is important to conserve the buy-in from all of these parties to increase the chances of success for the national strategy.

5.2 Overview of the Financial System in Kazakhstan

The financial sector in Kazakhstan is relatively small in terms of volume, which limits investment and the operations of companies, and hinders bank lending. These problems are mostly due to transition factors, including the economic cycle, the unsustainable use of international loans, and a period of unstable high exchange rates. Structural factors, such as uncertainty with regard to property rights and the judiciary, as well as the lack of transparent financial statements, also hamper financial development. However, the level of financial inclusion in Kazakhstan is comparable to that of other developing countries. The World Bank (2017) reports that in 2017, 59% of adults (aged 15+) had an account at a formal financial institution, 47% of adults (aged 15+) made or received digital payments, and 92% of small and medium-sized enterprises (SMEs) had an account at a formal financial institution. The financial sector in Kazakhstan is dominated by banks and, as a result, financial inclusion beyond banks remains modest.

Kazakhstan is well positioned in terms of the number of bank accounts, credit and debit cardholders (more than 17 million cards issued or one card per person), and ATMs. Household debt is low at 10% of gross domestic product (GDP). However, the insurance sector remains underdeveloped.

The availability of banking services differs from region to region, with the highest number of branches and premises per person in two major cities: Astana and Almaty. The lowest concentration is in the

Table 5.1 Overview of the Banking Sector in Kazakhstan

Total number of banks	33
of which:	
state-owned	1
with foreign participation	15
Assets, $ billion	77
as % of GDP	58
Total loans, $ billion	44
as % of GDP	35
Corporate loans (excluding SMEs), $ billion	20
Loans to SMEs, $ billion	15
as % of total loans	32
Retail loans, $ billion	11
of which:	
consumer loans, $ billion	8
Mortgages	3
Nonperforming loans (more than 90 days overdue) in retail loans, $ billion	1.3
as % of retail loans	11
Deposits, $ billion	52
of which:	
retail deposits, $ billion	24
retail deposits, as % of deposits	45

GDP = gross domestic product, SMEs = small and medium-sized enterprises.
Source: National Bank of Kazakhstan. 2017. *Tekushhee Sostojanie Bankovskogo Sektora Respubliki Kazakhstan*. 1 January. Almaty: National Bank of Kazakhstan.

southern regions with the largest populations: South Kazakhstan oblast,[1] Zhambyl oblast, Kyzylorda oblast, and Almaty oblast (Table 5.2).

According to the National Bank of Kazakhstan (NBK), there are currently two national payment systems: an interbank money transfer system and an interbank clearing system. In addition, international payment systems (Visa, MasterCard, American Express, and UnionPay) are operating in the country. Visa and MasterCard payment systems account for more than 95% of all transactions, and these firms issue debit and credit cards.

---

[1] Provincial administrative unit in Kazakhstan.

Table 5.2 Number of Commercial Bank Branches by Region in Kazakhstan

	Branches	Additional premises	Both	Per 10,000 persons
Almaty city	27	325	352	2.0
Karagandy oblast	31	177	208	1.5
East Kazakhstan oblast	30	176	206	1.5
Astana city	28	168	196	2.0
Pavlodar oblast	25	109	134	1.8
South Kazakhstan oblast	22	111	133	0.5
Aktobe oblast	19	96	115	1.4
Almaty oblast	21	89	110	0.6
Kostanai oblast	14	87	101	1.2
Mangistau oblast	22	78	100	1.5
Atyrau oblast	21	71	92	1.5
West Kazakhstan oblast	14	68	82	1.3
Akmola oblast	19	61	80	1.1
Zhambyl oblast	16	59	75	0.7
North Kazakhstan oblast	16	53	69	1.2
Kyzylorda oblast	13	40	53	0.7
Total	338	1,768	2,106	1.2

Note: An oblast is a provincial administrative unit in Kazakhstan.
Source: National Bank of Kazakhstan website. http://www.nationalbank.kz/?docid=3000&switch=russian. (accessed 21 September 2017).

There are 32 insurance companies registered in Kazakhstan, of which 22 are members of the state-owned Insurance Guarantee Fund. The assets of the insurance companies are relatively low at 2% of GDP. The average insurance premium amount is $60 (NBK. 2017a). According to the World Trade Organization accession requirements for Kazakhstan, foreign insurance companies will be allowed to establish branches 5 years after accession (i.e., not before 2020).

As of September 2017, there were 160 microfinance institutions (MFIs) registered in Kazakhstan. Their number has been increasing rapidly—in January 2017 there were 136 MFIs. Consumer lending by banks in Kazakhstan has decreased since 2015, following the devaluation of the national currency and the tightening of regulations. However, demand has shifted to payday loans and nonbank lending organizations, such as MFIs. In 2016, in just 1 year, the loan portfolio of MFIs had increased by 50% and reached $0.3 billion. In the first 6 months of 2017 the loan portfolio increased by 30% and reached $0.4 billion NBK (2017b). One of the reasons for this remarkable growth is that regulations for MFIs are not as tight as those for commercial banks. For example, licensing is not required for those MFIs that do not attract deposits from the population.

Online microlenders provided paycheck loans of almost T9 billion in 2016 compared to T2.5 billion in 2015, which shows the booming growth of the sector. In the 3 years since its inception the sector of online microlending has reached almost T34 billion (0.7% of total retail loans), disbursed in 543,000 microloans with an average size of T37,000 (equivalent of $100) and an average loan period of 23 days.

Currently there is only one pension fund operating in Kazakhstan—the Single Accumulative Pension Fund (*Edinyi Nakopitelnyi Pensionniy Fond*—ENPF), created in 2013. Every formally employed person in Kazakhstan pays 10% of their salary to the pension fund. In 2017 there were more than 9 million pension accounts, of which 5.6 million were active contributors (or 66% of the total employed population, including the self-employed) (ENPF, 2017). Almost none of those who are self-employed make mandatory or voluntary payments to a pension fund. The ENPF is the main source of local currency liquidity in the country and has accumulated nearly $21 billion (15% of GDP). Its funds are mostly invested in government securities (44%) and corporate bonds of local banks (20%). The ENPF is not listed and does not trade on the Kazakhstan Stock Exchange (KASE) (NBK. 2017c).

The KASE has been operating since 1993. After the pension reform and creation of private pension funds, the KASE experienced rapid growth in trade volumes. However, after the government's 2013 decision to consolidate all pension savings into a single state-owned fund, the number of listed companies dropped from 354 in 2010 to 142 in 2017. Currently the KASE's main operations concern foreign exchange (52%) and repurchase agreement transactions (46%), while the share of government and corporate securities remains negligible (1%). Stock market capitalization is at $47 billion and corporate bond market capitalization at $24 billion. The NBK owns 50.1% of KASE shares.

Kazakhstan has been a net exporter of remittances since 2000, and the annual amount of remittance outflows gradually increased from $47 million, peaked at $1.9 billion in 2012, and declined to $1.4 billion in 2017. Remittance outflows strongly correlate with oil revenues and are directly linked to oil prices. The amount of inflowing remittances since 2000 has been in the range of $3 million–$11 million per year and has not affected the financial situation in Kazakhstan.

Since 2011, Kazakhstan has had a law regulating the issuance of e-money, which can be issued only by the commercial banks. Private companies can act as operators for the banks to buy and sell e-money, and to provide transaction services using e-money.[2] E-money use has seen exceptional growth: in 2017, the volume of e-money transactions jumped 2.6 times to $1 billion (NBK website, 2018). Growth has also been seen in internet and mobile banking, with a 70% increase in the volume of transactions to almost $3 billion, equal to one-third of cashless payments using bank cards. The total number of registered internet and mobile banking users reached 7.8 million people or 60% of the population aged 16+ years in 2017.

5.3 Financial Inclusion

The Asian Development Bank defines financial inclusion as "ready access for households and firms to reasonably priced financial services." (ADB 2015, p 71). According to Demirgüç-Kunt et al (2017), 59% of adults (aged 15+) in Kazakhstan have an account at a formal financial institution (up from 54% in 2014). At the same time, only 46% of adults in the poorest 40% of households had an account at a formal financial institution (Demirgüç-Kunt et al 2014). In addition, the gap between richer and poorer in 2017 reached 17 percentage points (Table 5.3).

However, according to the Organisation for Economic Co-operation and Development (OECD), there is a difference between "unbanked" and "underserved" populations. To be considered banked, one only needs at least one open bank account, which can be an obligatory bank account opened as part of the social security or salary payment scheme. The underserved population comprises those who rarely use their accounts or do not know how to use them (OECD 2015). This is an important aspect for the analysis of financial inclusion in Kazakhstan as all current pensioners receive their pension payments on bank cards and use the cards mostly to withdraw cash. Hence, the 54% of the "banked" population can be treated as a supply-side measure, but it does not show the "demand" side, that is, the actual usage of financial services, which could be much lower. In addition, according to the legislation a retail bank account can be closed only if the client applies to close the account. Otherwise, accounts (both retail and corporate) will remain active. Thus, the total number of open bank

---

[2] Law of the Republic of Kazakhstan 21 July 2011 No. 466-IV "On Amendments and Additions to Certain Legislative Acts of the Republic of Kazakhstan Concerning Electronic Money."

Table 5.3 Accounts in Formal Financial Institutions in Kazakhstan

	2011	2014	2017
Account (% aged 15+)	42	54	59
Account, male (% aged 15+)	40	52	57
Account, in labor force (% aged 15+)	44	62	68
Account, out of labor force (% aged 15+)	37	42	46
Account, female (% aged 15+)	44	56	60
Account, young adults (% aged 15–24)	27	32	37
Account, older adults (% aged 25+)	47	61	66
Account, primary education or less (% aged 15+)	20	28	30
Account, secondary education or more (% aged 15+)	46	58	64
Account, income, poorest 40% (% aged 15+)	34	45	49
Account, income, richest 60% (% aged 15+)	48	60	65
Account, rural (% aged 15+)	37	49	57

Source: World Bank Global Findex (2017).

accounts does not represent the number of accounts that are being actively used. Unfortunately, the data reported by the NBK only show the number of bank accounts with a minimum amount of T1 million ($3,000 equivalent). This does not allow a proper estimation of how many accounts contain an insignificant amount (e.g., less than T30,000 or $100), and can therefore be considered abandoned.

According to the European Bank for Reconstruction and Development (EBRD), the share of people without bank accounts ("unbanked population") in Kazakhstan in 2014 was around 40%; the main reasons cited were "too expensive," "lack of money," and "lack of trust." The following factors did not play a significant role: "too far away," "religious reasons," and "lack of documentation" (EBRD 2017).

Although almost all SMEs have an account at a formal financial institution, the share of firms using bank loans remains relatively low. This applies to the share of firms using banks to finance investments (16%), firms using banks to finance working capital (13%), and firms with a bank loan or line of credit (20%). The main reasons for the low use of credit remain the restrictively high rates for loans and high requirements for collateral levels, usually in the form of real estate.

The official data on the number of accounts indicate the high concentration of retail deposits. In local currency, 99.6% of all demand deposit accounts are lower than $3,000. For term deposits, 86% of all deposit accounts in local currency amount to less than $10,000. Overall, there are currently 4.3 million demand deposit accounts and 3.0 million term deposit accounts in local currency. In value terms, the concentration level is lower, with only 93% of all demand deposit accounts and 60% of term deposits being lower than $3,000. For term deposits, 70% of all deposit accounts in United States (US) dollars hold less than $10,000. Overall, there are currently around 85,000 demand deposit accounts and over 900,000 term deposit accounts in US dollars.

Official statistics indicate relatively high levels of financial inclusion; however, it should be noted that one person could have several current and card accounts, and one depositor could have several deposit accounts in one bank, including demand deposits and different term deposits, and/or several deposits in different banks. According to the statistics, there are more than 24 million current accounts in banks and over 10 million card accounts with some cash balances. Despite the high number of current accounts and card accounts in banks, it is unclear whether these bank accounts are actually being used. According to Kazakhstan Deposit Insurance Fund (KDIF) data, the share of accounts with less than $3,000 (the minimum amount reported) is very high for cash balances on current accounts in local currency (96%), remains of money on card accounts in local currency (99%), as well as cash balances in current accounts in US dollars (92%) and remains of money on card accounts in US dollars (96%). Clearly, for a more comprehensive picture, further disaggregation of the data is needed

Bank cards in Kazakhstan are used relatively widely. There are over 17 million active bank cards; however, only half of all cards were being used during the reporting period. Most bank cards—around 87%—are debit cards mainly used to receive and withdraw government transfers. In 2017 there were almost 10,000 ATMs and more than 120,000 point-of-sale terminals; 30% of the ATMs and 45% of the point-of-sale terminals were located in two major cities: Almaty and Astana. In August 2017, for the first time, the number of transactions with cashless payments using bank cards equaled cash withdrawals. However, the monthly volume of the amount paid using bank cards ($0.8 billion) is still lower than the amount withdrawn ($2.8 billion). It is important to mention that every third cashless payment using a bank card was done on the internet (NBK website, 2017a).

According to the World Bank (2017) Global Findex survey, only 19% of adults (aged 15+) saved for old age (up from 6% in 2014), and only 14% saved in a financial institution (up from 8% in 2014). What is noteworthy is that the richest 60% of the population was twice as willing to save for old age compared to the poorest 40% (23% versus 12%) (Table 5.4) (World Bank, 2017).

Table 5.4 Financial Inclusion Indicators in Kazakhstan

	2011	2014	2017
Debit card ownership (% aged 15+)	31	32	40
Credit card ownership (% aged 15+)	9	11	20
Credit card used in the past year (% aged 15+)		5	17
Used a debit or credit card to make a purchase in the past year (% aged 15+)		15	26
Borrowed any money in the past year (% aged 15+)		45	46
Borrowed from a financial institution (% aged 15+)	13	16	20
Outstanding housing loan (% aged 15+)		15	21
Received domestic remittances in the past year (% aged 15+)		12	18
Received domestic remittances through a financial institution (% aged 15+)		2	8
Sent domestic remittances in the past year (% aged 15+)		14	16
Sent domestic remittances through a financial institution (% aged 15+)		5	9
Paid utility bills in the past year (% aged 15+)		65	64
Paid utility bills using a financial institution account (% aged 15+)		3	21
Received wages in the past year (% aged 15+)		45	44
Received wages in cash only (% aged 15+)		14	14
Deposit in the past year (% with a financial institution account, aged 15+)		72	83
Made or received digital payments in the past year (% aged 15+)		40	54
Made digital payments in the past year (% aged 15+)		23	38
Received digital payments in the past year (% aged 15+)		42	43

Source: World Bank Global Findex Database (2017).

Another issue is that access to financial services is not evenly distributed among different groups of the population, and some of them are almost totally excluded. For instance, only 5% of rural women had taken any loans from a bank in the last 12 months, according to a survey conducted by United Nations Women in 2015.

From 2020, foreign banks will be allowed to establish branches in Kazakhstan. This was a World Trade Organization accession requirement for the country. Foreign banks will be allowed to open retail deposits only for $120,000 or more. The government should take into account that, in countries with more foreign banks, banks focus disproportionately on "easy clients": white-collar workers with a stable job and a decent salary. Other groups benefit less from the presence of foreign banks.

5.4 Analysis of the Current Regulation of Financial Services

The NBK is the main state body responsible for regulating the financial sector. The NBK is responsible for the regulation and supervision of banks, insurers, pension funds, investment funds, credit bureaus, and securities markets. From 2004 to 2011, regulatory and supervisory functions were performed by the Agency on Regulation and Supervision of the Financial Market and Financial Organizations, an independent entity that reported directly to the President. During 2011–2013, the Committee for the Control and Supervision of the Financial Market and Financial Organizations performed the supervisory and regulatory functions. This committee later became a structural division of the NBK and continued to perform supervisory functions. Financial regulation is based on the dedicated Law on State Regulation, Control and Supervision of the Financial Market and Financial Organizations.[3]

Currently, regulation of the financial sector is conducted based on the goals set in the Concept for the Financial Sector Development of the Republic of Kazakhstan until 2030 (2030 Concept). According to the 2030 Concept, its main goal is to create a competitive and effective financial sector based on global practices and OECD standards (Resolution, 2014). To achieve this goal, the following tasks are envisaged:
 (i) reducing the costs of society and the state to maintain the stability of the financial system in the event of potential shocks;
 (ii) improving the efficiency of the financial sector in the context of economic integration and globalization;

---

[3]   Law of the Republic of Kazakhstan No. 474-II (4 July 2003): On State Regulation, Control and Supervision of the Financial Market and Financial Organizations.

(iii) improving the infrastructure and creating optimal conditions for the qualitative development of the financial system;
(iv) expansion of financial sector growth resources, including through financial products that meet the needs of the economy; and
(v) maintaining a balanced economic environment and reducing credit risks in the economy.

The Law on Payments and Payment Systems (effective 10 September 2016) regulates the payments system in Kazakhstan. This law regulates relations in the sphere of payment system operations and the market, as well as improving practice for the performance of payments and money transfers. The law defines several new participants in the payment services market, including nonbank suppliers of payment services, such as payment organizations, payment agents, and subagents. New participants were added to facilitate and promote the development of e-money in Kazakhstan (Signum Law, 2017).

To increase the level of trust in banking services, the NBK created the KDIF in 1999. All commercial banks in Kazakhstan are members of the KDIF system. The KDIF provides a guarantee of up to T10 million ($30,000) for each deposit denominated in local currency and up to T5 million ($15,000) for deposits denominated in foreign currency. Currently, due to the small size of deposits, the KDIF system covers 99% of accounts (KDIF, 2017). The KDIF guarantee is valid for only one deposit account per person per bank. This threshold can stimulate big depositors to split their deposits between several banks and accounts to guarantee their safety. This factor should be taken into account when analyzing the concentration of retail deposits.

Aside from deposit insurance, the NBK has implemented several measures aimed at consumer protection, including the following:
(i) refinancing for mortgages denominated in foreign currency to support consumers who obtained loans in US dollars and suffered high payments after the series of devaluations of the national currency;
(ii) bank ombudsmen dealing with mortgage loans;
(iii) insurance ombudsmen dealing with transportation insurance issues; and
(iv) online calculators to estimate the effective annual interest rate on loans and deposits.

In addition to the state regulation of financial services, there have been attempts to impose self-regulation on different areas of the financial sector. For instance, the FinTech Association, which unites online microlenders, has imposed a voluntary threshold on the maximal penalty amount for its debtors of 300% of the amount of the principal balance.

5.5 Evaluation of Barriers to the Availability of Financial Services

There are many barriers to financial inclusion that are widely recognized. Among those most relevant to Kazakhstan's case are the following factors:

(i) historical circumstances among societies that for various reasons do not have a tradition of wide use of financial services, such as commercial loans and mortgages, in the post-Soviet countries;

(ii) negative perceptions and a lack of trust in general concerning financial agents based on previous negative experience, especially in countries that have undergone radical economic reforms;

(iii) regulatory constraints, mostly based on the risk management requirements promoted by regulatory agencies;

(iv) employment status, based on the ability to confirm income officially, which is especially important in developing countries with a larger informal sector;

(v) low awareness of financial services, mostly due to information asymmetry;

(vi) limited knowledge of how to conduct risk assessment of financial services, which prevents their use;

(vii) financial services and products that capture those in the unbanked population, and do not allow them to move to traditional services and products (e.g. loan sharks);

(viii) the focus of financial service providers on parts of the population with higher income that represent a lower risk, excluding the rest through prohibitive fees and credit history requirements;

(ix) geographical, physical, and information and communication technology barriers, especially for populations living in rural and low-income areas;

(x) digital discrimination, which is becoming a more important factor as more financial services move to online platforms, hence excluding those groups of the population with limited access to the internet; and

(xi) the general educational level, which can prevent the less-educated part of the population from using "complicated" (in their view) financial services.

5.6 Overview of State Policy to Promote Financial Inclusion

Financial inclusion for firms and SMEs is an important issue for Kazakhstan. As a response to the financial crisis in 2008, Kazakhstan widened its schemes to support firms' access to financing through interest rate subsidies and loan guarantees. These measures were effective during the financial crisis, but in the long run they have had limited benefits. Strengthening the ability of banks to access wholesale financing will contribute to sustainable improvement in their ability to provide loans. In the short term, improved access to international wholesale financing could solve this problem with a good credit rating. Joint ventures and the sale of shares to international banks could also improve the access of banks to international financing, while strengthening their management. At the same time, it is necessary to continue other efforts to develop domestic savings, giving priority to improving the management strategies and long-term investments of the pension fund. In the longer term, the institutional environment of the financial sector should become stronger to provide investors with greater confidence in their ability to protect their investments and in the reliability of financial information.

In areas where a number of banks are already competing with each other, some population segments may remain underserved because they do not meet the strict requirements imposed by these institutions. In this case, other types of financial service providers can pick up those clients that are left behind by banks and help ensure financial inclusion. Evidence from MFIs suggests that they may pick up some clients who are not served by formal banks. Moreover, the opening of new branches of MFIs in locations with a large percentage of low-income households in most cases eventually leads to an increase in the number of households with bank accounts. Therefore, the financial inclusion policy should take into account the role of MFIs as "enablers" of the first step for people to become formally "banked." Currently, there is no such state policy in place and the MFI sector is not regulated thoroughly, probably due to its relatively small size.

5.7 Financial Education

The 2030 Concept stated that work on increasing the level of financial education should be continuous and include various aspects. The 2030 Concept also acknowledged the fact that most developed and an increasing number of developing countries have permanent state programs aimed at increasing financial literacy levels. However, despite this acknowledgement, the 2030 Concept did not set a target for developing such a national strategy, but rather tasked the NBK with a list of measures, including launching a call center for consumers of financial services, producing educational animated cartoons on related topics, and adding information related to financial literacy to school and university teaching programs. Naturally, given their scope, these measures have had a limited effect on promoting financial inclusion among the population.

During 2007–2011, the State Program for Enhancing the Investment Culture (2007–2011 Program) was implemented. It had a budget of $30 million over 5 years, and expressly focused on increasing the knowledge of the population concerning investment opportunities in Kazakhstan with the aim of attracting private funds to be used for economic growth. The official goal of the program was to "increase the investment activity level of the population and to attract retail savings to promote economic growth." The NBK participated through the promotion of financial education and "the emphasis was on television projects, as the most popular communication tool at that time." (NBK, 2017d). However, despite the intention to increase the investment culture and financial literacy of the population in Kazakhstan, it focused more on promoting demand from retail investors as a necessary factor for the successful implementation of the "People's IPO [initial public offering]" program. After the completion of this program, there was effectively no other wide-scale policy action aimed at increasing financial inclusion.

Currently, the NBK, together with some commercial banks and MFIs, is carrying out financial education in Kazakhstan. However, these efforts are not regular and lack coordination. Therefore, it is hard to estimate the impact of these measures. To date, the NBK's activities in financial education for schoolchildren and students have included the following:

(i) in 2013, broadcasting the television programs *Kyzykty Karzhy* and *Fascinating Finances*, incorporating elements of a television journal and aimed at children's cognitive development;

(ii) broadcasting the television program *Smart Game* (2012), an intellectual quiz for students, the jury of which included employees of the NBK and its subsidiaries, and where the main prize was studying on the NBK's Master Program;

(iii) publication of special editions in the Republican newspapers *Ulan* and *Druzhnye Rebyata* for children on financial topics in 2012–2013;

(iv) in 2013, release of an animated film on the history of the tenge;

(v) in 2013, publication of *The History of Money*, a book for children with vivid illustrations;
(vi) in 2013, a children's competition held throughout the country for the best coin design; and
(vii) a number of educational events for students and schoolchildren conducted jointly with the Republican Children's Library, including meetings and lectures on financial literacy.

The main website of the NBK does not have a dedicated section on financial literacy, nor does it provide educational materials on financial services adapted for the wider population. Instead, the NBK launched a website, FinGramota, specifically dedicated to financial education. However, the content of the website remains limited, and can be considered informative rather than interactive and educational. The main page of the NBK's official website does not have a link to this website. Moreover, some of the advice given on the website could potentially raise questions. For example, the first piece of advice in the Family budget section states, "Get rid of credit cards and try not to take loans." (Fingramota website).

It is worth noting that while the 2007–2011 Program was adopted as a government decree, the newly adopted Program to Improve the Financial Literacy of the Population for 2016–2018 (2016–2018 Program) was approved by the board of the NBK (NBK 2016). The new program has the following goals:
(i) the development and accumulation of skills in financial planning;
(ii) the formation of active economic behavior among citizens, corresponding to their financial capabilities;
(iii) a reduction in overstated expectations for state financial support;
(iv) an increase in the confidence of consumers of financial products and services in the financial sector; and
(v) an increase in the overall economic activity of the population.

The 2016–2018 Program has the following key performance indicators (KPIs):
(i) Increase the savings of the population from T13 billion in 2016 to T14 billion in 2018.
(ii) Increase loans to the economy from T17 billion in 2016 to T20 billion in 2018.

These KPIs primarily describe the growth of the economy, and can only indirectly represent an increase in financial literacy levels and the adoption of financial services by the wider population. Hence, it is crucial that the new National Financial Inclusion Strategy includes independently measured KPIs that are more closely related to financial inclusion and financial literacy, possibly based on the World Bank Findex indicators and OECD Programme for International Student Assessment test results.

To gain a better picture of the financial literacy level, in 2018 the NBK is planning to commission sociological research. In addition, the NBK plans to (i) continue to hold press conferences for the media on financial literacy topics; (ii) give lectures at schools, libraries, and universities; and (iii) organize seminars for the media, NGOs, and governmental agencies. In particular, according to Atkinson and Messy (2013), education for financial inclusion should target the following three groups: (i) those with no formal financial products; (ii) those using a very limited range of products; and (iii) inexperienced, newly included consumers.

It is important to note that increased financial inclusion needs to be accompanied by growing financial education. New opportunities to borrow and invest can pose risks for the savings of households, and a proper level of understanding of how markets operate is required to avoid insolvency and wide-scale losses. Moreover, improved access to infrastructure must be matched by wide-scale investments in financial education. This is needed to address the issues that arose in Kazakhstan in 2007–2008, when the supply of loans increased sharply over a short period of time and borrowers paid little attention to the terms of the loans, which eventually led to defaults on mortgages, and retail and corporate loans denominated in foreign currency. The low level of financial education at the time spurred the banking and financial crisis in the country.

The risk of irresponsible over-borrowing by the population is especially relevant for markets during a post-economic boom period, when it takes time for households to adjust their consumption to new lower levels of income; this leads to growth in consumer loans, mostly from MFIs, and possibly to eventual over-indebtedness.

In an attempt to increase public interest in investing in the stock exchange, in 2012 the government initiated the so-called "People's IPO," a wide-scale privatization program, through which it was planned to include IPOs of shares in the country's most attractive national companies and monopolies in the infrastructure and energy sectors. The move was considered a major economic reform aimed at increasing the country's profile, liquidity, and economic development over the coming decade, and providing Kazakhstan's population with a larger stake in the national wealth. The successful implementation of the program, reflected in the level of involvement of retail investors, could potentially strengthen social stability in the country and spur economic growth. The plan was to place 5%–15% stakes locally to raise $100 million–$200 million from more than 5,000 retail investors. The total estimated domestic demand from retail investors at the time was estimated at $1.3 billion–$2.6 billion (Renaissance Capital Research 2011).

5.8 Conclusions and Recommendations

In general, we can conclude that, since independence in Kazakhstan, there has been no systematic, wide-scale financial inclusion strategy or policy. The general informal understanding was that economic growth would lead to a reduction in poverty, and higher income levels would in turn lead to higher levels of financial education and inclusion. Indeed, the development of the banking sector, driven by access to the global finance market prior to 2007, led to greater access to the financial sector for the population. However, the access to infrastructure was not matched by improved financial education. This in turn led to cases of insolvency for mortgages, retail and corporate loans denominated in foreign currency, and eventually to the banking crises in the country. As a result, the government had to use taxpayers' money to save some parts of retail, the corporate clients of banks, and not least the banks themselves. This led to an increase in critical voices among the population, and the president had to announce several times that the government would not be bailing out the banks. Nonetheless, in 2017 the government spent nearly $6 billion to help banks lower their nonperforming loan levels, which had been dragging the sector down since 2008.

There has been no state-level policy document on financial inclusion and education in Kazakhstan. The 2007–2011 Program, which aimed to increase the investment culture and financial literacy of the population in Kazakhstan cannot be considered such a policy as it was mostly focused on promoting the number of retail investors in the local stock market and did not take into account other sectors of the financial market. The 2016–2018 Program, which aimed to improve the financial literacy of the population, also cannot be considered a strategic document as it only defines the actions of the NBK and is an internal document, lacking sufficient authority to coordinate other state agencies.

A national financial strategy is needed in Kazakhstan for several reasons. First, there is a great need to provide the unbanked population access to existing financial services. This will reduce the informal sector, and provide new opportunities for the population with a lower income (including those employed in the healthcare and education sectors), as well as microentrepreneurs. Second, current policy for promoting financial inclusion and education in Kazakhstan is fragmented, and constitutes half measures at best. The activities of the NBK in enhancing financial literacy have been nonexistent since 2011, and those implemented predominantly employed non-systematic and non-institutional tools, such as television campaigns (mostly targeting children and youth). Although such measures may play some role in contributing to an increase in financial literacy, it is clear that they are not game changers. Third, there is a need to define clear goals for the government's efforts at financial inclusion. Moreover, there is no link to the level of financial education and how this should be co-promoted with financial inclusion. Improved access to financial services should be matched by an increased understanding of the risks, costs, and benefits of the use of financial services.

In summary, there is a great need to have a national financial inclusion strategy, and this should be based on a nationwide discussion of what such a strategy should include and focus on. There are several requirements for a national financial strategy in Kazakhstan, some of which are listed below.

(i) It is necessary to set clear goals for the strategy and identify clear KPIs to measure their achievement. It is important to link the goals of financial inclusion to the goals on the government's agenda, such as the attainment of higher levels of economic growth and social development. This will help ensure that financial inclusion remains on the government's agenda over the long term and secures the needed funding.

(ii) There must be a strong linkage with financial education and regular measurement of financial literacy levels based on the OECD methodology (OECD/International Network on Financial Education 2015).

(iii) Coordination is needed among the implementing governmental agencies (beginning with the NBK and the Ministry of Education).

(iv) There must be civil society participation in all stages of the strategy: design, discussion, implementation, and assessment. This will ensure that the needs of various groups of the population will be taken into account in the policy for financial education and financial inclusion.

(v) National statistics measuring financial literacy and financial education need to be developed that can be comparable at national and international levels. Existing statistical indicators should be updated and broadened to include new financial services, especially those that are online and semi-formal.

(vi) The national strategy should be based not only on the "ready-made, out-of-the-box" solutions proposed by international experience, but also on local knowledge and understanding of the behavioral patterns of local consumers of financial services. This will require conducting a series of sociological studies to identify the role of traditions, habits, and previous experience in the adoption and use of financial services.

(vii) "Push" and "pull" factors should be combined when designing the national strategy. The government's role should not be focused on providing free-of-charge training and the dissemination of educational information; rather, it should focus on organizing, stimulating, and coordinating society's efforts to make financial sectors and their services more available to larger numbers of those who would use them responsibly. Working closely with the main stakeholders—financial institutions and NGOs—should be at the core of the new strategy to ensure buy-in from a wider range of population groups.

References

Asian Development Bank (ADB). 2015. *Asian Development Outlook 2015. Financing Asia's Future Growth.* Manila: ADB.

Asian Development Bank Institute (ADBI). 2017. *Financial Inclusion, Regulation, and Education. Asian Perspectives.* Tokyo: Asian Development Bank Institute.

Atkinson, A., and F. Messy. 2013. Promoting Financial Inclusion through Financial Education: OECD/INFE Evidence, Policies and Practice. Organisation for Economic Co-operation and Development Working Paper on Finance, Insurance and Private Pensions 34. Paris: OECD Publishing. http://dx.doi.org/10.1787/5k3xz6m88smp-en

Resolution of the Government of the Republic of Kazakhstan dated August 29, 2014 N954. Concept for the Financial Sector Development of the Republic of Kazakhstan till 2030.

Demirguc-Kunt, A., L. Klapper, D. Singer, and P. Van Oudheusden. 2014. The Global Findex Database 2014. Measuring Financial Inclusion around the World. World Bank Policy Research Working Paper 7255. Washington, DC: World Bank.

Demirguc-Kunt, A., L. Klapper, D. Singer, S. Ansar, and J. Hess. 2017.*The Global Findex Database 2017. Measuring Financial Inclusion and the Fintech Revolution.* Washington, DC: World Bank.

EBRD. 2017. *Transition Report 2016-17. Transition for all: equal opportunities in an unequal world.* London, 2016.

ENPF. 2017. Presentation at Round Table on Pension System Development on 12 April 2017. Almaty.

Fingramota. http://fingramota.kz/budget/budget/ (accessed 3 October 2017). In Russian

Gardeva, A., and E. Rhyne. 2011. *Opportunities and Obstacles to Financial Inclusion.* Survey Report. Washington, DC: Center for Financial Inclusion at ACCION International. http://centerforfinancialinclusionblog.files.wordpress.com/2011/07/opportunities-and-obstacles- to-financial-inclusion_110708_final.pdf

KDIF. 2017. Kazakhstan Deposit Insurance Fund. *Deposit insurance system in Kazakhstan.* http://www.kdif.kz/en/sistema-garantirovaniya-depozitov-v-rk (accessed 25 November 2017).

Law of the Republic of Kazakhstan 21 July 2011 No. 466-IV "On Amendments and Additions to Certain Legislative Acts of the Republic of Kazakhstan Concerning Electronic Money."

National Bank of Kazakhstan (NBK). 2016. *Resolution of the Board of the National Bank of Kazakhstan of 30 September 2016 No. 244.* Almaty: NBK. http://nationalbank.kz/?docid=1544&switch=russian (accessed 20 April 2018).

NBK. 2017a. *Tekushcheye Sostoyaniye Strakhovogo Sektora Respubliki Kazakhstan po Sostoyaniyu na 1 Yanvarya 2017 goda*. January 2017. Almaty: NBK.

NBK. 2017b. *Tekushhee Sostojanie Mikrofinansovyh Organizacij Respubliki Kazahstan po Sostoyaniyu na 1 Julya 2017 goda*. July 2017. Almaty: NBK.

NBK. 2017c. *Tekushcheye sostoyaniye nakopitel'noy pensionnoy sistemy Respubliki Kazakhstan po sostoyaniyu na 1 yanvarya 2017 goda*. January 2017. Almaty: NBK.

NBK. 2017d. *Obucheniye Finansovoy Gramotnosti Tselesoobrazno Nachinat' v Rannem Vozraste*. September 2017. Almaty: NBK.

NBK. 2017e. *Tekushhee Sostojanie Bankovskogo Sektora Respubliki Kazakhstan*. January 2017. Almaty: NBK.

NBK website (2017). *Statistika po Platezhnym Kartochkam*. http://nationalbank.kz/?docid=786&switch=russian (accessed 12 September 2017).

NBK website (2018). *Elektronnyye Den'gi*. http://www.nationalbank.kz/?docid=3453&switch=russian (accessed 10 April 2018).

OECD. 2005. *Improving Financial Literacy: Analysis of Issues and Policies*. Paris: OECD.

OECD/International Network on Financial Education. 2015. *National Strategies for Financial Education. OECD/INFE Policy Handbook*. Paris: OECD.

Renaissance Capital Research. 2011. *Kazakhstan: Privatization of "Holy Cows" to Start in 2012*. 10 October. Renaissance Capital Research.

Reserve Bank of India. 2009. *National Strategy for Financial Education of India*. Mumbai: Reserve Bank of India.

Signum Law. *Regulation of Payment Systems and Market of Payment Services*. http://signumlaw.com/regulation-of-payment-systems-and-market-of-payment-services/?utm_source=Mondaq&utm_medium=syndication&utm_campaign=View-Original (accessed 1 December 2017).

World Bank. 2003. *Policy Research Report: Land Policies for Growth and Poverty Reduction*. Oxford: Oxford University Press.

World Bank. 2017. Financial Inclusion Data. Global Findex. https://globalfindex.worldbank.org (accessed 20 April 2018).

6
Kyrgyz Republic

Savia Hasanova

6.1 Introduction

After declaring its independence from the Soviet Union in 1991, the Kyrgyz Republic followed a path toward democratic and economic reforms. The country signed multiple agreements with international donors, introduced a national currency, and followed macroeconomic reforms according to the structural adjustments of the International Monetary Fund (IMF). Since then, the Kyrgyz Republic is considered the most open economy in the region and is a member of more than 75 international organizations and cooperation agreements. After the Russian Federation crisis in 1998, the Kyrgyz Republic experienced an overall economic decline, and in 2000, the poverty rate hit a peak of 62.6%. To address economic and social problems, a donor community supported the development of a microfinance sector. A large number of microfinance organizations (MFOs) and credit unions emerged, and these have been helping to reduce poverty. At the same time, the banking system was evolving quite quickly. During 1990s, the National Bank of the Kyrgyz Republic (NBKR) issued a license to over 30 commercial banks. Impetuous transformations in the banking sector, along with management problems, eventually led to a huge lack of adequate capital, and the regulator withdrew almost half of the licenses. After that, the Kyrgyz Republic's banking and microfinance sectors evolved gradually, and the share of foreign capital started to increase.

While financial inclusion is considered one of the key drivers of today's development, it is quite new to the Kyrgyz Republic. The first attempts to introduce the notion of financial inclusion arose after a violent power shift in 2010. A large number of entrepreneurs suffered from pogroms and there was an overall decline in the economy after events in April 2010. The majority of entrepreneurs operated small and medium-sized enterprises (SMEs) in the retail, construction, and services sectors. The banking sector suffered from the expropriation of former president-affiliated banks and their capital. These events induced people to protest against the high interest rates of microfinance companies and banks. At that time, many MFOs charged interest rates of 50%–100%, which led to the bankruptcy of many borrowers and social unrest in many regions of the country. Some distressed borrowers created associations and initiated protests against microfinance institutions (MFIs) and banks in front of the Parliament.

After these events, the Government of the Kyrgyz Republic began discussions on adopting a program to increase financial literacy, provide financial education, and reform regulatory frameworks. Many donors, private banks, and financial institutions supported these initiatives. A donor community began its own projects on improving financial literacy and promoting financial inclusion; however, the government initiatives were never realized. The majority of efforts implemented by the government included the improvement of legislation, simplification of procedures, and increasing consumer protection. Only in 2016 was the program on increasing financial literacy in the Kyrgyz Republic adopted.

Today, unstable economic growth, a high poverty rate, and weak governance are key vulnerabilities of increased inclusivity of financial products and services. Over 25% of the Kyrgyz Republic's population lives below the poverty line, with 13.9% living in multidimensional poverty (UNDP 2016). Income inequality, especially when comparing rural and urban areas, is substantial and restricts access to financial services for the rural population. This analysis suggests that there is an urgent need for consolidated efforts to include the poor in financial activities, mobilize their savings, and improve access to credit.

This chapter provides an overview of the financial sector in the Kyrgyz Republic, recent trends in its development, and discusses vulnerabilities and perspectives of the banking and microfinance sectors. The chapter also discusses the status of financial inclusion, penetration of financial products, and accessibility of finance to SMEs. Among other topics, the chapter focuses on financial literacy and financial education, and discusses some policies to promote financial inclusion in the Kyrgyz Republic. The final section provides concluding remarks and recommendations.

6.2 Overview of the Financial Sector

The financial sector in the Kyrgyz Republic is represented by the banking sector and nonbank financial institutions (NBFIs), including MFOs, insurance companies, the stock exchange, and other minor financial institutions. For the past decade, the financial sector has been evolving moderately, but stably. At the end of 2016, assets of the financial sector amounted to Som195.2 billion,[1] or 42.6% of gross domestic product (GDP). Although there are a substantial number of NBFIs, banks dominate the financial sector. Of the country's total financial assets, banks hold 91.2%, NBFIs 7%, and others 1.8%. Of the non-cash money stock of the economy, 80% is concentrated in commercial banks. As a result of macroeconomic conditions, social development, and a lack of financial literacy and education, other financial markets and institutions are poorly developed, weakly integrated in the world financial system, and do not play a significant role in the country's economy.

6.2.1 Banking Sector

As of 2016, the assets of commercial banks constituted 39% of GDP; and there were 25 banks, two of which were state-owned. Five major banks hold 55% of the banking sector's assets and 49% of the credit portfolio.

The amount of both loans and deposits has been increasing and the level of financial intermediation is rising (Figure 6.1). The share of loans to GDP increased from 14% in 2006 to 21% in 2016, while that of deposits increased from 15% to 23%. For the first half of 2017, the NBKR reports that individual deposits increased by 11%, credit by 9%, and total banking assets by 3.2%. The level of liquidity of the banking sector is 64.4% compared to the 45.0% NBKR requirement.

The slowdown in 2008–2011 is attributed to overall economic decline due to the financial crisis in 2008 and political events in 2010. After the violent power shift in April 2010, the volume of deposits in commercial banks declined by 31% within a few months (Gaidarov, Alamanova, and Kasymov 2015). This sharp decline in the number of deposits occurred because the five banks related to the former president and his affiliates were running money out of the country, and because the population withdrew their deposits. As for the credit volume, major contributors to the increase in the credit portfolio from 2013 are three former large microfinance companies, which obtained banking licenses. Despite some positive trends, the level of savings mobilization and credit to GDP is still low relative to the Caucasus and Central Asian regions, particularly when compared with the lower middle-income country average (IMF 2016).

---

[1] The average exchange rate in 2016 was Som69.00 = $1.00.

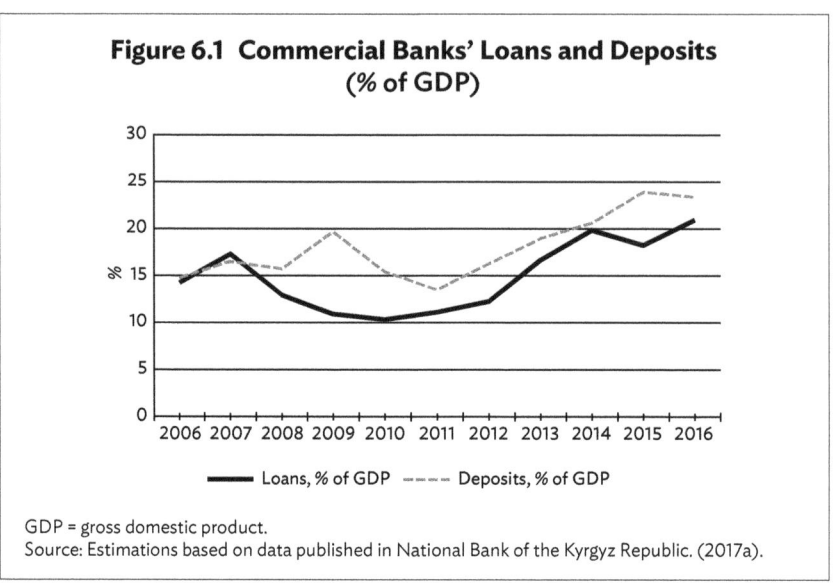

Figure 6.1 Commercial Banks' Loans and Deposits (% of GDP)

GDP = gross domestic product.
Source: Estimations based on data published in National Bank of the Kyrgyz Republic. (2017a).

Vulnerabilities of the Banking Sector

The economic slowdown in 2015–2016, attributed to the entry of the Kyrgyz Republic into the Eurasian Economic Union, affected the banking sector as well. Customs duties for one of the country's main trade partners—the People's Republic of China—increased, the level of international trade turnover dropped, and the amount of remittances decreased substantially, causing a decline in aggregate demand and the purchasing power of the population. Furthermore, the devaluation of the national currency imposed additional risks on the repayment of United States dollar loans and increased the number of nonperforming loans (NPLs). According to the Credit Bureau, NPLs as a share of total bank loans amounted to 8% in 2016.[2] Of the NPLs, 3% were nonperforming within 90 days or more. The share of NPLs is somewhat higher in the trade, construction, and mortgage sectors. NPLs are sensitive to exchange rate movements, reacting with a 1-month lag (IMF 2016). There is also a risk of borrower insolvency: 10% of commercial banks' borrowers have active parallel credits in one or two credit organizations.

---

[2] The Credit Bureau's purpose is to collect, process, and store the credit information of borrowers, their liabilities, and credit history in order to forecast and minimize credit risks in the financial sector.

Dollarization of loans has been declining since 2006, but remains high. As of 2016, the share of dollar credits decreased by 10.5%, and constituted 44.5% of the credit portfolio. After a sharp depreciation of the national currency in 2015 (over 50% within 1 year), borrowers with dollar credits struggled to repay their loans. To ease the burden on the population, the government issued a decree on the conversion of dollar mortgage loans into the national currency. Along with that, a number of de-dollarization initiatives were implemented by the NBKR, including a ban on lending in foreign currency for mortgage and consumer credits, higher reserve requirements for loans in dollars, and the conversion of mortgage loans from dollars to the national currency under a lower exchange rate.

With that, there are a number of vulnerabilities emerging from structural problems in the sector, including:

(i) **High credit concentration.** The role of banks in the Kyrgyz Republic economy is a bit confused. Commercial banks are not viewed as locomotives of the real sector's development; instead, banks follow the most developed sectors to gain the highest profit and maximal clients share. Loans in retail trade, agriculture, and industry constitute 68% of the total credit portfolio, and the concentration is growing (Figure 6.2). Given the fact that key bank clients may be connected, and there is a risk of potential default of the largest borrowers, this may become a source of vulnerabilities for commercial banks in the case of economic external and internal shocks.

(ii) **Lack of long-term finance is a big problem.** For the past 3 years, the weighted average interest rate on loans in national currency has been increasing, which is attributed to the rising costs of credit resources (the weighted average interest rate for loans in national currency increased by 4.4 percentage points to 24.5% in 2016). Commercial banks have a deficiency of long finance; therefore, long-term loans over 3 years constitute only 7% of total loans (10% in 2014). In fact, the dynamics of interest rates on loans correlate with deposit interest rates, meaning that banks lack sufficient resources to satisfy the demand. At the same time, the majority of deposits are demand deposits (about 55%), and only 12% of total deposits have a maturity of over a year (IMF 2016). Banks are in high demand for attracting additional cheap credit resources.

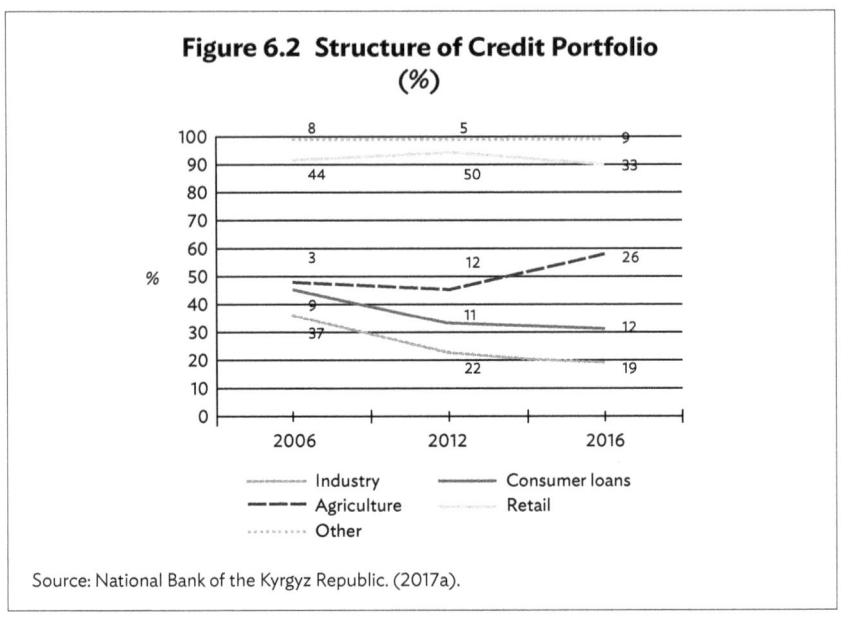

Figure 6.2 Structure of Credit Portfolio (%)

Source: National Bank of the Kyrgyz Republic. (2017a).

6.2.2 Development of Microfinance

The development of the microfinance sector in the Kyrgyz Republic started in the mid-1990s, when international donors supported the majority of MFIs, particularly credit unions. Relatively liberal requirements for MFIs' registration led to the transformation of an informal microfinance sector into formally operating businesses (Davlesov and Ibrayev 2014). Most MFIs have been practicing group lending. According to the estimates, over half of MFIs' credit portfolios are group, collateral-free loans (53%–71% of the total loans).[3] Having restricted access to collateral, women became the majority of MFIs' borrowers—70% on average during 2006–2016. The accessibility of loans, simplified procedures of obtaining them, and branches in rural areas have made microfinance attractive for the low-income rural population.

By 2011, the number of MFIs reached its peak of 651 units, and the share of loans reached 8% of GDP. A number of political events and economic conditions in 2010 caused the NKBR to tighten regulations. As

---

[3] Estimates based on data from the Kyrgyz Stock Exchange. http://www.kse.kg/ru/IndexAndCapitalization (accessed 20 December 2017).

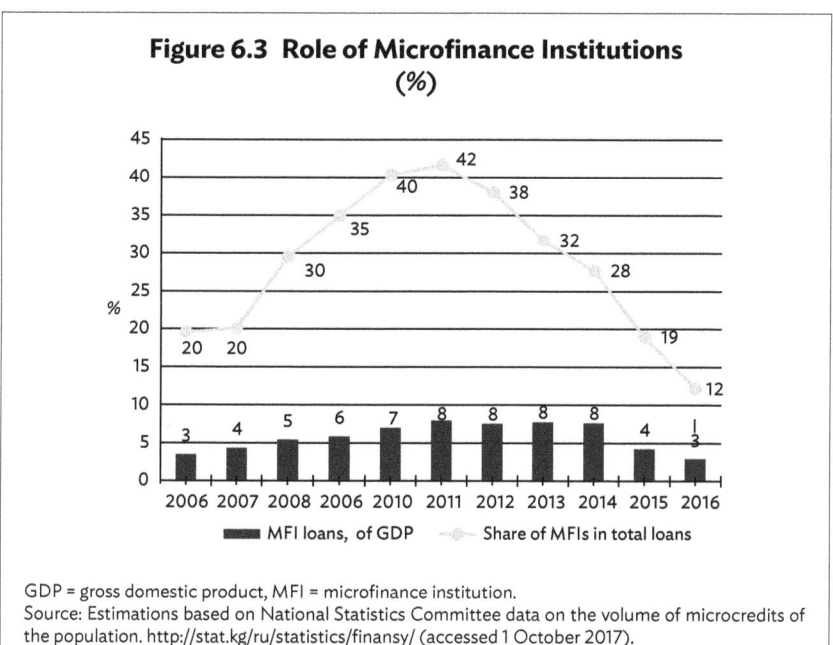

Figure 6.3 Role of Microfinance Institutions (%)

GDP = gross domestic product, MFI = microfinance institution.
Source: Estimations based on National Statistics Committee data on the volume of microcredits of the population. http://stat.kg/ru/statistics/finansy/ (accessed 1 October 2017).

a result, the NBKR withdrew the licenses from 117 MFIs, most of which were small and had few clients (Davlesov and Ibrayev 2014). Furthermore, after 2013, the three largest MFOs started to obtain banking licenses, and the microfinance sector began to shrink. As of 2016, the share of MFO loans to GDP is less than 3%, and the share of total loans is 12% (see Figure 6.3). With the transformation of three MFOs—Bai Tushum, Finca, and Companion—into banks, their clients have also been transformed, leading to a drop of almost 275,000 borrowers in the microfinance sector. The number of credit unions has been declining as well. Since the beginning of the credit union system, the main lender to the system was a company funded by the Asian Development Bank (ADB) project. With the end of the project in 2006, the financial resources of credit unions decreased, as did the number of credit unions. As of 2016, there were 278 operating MFIs, of which 162 are MFOs and 116 are credit unions.

Perspectives of Microfinance Institutions
The major problem of MFIs is access to financial resources. Half of the credit resources of MFIs are loans. Most of the funding comes from international donors, who were co-founders of the largest and oldest MFIs in the Kyrgyz Republic. At the same time, according to

Kyrgyz laws, MFIs may perform only a limited number of activities. For example, until 2013, MFIs were not allowed to lend in foreign currency, and therefore their costs for hedging resources were high. Today, only microfinance companies (6 out of 162) and credit unions are allowed to attract deposits, and to do so, they are required to obtain a license. Therefore, it is not surprising that large microfinance companies with a substantial number of borrowers tend to transform their statuses to banks to access a wider range of financing sources. Experts believe that this tendency will slow, because there are only one or two microfinance companies left that are able to comply with the NBKR requirements of applying for a banking license.

Lack of capital and an absence of free money resources affect the interest rate as well. On top of that, operating costs of MFIs are quite high (20% of the credit portfolio, on average). Consequently, the interest rate on microcredits is higher by an average of 10%. At the end of 2016, the weighted average interest rate of MFIs was 31.42%. On the one hand, borrowers benefit from ongoing transformation. Although the new banks continue to work with their borrowers on previous terms, one former microfinance company reported that it was ready to refinance loans for its borrowers at a reduced rate. On the other hand, it is still hard for banks to compete with MFIs in terms of simplicity of procedures, paperwork, collateral-free loans, and accessibility of credit in remote areas. This means that MFIs and credit unions have room for development in the future. MFIs will cover the niche of microloans, which banks cannot cover while complying with the strict standards of the NBKR; while small MFIs will be transformed into pawnshops, which are not subject to the NBKR's license requirements. Whether or not borrowers will come back to MFIs depends on commercial banks' willingness to cover the microloan segment. Meanwhile, MFIs should concentrate their efforts on attracting new borrowers.

6.2.3 Other Financial Institutions and Markets

Except for the banking and microfinance sectors, other financial institutions play a marginal role. Capital markets (e.g. bonds and securities, government securities, and the insurance market) are very shallow. The stock of government securities accounts for 3% of GDP; banks hold 1.3% of GDP, and institutional investors (social fund and deposit protection agency) hold 1.4% (IMF 2016). In 2016, the trading volume of the stock market reached its peak of Som9.9 billion (Senti 2017), but the market capitalization of the stock market constituted only 4% of GDP in 2017.[4]

---

[4]   Estimates based on data from the Kyrgyz Republic's Stock Exchange. http://www.kse.kg/ru/IndexAndCapitalization (accessed 20 December 2017).

The gradual development of a stock market started in 2008–2009. Since then, the State Service for Financial Market Regulation and Supervision has registered 15 issues of corporate bonds, of which eight are effective. The issuance of corporate bonds allowed domestic companies to attract home investments and, as a result of investing in the stock market, investors were able to improve their financial wellbeing. The investors' interest amounted to Som240 million, of which individuals received 80%.[5]

All corporate bonds at today's bond market are present on a Kyrgyz Stock Exchange listing. The majority of investors in corporate bonds are individuals (68%), followed by companies (25%), and commercial banks (7%). The procedure for buying corporate bonds is very simple—one can just show up at a financial company with one's identification card and become an investor. Unfortunately, public demand for corporate bonds is very low, and there are problems from the supply side as well.

Experts[6] point out several reasons for this. From the investors' perspective, these include low financial literacy, lack of awareness of the bond market, unwillingness to take risks, desire for quick gains, and lack of access to financial companies in the provinces (the majority of financial companies have branches in Bishkek only). From the issuer's side, there is a large shadow economy, and a company must reveal all of its money flows to get into the listing. Based on recent events (2010), many enterprises do not believe in legislation on property rights, and are afraid of illegal corporate raids. Lack of free float at the shares market is also an issue—only 6%–7% of large companies' shares are available for public investors. Furthermore, some of the initiatives of the legislature are controversial. In 2016, legislators proposed to revoke preferential terms on paying income taxes for individuals who buy securities. Fortunately, these amendments were not introduced; otherwise, it would have negatively affected further development, popularization, and promotion of the stock market in the country. Finally, there is a lack of trust in the system as whole.

The insurance market does not play an essential role in the economy. Despite some positive tendencies—the number of insurance companies increased from 12 in 2006 to 19 in 2016—assets of the insurance sector

---

[5] Program to Increase the Financial Literacy of the Population of the Kyrgyz Republic for 2016–2020. Approved by Resolution of the Government of the Kyrgyz Republic No. 319 (15 June 2016).

[6] Interview with representatives of financial companies.

constitute only 0.6% of GDP.[7] The majority of insurance contracts are personal voluntary insurance (i.e. life, medical, and accident insurance). Unfortunately, low income levels, lack of demand, and lack of insurance culture among the population restrict the development of the insurance market. There are also legislation gaps and a lack of investment opportunities for insurance companies and professional actuaries. The government is implementing a number of concepts and strategies for the development of stock and insurance markets, but their sustainable development depends on macroeconomic and social conditions, development of the financial sector as a whole, financial literacy, and a revival of the population's trust. Another problem is that the development of the stock and bonds market in the Kyrgyz Republic is part of the government's activities. The State Service for Financial Market Regulation and Supervision is currently a key state body for developing the stock market and insurance and pension sectors. However, this agency does not have the human or financial capacity to develop the financial market.

6.2.4 Status of Financial Inclusion in the Kyrgyz Republic

Financial inclusion in the Kyrgyz Republic can be assessed mainly by the levels of credit and deposit coverage, the number of bank branches, and the number of ATMs and bank cards per 100,000 adults (see Table 6.1). According to the Credit Bureau,[8] there were 329,151 active commercial borrowers in 2016, and the preliminary data for 2017 indicate that the number of borrowers exceeded 550,000. This constitutes 14% of the adult population, or 13,598 per 100,000 adults. Of total loans, 32% are microloans of up to Som50,000 (approximately $725), 57% are loans of up to Som500,000 (approximately $7,250), and 10% are large credits.

The number of depositors is currently 49,254 per 100,000 adults, but the NBKR's regulations classify payroll money as a deposit, which exaggerates the statistics on the number of deposits. Given the high level of poverty in the Kyrgyz Republic (officially 25.4% in 2016), many people do not have enough income to make savings, and the majority of depositors are from the upper-middle class. Furthermore, as indicated

---

[7] Estimated based on the data published in National Statistical Committee of the Kyrgyz Republic. Report on Activities of Insurance Companies. Statistical publication. Bishkek: National Statistical Committee of the Kyrgyz Republic. http://www.stat.kg/ru/news/o-deyatelnosti-strahovyh-kompanij-kyrgyzskoj-respubliki-v-2010-2014gg/ (accessed 20 September 2017).

[8] Data of the Credit Bureau may differ slightly from that of the National Bank and official statistics. The Credit Bureau collects data from banks and NBFIs registered in the bureau's database. Today all major banks, MFOs, and credit unions are members of the Credit Bureau.

by the Global Findex, the population is reluctant to use formal financial institutions for borrowing and saving (World Bank Group 2018). Around 40% of the adult population had an account at financial institution in 2017, and 6% of these accounts were identified as inactive. Only one-third of the population borrowed any money in the past year, and only 10% of borrowers borrowed from a financial institution. Almost one-fourth of the population saved some money, but only 3% of them saved it at a financial institution (see Table 6.2).

Table 6.1 Status of Financial Inclusion

	2006	2012	2016
Deposits[a] per 100,000 adults	7,075	24,645	49,254[b]
Borrowers per 100,000 adults	NA	NA	13,598[c]
MFO borrowers per 100,000 adults	4,991	14,096	5,968
Women per MFO borrowers	78%	72%	57%
Number of branches per 100,000 adults	5	7	8
Bank cards per 100,000 adults	973	7,210	40,276
ATMs per 100,000 adults	1	12	32
POS terminals per 100,000 adults	14	54	195

MFO = microfinance organization, NA = not applicable, POS = point-of-sale.
[a] The National Bank's regulation classifies payroll money as a deposit, which exaggerates the statistics on the number of deposits.
[b] Estimations based on national statistics.
[c] Preliminary data for 2017.
Note: An adult is a person aged 16 and above.
Sources: Estimations based on data published in National Bank of Kyrgyz Republic. 2017. Report on the Status of the Payment System of the Kyrgyz Republic for the 1st Quarter of 2017. Bishkek: National Bank of the Kyrgyz Republic. http://www.nbkr.kg/index1.jsp?item=98&lang=RUS (accessed 1 October 2017); Statistical reviews of the Credit Bureau. http://www.ishenim.kg/ru/Page/statisticalreviews (accessed 1 October 2017).

Table 6.2 Selected Indicators of Financial Inclusion in the Kyrgyz Republic, Global Findex

Financial Inclusion Indicator	% of those aged 15+
Financial institution account	38.3
No deposit and no withdrawal from a financial institution account	6.1
Saved any money	23.7
Saved at a financial institution	3.0
Borrowed any money	32.2
Borrowed from a financial institution or used a credit card	10.2

Source: World Bank (2018).

Indeed, the research shows that the population prefers to borrow rather than save. The official data show that the ratio of debt to disposable income doubled from 13.2% in 2008 to almost 26% in 2016 (NBKR 2016). On the one hand, given the socioeconomic conditions of the Kyrgyz Republic, a high share of the population simply does not have enough income to save. On the other hand, given the low level of financial literacy and trust in the financial system, many people prefer to keep their money "under the mattress". Given such philosophy, the most popular financial product for households is consumer credit, and the use of other financial products is very low (Figure 6.4).

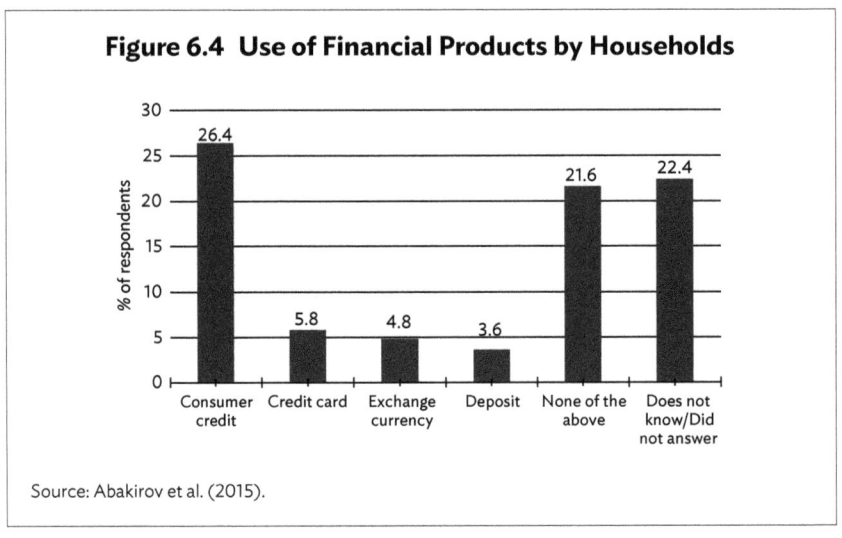

Figure 6.4 Use of Financial Products by Households

Source: Abakirov et al. (2015).

Penetration of bank services is expanding, but remains low. The number of commercial bank branches increased slightly over the past decade, from five in 2006 to eight per 100,000 adults in 2016, which is significantly lower than in the developed world. Furthermore, access to banking services, especially to ATMs and payment terminals in the capital region, is significantly higher than in the other regions (see Table 6.3). Credit is mostly concentrated in big cities; over half of loans and over 80% of deposits are registered in Bishkek, the capital city. Except for bank branches, the number of bank cards, ATMs, and POS terminals is highest in Bishkek. The southern oblasts—Batken, Jalal-Abad, and Osh—have the lowest rates of bank services penetration. Chui oblast also has low access to bank services, but this is explained by its proximity to Bishkek (Bishkek is a part of Chui oblast).

Table 6.3 Penetration of Bank Services

Region	Bank Cards per 100,000 Adults	ATMs per 100,000 Adults	Payment Terminals per 100,000 Adults	Branches per 100,000 Adults
Batken *oblast*	26,105	16	48	8
Jalal-Abad *oblast*	29,891	19	64	7
Osh (and Osh city)	25,891	18	74	6
Issyk-Kul *oblast*	37,969	37	174	13
Naryn *oblast*	48,060	26	69	12
Talas *oblast*	35,217	28	76	11
Chui *oblast*	23,258	17	117	7
Bishkek city	94,064	88	720	9
Kyrgyz Republic	40,276	32	195	8

Note: An oblast is a provincial administrative unit in the Kyrgyz Republic.
Source: Estimations based on data published in National Bank of Kyrgyz Republic. 2017. Report on the Status of the Payment System of the Kyrgyz Republic for the 1st Quarter of 2017. Bishkek: National Bank of Kyrgyz Republic. http://www.nbkr.kg/index1.jsp?item=98&lang=RUS (accessed 1 October 2017).

To increase non-cash payments, a Unified Interbanking Processing Center was established in 2006 as a step toward the creation of a centralized system for non-cash payments, and the first national payment system—Elcart—was introduced. State workers started receiving their wages on payroll cards, and a significant number of bank cards were issued (nearly 40% of bank cards in the country belong to Elcart) (NBKR 2017c). The majority of account holders have two or more cards; due to the expansion of the national system Elcart and Golden Crown, they have one card for national currency accounts and another for foreign currency accounts.

Nevertheless, the problem persists, and the economy of the Kyrgyz Republic remains cash-based. The NBKR is currently attempting to increase the non-cash turnover by obliging the retail trade sector to introduce non-cash payments.[9] However, despite all the measures to introduce non-cash payments, cash withdrawal constitutes 90% of operations with bank cards (over 96% of the volume).

The development of internet banking began in 2012, and in 2013 only 13 of 24 commercial banks provided internet banking services to

---

[9] On Measures of Consumer Protection Rights. Resolution of the Government of the Kyrgyz Republic No. 869 (23 December 2015).

their clients (Khikmatov and Koichueva 2015). At that time, the costs associated with introducing internet banking were quite high, as public awareness of the service was insufficient. As of 2017, almost every bank has its own internet banking services, but few provide services for mobile banking (e.g. internet banking access through mobile applications). According to the Global Findex data, only 5.8% of the adult population uses a mobile phone or internet to access their accounts. The same development patterns are observed with electronic wallets. According to the Union of Banks of the Kyrgyz Republic, commercial banks offer six electronic wallets (including the most popular, Elsom), two of which were only developed in 2017. At the end of 2015 Elsom had almost 285,000 users, or 7% of the adult population.

The Kyrgyz Republic still favors stationary self-service payment terminals. Self-service payment terminals have been established all over the country's regions in shopping centers and small shops, government agencies, and financial institutions. There are 20 licensed providers of self-service payment terminal services, over 4,000 terminals, and nearly 30,000 agents. The volume of operations with self-service terminals in 2016 exceeded Som23 billion and constituted 52% of the non-cash money stock.

6.2.5 Small and Medium-Sized Enterprise Finance

Consistent development of the SME sector is an essential driver of the Kyrgyz Republic's economic development. SMEs stimulate domestic demand, create jobs, and facilitate competition. There are approximately 400,000 SMEs in the Kyrgyz Republic (including individual entrepreneurs). In 2016, SMEs contributed 40.8% of GDP, of which individual entrepreneurs (microbusiness) have the highest share of value added—21.7%. For the past 10 years the number of SMEs has grown on average by 5% annually; however, their contribution to GDP has somewhat declined (see Figure 6.5).

The national statistics do not provide data on the amount of SME loans as a share of total loans. According to some estimates, 20% of small firms and 27% of medium firms use bank loans as a source of business financing (OECD 2013). In the Kyrgyz Republic, every bank has several types of loans and credit lines for small and medium-sized businesses, and many SMEs, especially micro-firms, borrow from MFIs; however, borrowing based on informal deals is fairly common (Neufeld and Earle 2014).

The bank-dominant system makes SMEs more vulnerable to financial shocks because these firms do not have an opportunity to diversify their funding during crises (United Nations 2014). Banks in the

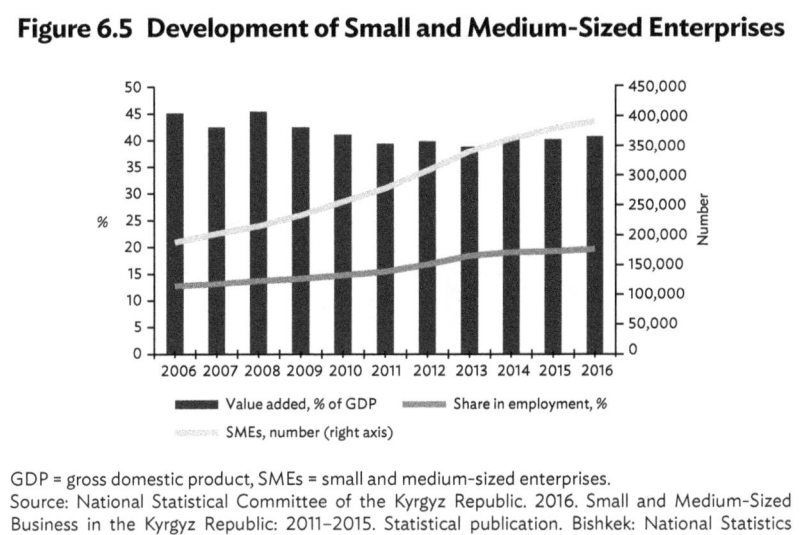

Figure 6.5 Development of Small and Medium-Sized Enterprises

GDP = gross domestic product, SMEs = small and medium-sized enterprises.
Source: National Statistical Committee of the Kyrgyz Republic. 2016. Small and Medium-Sized Business in the Kyrgyz Republic: 2011–2015. Statistical publication. Bishkek: National Statistics Committee. p. 24.

Kyrgyz Republic remain reluctant to lend to small firms due to a higher perceived risk and high transaction costs for the bank. The majority of credit lines are offered for 12 months, and there are loans which can be repaid in 5 years. The most popular credits are express business credits provided for 3 to 18 months that do not exceed $5,000. Almost every commercial bank is required to provide a list of confirmation documents (up to 10) and collateral in the form of real estate, movable property or, rarely, a personal guarantee. At least 44% of businesses need a financing purchase of their input materials, and only 39% of firms indicated that access to finance was not a problem for them (World Bank 2014).

6.2.6 Financial Inclusion of Migrants

For the past 10 years, the inflow of remittances to the Kyrgyz Republic has been increasing (see Figure 6.6), contributing significantly to poverty reduction in the country. During 2003–2007, the increasing amount of remittances contributed to a 15% reduction in absolute poverty in the country (Braunbridge and Kanagaraja 2010). Approximately 1 million migrants work abroad, predominantly in the Russian Federation, and the macroeconomic impact of remittances in the Kyrgyz Republic is very high. The devaluation of the ruble, sanctions, and the recession of the Russian Federation's economy in 2015 led to a decline in migrants'

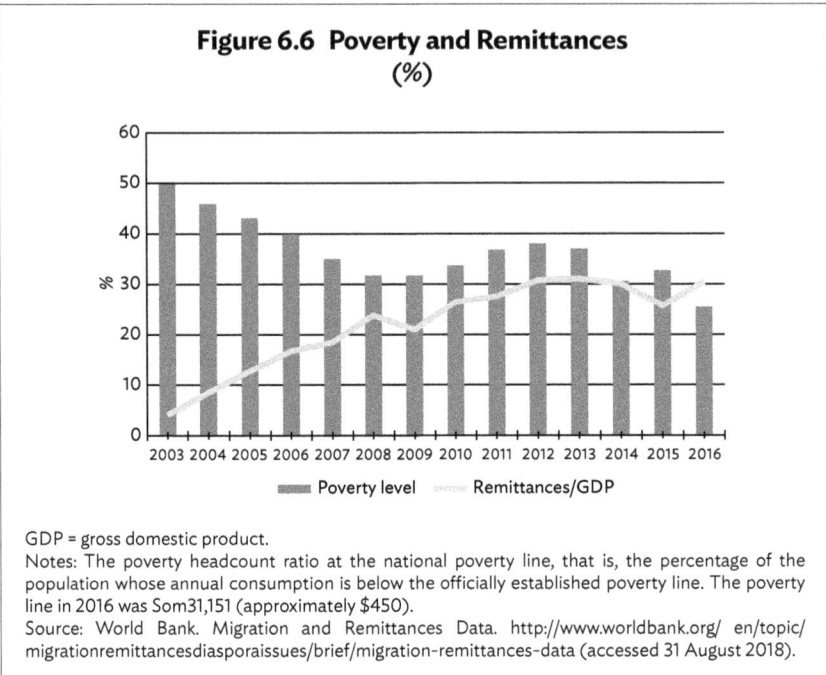

Figure 6.6 Poverty and Remittances (%)

GDP = gross domestic product.
Notes: The poverty headcount ratio at the national poverty line, that is, the percentage of the population whose annual consumption is below the officially established poverty line. The poverty line in 2016 was Som31,151 (approximately $450).
Source: World Bank. Migration and Remittances Data. http://www.worldbank.org/ en/topic/migrationremittancesdiasporaissues/brief/migration-remittances-data (accessed 31 August 2018).

remittances. However, partly because of its membership in the Eurasian Economic Union, the Kyrgyz Republic became the only country in Central Asia whose remittances increased in 2016, reaching $1.99 billion. The amount of remittances as a share of GDP reached 30.5% and the Kyrgyz Republic ranked first in the world in terms of remittances as a share of GDP (World Bank Group 2017).

Some positive anticipated effects from growing remittances are the development of the banking sector, increased deposits and savings, and the growth of internal investments. The extent to which positive effects are realized depends on spending patterns. Given the high poverty rates in the country, most remittances were spent on current consumption needs. Since 2010, spending patterns have changed slightly. According to an NBKR study, households receiving remittances spend 2.7% less on food products (Muktarbekkyzy, Seyitov, and Zhenish 2015). The study also argues that remittance-receiving households tend to spend more on education and healthcare, as well as invest in construction. The study concludes that, under certain assumptions, the investment potential of remittances is realized, but the effect is very small in comparison with other remittance-dependent countries. Other studies suggest that 63% of migrants spend money on consumption, only 2% invest in the education of their family members, and 3% open their own business and make savings (Esipova and Pugliese 2012). There is also a tradition, especially in rural areas, to invest extra income in livestock (Lukashov and Makenbaeva 2011). Overall, migrant families prefer non-deposit forms of savings, such as cars, livestock, or keeping cash "under the mattress." Therefore, the population is reluctant to bring this additional money to the financial sector.

Banks currently lack special financial products for migrants. Given the increasing amounts of remittances, banks are more interested in establishing money transfer systems or providing services on money transfers and earning commission income. Migrants send money via money transfer services without opening an account, and their families receive cash. Only a few banks are trying to introduce special services for migrants in order to attract this money to banks. They are explaining to migrant families the advantages of opening an account and offering them different kinds of deposits either in national currency or rubles. However, these instruments have not become popular among migrants and, given the low propensity to invest remittances, their impact on the development of the financial system is minor.

6.3 Barriers to Financial Inclusion

Opportunities to improve financial inclusion in the Kyrgyz Republic depend on many objective and subjective factors. The current economic and social development patterns, lack of institutional capacity, high level of corruption, lack of political will, and continuity of ongoing reforms limit advancing financial inclusion in the country. The large informal sector is one of the most influential factors—according to surveys, the shadow economy accounts for 40% of GDP. Many entrepreneurs operate in the quasi-formal sector. Not having completely transparent accounts and activities makes it difficult for entrepreneurs to get sufficient finance, and the members of the population that receives informal wages cannot prove their creditworthiness and would therefore rather borrow from pawnshops or relatives.

Low standards of living, poverty, and lack of financial literacy hold back the growth of savings and internal investment opportunities. Current consumption constitutes over 80% of households' expenditures (NBKR 2016). Data suggest that transfers, including migrants' remittances, can account for poverty reduction of 15% on average in rural areas (NSC 2016a). With that, rural households' dependence on remittances imposes risks on those households in the case of a reduction of this source of income. Research suggests that remittances finance over half of total expenditures in rural areas.

Table 6.4 Index of Trust for Government Financial Institutions

	Kyrgyz Republic	Bishkek	
Ministry of Internal Affairs	13.0	3.0	Lowest
Ministry of Finance	19.9	5.8	
Ministry of Economy	19.1	6.0	
State Tax Service	18.5	−0.9	
State Service for Financial Market Regulation and Supervision	19.3	7.4	
Financial Police	12.9	−2.5	
State Information Technology Committee	49.4	−9.9	Highest
State Agency for Youth, Culture, and Sports	48.6	43.6	

Note: The scores take values from −100 to 100.
Source: Statistical data from National Statistical Committee of the Kyrgyz Republic. Index of Trust in the 1st Quarter of 2017. Bishkek: National Statistical Committee of the Kyrgyz Republic. http://stat.kg/ru/indeks-doveriya-naseleniya/ (accessed 8 October 2017).

Another major problem is the population's low level of trust in the financial system. Political instability, high corruption, and poor implementation of laws undermine the population's trust in governance institutions. According to the National Statistics Committee's Index of Trust, state institutions regulating the financial sector have the lowest level of trust after the police service.[10] The Ministry of Finance, Ministry of Economy, and State Service for Financial Market Regulation and Supervision have a score of 19 (out of a maximum of 100) for population trust, while the Financial Police have only 12.9. In Bishkek, where the population has more of a tendency toward critical thinking and higher education, the level of trust is much lower and even shows negative signs (Financial Police and Tax Service). In comparison, other institutions, such as those regulating culture and sports, score 2.5 times higher (Table 6.4).

After the violent power shift in April 2010 (the so-called "revolution"), the expropriation of banks affiliated with the former president led to uncertainty in the banking sector. Due to the instability of the situation, the NBKR took over six commercial banks. Two of them—Asia Universal Bank and Manas Bank—were afterwards nationalized. The interim government claimed that these two banks were affiliated with Maksim

---

[10] The NBKR is not a member of the Government of the Kyrgyz Republic.

Bakiyev, the son of the previous president Kurmanbek Bakiyev, and were engaged in money laundering and criminal activities. At the end of 2010, the government attempted to restructure and restore the assets of Asia Universal Bank but, as this laid a big burden on the budget, a liquidation process was initiated. The government also filed a claim in court about the main shareholder of Manas Bank, a Latvian citizen. He and his team were accused of affiliation with Maksim Bakiyev, money laundering, and other criminal schemes. The arbitrage court proceedings are still ongoing.

The situation in the banking sector had a negative effect on level of trust—many depositors withdrew their money from banks and the demand for bank services declined sharply. The volume of deposits decreased by 14% and the credit portfolio grew by only 3.7% (in contrast, a year later in 2012, the credit portfolio increased by 40%). The decline in deposits was also due to the running of money out of the country by the former president and his affiliates.

Political instability and low levels of trust are not the only factors affecting levels of financial inclusion. SMEs face a substantial number of barriers in getting sufficient finance, including a lack of collateral; 40%–50% of borrowers[11] asking for credit do not get a sufficient amount of lending because they cannot provide the required collateral. Prices for real estate vary in rural areas and the market is unstable, which leads to an inadequate assessment of collateral. Some banks revise collateral when real estate prices fall, and occasionally ask borrowers to pledge additional collateral or repay the loans (IMF 2016). Most collateral is in the form of real estate, which is mostly owned by men. This restricts the access of women to finance.

More obstacles to SME growth have been identified, such as weak regulatory frameworks, few other alternatives for financing start-ups, young SMEs, and lack of long-term finance. In the early growth stage, SMEs attract finance from family and friends, or, for many in the Kyrgyz Republic, from MFIs. Growth-oriented SMEs need long-term finance, while the banking sector provides mostly short-term credit. Entrepreneurs simply do not have enough time to make a profit and start repaying the loans. This indicates a strong need to develop adequate measures to support finance for SMEs.

While the factors listed above are of great importance, the main problem remains a lack of financial knowledge and insufficient knowledge of business processes. Both entrepreneurs and the general population do

---

[11] Concept of Development of Guarantee Funds of the Kyrgyz Republic until 2020. Approved by the Resolution of the Government of the Kyrgyz Republic No. 325 (15 June 2016).

not use bank accounts or non-cash payments. This lowers their credit limits or even leads to rejections. Starting from business-plan preparation, entrepreneurs lack knowledge of how to open, run, and operate a business effectively. They do not know how to manage financial resources or plan costs and revenues, which leads to parallel borrowing.

6.4 Regulation and Consumer Protection

The NBKR is a central bank and a main regulator of financial institutions in the country. The powers and function of the NBKR include (i) the determination and implementation of monetary policy in the Kyrgyz Republic; (ii) the issuance of licenses for all types of banking operations; (iii) the exercise of currency regulation, including issuance of guidelines for foreign currency transactions as well as the purchase, sale, and exchange of foreign currency in accordance with Kyrgyz law; and (iv) the exercise of other functions and powers in accordance with Kyrgyz law.

There are no regulations or targeted programs for financial inclusion in the country. The majority of efforts implemented in this regard are de-centralized; a large number of projects are implemented with donor support. Accessibility of financial products and services depends mainly on the expansion of banking and microfinance sectors subject to the NBKR's regulation and supervision.

Kyrgyz legislation establishes the ground for the operation of banks, MFOs, and other financial institutions. Activities of MFIs are regulated in accordance with the main law on MFOs and a number of supplementary acts, which were adopted with the expansion of microfinance at the beginning of the 2000s. These include the Law on Credit Unions in 1999 and the Law on Microfinance Organizations in 2002. According to the Law on Microfinance Organizations, the term "microcredit" only applies to a loan provided by MFOs. Depending on its scope of activities, an MFO can be registered as a microfinance company, microcredit company, or microcredit agency. A microfinance company is a company licensed by the NBKR that has a right both to provide credit and to attract deposits. Microcredit companies and microcredit agencies have the right to provide credit only, and the difference between them is that a microcredit company has the right to make currency exchange operations and perform factoring and some other retail banking services. Microcredit agencies' operations are mostly limited to providing credit.[12]

---

[12] Law of the Kyrgyz Republic No. 124 (23 July 2002): On Microfinance Organizations in the Kyrgyz Republic.

Since 2010, the NBKR has been strengthening control over MFIs. The first initiative of the NBKR was to consolidate the microfinance market by introducing higher requirements for capital. This was done to reduce number of non-working and small MFOs.

Another issue to control was the fact that MFIs' existing group-lending technique does not take into account the financial position of borrowers. This led to a high rate of parallel borrowing, in which a borrower had two or more loans. MFIs tend to encourage people to apply for more loans, which are usually repaid by obtaining new loans from other MFIs or banks. The NBKR implemented a number of measures to reduce multiple borrowing by focusing on client protection activities, limiting interest rates, and introducing a maximum level of fines (20% of the principal amount) that could be charged to the borrower.

Banking activities are regulated by the Law of the Kyrgyz Republic on the National Bank, Banks and Banking Activities. Starting in 2013, banking legislation has been completely revised and an attempt to introduce a bank code was made. In 2016, the Law on the National Bank was combined with the Law on Banks and Banking Activities into one complete document: the Law on National Bank of the Kyrgyz Republic, Banks and Banking Activities. Under the new law, banking regulations are structured and optimized, control over commercial banks is strengthened, and consumer protection is improved.[13]

The NBKR regulates the interest rates of loans for both commercial banks and MFIs. Under the law, the maximum allowable interest rate on loans is set according to the weighted average nominal interest rate calculated by the NBKR, plus 15%. The weighted average nominal interest rate is a weighted average of interest rates on loans in national and foreign currency of commercial banks, MFOs, and credit unions. The NBKR sets minimal collateral size and maximal ratio of credit payments to borrower's income, among others.

A number of legislative acts regulate the protection of financial consumers' rights. The Deposit Protection Agency under the government, special department for consumer rights protection under the NBKR, and State Service for Financial Market Regulation and Supervision are members of the consumer protection system. There is also a Credit Bureau, which was established in 2003. Its main function is to manage a database of borrowers and their credit history. The Deposit Protection Agency was established in 2009. Participation in the deposit protection system is mandatory for all resident and non-resident commercial banks. Banks' annual contribution to the deposit protection system constitutes 0.2% of their deposit base. In 2013 the level of adequacy

---

[13] Law of the Kyrgyz Republic No. 206 (16 December 2016): On National Bank of the Kyrgyz Republic, Banks and Banking Activities.

Table 6.5 Regulation of Financial Consumers' Rights

	Regulator	Legislation	Functions
Deposits	Deposit Protection Agency under the Government of the Kyrgyz Republic	Law on Deposit Protection (2008)	Guaranteed amount of Som200,000 (approximately $2,900)
Interest rate	NBKR	Law on Limitation of Usury (2013)	Cap: 15% limit over weighted average interest rate, calculated by the NBKR
Credit risk	NBKR	Regulations on assets classification and minimal reserves	Assets must be regularly classified. Reserves are created to cover unexpected expenses.
Collateral		Civil Code, Law on Collateral (2005)	The only dwelling cannot be foreclosed upon court proceedings.
Transparency of information	Department of Rights of Banking and Microfinance Services Consumers under the NBKR (2014) Credit Bureau (2003)	Law on Microfinance Organizations (2002), Order of NBKR on Minimal Requirements for Financial Services Provision and Consumer Complaints (2015), Law on National Bank, Banks and Banking Activities (2016)	Department handles complaints, participates in development of legislation, and interacts with the supervision department. Financial institutions must ensure clear contracts, transparent information; the amount of fines must not exceed 20% of the loan; complaints must be responded to within 10 working days; and the contract must have a list of rights and schedule of all payments, including fines and commissions.
Bonds and securities	Stock Exchange	Law on Stock Market (2009)	Listing
Bank secrecy	National Bank State Service for Financial Market Regulation and Supervision	Law on National Bank, Banks and Banking activities (2016) Law on Counteracting Terrorism Financing and Legalization (2006)	Sets the requirements for bank secrecy disclosure, responsibilities

NBKR = National Bank of the Kyrgyz Republic.
Source: Based on the author's analysis of the Kyrgyz Republic legislation listed here.

of deposit protection system was insufficient, amounting to only 8.5% of the deposit base (Gaidarov, Alamanova, and Kasymov 2015). To increase the coverage of deposit protection, the amount of guaranteed deposits was doubled from Som100,000 to Som200,000 in 2016. Table 6.5 summarizes the activities of financial consumer protection in the Kyrgyz Republic.

The activities of the NBKR with regard to consumer protection are based on new amendments to the Law on National Bank, Banks and Banking Activities and other regulatory acts. These measures are based on client complaints, not on a systematic approach or research and/or analysis of specific services and products. In fact, some experts point out that measures proposed by the NBKR are considered excessive, distorting the market, increasing the complexity of services provided to final consumers, and increasing the number of documents that a client needs to read, understand, and sign.

6.5 Policies to Promote Financial Inclusion

The notion of financial inclusion in the Kyrgyz Republic was introduced by donor organizations. The majority of efforts to promote financial inclusions were implemented with their support. There are no regulations or programs that target financial inclusion in the country. The accessibility of financial products and services depends mainly on the expansion of the banking and microfinance sectors. Nevertheless, the government is implementing a number of sectorial programs aimed at developing the microfinance and banking sectors, increasing the accessibility of financial products, and expanding the coverage of the vulnerable population. Most efforts in this regard are concentrated around improving legislation, simplifying collateral and application procedures, and improving the capacity of local authorities and financial consumer protection. Over the past decade, two strategies for the development of the microfinance sector were implemented (2006–2010, 2011–2015),[14] as well as a number of midterm strategies for the development of the banking sector (2006–2008, 2009–2011).

Facilitating non-cash payments in the Kyrgyz Republic is a priority. The 5-year state program aimed at increasing the share of non-cash payments in the economy has just ended. The program attempted to introduce non-cash payments in favor of the state (taxes, customs duties,

---

[14] Microfinance Development Strategy for 2011–2015. Approved by Resolution of the Government of the Kyrgyz Republic and the National Republic of the Kyrgyz Republic No. 150/40/6 (28 February 2012).

and utility bills), transfers of wages, and payments for goods and services, by population. The program succeeded in terms of infrastructure—the number of payment terminals, POS terminals, and bank branches has grown. Banks have created multiple opportunities for digital payments for utilities, fines, and taxes, among others, including internet and mobile banking. The number of issued bank cards increased by six times. However, as discussed previously, 90% of operations using bank cards are still cash withdrawal. The population prefers to withdraw money from their accounts and pay for their goods and services in cash. This is the same with the development of financial markets. A number of strategies and programs were implemented in financial markets, including the Concept for Stock and Bonds Market Development until 2018, and the Concept for Insurance Market Development for 2013–2017.[15] However, the population rarely invests in stock and bond markets, and buys insurance reluctantly.

Another priority of the government is to boost the provision of cheap access to finance for businesses and individuals. In 2015 the government registered a State Mortgage Company and adopted a government program on affordable dwelling for 2015–2020. The program is aimed at providing cheap mortgages for state workers by subsidizing the mortgage rate. For now, this program is not available to the general population, which has become one of its main criticisms. At the end of 2017 some light but positive impacts were observed: the amount of mortgage loans more than doubled, and mortgage loans as a share of total loans increased from 3% in 2016 to 6% in 2017.

In 2017, the president announced the adoption of the program Taza Koom, which is aimed at the digital transformation of the Kyrgyz economy within the framework of the National Development Strategy 2040. At the same time, the government adopted the supplementary program Forty Steps for 2018–2023. Both initiatives are aimed at establishing an open government, introducing a digital government and institutions, and boosting non-cash payments. It is too soon to assess the results of these initiatives.

Meanwhile, while some gradual improvement in financial inclusivity in the Kyrgyz Republic is observed, the majority of efforts are decentralized and programs are rather fragmented, while financial inclusion requires a complex touch. This indicates that more complex measures are needed to improve the financial literacy of the population and increase the level of their trust in the financial system, as well as to motivate people to keep their savings in financial institutions.

---

[15] The Concept of Development of the Securities Market in the Kyrgyz Republic for the Period until 2018. Approved by the Decree of the Government of the Kyrgyz Republic No. 33 (26 January 2016).

6.5.1 State Support of Small and Medium-sized Enterprises

The government has always recognized the role that SMEs play in the country's development. In the late 1990s, a number of legislative acts were adopted to support the development of SMEs, followed by the Concept for SME Development for 2001–2005, and a state program for entrepreneurship development for 2004–2005. These documents underlined the necessity of reforms aimed at reducing administrative barriers, creating a favorable investment environment, and promoting export opportunities for SMEs. Later, the program underlined that there is a need to consolidate financial resources and integrate SME finance mechanisms into the financial system.

In 2007, the president signed a law on state support of small enterprises. Among other measures, the law laid the foundation for annual implementation of state programs on SME support, and the establishment of the Entrepreneurship Development Fund (EDF), as well as grounds for cheap lending. However, most SME support efforts included the reduction of administrative barriers and simplified taxation regimes.

The majority of efforts for state support of SME finance began in the past 3–4 years. These initiatives included a number of sectorial strategies, the establishment of guarantee funds, and agreement with the Government of the Russian Federation.

6.5.2 Guarantee Funds

To support SMEs, the law Guarantee Funds in the Kyrgyz Republic was signed in 2013.[16] Guarantee funds act as mediators between borrowers and commercial banks to provide guarantees when a borrower does not have sufficient collateral. As of 2016, six guarantee funds were operating in four regions. In 2017, the government established an open joint stock company "Guarantee Fund" with capital formed from the budget (25%) and ADB (75%). The fund has representatives in every region, working with seven commercial banks and the Russian Kyrgyz Development Fund (RKDF). As of September 2017, the Guarantee Fund had issued 140 guarantees, of which 114 were provided to SMEs and 51 to projects run by women. The total amount of lending provided by commercial banks under the guarantees of the fund reached almost Som651 million.

---

[16] Law of the Kyrgyz Republic No. 167 (30 July 2013): On Guarantee Funds in the Kyrgyz Republic.

The majority of entrepreneurs were supported in retail trade (31%), the manufacturing sector (24%), and agriculture (15%) (Guarantee Fund).

Currently guarantee funds in Kyrgyzstan are not well developed due to the lack of trust from commercial banks and the National bank. Activity of the guarantee funds is subject to similar risks of borrowers' insolvency as commercial banks are. Therefore, the National bank has to impose additional restrictions on guarantee funds' activities, which limits the potential of their development.

6.5.3 Russian Kyrgyz Development Fund

At the end of 2014, the RKDF was established through an agreement between the governments of the Russian Federation and the Kyrgyz Republic. The RKDF's mission is to contribute to the economic development of the Kyrgyz Republic by lending in priority sectors at interest rates below market rates, and to contribute to financial sector development by introducing new products and services. The capital of the fund is $500 million and it is formed solely from the resources of the Government of the Russian Federation.

In 2016, the RKDF supported 614 SMEs with a total of $82 million in finance. The fund, via nine commercial banks, has credited SMEs in the agricultural, textile, manufacturing, and transport sectors. Credits were issued at a final rate of 12% for national currency, and 5% for foreign currency, 2.5 times less than the market level (RKDF 2017). According to the development strategy of the fund, it will operate within the framework of Eurasian integration at least up until 2021.

6.5.4 Support of Agricultural Sector

The agricultural sector remains an important employment sector. Although its share of GDP declined from 29% in 2006 to 14% in 2016, it still holds the highest share of the employed population—around 30%. The number of small farmers ("peasant farms") in 2016 reached 414,000, and their contribution to GDP reached 8.4%. In 2013, the government launched a project, Financing the Agricultural Sector (FAS), to support the development of manufacturing agriculture by subsidizing the interest rates on loans provided by commercial banks. The final rate on the loans was 10%.

Currently, the fifth phase of the FAS (FAS 5) is being implemented.[17] Along with 10% lending in the sphere of cattle breeding and plant

---

[17] State Program on Financing of Agriculture-5. Approved by the Resolution of the Government of the Kyrgyz Republic No. 58 (3 February 2017).

growing, FAS 5 provides lending to export-oriented agricultural production at a rate of 6%. According to the Ministry of Finance, 53,590 farmers received loans of a total amount of Som17.1 billion since 2013.

6.5.5 Entrepreneurship Development Fund

The EDF was established in the early 1990s; since then it has been reorganized several times. Today the EDF has the status of a microcredit company with 100% capitalization of the Government of the Kyrgyz Republic. The EDF provides lending to SMEs and farmers, and consumer credits to the population. The fund is a profit-making microcredit company. There are no preferential interest rates and the fund operates by market rules. In 2015, a discussion began about transforming the EDF's status from a microcredit company to the EDF under the government and providing interest-free loans to SMEs. The discussion is ongoing.

6.5.6 Warehouse Receipts and Contract Financing

Alternative collateral instruments, such as warehouse receipts and contract financing, are not common for the Kyrgyz Republic. There have been attempts to introduce contract financing in the agricultural sector's value chain. The project is supported by the donor organizations, and now covers only few chains.

Another pilot project is using warehouse receipts as a form of collateral. Within this pilot, commercial banks agree to use warehouse receipts proving that a farmer has a certain amount of agricultural commodities stored in a warehouse, as collateral for a loan. In March 2018, the President signed a law on Warehouses and Warehouse Receipts, establishing a legal ground for the introduction of this type of collateral.

Table 6.6 summarizes the coverage of major state initiatives providing support for SME financing. Evidently, the coverage is extremely small. So far, less than 6% of SMEs are financed through the Guarantee Fund and RKDF. Meanwhile the total coverage of the FAS 5-year program is 13% of small farmers in the country. Despite government proclamations about the importance of SME development and the law on SME support,[18] there are no centralized efforts that support SME financing. Even though there is a government EDF, it operates as a profit-making MFO. The national strategy for sustainable development for 2013–2017 envisaged measures for

---

[18] Law of the Kyrgyz Republic No. 73 (25 May 2007): On State Support of Small Business.

Table 6.6 Coverage of State Support

	Number of SME Borrowers	Sum, Som million
Guarantee Fund	114	651
Russian Kyrgyz Development Fund	614	5,732.9 ($82 million)
Financing of the agriculture sector: total for 5 years	53,590	17,100
	Share in SMEs	Share in total loans
Guarantee Fund	0.03%	0.60%
Russian Kyrgyz Development Fund	0.16%	5.25%
Financing of the agriculture sector: total for 5 years	12.92%	15.65%

SME = small and medium-sized enterprises.
Source: Author's analysis based on data from the Russian Kyrgyz Development Fund, and Guarantee Fund.

SME development, improving access to long-term loans for women entrepreneurs, and encouraging the development of the program for women's entrepreneurship development. So far, none of these measures have been implemented. The majority of state measures on SME development involved reducing administrative barriers and introducing preferential taxation regimes. Additional efforts are necessary to ensure adequate access to financing resources for SMEs.

6.6 Financial Literacy and Financial Education in the Kyrgyz Republic

Financial literacy is one determinant of success in the development of not only the financial system, but of the country as a whole. Financial literacy contributes to a person's financial wellbeing and affects the level of financial involvement (inclusion) and development of fair and efficient financial institutions that offer suitable and acceptable financial services and consumer protection systems, ensuring protection against financial fraud.[19]

The institutionalization of financial literacy and education has only recently become popular among policy makers. There have been

---

[19] Program to Increase the Financial Literacy of the Population of the Kyrgyz Republic for 2016–2020. Approved by Resolution of the Government of the Kyrgyz Republic No. 319 (15 June 2016).

a number of projects implemented by international organizations and commercial banks aimed at increasing financial literacy among the population and providing financial education. These include the European Bank for Reconstruction and Development, ADB, and World Bank initiatives on increasing financial inclusion starting in 2012, participation in the Global Money Week from 2014, and cooperation with the Organisation for Economic Co-operation and Development on the development of the national strategy for financial education.

6.6.1 Financial Literacy

In 2015, the NBKR conducted a study on financial literacy. The study covered respondents in all regions, representative of levels of income, age, and education. It included a survey on various aspects of financial markets and a test to determine the level of basic financial knowledge.

Overall, the study revealed insufficient level of financial knowledge among the population. Only 19.3% assessed their level of financial knowledge as good, and 40.3% of respondents stated that they did not have any financial knowledge, or possessed a low level of it.

The test scores showed that only 17% of respondents managed to answer two-thirds of the questions correctly, while only 1% gave correct answers to all of the assignments. The study concluded that 22% possess unsatisfactory knowledge, while 12% do not have any knowledge at all. Furthermore, almost half of the population does not keep a record of their expenses and income, 74% borrowed to repay their loans, and almost 40% have financial liabilities, including bank or microfinance credits (Table 6.7).

There is a high correlation between the level of financial literacy and income, which is reasonable. Individuals with low income are deprived of savings and investments, and therefore have fewer incentives to learn

Table 6.7 Basic Results of the Survey on Financial Literacy

	% of Respondents
Do not have any financial knowledge, or have poor knowledge	34
Financial test: 66% of correct answers	17
Do not keep record of income and expenses	45
Borrowed to pay back debt	74
Have debt	39

Source: Abakirov et al. (2015).

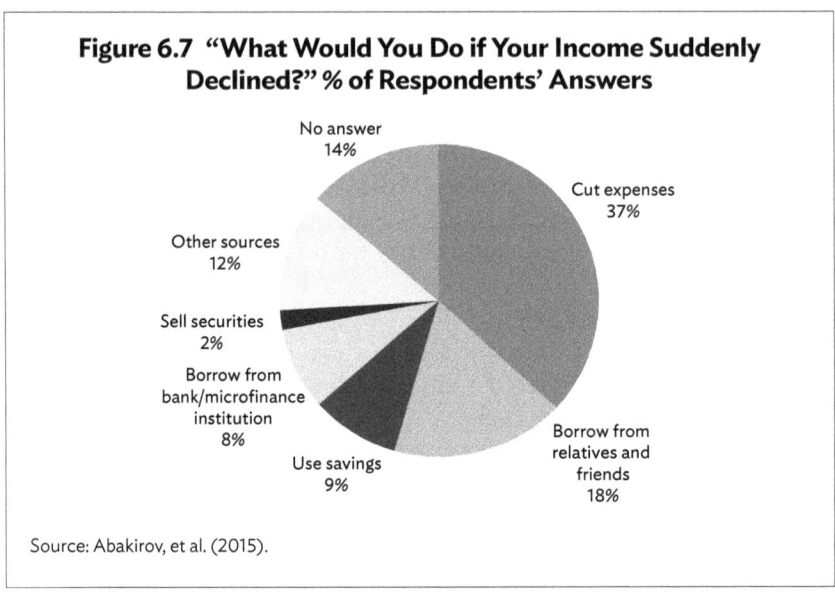

Figure 6.7 "What Would You Do if Your Income Suddenly Declined?" % of Respondents' Answers

Source: Abakirov, et al. (2015).

about financial products. There is also a correlation between financial literacy and level of education in the Kyrgyz Republic. Individuals with a higher level of education are more likely to diversify the use of their money. The level of basic financial knowledge is also higher due to a higher level of general knowledge.

The population also tends to use passive forms of savings (Figure 6.7). Only 11% had a "safety cushion" and are able to afford unexpected expenses.

However, the majority of the population is passive and not interested in obtaining information about financial markets, services, and products. To quote Abakirov et al. (2015), "it feels contradictory, but despite having a low level of financial literacy, the majority of Kyrgyz citizens are not interested in any financial topics." There is a need for complex measures aimed at stimulating and motivating people to exploit the advantages of financial literacy.

6.6.2 Financial Education in the Kyrgyz Republic

Centralized initiatives to provide financial education are new for the Kyrgyz Republic. The first attempt to institutionalize the problem of financial literacy in the Kyrgyz Republic was in the Microfinance Development Strategy for 2011–2015. The strategy emphasized the need for national efforts to improve financial literacy, and for inter-ministerial coordination. In 2016, the Program to Improve Financial Literacy in the Kyrgyz Republic for 2016–2020 was adopted. Before that, several participants of the stock market had attempted to create a saving and investment culture among citizens of the country. A small number of existing financial companies and brokers issued corporate bonds and conducted public relations campaigns to attract investors to market. Further, one of the companies has been systematically organizing training to improve the basic financial knowledge of the population. Commercial banks and MFIs periodically inform their clients about financial products by providing consultations and trainings, and disseminating information materials. In 2015, a former microfinance company published *Basics of Financial Literacy* (Khikmatov and Koichueva 2015). Of course, the coverage, particularly of the rural population, by the private sector's initiatives was rather small, and the effect was not sustainable. In an attempt to increase financial literacy, most projects and initiatives were implemented with the support of international donors.

As a preliminary stage for the implementation of the program,[20] the government established a working group to deal with issues related to financial education. The NBKR launched the specialist financial literacy website, *Monetary ABC*, and carries out various educational activities on financial literacy.

The Program to Improve Financial Literacy targets three pillars: encouraging financial literacy among schoolchildren and youth, encouraging financial literacy among adults, and ensuring equal and full access to financial information and services for all citizens. The program will employ an inter-sectoral approach and will involve multiple governmental bodies, the private sector, and donors.

One of the most important things is the introduction of a new curriculum for schools to inculcate responsible financial behavior at a young age. Financial education centers are planned in every rural district, where trainers will include representatives of local authorities and teachers. Several online instruments will be developed to determine citizens' level of credit stability. A set of activities aimed at increasing trust in financial institutions and an inventory of the legislative and regulatory framework regarding the protection of the rights of financial service consumers are also on the list (see Figure 6.8).

So far, the program is lacking a description of detailed measures and activities. It is not clear from the action plan, for example, how and

---

[20] Program to Increase the Financial Literacy of the Population of the Kyrgyz Republic for 2016–2020. Approved by Resolution of the Government of the Kyrgyz Republic No. 319 (15 June 2016). http://www.gov.kg/?p=77010&lang=ru (accessed 31 August 2017).

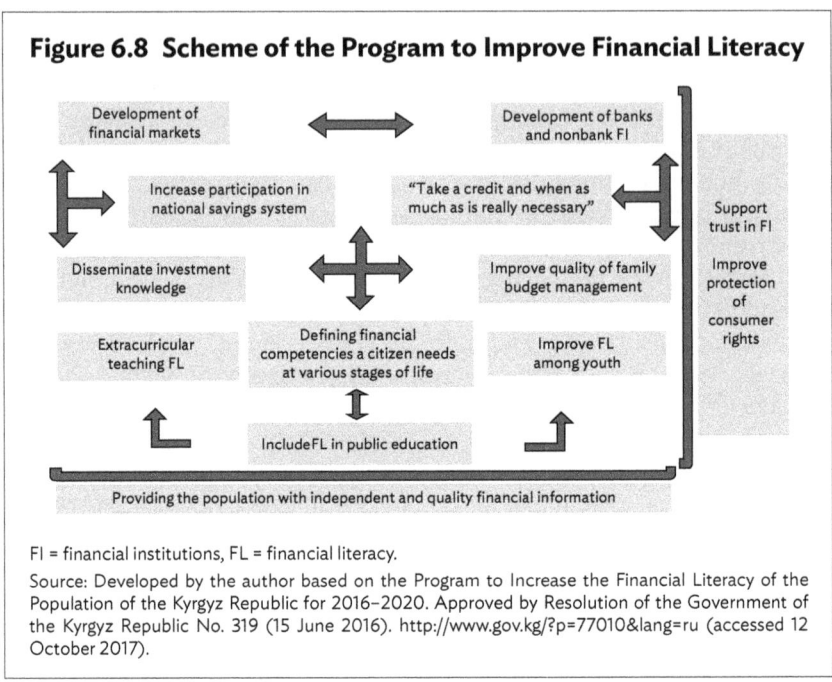

Figure 6.8 Scheme of the Program to Improve Financial Literacy

FI = financial institutions, FL = financial literacy.
Source: Developed by the author based on the Program to Increase the Financial Literacy of the Population of the Kyrgyz Republic for 2016–2020. Approved by Resolution of the Government of the Kyrgyz Republic No. 319 (15 June 2016). http://www.gov.kg/?p=77010&lang=ru (accessed 12 October 2017).

which amendments will be introduced to the legislation to increase consumer protection. It is the same with other measures—the NBKR plans to call for proposals while achieving one program task or another. There is no clear plan to monitor and assess the program's effectiveness. Furthermore, improved financial literacy is not a magic solution for financial and economic development. There should be complex measures, not just to improve financial literacy, but also to raise financial inclusion. The government should initiate a discussion with interested parties and stakeholders to identify a complex strategy and systematic approach toward increasing financial literacy in the Kyrgyz Republic.

6.7 Conclusion and Recommendations

While there has been progress toward financial inclusion in the Kyrgyz Republic, access to financial products and services remains insufficient. Since 2006 the shares of credit and deposit to GDP have increased, but numbers remain low compared to other lower middle-income countries. As banks account for 90% of the financial sector assets, they are now the main providers of financial services to the population. Penetration of bank services is expanding, but access to financial services differs across regions. Credit is mostly concentrated in the capital region. The southern regions have the lowest rates of bank services penetration. The use of mobile banking is rare—research suggests that only slightly over 12% of the population use mobile phones to conduct bank operations. The accessibility of digital services is also limited by restricted access to broadband internet in rural areas.

Up until 2011, the microfinance sector played an important role in providing inclusive finance to the population. Relatively liberal registration requirements for MFIs led to the transformation of the informal microfinance sector into a formally operating business. Having restricted access to collateral, women have become the majority of borrowers from MFIs. The accessibility of loans, simplified procedures for obtaining them, and branches in rural areas have made microfinance attractive for the low-income rural population. After 2010, a number of regulatory measures decreased the number of MFIs, and after 2013, three of the largest microfinance companies obtained banking licenses. As a result, the share of MFO loans dropped from 42% of total loans to 12%, and over half of MFOs' clients have become clients of the banking sector.

With that being said, "real" financial inclusion does not imply lending by banks and MFIs only. Access to other financial institutions, such as insurance companies, pension funds, and the stock and bonds market, is very limited. Financial markets are poorly developed and very shallow: insurance sector assets are less than 1% of GDP, and the volume of operations in the stock market is slightly more than 2% of GDP.

Boosting financial inclusion in the Kyrgyz Republic has many challenges, including current economic and social development patterns, lack of institutional capacity, high level of corruption, lack of political will, and continuity of ongoing reforms. The large informal sector is one of the most influential factors. Not having completely transparent accounts and activities prevents entrepreneurs from getting sufficient finance, and the members of the population that receive informal wages cannot prove their creditworthiness and would rather borrow from pawnshops or relatives.

The development of SME finance has its own bottlenecks. Lack of collateral, lack of long-term credit, and lack of financial knowledge significantly restrict access to finance. Despite the proclaimed importance of the SME sector for economic development, the government does not have any state programs for supporting SME finance. With the Kyrgyz Republic entering the Eurasian Economic Union, the RKDF was established, which now acts as the main provider of cheap credit resources to small and medium businesses.

Financial literacy is an important issue. Many people do not have basic financial knowledge, do not keep records of their cash flows, and do not have formal savings. Over 90% of transactions with bank cards are cash withdrawals. The population prefers to withdraw money from their accounts and pay for their goods and services in cash. The positive anticipated effects from growing remittances, such as the development of the banking sector, increased deposits and savings, and the growth of internal investments have not been realized in the Kyrgyz Republic. Remittances have played a significant role in poverty reduction, but their investment potential is very low. Few banks have financial products oriented toward migrant families. Moreover, the financial behavior of the population is such that it prefers to invest in real estate, livestock, or spend remittances on current consumption.

The Kyrgyz Republic has not implemented any centralized efforts for providing financial education. The majority of initiatives for improving financial literacy were implemented in a disjointed fashion by the private sector and donors. In 2016, the NBKR launched a midterm program on improving financial literacy. However, it is not clear from the program's action plan exactly which measures will be implemented to achieve its objectives.

Financial inclusion should become part of the government's strategy, which should aim to increase the level of public involvement in economic activities, improve access to SME finance, and create opportunities for inclusive growth. The strategy should have a component for spreading the complex knowledge about financial institutions and markets to encourage the population to make formal savings and to invest in financial instruments.

Financial inclusion requires efforts to improve financial literacy at all levels of secondary, graduate, and postgraduate education. At the same time, financial literacy should form part of the day-to-day efforts of all levels of society, media, and financial intermediaries.

Greater financial inclusion can help reduce income inequality and raise the incomes of poor families, which is particularly important for the Kyrgyz Republic given its high poverty and inequality rates (Yoshino and Morgan 2017). Therefore it is necessary to increase the financial inclusion level of migrants and their families. Efforts to provide financial education and promote a culture of formal saving among remittance recipients are necessary to mobilize this huge amount of money.

The government should develop state programs for the development of entrepreneurship among women and for SME development (as proclaimed in the National Sustainable Development Strategy for 2013–2017). Instead of relying on donor funding, the government should find opportunities to establish a state SME-development fund, or transform the existing EDF into a nonprofit company to provide cheap SME finance. Given the importance of collateral issues, it is necessary to consider broad (not just pilot) introduction of alternative collateral instruments. Overall, policies to promote financial inclusion must be in line with the government's proclamation of a path toward the digitization of the economy. Such efforts, along with newly adopted strategic documents, will enhance financial inclusion, reduce cash payments, and boost the financial sector.

References

Abakirov, M. et al. 2015. *Financial Literacy of the Population of the Kyrgyz Republic: Facts and Conclusions*. Bishkek: National Bank of the Kyrgyz Republic.

Braunbridge, M., and S. Kanagaraja. 2010. Remittances and the Macroeconomic Consequences of the Global Economic Crisis in the Kyrgyz Republic and the Republic of Tajikistan. *China and Eurasia Forum Quarterly* 8(4): 5.

Davlesov, A., and N. Ibrayev. 2014. *The Role of the Microfinance Market in the Kyrgyz Republic: Prospects and Threats*. Bishkek: National Institute for Strategic Studies of the Kyrgyz Republic.

Esipova, N., and A. Pugliese. 2012. Labor Migration Doesn't Always Pay Off for FSU Migrants. Gallup. 27 December. https://news.gallup.com/poll/159572/labor-migration-doesn-always-pay-off-fsumigrants.aspx

Gaidarov, R., C. Alamanova, and G. Kasymov. 2015. *Formation and Development of the Deposit Protection System in the Kyrgyz Republic*. Bishkek: Kyrgyz-Russian Slavic University.

Khikmatov, U., and M. Koichueva. 2015. *Fundamentals of Financial Literacy*. Bishkek: Kyrgyz-Russian Slavic University.

International Monetary Fund (IMF). 2016. *Kyrgyz Republic: Selected Issues*. IMF Country Report 16/56. Washington, DC: IMF.

Lukashova, I., and I. Makenbaeva. 2011. *Prospects for the Development of Banking Products for Labor Migrants. Experience of Kyrgyz Republic*. Bishkek: The Organization for Security and Co-operation in Europe Center in Bishkek.

Muktarbekkyzy, A., C. Seyitov, and N. Zhenish. 2015. *Effect of Remittances on the Household Expenditure Structure in the Kyrgyz Republic*. Bishkek: NBKR, Center for Economic Research.

National Bank of the Kyrgyz Republic (NBKR). 2007. *Trends in the Development of the Banking System. The Second Half of 2006*. Bishkek: NBKR. http://www.nbkr.kg/DOC/06082009/000000000001882.pdf.

NBKR. 2016. *Report on the Stability of the Financial Sector of the Kyrgyz Republic*. Bishkek: NBKR. http://www.nbkr.kg/DOC/30062016/000000000042895.pdf (accessed 12 October 2017).

NBKR. 2017a. *Bulletin of the National Bank of the Kyrgyz Republic*. Bishkek: NBKR. http://www.nbkr.kg/index1.jsp?item=137&lang=ENG (accessed 12 October 2017).

NBKR. 2017b. *Report on the Status of the Payment System of the Kyrgyz Republic for the 1st Quarter of 2017*. Bishkek: NBKR. http://www.nbkr.kg/index1.jsp?item=98&lang=RUS (accessed 1 October 2017).

NBKR. 2017c. *Main Directions of the Payment System Development in the Kyrgyz Republic for 2018–2022*. Bishkek: NBKR. http://www.nbkr.kg/DOC/26122017/000000000048958.pdf (accessed 12 October 2017).

National Statistical Committee (NSC) of the Kyrgyz Republic. 2015. *Report on Activities of Insurance Companies*. Statistical Publication. Bishkek: NSC. http://www.stat.kg/ru/news/o-deyatelnosti-strahovyh-kompanij-kyrgyzskoj-respubliki-v-2010-2014gg/ (accessed 20 September 2017).

NSC. 2016a. *Level of Poverty in Kyrgyz Republic*. Bishkek: National Statistical Committee. Bishkek: NSC. http://stat.kg/media/publicationarchive/01b28ef9-9e8c-4d84-9fae-4b1b58b1aa5a.pdf (accessed 20 December 2018).

NSC. 2016b. *Small and Medium-Sized Business in the Kyrgyz Republic: 2011–2015*. Statistical Publication. Bishkek: NSC.

Neufeld, B. M., and J. Earle. 2014. *The Growth of Export-Oriented Small and Medium Enterprises in Afghanistan, Kyrgyz Republic and Tajikistan*. Working Paper 30. Bishkek: University of Central Asia, Institute of Public Policy and Administration.

Organisation for Economic Co-operation and Development (OECD). 2013. *Improving Access to Finance for SMEs in Central Asia through Credit Guarantee Schemes. Private Sector Development Policy Handbook*. Paris: Organisation for Economic Co-operation and Development.

Russian Kyrgyz Development Fund. 2017. *Annual Report 2016*. Bishkek: Start Ltd. http://www.rkdf.org/ru/o_nas/otchety (accessed 30 September 2107).

Senti. 2014. *Financial Market of Kyrgyz Republic—Development Prospects*. Bishkek: Senti. http://www.senti.kg/article/financoviy_rinok_kirgizctana_percpektivi_razvitiya (accessed 1 September 2017).

Statistical Reviews of the Credit Bureau. http://www.ishenim.kg/ru/Page/statisticalreviews (accessed 1 October 2017).

The Guarantee Fund. Information about Issued Guarantees. http://gf.kg/about/informatsiya-po-vydannym-gara/ (accessed 20 December 2017).

United Nations. 2014. *Small and Medium Enterprises Financing*. Bangkok: United Nations Economic and Social Commission for Asia and the Pacific.

United Nations Development Programme (UNDP). 2016. *National Human Development Report: Human Development and Trade in Kyrgyz Republic*. Bishkek: United Nations Development Programme.

World Bank. Migration and Remittances Data. http://www.worldbank.org/en/topic/migrationremittancesdiasporaissues/brief/migration-remittances-data (accessed 31 August 2018).

World Bank. 2013. *Kyrgyz Republic: BEEPS at a Glance* 2013. Bishkek: World Bank.

World Bank. 2017. *Migration and Remittances: Recent Developments and Outlook. Special Topic: Global Compact on Migration.*

World Bank. 2018. *The Little Data Book on Financial Inclusion.* Global Findex. 2018. https://globalfindex.worldbank.org/#data_sec_focus (accessed 10 March 2018).

Yoshino, N., and P. Morgan. 2017. *Financial Inclusion, Regulation, and Education Asian Perspectives.* Tokyo: Asian Development Bank Institute.

7
Tajikistan

Roman Mogilevskii and Shokhboz Asadov

7.1 Introduction

This chapter has been prepared in the framework of the Asian Development Bank (ADB) Institute study on financial inclusion in the countries of Central Asia and the South Caucasus. It covers topics related to financial inclusion and associated matters in the Republic of Tajikistan.

The chapter is organized in the following way: Section 7.2 provides a brief overview of the financial system of Tajikistan. Section 7.3 describes the financial inclusion status of individuals and small and medium-sized enterprises (SMEs). Section 7.4 discusses the key barriers to financial inclusion that exist in Tajikistan. Section 7.5 briefly describes the financial sector's regulatory framework in the country. Sections 7.6 and 7.7 analyze the government policies and financial sector stakeholders' activities aimed at promoting financial inclusion and financial education. Section 7.8 summarizes the key findings and provides recommendations for the development of financial inclusion.

The chapter expresses the views and opinions of its authors only, and does not reflect the position of the ADB Institute, the University of Central Asia, or any other organizations.

7.2 Overview of Financial System

7.2.1 The Economy

The Republic of Tajikistan has a territorial area of 141,400 square kilometers and a population of 8.7 million (2016). The country's gross domestic product (GDP) is $7.0 billion (at the current exchange rate) and GDP per capita is $796 (both values for 2016). In purchasing power parity terms, GDP per capita is 2,980 international dollars, and gross national income (GNI) per capita is 3,500 international dollars (2016).

The significant difference between GDP and GNI values is related to the fact that Tajikistan is one of the most remittance-dependent countries in the world: for several years it was number one in the world in terms of remittances-to-GDP ratio (last time in 2014), but in 2016 it slipped to fourth position due to the decline in remittances from the crisis-affected Russian Federation.

The fall in international energy prices that caused the crisis in the Russian Federation and some other countries in the region had a major spillover effect on the economy and financial sector of Tajikistan. Remittances of labor migrants to Tajikistan fell from $3.7 billion in 2013 and $3.4 billion in 2014 to $2.3 billion in 2015 and $1.9 billion in 2016 (half the 2013 level) (World Bank 2017c). This required a major devaluation of the Tajik currency, the somoni, from TJS4.77 per United States (US) dollar at the end of 2013 to TJS7.87 per dollar at the end of 2016. This created serious challenges for all financial and nonfinancial institutions, which had a mismatch between assets and liabilities denominated in national and foreign currencies.

The key sectors of the economy of Tajikistan are agriculture and industry (of which a single enterprise—the aluminum melter Talco—is a large part); construction and mostly nontradable services are also large sectors of the economy (Figure 7.1). A very large part of the economy is informal (especially in agriculture, retail trade, and consumer services) and based on cash settlements. This economic structure, of course, has

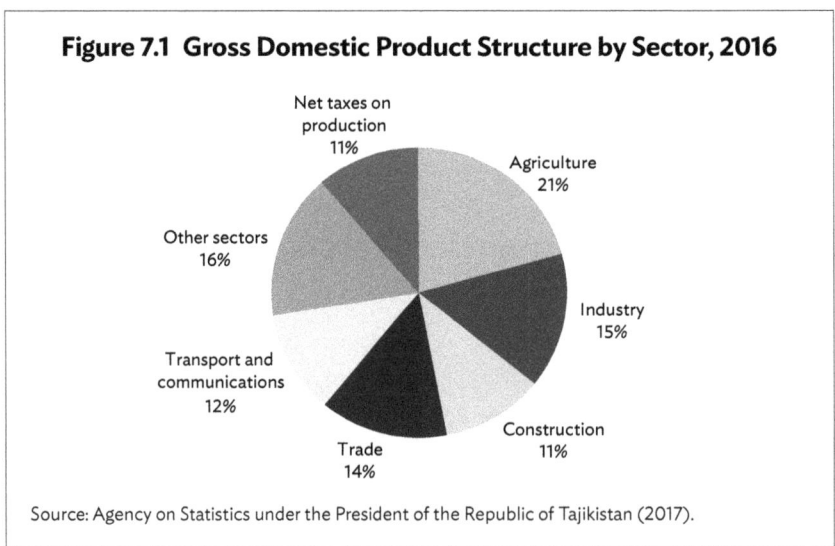

Figure 7.1 Gross Domestic Product Structure by Sector, 2016

Net taxes on production 11%
Agriculture 21%
Other sectors 16%
Industry 15%
Transport and communications 12%
Trade 14%
Construction 11%

Source: Agency on Statistics under the President of the Republic of Tajikistan (2017).

major implications for financial sector development and objectively limits its depth and pace of development. As already mentioned above, Tajikistan is a labor-migrant-sending country; the total number of labor migrants is not known, but available estimates have in the order of 1 million people (± several 100,000) or some 30%–40 % of the country's total labor force.

The relatively low level of GDP per capita, with the population having little ability to save, results in a rather small national savings rate of 11.4% of GDP in 2013 (World Development Indicators)—perhaps the lowest in Central Asia and the South Caucasus.

7.2.2 Key Financial Development Indicators

As of 30 June 2017, the credit system of Tajikistan comprises the National Bank of Tajikistan (NBT), the regulatory and supervisory body; 16 commercial banks; and 80 microfinance organizations (MFOs) (NBT 2017a). Of these banks, one belongs to the state, five are private and domestic, and 10 have foreign participation in the statutory capital. The microfinance institutions (MFIs) include 34 microcredit deposit organizations (MDOs), 13 microcredit organizations (MCOs), and 33 microcredit funds (MCFs).

The commercial banks have 274 branches (compared to 355 at the end of 2015) and 1,122 banking service centers. Until the end of 2015, there were also currency exchange points and money transfer points. In December 2015, the board of the NBT issued instructions on the procedure for carrying out foreign currency transactions, which required the closure of all currency-exchange points in the country. All foreign currency transactions, including currency exchange, must be carried out at banking service centers, regional bank branches, and head offices of lending agencies. The NBT ordered the closure of private currency-exchange points on the grounds that some employees of currency-exchange points overvalued foreign currency.

The level of deposits in the financial system of Tajikistan is relatively low; it had been growing slowly until 2015 (Figure 7.2), but somewhat declined in 2016. About two-thirds of these deposits are denominated in foreign currency, and 96% are kept in commercial banks; some 60% of them belong to individuals, with the rest being owned by legal entities. The dollarization of deposits is gradually declining, from 68% of total deposits in 2013 to 62% in 2016 (NBT 2017a).

Similar to deposits, the amount of loans issued by commercial banks was growing until 2015, but it declined in 2016 (Figure 7.3). This dynamic of both deposits and loans is related to the negative shock affecting the financial system as a result of the fall in remittances and associated devaluation of the somoni.

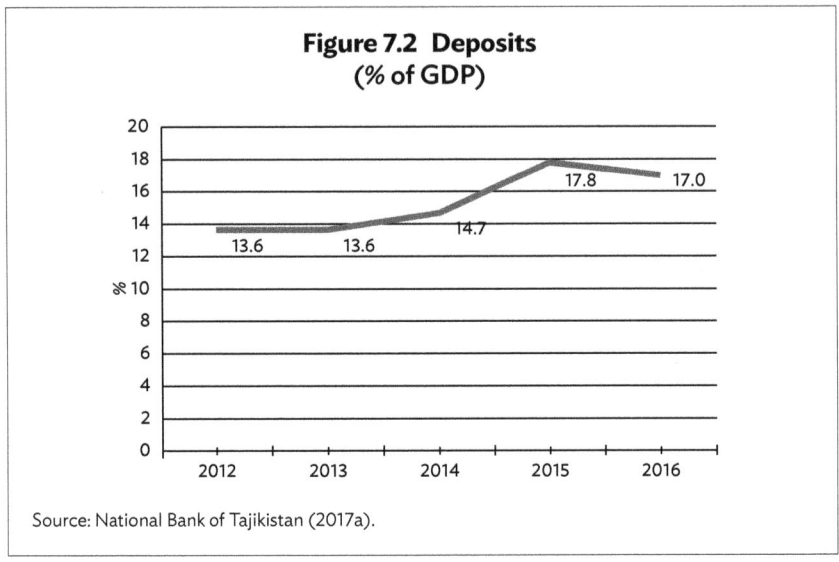

Figure 7.2 Deposits (% of GDP)

Source: National Bank of Tajikistan (2017a).

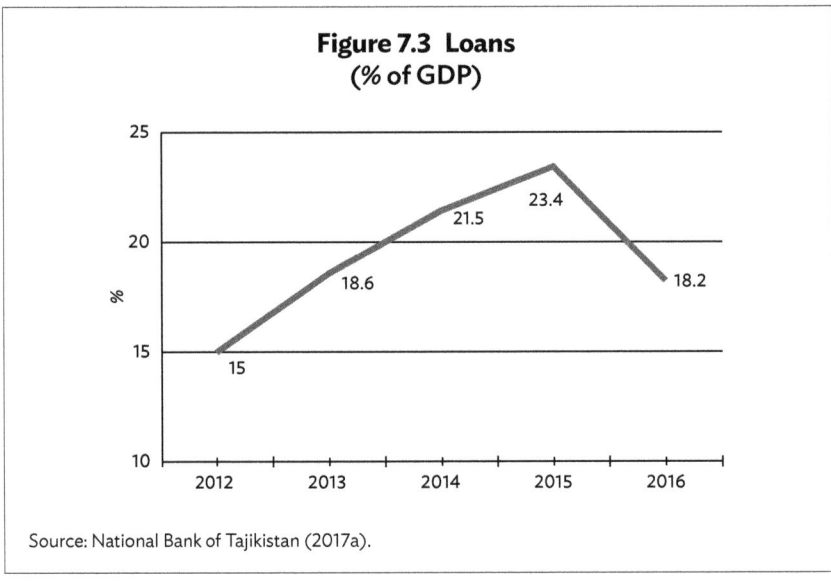

Figure 7.3 Loans (% of GDP)

Source: National Bank of Tajikistan (2017a).

The loans are mostly denominated in foreign currency (62% in 2016). The role of MFOs in credit activity is higher than in deposits (17% of the total amount of loans versus 4% of the total amount of deposits). The main types of borrowers are private enterprises, individual entrepreneurs, and individuals; however, in 2016, their joint share in the total loan amount contracted, so the share of loans to state-owned enterprises somewhat increased (from 14% in 2015 to 17% in 2016). The key sector of the economy receiving loans is industry (27% of the total amount of loans), with agriculture, construction, foreign trade, and personal consumption also being large loan recipients.

As of 2017, the six largest banks accounted for 81% of total bank assets, and the majority of foreign-owned banks accounted for just 10.5%. Two commercial banks have been announced as bankrupt, and their licenses were revoked by the NBT. In the microfinance sector, the five largest MFIs accounted for around 70% of total assets, which is comparable with the share of banks in the SME sector.

Due to the crisis, the quality of loans has deteriorated dramatically (Figure 7.4). Standard banking loans constitute just one-third of all loans, while different nonperforming loans (NPLs) account for some 66% of the total amount of loans. These NPLs have been mostly issued to large borrowers—industrial and other enterprises. The credit portfolio of MFIs is much healthier, with NPLs accounting for 16% of the total amount of loans issued by these institutions.

The size of loans also varies according to the types of credit organizations. For instance, MCFs can provide up to TJS250,000 ($28,375) to individuals and TJS350,000 ($39,727) to legal entities; MCOs can provide up to TJS250,000 ($28,375) to individuals and TJS400,000 ($45,402) to legal entities; MDOs can provide up to

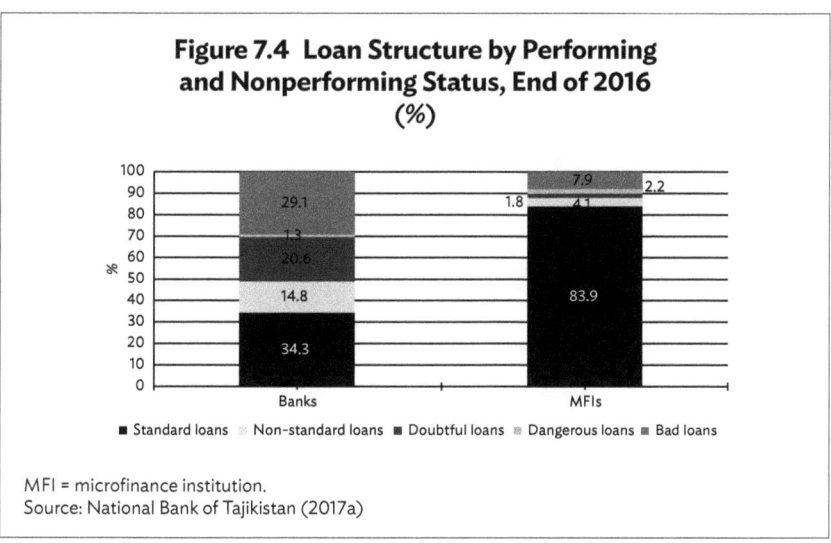

Figure 7.4 Loan Structure by Performing and Nonperforming Status, End of 2016 (%)

MFI = microfinance institution.
Source: National Bank of Tajikistan (2017a)

TJS250,000 ($28,375) to individuals and TJS500,000 ($56,753) to legal entities; and commercial banks can provide credit of up to 20% of regulatory capital (NBT 2012, 2017a, 2017b.) As of mid-2017, the credit organizations of Tajikistan had provided TJS9,561 million ($1,085 million) in loans (NBT 2017a). MFOs can provide loans of up to $3,000 to individuals without collateral; over this amount, they require a warrantor or collateral. For SMEs, this limitation starts from $500. The banks provide credit to individuals and SMEs for up to $500 without collateral or a warrantor; over that amount, collateral and a warranty are needed.

The average annual interest rates on bank loans are 30.04% in local currency and 20.80% in foreign currency (NBT 2017a). For MFIs, these rates are 38% in local currency and 28% in foreign currency (Association of Microfinance Organizations of Tajikistan [AMFOT] 2016). The number of borrowers from MFIs and banks at the end of 2016 is shown in Figure 7.5.

Interest rates are high in Tajikistan because most of the MFIs' resources are attracted from abroad; hedging of most investments is conducted by the Currency Exchange Fund (The Currency Exchange Fund 2017), which considers Tajikistan to be a high-risk economy. The current rate of hedging for Tajikistan is 15.3%, down from 33.0% in 2009. From the beginning of 2017, the somoni devalued 10% against the dollar (NBT 2017b), which confirms the high-risk perception. About 60% of the credit portfolio of MFIs are foreign investments.

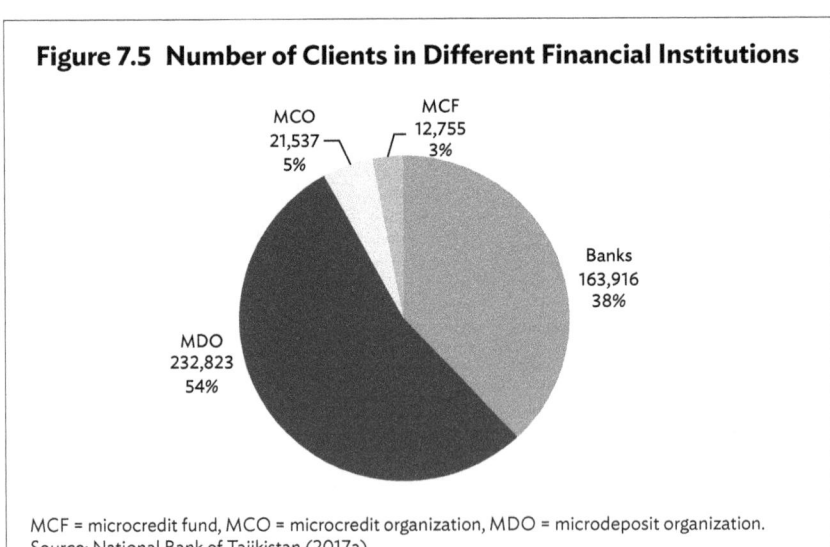

Figure 7.5 Number of Clients in Different Financial Institutions

MCF = microcredit fund, MCO = microcredit organization, MDO = microdeposit organization.
Source: National Bank of Tajikistan (2017a).

7.2.3 Cards

Currently, credit institutions issue payment cards for the national payment system Korti Milli, the international payment systems Visa and Mastercard, co-branding cards for the payment systems UnionPay and Korti Milli, and payment cards for local systems of credit institutions. As of 1 July 2017, credit institutions had issued 1.69 million payment cards, 8.1% more than a year ago. Among these cards, the share of Korti Milli reached 80.5%, Visa and MasterCard 14.3%, payment cards for local credit institutions 4.7%, and UnionPay-Korti Milli 0.5% (Figure 7.6).

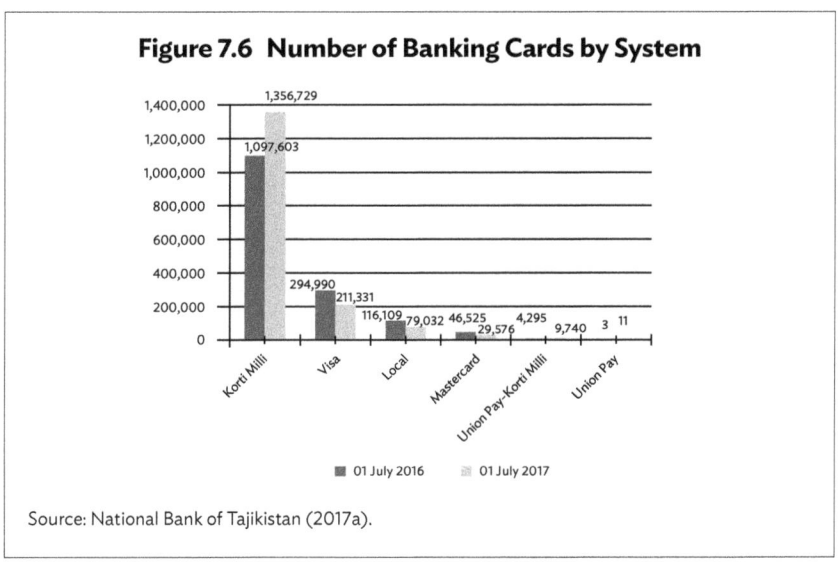

Figure 7.6 Number of Banking Cards by System

Source: National Bank of Tajikistan (2017a).

The majority of payment cards in circulation have been issued by the state savings bank Tajikistan Amonatbank, which serves pensioners. The total share of cards issued by Amonatbank is 75.9%. In 2009, Tajikistan introduced an electronic system of payments for pensioners; this was one of the first experiences with such a system in Central Asia. The Ministry of Labor and Social Protection of the Population and Amonatbank later decided to (i) reduce the average time for releasing funds from the State Agency for Social Insurance and Pensions to beneficiaries, (ii) improve the quality of services provided to pensioners, (iii) reduce the costs of administering pension payments and eliminate opportunities for fraud and misuse of funds through a secure channel of automation, and (iv) promote financial inclusion. By 2012, the electronic system had been implemented in 15 out of 68 districts, covering roughly 192,000 of Tajikistan's 596,000 pensioners. Districts were selected for the new system according to the local availability of financial infrastructure and a stable electricity supply to ensure that pensioners would have a sufficient number of points where they could access their funds (ADB 2013).

The cards are used mostly for cash withdrawals, although the amount of payments with cards is increasing (Figure 7.7). The number of ATMs did not grow between 1 July 2016 and 1 July 2017, while the number of point-of-sale (POS) terminals increased (Figure 7.8).

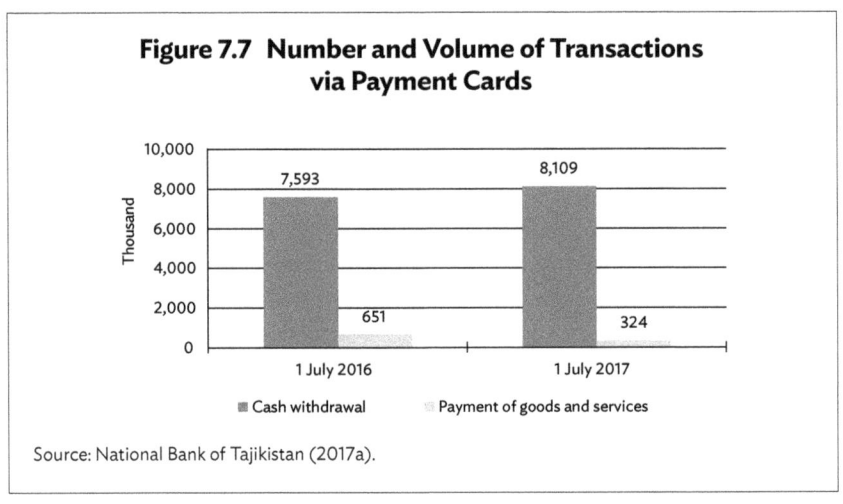

Figure 7.7 Number and Volume of Transactions via Payment Cards

Source: National Bank of Tajikistan (2017a).

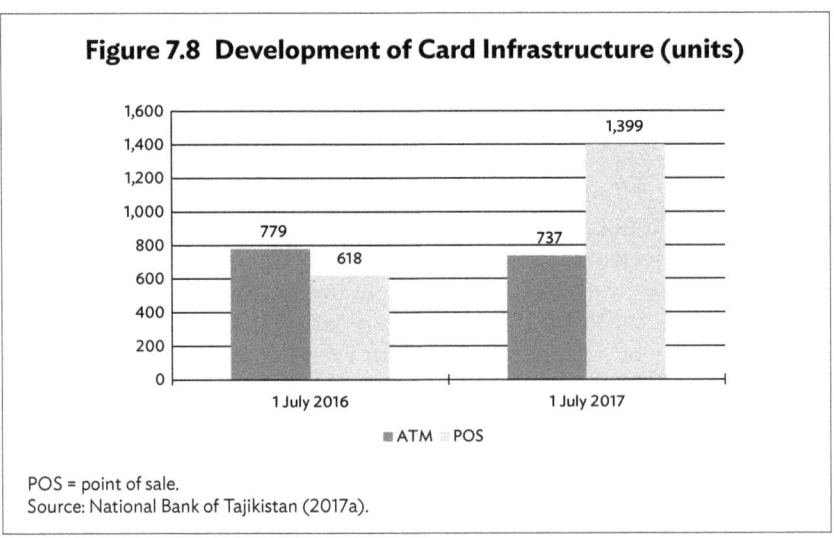

Figure 7.8 Development of Card Infrastructure (units)

POS = point of sale.
Source: National Bank of Tajikistan (2017a).

The number of POS terminals and the volume of transactions through them will continue to grow, as several large state-owned utility companies, including Barqi Tojik (power supply), Vodokanal (water), and Tajik Telecom (fixed-line telephone operator), focus on electronic payments via POS terminals throughout the country.

7.2.4 Insurance

Insurance companies in Tajikistan conduct their activity based on the Law on Insurance Activity (No. 681, in the new edition, 29 December 2010). There are 21 insurance companies registered in Tajikistan. Previously, insurance companies were supervised by the State Insurance Supervisory Service of the Ministry of Finance; on 1 January 2017, in accordance with the Order of the President of the Republic of Tajikistan No. 851 dated 13 March 2017, the supervisory role was transferred to the NBT. Based on the law, the minimum capital requirement for insurance companies is TJS500,000 ($56,753). Of the 21 insurance companies, two are state-owned and one is foreign-owned. The total assets of these companies were TJS197.2 million in 2014 (World Bank and International Monetary Fund 2015). The sector collected TJS138 million (0.34% of GDP) in 2013 in insurance premiums. Two state-owned companies mostly concentrate on vehicle insurance, which is mandatory in Tajikistan. There are a few reasons why the population hesitates to cooperate with them. Firstly, individuals and SMEs do not trust these companies, because there have been situations where costs have not been covered in insurance cases. The costs of their services are also very high. Obtaining information about the costs of services of insurance companies is not a simple process (the companies do not provide this information online), which is a barrier for individuals and SMEs in gaining access to insurance services. Moreover, the sector suffers from the absence of actuaries, underwriters, and loss adjustors.

Currently, reinsurance services are provided by foreign insurance companies. Recently, the NBT informed local insurance companies about the plan to establish a new local reinsurance company with initial capital of TJS5 million ($576,536). As this company will be too small to cover the claims of large clients, the insurance companies may have issues with reinsurance after this plan has been implemented.

7.3 Status of Financial Inclusion for Individuals and Small and Medium-Sized Enterprises

7.3.1 Accounts

There are no complications in opening an account at credit organizations in Tajikistan. Servicing accounts is based on the Law on Banking Activities and Law on Microfinance Organizations (NBT 2017d), which allow commercial banks and MDOs to service banking accounts. Data on access to different financial instruments in Tajikistan are provided in Table 7.1, which shows the results of the Global Findex Study 2017 (World Bank 2018).

Table 7.1 Financial Inclusion Indicators, 2017

	Tajikistan	Europe and Central Asia
Account (% aged 15+)		
All adults	47.0	65.3
All adults, 2011	2.5	43.3
Women	42.1	62.5
Poorest 40%	38.5	56.3
Rural	46.3	61.7
Young adults (% aged 15–24)	49.3	50.1
Debit card (% aged 15+)		
Has debit card	15.9	51.1
Has debit card, 2011	1.8	36.4
Use of account in the past year (% aged 15+)		
Used an account at a financial institution to pay utility bills	21.7	23.3
Used an account to receive government transfers	8.4	12.5
Used an account to receive wages	13.7	30.8
Other digital payments in the past year (% aged 15+)		
Used a debit or credit card to make payments	10.8	38.5
Used the internet to pay bills or buy things	12.8	30.6
Domestic remittances in the past year (% aged 15+)		

continued on next page

Table 7.1 continued

	Tajikistan	Europe and Central Asia
Sent remittances	19.5	19.2
Received remittances	20.9	18.4
Received remittances through a financial institution (% of recipients)	45.3	43.0
Received remittances through a mobile phone (% of recipients)	10.8	21.3
Received remittances through a money transfer service (% of recipients)	8.1	6.8
Saving in the past year (% aged 15+)		
Saved at a financial institution	11.3	14.4
Saved at a financial institution, 2011	0.3	6.9
Saved using a savings club or a person outside the family	8.8	5.0
Saved any money	32.8	37.0
Saved for old age	11.2	15.0
Saved to start, operate, or expand a farm or business	13.2	8.1
Credit in the past year (% aged 15+)		
Borrowed from a financial institution	14.7	12.8
Borrowed from a financial institution, 2011	4.8	7.8
Borrowed from family or friends	21.6	24.5
Borrowed from an informal savings club	3.0	1.8
Borrowed any money	33.7	44.0
Borrowed to start, operate, or expand a farm or business	12.6	11.6
Borrowed for health or medical purposes	7.2	8.5
Outstanding mortgage	12.6	11.6

Source: World Bank (2018).

According to these data, as of 2017, 47.0% of the population aged over 15 had a bank account (2.5% in 2011). According to the NBT statistics, at the end of June 2017 the number of individual accounts reached 3.28 million (there are 5.8 million people aged over 15 in the country). Even considering the fact that one individual can have more than one account, the comparison of the Findex data with official statistics hints at a dramatic increase in the number of accounts between 2011 and 2017. This increase is mostly due to the Government of Tajikistan's efforts to transfer pensions and other payments to individuals to the banking system.

A few banks and large MFOs provide internet and mobile banking services; as of 30 June 2017, there were 67,700 online managed accounts and 59,300 accounts accessible from mobile devices (NBT 2017a).

The dynamics of banking service penetration is presented in Figure 7.9. While the number of banking accounts is growing fast, the number of borrowers from MFOs went down, with the number of bank

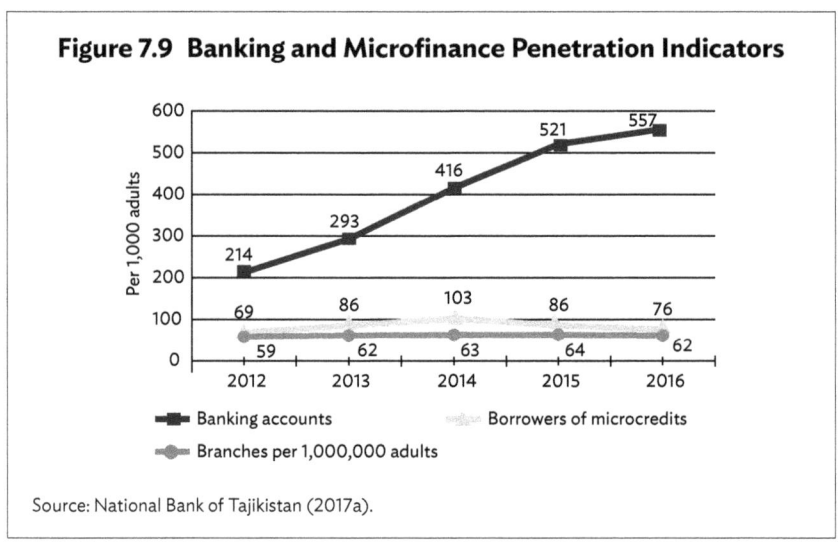

Figure 7.9 Banking and Microfinance Penetration Indicators

Source: National Bank of Tajikistan (2017a).

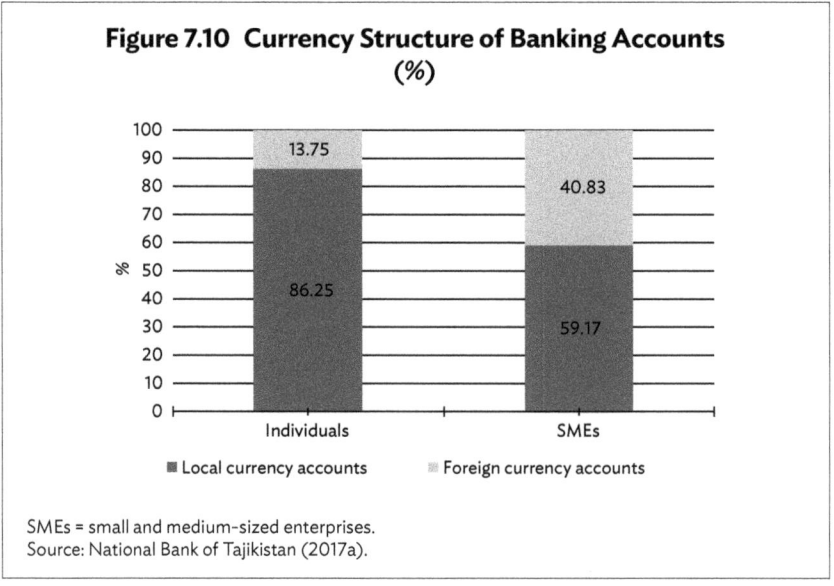

Figure 7.10 Currency Structure of Banking Accounts (%)

SMEs = small and medium-sized enterprises.
Source: National Bank of Tajikistan (2017a).

branches remaining more or less stable over the last 5 years. The decline in the number of borrowers can be attributed to the financial crisis associated with the fall in remittances and devaluation of the national currency (see Section 7.2.1).

Individuals' banking accounts are mostly denominated in somoni (Figure 7.10), while SMEs use foreign currency accounts more frequently than individuals.

In Tajikistan, only legal entities can use a checkbook, and checks are only used for cash-out operations at banks. No businesses, grocery stores, or shops accept checks instead of cash.

7.3.2 Pensions

Pensions are provided based on the Law about Pension Support of Population of Republic of Tajikistan (adopted 25 June 1993). In Tajikistan, retirement compensation is paid from the Pension Fund. As of the end of 2016, there were 642,000 pensioners (7.6% of the population), and the average monthly pension was TJS274 ($35 or 23% of the average wage in the country). The retirement age is 63 for males (with a registered working history of at least 25 years) and 58 for females (with a registered working history of not less than 20 years). According to the Law on State Social Insurance (1997), 1% of the deductions from the gross salaries of employees are forwarded to the Pension Fund.

The transition to electronic payments to pensioners has had positive effects, especially on perceived convenience and wait times. However, not all pensioners have benefited equally from the change in the payment system. In particular, rural pensioners have faced challenges and experienced increased wait and travel times. Although all pensioners have been moved to an electronic system of payment through the state-owned bank, not all pensioners know how to use this system and face long lines with only one ATM at each banking branch. Sometimes ATMs are out of money, and the pension payments often arrive late.

The Law about Pension Support of Population of Republic of Tajikistan provides no room for private pension funds. To make any changes in this area, the government first needs to develop a legal base.

7.3.3 Remittances

As noted above, Tajikistan depends heavily on remittances. Some 66% of remittances come through commercial banks, and the rest through the largest MDOs. Remittances are closely connected with loans, since households use loans as a source of cash until they receive the next money transfer from abroad. According to a survey conducted in 24 regions of Tajikistan, 80% of remittances are transferred from the

Russian Federation, 7% from Kazakhstan, 3% from Belarus, and 10% from other countries. As most of the remittances come from the Russian Federation, the recent devaluation of the Russian ruble against the US dollar and somoni decreased the amount of remittances received by households. However, according to the NBT's balance of payments (NBT 2017a), the amount of remittances received by the country in the first half of 2017 increased by 25% compared to the same period in 2016. This is due to the nominal appreciation of the Russian ruble and the return of the Russian Federation economy to positive growth rates.

At the beginning of 2017, the NBT ordered all credit organizations to pay all Russian ruble incoming transfers in local currency using the official NBT exchange rate (which coincides with the market rate).

7.3.4 Inclusion-Related Financial Products and Issues

Based on market demand and the availability of financial sources, credit organizations are trying to decrease interest rates and offer products and services based on new technologies, including internet banking and mobile banking. Only a few banks and large MFIs are providing these services and the products are not yet well developed. For instance, in some countries, including the Russian Federation, credit organizations cooperate with mobile operators to improve the accessibility of financial services to enable clients to obtain credit through a mobile operator system that would transfer the loan amount to the client's balance, and the client can cash out the balance at the mobile operator's branches. Deutsche Gesellschaft für Internationale Zusammenarbeit proposed that this scheme be introduced in Tajikistan in 2010, but the NBT did not accept it, as this would imply involving mobile operators in banking activity, for which they need a banking license. The issue remains unresolved.

In 2014, the International Finance Corporation (IFC) conducted a survey to help understand the existing channels for delivering mobile banking services (Table 7.2) (IFC 2014). It follows from the data that most of the mobile transactions are related to mobile top-up operations. Most of the respondents participating in the survey provided their own description of the potential uses of mobile banking services (Figure 7.11).

Currently, very few types of operations are available online; the software used by banks and MFIs does not allow some operations to be implemented. For instance, the foreign exchange operations of the First MicroFinance Bank should be done in both mobile and paper-based form. Orienbank requires more than a week to transfer resources. Bank Eskhata offers an option for money transfer that requires opening an account and transferring resources to this account via any money transfer system. Payment service providers (PSPs) work through cash-in terminals and an agent network, and they use mobile phone applications and computer software for payment processing. Some 60% of PSP agents are in rural areas, and 80% of transactions are for airtime top-up. Mobile money deployment exists, but services are limited (mostly focused on e-wallets). Several of the largest MFIs (Imon, Humo, Arvand, and Finca) have started using PSP terminals for loan repayment, and some MFIs (e.g. Humo) have launched mobile applications accessible via the App Store or PlayMarket, thereby facilitating person-to-business and person-to-person money transfer transactions.

Table 7.2 Use of Mobile Payment Services

Services	Service Channels	Market Segment	Current Scope of Activities
Payments for a wide range of services (mobile phone credit, internet service provider, utilities, microloans, social networks, online games, betting, and electronic wallets) in the Russian Federation	Terminals and agents equipped with a computer or mobile phone; directly from a mobile wallet (Expresspay)	P2B (in theory Expresspay also allows P2P)	Mostly mobile top-up and internet service payments; few mobile wallets held by individual customers
Repayment of loans	Mostly terminals and some agents (only Arvand)	P2B	Still limited, maximum 20% of repayments via terminals
Mobile top-up	Terminals and agents	P2B	Majority of payments through this channel
Sending airtime from the Russian Federation to Tajikistan and transferring it between airtime accounts of the same provider	Mobile phone	P2P, but only airtime	Reportedly not very popular
Agroinvest bank has launched a mobile banking application that allows transactions initiated from a phone	Mobile phone	P2P between card accounts of different banks; P2B	No usage data available

P2B = person-to-business, P2P = person-to-person.
Source: International Finance Corporation (2014).

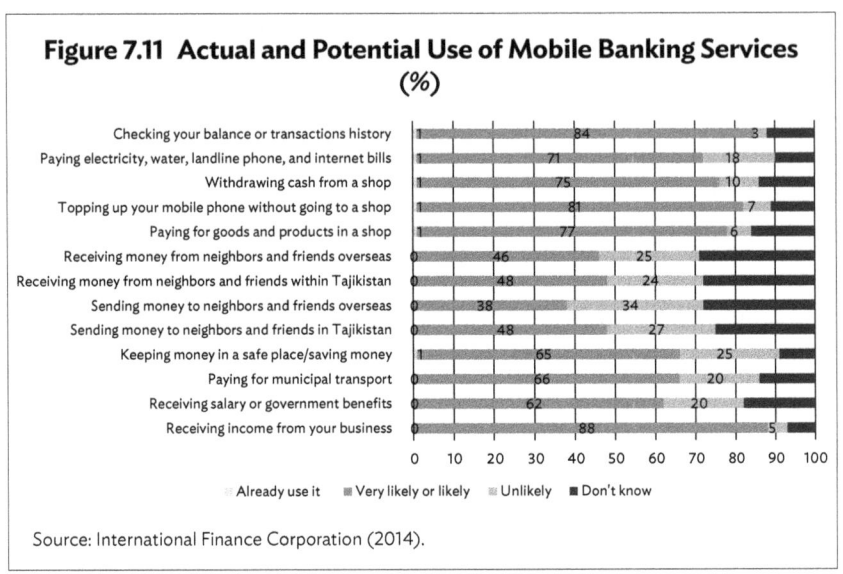

Figure 7.11 Actual and Potential Use of Mobile Banking Services (%)

Source: International Finance Corporation (2014).

7.4 Barriers to Financial Inclusion

According to the Life in Transition III survey, 38% of respondents in Tajikistan referred to access to finance as the top obstacle to the operation and growth of a business (the most frequent answer). Access to finance is low in Tajikistan due to a number of factors, as discussed below.

Macroeconomic stability and vulnerability to external shocks. The economy of Tajikistan is dependent on remittance inflows and other external sources of income (exports, foreign aid, and foreign direct investments). The recent experience of the negative remittance shock associated with the economic decline of the Russian Federation shows that many macroeconomic variables, especially the somoni exchange rate, are very sensitive to these kinds of shocks. A sharp devaluation of the somoni against the dollar resulted in a full-fledged banking crisis and a hike in the number of NPLs (see Section 7.2.2). The issues in the banking sector refueled the population's perception of the country's financial sector as insecure.

Low domestic savings and a lack of affordable credit resources. The low (albeit fast-growing) level of GNI per capita in Tajikistan does not permit the accumulation of sufficient domestic savings to satisfy the domestic demand for financial resources. As a result, many financial institutions have to rely on foreign sources of financing, which are (i) expensive for a country with a relatively low credit rating,[1] and (ii) provided in foreign currency, which exposes all financial institutions to a high exchange rate risk. To reduce this risk, financial institutions tend to issue loans to their clients in foreign currency (mostly US dollars), including clients with no foreign currency-denominated income streams. This shifts the risk to the clients. The capital of all MFIs and many banks is not large, which is an additional limiting factor in attracting credit resources. The high costs of credit resources for financial institutions coupled with high inflation expectations, weakness, and insufficient transparency of borrowers and administrative costs lead to very high interest rates and strict collateral requirements for clients. Many clients, especially households and SMEs, cannot afford to borrow at such rates and collateral requirements. In the Life in Transition survey, 44% of the respondents who provided reasons for not borrowing any money indicated high interest rates, collateral requirements, and administrative costs as the main reasons.

Insufficient autonomy of the NBT and financial institutions. The previous practice of directed lending and limited NBT autonomy have undermined financial intermediation progress. Loans to related parties and directed lending to the agricultural sector, industrial enterprises, and especially large state-owned enterprises, have adversely impacted the banking sector's profitability over the last 5 years with a return-on-assets ratio of -4.4% (International Monetary Fund 2015). NPLs have increased dramatically (see section 7.2), and the capital adequacy ratio fell from 24.5% in 2010 to 12.0% as of the end of 2014, which is the minimum level set for commercial banks and MFIs in Tajikistan. Administrative interference, coupled with banks' weak corporate governance and risk management capacity, poses significant credit, liquidity, and integrity risks for the sector.

Insufficient transparency of financial institutions and lack of clients' confidence in them. According to the NBT requirements, MFIs should regularly publish their financial statements. However, they do not meet this requirement, leaving the population short of necessary information about MFIs' activities and financial situation. NPLs accumulation at large commercial banks (Agroinvest bank and Tojiksodirot bank; two others—Tajprombank and Fononbank—are under bankruptcy procedures) and the lack of understanding of MFIs' situation worsen the entire financial sector's reputation and makes clients hesitate even to have a current account with any financial institution. The deposit insurance scheme has never been tested in practice, and this

---

[1] On 28 August 2017, Moody's assigned a sovereign long-term rating of B3 to Tajikistan. This is the lowest of the "B" ratings, meaning a high credit risk.

does not add to the system's credibility. The NBT, as the regulatory and supervisory body, should ensure that the population has accurate and full information about the financial sector agents' situation to protect the population from poor decision-making on deposit operations.

Insufficient geographical accessibility of, and underdeveloped infrastructure for, financial services. To reduce operation costs, different types of products and services tailored to individuals, households, and SMEs offered by credit organizations are provided mainly at banking service centers, which are located mostly in urban and administrative centers where people and economic activities are concentrated. Thus, the services are insufficiently accessible for the majority of the population dispersed in rural and/or remote areas. For instance, the mountainous Pamir area of Tajikistan (the Gorno-Badakhshan Autonomous Region) is covered very little by credit organizations. Of course, mobile banking could be the solution here. Payment infrastructure is also underdeveloped, and the number of ATMs, POS terminals, and internet and mobile banking users is low compared with regional and income group averages.

Reluctance of the regulator to experiment with new technology-based financial products. The regulator is challenged to understand the evolution of the market and ensure that appropriate regulation is provided. At the same time, innovation should not be held up until the regulator has had a chance to "catch up." The experience of other countries shows that regulators may want to allow innovation on an experimental basis and regulate on an "as needed" basis, provided there is full transparency on the activities of market participants. This is best achieved through an ongoing dialogue, by keeping the regulator abreast of developments and plans. In Tajikistan, the implementation of e-services is impossible without the close cooperation of mobile operators and financial institutions in the accomplishment of payment transactions. The current legislation requiring operators of such transactions to have a credit organization's license effectively blocks the development of a payment system with the participation of mobile operators as they cannot obtain this license. Without amending this legislation, significant progress in this area cannot be expected.

7.5 Regulatory Framework

7.5.1 Regulatory Issues

Banking legislation in Tajikistan represents the system of legislative and normative acts regulating banking activities. The legal basis for banking activities is established by the Law about National Bank of

Tajikistan (No. 722, 28 June 2011) and the Law about Banking Activities (No. 524, 19 May 2009). Microfinance activities are regulated by the Law about Microfinance Organizations (No. 816, 16 April 2012). The NBT is in charge of licensing, regulation, and supervision in Tajikistan; it is authorized to issue normative acts for banks and MFIs, establish financial standards, impose sanctions and penalties, and request reports. This legislation stipulates that credit organizations should provide the population with access to affordable sources of finance and improve the quality of financial services and products. To support improvement in the quality of services and protect clients' interests, the NBT established a consumer protection division. This division's procedures and internal regulations are currently under development.

The legislation identifies three types of MFIs: MDOs, MCOs, and MCFs. Of these three, only MDOs are allowed to offer deposit products based on a license issued by the NBT. MDOs can engage in most forms of financial intermediation, including cash transactions, the issuance of guarantees, operations with payment cards, and clearing and settlement operations. MDOs become eligible to conduct foreign currency operations after 1 year of operations and after obtaining a supplementary license. An MCO is defined as a commercial MFO licensed by the NBT and engaged in providing microloans and swap operations for themselves. MDOs and MCOs can be closed joint-stock companies or limited liability companies. An MCF is a noncommercial organization in the form of a public foundation. MCFs should also have a license from the NBT to engage in providing microloans and swap operations for themselves. Other important pieces of legislation regulating MFIs' activities include the NBT's Regulation on Procedures Regulating the Activities of Microcredit Deposit Organizations (No. 135), Regulation on Microcredit Organizations (No. 136), and Regulation on Microcredit Funds (No. 137).

An MFO can be established by individuals and/or legal entities, residents, and/or nonresidents. Any individual, legal entity, or group of individuals and legal entities acting in concert intending to enter into a transaction that would result in such an individual, legal entity, or group controlling more than 20% of the voting shares of an MDO shall submit a written application for approval to the NBT. To transform into a bank, MFOs must meet prudential normative and other compulsory norms established by the NBT. The NBT's prudential norms, which are mandatory for banks, include (i) a minimum amount of statutory capital for a bank; (ii) a cap on the nonmonetary part of the statutory capital, which should not exceed 20% of a bank's statutory capital; (iii) a maximum risk for one borrower or a group of related borrowers; (iv) liquidity ratio; (v) capital adequacy ratio; (vi) caps on foreign exchange, interest, and other risks; (vii) a ratio of bank's own funds used for the acquisition of shares or stocks of other legal entities; and (viii) a maximum size of credits, guarantees, and warranties extended by banks to their shareholders. Similarly, if an MCO would like to transform into an MDO, it must meet the NBT's prudential and other compulsory norms concerning (i) minimum statutory capital requirements; (ii) a minimum nonmonetary part of the statutory capital; (iii) liquidity requirements; (iv) the capital adequacy ratio; (v) the size of foreign exchange, interest, and other risks; (vi) the ratio of the MDO's capital to its equity investments in other legal entities; (vii) requirements for transactions with affiliates; (viii) the maximum ratio of the MDO's deposits to its capital; and (ix) a minimum size of total capital. According to the existing regulations, both MCFs and MCOs have a right to perform two types of operations only: providing credit, and conducting swap operations. The difference between MCFs and MCOs is their status (noncommercial for MCFs and commercial for MCOs) and size (MCOs are supposed to be much larger than MCFs).

Since 2004, the requirements for initial capital for MFOs have been changed several times (Figure 7.12) to cleanse the market of too small, unsustainable, and nontransparent MFIs.

Some 30% of MFIs were unable meet the latest increase in capital requirements, and most of these have closed or are in the process of liquidating. In one case, three MFIs consolidated, but still barely met

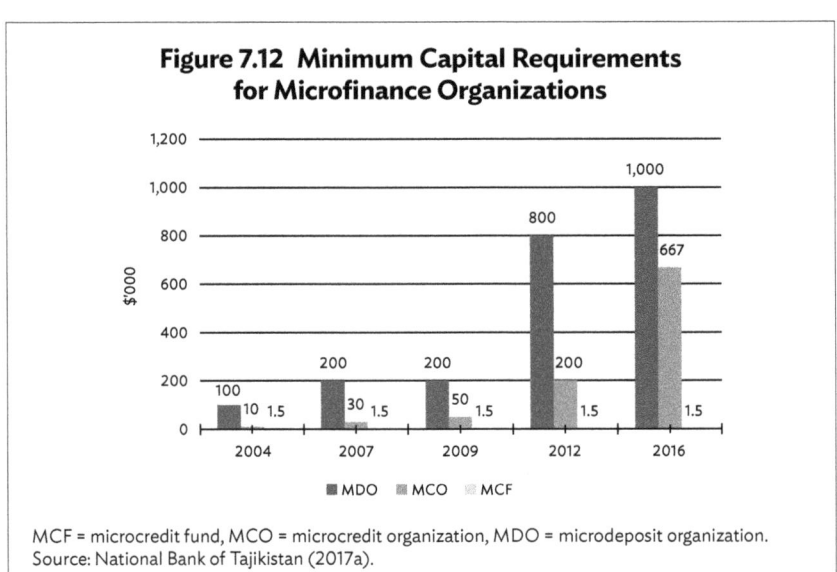

Figure 7.12 Minimum Capital Requirements for Microfinance Organizations

MCF = microcredit fund, MCO = microcredit organization, MDO = microdeposit organization.
Source: National Bank of Tajikistan (2017a).

the requirements, as most investors now tend to cooperate with large MFIs with a credit portfolio of over $5 million. Six large MFIs meet the capital requirements, and are able to compete with commercial banks in terms of quality of service and the implementation of new products and services; but small and medium-sized MFIs were unable to do this.

The NBT has a right to revoke an MFI's license if (i) cases of submission of unreliable information or reporting have been identified; or (ii) over the 12-month period from the date of being granted a license, the MFO has not begun activity or, after the beginning of its activity, the MFO independently decided to stop activity for a period of more than 6 months.

The financial sector has deepened in recent years, albeit from a low base (World Bank 2009). This is reflected in the overall growth of the financial system, greater diversification, and the expansion of lending to previously underserved sectors, such as agriculture and SMEs. Since the expansion, the financial sector has remained small and cannot serve all of the financing needs of the economy. Banks have better liquidity and their rapid growth has brought new risk exposures that should be carefully monitored and appropriately addressed. In particular, rapid loan growth has brought unrecognized high credit risk and led to an increase in NPLs (see section 7.2.2). Because of extensive dollarization, banks' exposure to exchange rate-induced credit risk is another significant source of concern. To control this tendency, the NBT is strengthening the regulatory and supervisory framework to sustain the system's health in the face of rapid growth. The governance of a few commercial banks was temporarily strengthened by the NBT. The NBT also started ensuring the integrity of the regulatory bodies, and guaranteed that all financial transactions would be priced on a market basis.

Supervision at financial institutions is still mainly compliance-based, with little focus on good governance and risk management. Regulation and supervision need to be strengthened to better manage credit, market, operation, concentration, interest rate, and liquidity risks; and to improve the corporate governance and internal control systems of the financial institutions. Adaption of the international financial reporting standards, more advanced risk assessment tools, stress testing, and crisis management tools are among the primary measures that need to be introduced immediately (ADB 2016).

Based on the World Bank's 2007 Financial System Assessment Program, on 28 May 2010 the government passed Resolution No. 261, which brought into effect the Tajikistan Banking Sector Development Strategy and Action Plan 2010–2015. The key component of this strategy was strengthening the NBT's oversight of the payment system.

A dedicated unit with the capacity and responsibility for supervising the payment system has been established, with capacity building provided by the World Bank.

Farmers in recent years have benefited from the adoption of new laws and amendments to the Land Code and other land legislation, which were adopted to expand farmers' use rights to include the right to buy, sell, mortgage, lease, transfer, and exchange land rights, as well as to pass them on through inheritance. However, in practice the registration of farmers' land use rights has been limited to "lifelong-inheritable use" rights that do not include rights of alienation.

Insurance companies in Tajikistan need not go through certification of the quality of provided services.

Insolvency. The number of insolvency cases that are resolved in economic courts in Tajikistan is fairly small due to, perhaps, the insolvent entities having insufficient assets to cover the costs of the insolvency processes. Tajikistan is ranked 144th in the World Bank's annual Resolving Insolvency rate of 2017 Doing Business Index, with no change from the previous year (World Bank 2017a). The latest index value is based on data for June 2016. This is a fairly poor position compared to its neighboring countries in Central Asia. The recovery rate index is 35.9, slightly lower than the average score for Europe and the Central Asia region.[2] It has been strongly proved that the existence of strong legislation on insolvency may lead to growth in entrepreneurial activities (specifically on self-employment). Tajikistan's insolvency legislature has improved, following enacting amendments to the Law on Bankruptcy in 2009. Specifically, the insolvency procedure was burdensome for enterprises, both financially and timewise. In some instances, the procedure lasted more than 3 years, although in some cases disputing parties reached amicable agreements. The Resolving Insolvency Index for 2017 depicts the necessary improvement in the period to recover credits, recording it at 1.7 years. This timing applies for large-scale enterprises, whereas SMEs' insolvency procedures are limited to 6 months. Another area for improvement lies in the insolvency management process in the case of bankruptcy of a debtor. The lack of objective information about the financial situation of the debtor, the latter's possible opportunity for further entrepreneurial operation, information on the stage of crisis development, and the consequences of enforcing one or another bankruptcy procedure make it necessary to consider introducing a pre-trial diagnosis in bankruptcy procedures.

---

[2] The recovery rate is a function of the cost, time, and outcome of insolvency proceedings involving domestic legal entities according to the Methodology of Doing Business Index.

7.5.2 Consumer Protection

At the end of 2015, the NBT launched a new initiative that should improve customer protection in the finance industry. With the support of the IFC, the NBT has developed a strategic plan for 2017–2021, in which it listed a range of outstanding issues in this area, from the lack of transparency to the need for improvements in the institutional framework, such as the creation of a financial ombudsman. Most MFIs have adopted Smart Campaign Principles (Smart Campaign 2011), according to which MFIs should set the pricing, terms, and conditions in a way that is affordable for clients while allowing the financial institutions to be sustainable. These seven client protection principles have also been included in the strategic plan. At the same time, credit organizations are recommended to provide detailed information on the composition of an effective interest rate on loans.

Since 2016, the NBT has had a customer compliance department that should keep track not only of complaints and their outcome, but also customer feedback on financial institutions' activities. Once every 2 years, each organization is recommended to go through client protection certification (Social Performance Task Force website), which could be conducted by the NBT's customer compliance department; two MFIs have already been through it. This initiative would benefit both the NBT and MFIs, with the latter using it to develop a social strategy. In addition, the NBT's consumer protection division conducts roundtables and training sessions on financial literacy, and encourages credit organizations to join Global Money Week.

7.5.3 Deposit Insurance

The Deposit Insurance Fund was established in 2003. Its assets reached TJS260 million, or 6.3% of total deposits at the end of 2016. In Tajikistan, the deposit amount covered by the fund in the case of bankruptcy of a credit organization has been increased from the initial TJS7,000 to TJS14,000 in 2015 and TJS17,500 in 2017 (approximately $2,100). As of the end of 2014, 14 banks and 40 MDOs were members of the Deposit Insurance Fund. The largest savings bank, Amonatbank, does not participate in the scheme, as its deposits are fully guaranteed by the government by separate legislation.

In addition to having a low coverage level, compensation provided in local currency is seen as insufficiently attractive by market participants in a country with extensive dollarization and foreign currency remittances from abroad. While the DIF has put in place a variety of communication tools (e.g. website, posters, and handouts) to inform the public of its existence, it has not conducted any surveys on public awareness of the deposit insurance scheme.

7.6 Policies to Promote Financial Inclusion

Cheap resources. Today ADB, the European Bank for Reconstruction and Development (EBRD), the United Nations Development Programme, and the World Bank in the framework of their programs provide Tajik commercial banks and MFIs with low-cost financial resources that are channeled to the population at relatively low interest rates; however, these resources are not very large in comparison to the high demand in rural areas of Tajikistan. Since MFOs need many branches, their operational costs range from 10% to 17% (AMFOT 2016). The cheapest resources were provided by the United Nations Development Programme with a rate for clients of 12% per year.

Some international financial organizations sometimes implement financial inclusion programs and provide sources of finance to credit organizations aimed at specific groups of the population; for example, the commercial bank Eschata recently received $1 million from the EBRD for the implementation of the "Women in Business" initiative aimed at improving women's access to finance, which is even more constrained than that of men.

Credit databases. Two credit information bureaus provide services to credit organizations in Tajikistan: the Credit Information Bureau of Tajikistan (CIBT) and the Bureau of Credit History Somonion. The CIBT cooperates with 17 banks and 56 MFIs and holds information on 602,000 individuals and 25,000 firms representing 887,000 credit transactions. The second bureau covers five banks and 80 small MFIs, and holds information on 120,000 individuals and 8,500 firms representing 332,000 credit transactions (World Bank 2015). Both credit bureaus have their own clientele but it is not sufficient, since the scoring at the CIBT is not reliable and credit organizations do not use it. Second, not all financial institutions provide information on all their clients, so there are risks associated with the information gap. Third, the prices for CIBT services are high, which might be related to the operational or technical support costs as the CIBT rents in its software. The NBT recently started collecting full data sets from credit organizations, and is going to establish a national registry where all necessary data from the entire sector will be stored; this registry is expected to provide information to market participants on a fee basis.

Credit guarantees. Credit Guarantee Fund Tajikistan was established in 2014 to address financial institutions' strict collateral requirements. This fund is dedicated to improving access to finance for Tajik SMEs by sharing credit risk through credit guarantees and providing technical assistance to Tajik partner financial institutions (PFIs). The fund uses credit guarantees as instruments to provide benefits for borrowers (SMEs) through intermediaries (PFIs). It issues individual letters of guarantee for PFIs' loans to SMEs. The value of eligible loans ranges from $10,000 to $500,000, or the equivalent value in somoni. Eligible loan purposes are investments in fixed assets and working capital. In the case of default of borrowers on guaranteed loans and after having carried out the contractually agreed delinquency management procedures without success, the PFIs can claim the guarantee after 180 days past due. The fund then appraises the guarantee claim and pays out its share of the lost principal in the amount of 60% of the credit's value. Recoveries collected by the PFIs after the claim payout are shared with the fund. Currently, the fund provides individual guarantees; however, it plans to transition to blanket guarantees. Credit guarantees can also be offered in the form of investment guarantees rather than loan guarantees. Of the 23 largest microfinance investment funds, three offer investment guarantees on MFI or SME loan portfolios.[3]

To expand to rural areas at a reasonable cost, financial institutions are considering harnessing technology and branchless banking. This could be done through partnerships with PSPs, allowing use of their networks for expansion and further development of card-based payment systems as a cost-effective way to service rural clients. Support for agricultural finance could be enhanced by the electronic disbursement of funds to the suppliers of necessary agricultural inputs (ADB 2013b).

7.7. Financial Education and Financial Literacy

Financial literacy activities. The National Development Strategy (NDS) of Tajikistan 2030 (NDS Section 5.3) places emphasis on improving the protection of the rights of consumers of financial services. Among other policy measures related to the financial sector of the country, it stipulates the need for the development and implementation of a state program on improving the population's financial literacy.

In the framework of the NDS implementation, the NBT, in collaboration with international experts, developed the Strategic Priorities in the Development of a Mechanism on the Protection of the Rights of Consumers of Financial Services for 2017–2019. This document

---

[3] The Netherlands' Hivos-Triodos Foundation offers 8% of its total MFI investment funds as guarantees. The share is smaller for the church-based and very innovative Oikocredit (also the Netherlands) investments and the French Solidarité Internationale pour le Développement et l'Investissement.

requires the development of a state program that should become an effective framework to coordinate the efforts of various government agencies, ensure efficient distribution of budget financing, and formulate a systemic approach through various channels and initiatives. Further, the NBT is expected to continue initiatives on improving financial literacy, including the coordination of annual international financial literacy weeks among children and young people, the organization of workshops and training sessions for elementary school teachers, the placement of information and video materials on the official website of the NBT, and participation in television and radio shows. The most vulnerable target groups are defined as priority groups for the development and implementation of financial education initiatives. At the same time, the opportunity to gain financial knowledge should be available for all citizens. Financial education will be offered mostly through the provision of basic knowledge using mass media outlets. In particular, the NBT plans to carry out activities related to the development and distribution of informational materials on key financial products and services, bearing in mind the properties and risks for the population. For their part, financial institutions and their associations will continue their efforts to improve the financial literacy of consumers.

Over the last decade, different international organizations in Tajikistan have implemented and conducted many activities and training sessions in the area of financial literacy. In the framework of the coordination council on improving the investment climate under the President of the Republic of Tajikistan, a donor committee has been established that should coordinate a tailored and sequenced support package to fit national financial development strategies and work within financial inclusion coordination mechanisms, such as the national platforms recommended in this framework. It is important that all stakeholders are consulted so that they are actively involved in the development and implementation of a financial literacy strategy and program. Stakeholders will benefit from improved financial literacy, and can contribute by determining priorities, funding initiatives, developing materials, and undertaking projects, among other things (World Bank 2014). The module of financial literacy training and programs should be standardized and the most important information compiled to enable understanding of financial institutions' rights and responsibilities, financial disclosure rules, and the risks and rewards of financial products.

According to the IFC, more than 40% of respondents spend all their income, while only half make regular savings (IFC 2015). In addition, 83% cannot explain basic banking terms, about 90% have never heard of the credit bureau, and only about 40% would agree to provide their credit information to the credit bureau. This leads to debt and high default rates, and delays home purchases and investments in children's education.

Several donor organizations undertake financial literacy activities in collaboration with the AMFOT, the Center for Training and Microfinance Development, the Association of Banks of Tajikistan, and specific financial institutions; they work to train clients in financial literacy topics in specific regions of the country. However, until now Tajikistan has had no financial education strategy. There is no comprehensive financial education program led by the NBT or any other government agency. Also, the Consumers Union of Tajikistan does not deal with financial service issues and has not been involved in financial literacy activities.

Credit organizations should have an important role in supporting and delivering financial education programs, as long as they are trusted by consumers and do not mix marketing and educational messages. Often it is reported that the programs run by credit organizations are used for marketing purposes. Financial education provided by credit organizations should be regularly assessed to ensure it meets consumer needs. This may be achieved through partnerships with independent, not-for-profit financial advisory bodies that may have better a connection with consumers, particularly those facing disadvantages in their participation in financial markets (OECD 2015).

In February of 2015, the IFC launched a financial infrastructure development program in Tajikistan involving several credit organizations. The program includes educational materials on household budgets and personal finance management, smart borrowing rules, preventing overindebtedness, saving strategies, managing remittances, and the benefits of credit information reporting. The program has been delivered through various delivery channels, including training for the adult population, in-depth consultations for borrowers, and broadcasting of educational video clips and radio programs.

7.8 Conclusions and Recommendations

In recent years, public access to financial services measured by the volume of deposits, loans, card transactions, and infrastructure density has improved significantly (albeit from a low base). However, the external shock associated with the decline in remittances from the Russian Federation has adversely affected the financial system in Tajikistan, leading to a very sensitive devaluation of the somoni against the US dollar, an explosive accumulation of NPLs in the country's banking system, serious issues in several banks, a reduction in the total amount of loans for the nonfinancial sector, and reduced trust of the population in the financial system.

The key barriers to financial inclusion in Tajikistan are (i) the macroeconomic instability and vulnerability of the economy and financial system to external shocks; (ii) low domestic savings and the need for financial institutions to rely on foreign sources of financing, which make financial resources expensive and unaffordable for a large proportion of households and SMEs; (iii) insufficient autonomy of the NBT and financial institutions leading to directed lending practices; (iv) insufficient transparency of financial institutions and an associated lack of client confidence in them; (v) underdevelopment of financial infrastructure and low accessibility of financial services in rural and remote areas of the country; and (vi) the reluctance of the NBT to encourage the introduction of new technologies in the financial sector.

A regulatory framework for the financial sector in Tajikistan is mostly in place, while there are different issues related to banking supervision, the regulator's independence, and the openness of the system to technological innovations (as mentioned in section 7.3.4). The NBT and other government agencies are paying increasing attention to the financial education and financial literacy of the population with the support of different international organizations; nevertheless, the country has a long way to go for the population to achieve a sufficient level of familiarity with, and understanding of, different financial products. Recent issues in the financial sector have distracted the authorities from developing a comprehensive strategy or action plan for financial inclusion and education, which is explicitly demanded by the NDS. As the situation stabilizes, the financial inclusion agenda is coming to the forefront of the government's policy towards the financial sector.

The following are the key recommendations for improved financial inclusion in Tajikistan.

(i) Ensure macroeconomic stability in the country; refrain from attempts to regulate the somoni/dollar exchange rate (other than smoothing sharp fluctuations caused by external shocks).

(ii) Increase the independence of the NBT; refuse to force the banking system to run quasi-fiscal operations and directed lending.

(iii) Increase the transparency of, and proper information disclosure by, both commercial banks and MFIs.

(iv) Encourage financial institutions to develop financial infrastructure, especially associated with the utilization of new technology-based products, including mobile and internet banking.

(v) Resolve issues related to the participation of mobile network operators in the delivery of financial services using the experience of other countries.
(vi) In accordance with the NDS, develop and run the well-coordinated long-term State Programme on Improving Financial Literacy of the Population and advocacy campaign to increase the utilization of financial services by the population.
(vii) Similarly, develop and implement the State Programme on Financial Inclusion with a focus on reducing risks in the financial sector and providing financial products that are more affordable for the population, promoting modern financial technologies, and fostering and properly supervising retail financial institutions, especially aimed at rural areas and migrants.
(viii) Support the financial inclusion agenda institutionally by creating a separate unit at the NBT in charge of inclusion issues and establishing a body or task force consisting of all public and private stakeholders dealing with financial inclusion issues (e.g. under the umbrella of the Investment Council under the President of the Republic of Tajikistan).
(ix) Strengthen general education, especially in the area of numeracy, to equip young people with the necessary knowledge and skills to utilize financial products effectively.

References

Agency on Statistics under President of the Republic of Tajikistan (ASPRT). 2017. Dushanbe: ASPRT. http://www.stat.tj (accessed 20 December 2017).

Asian Development Bank (ADB). 2014. *Making Mobile Financial Services Work for Central and West Asian Countries*. Manila: ADB. https://www.adb.org/sites/default/files/project-document/173360/43359-012-tacr-07.pdf (accessed 20 December 2017).

ADB. 2016. *Country Partnership Strategy: Tajikistan, 2016–2020, Sector Assessment Summary: Finance*. Manila: ADB. https://www.adb.org/documents/tajikistan-country-partnership-strategy-2016-2020 (accessed 20 December 2017).

Association of Microfinance Organizations of Tajikistan. 2016. *Quarterly Analysis of Microfinance Sector, 4th Quarter*. Dushanbe: Association of Microfinance Organizations of Tajikistan. http://amfot.tj/en (accessed 20 December 2017).

Countrymeters. Tajikistan. http://countrymeters.info/ru/Tajikistan (accessed 20 December 2017).

Currency Exchange Fund. 2017. https://www.tcxfund.com/countries/tajikistan (accessed 20 December 2017).

European Bank for Reconstruction and Development (EBRD). 2017. *EBRD is Expanding its Award-Winning Women in Business Program to Tajikistan*. 28 July. Dushanbe: EBRD. http://www.ebrd.com/news/2017/ebrd-launches-women-in-business-programme-in-tajikistan-.html (accessed 20 December 2017).

European Bank for Reconstruction and Development (EBRD). 2017. *Life in Transition: A Decade of Measuring Transition*. Dushanbe: EBRD. http://litsonline-ebrd.com/ (accessed 20 December 2017).

Food and Agriculture Organization of the United Nations. 2013. *Credit Guarantee Systems for Agriculture and Rural Enterprise Development*. Rome: Food and Agriculture Organization of the United Nations. https://europa.eu/ capacity4dev/file/52505/ download?token=iS5-SF3a (accessed 20 December 2017).

International Finance Corporation (IFC). 2010. *Comparative Analysis of Microfinance Policy Frameworks and Legislation*. Washington, DC: International Finance Corporation. http://www.ifc.org/wps/wcm/connect/c afb7e004cb6bffbbf8bfff81ee631cc/ PublicationCA-MicrofinancePolicy2010.pdf? MOD=AJPERES (accessed 20 December 2017).

IFC. 2014. *Money Flow Mobile Money Market Survey*. Washington, DC: International Finance Corporation.

IFC. 2015. *World Bank Group, Financial Institutions Help Tajik Population Increase Financial Literacy*. Press Release, Dushanbe,

Tajikistan, February 20, 2015. Washington, DC: International Finance Corporation. https://ifcextapps.ifc.org/IFCExt/Pressroom/IFCPressRoom.nsf/0/30C5DD67A6047D5F85257DF20031E744?OpenDocument (accessed 20 December 2017).

International Monetary Fund (IMF). 2000. The Impact of Monetary Policy on the Exchange Rate: Evidence from Three Small Economies. IMF Working Paper 00/14. Washington, DC: IMF.

IMF. 2015. *Statistical Appendix. Regional Economic Outlook Update: Middle East and Central Asia*. Washington, DC: IMF. https://www.imf.org/en/Publications/REO/MECA/Issues/2017/04/18/ mreo0517 (accessed 20 December 2017).

IMF. 2017. Deposit Insurance, Remittances, and Dollarization: Survey-Based Evidence from a Top Remittance-Receiving Country. IMF Working Paper 17/132. Washington, DC: IMF.

National Bank of Tajikistan (NBT). 2012. On Procedures for Regulating the Activities of Microcredit Funds. Instruction No. 198. 30 August. Dushanbe: NBT. http://nbt.tj/upload/iblock/796/Ins_198_en.pdf (accessed 20 December 2017).

NBT. 2015a. On Procedures for Regulating the Activities of Microcredit Deposit Organizations. Instruction No. 196. 28 May. Dushanbe: NBT. http://nbt.tj/upload/iblock/b1e/Ins_196_en.pdf (accessed 20 December 2017).

NBT. 2015b. On Procedures for Regulating the Activities of Microcredit Organizations. Instruction No. 197. 28 May. Dushanbe: NBT. http://nbt.tj/upload/iblock/6ab/Ins_197_en.pdf (accessed 20 December 2017).

NBT. 2017a. *Banking Statistics Bulletin*. No. 7. July. Dushanbe: NBT. http://nbt.tj/en/statistics/statistical_bulletin.php (accessed 20 December 2017).

NBT. 2017b. Exchange Rate of Tajik Somoni to other Currencies, Database. 1 July. Dushanbe: NBT. http://nbt.tj/en/kurs/kurs.php?date=01.01.2017 (accessed 20 December 2017).

NBT. 2017c. *Strategic Priorities of NBT on Development of Mechanisms on Protection of the Rights of Consumers of Financial Services in the Republic of Tajikistan for 2017–2019*. Dushanbe: NBT. http://nbt.tj/files/Protection/strategiya/Strategiya_en.pdf (accessed 20 December 2017).

NBT. 2017d. *Banking laws*. Dushanbe: NBT. http://nbt.tj/en/laws/ (accessed 20 December 2017).

Organisation for Economic Co-operation and Development (OECD). 2015. *National Strategies for Financial Education*. Paris: Organisation for Economic Co-operation and Development. http://www.oecd.org/finance/financial-education/nationalstrategiesforfinancialeducation.htm (accessed 20 December 2017).

Smart Campaign. 2011. *Client Protection Principles.* http://www.smartcampaign.org/about/smart-microfinance-and-the-client-protection-principles (accessed 20 December 2017).

Social Performance Task Force. 2017. https://sptf.info/universal-standards-for-spm/assess-and-plan (accessed 20 December 2017).

United States Agency for International Development. 2009. *Analysis of Implementation of Insolvency Law of the Republic of Tajikistan.* Washington, DC: United States Agency for International Development. http://www.namsb.tj/phocadownload/beilibrary/analysis_on_insolvency_rus.pdf (accessed 20 September 2017).

World Bank. 2009. *Financial Sector Assessment: Republic of Tajikistan.* Washington, DC: World Bank. https://openknowledge.worldbank.org/handle/10986/3026 (accessed 20 December 2017).

World Bank. 2012. *Financial Inclusion Strategies Reference Framework.* Washington, DC: World Bank. http://documents.worldbank.org/curated/en/801151468152092070/Financial-inclusion-strategies-reference-framework (accessed 20 December 2017).

World Bank. 2014. *Diagnostic Review of Customer Protection and Financial Literacy. Oversight Frameworks and Practices in 114 Economies.* Washington, DC: World Bank. http://responsiblefinance.worldbank.org/~/media/GIAWB/FL/Documents/Publications/CPFL-Global-Survey-114econ-Oversight-2014.pdf (accessed 20 December 2017).

World Bank. 2017a. *Doing Business Index. Ease of Doing Business in Tajikistan.* Washington, DC: World Bank. http://www.doingbusiness.org/data/exploreeconomies/tajikistan#resolving-insolvency (accessed 19 September 2017).

World Bank. 2017b. *Survey: Listen to Tajikistan.* Washington, DC: World Bank. http://blogs.worldbank.org/europeandcentralasia/why-low-oil-prices-are-also-bad-news-poor-central-asia (accessed 20 December 2017).

World Bank. 2017c. *World Development Indicators.* Washington, DC: World Bank. https://databank.worldbank.org/data/source/world-development-indicators (accessed 20 December 2017).

World Bank. 2018. *Financial Inclusion Data/Global Findex Database.* Washington, DC: World Bank. http://datatopics.worldbank.org/financialinclusion/ (accessed 5 April 2018)

World Bank and IMF. 2015. *Finance Sector Assessment, Republic of Tajikistan.* Washington, DC: World Bank and IMF. http://documents.worldbank.org/curated/en/595671468189271129/pdf/100521-FSAP-SecM2015-0311-Box393232B-OUO-9-add-FSAP-series.pdf (accessed 20 December 2017).

8
Uzbekistan

Muzaffarjon Ahunov

Abstract

8.1 Introduction

In his speech at the General Assembly of the United Nations Organization in 2017, the President of Uzbekistan, as one of his key messages, outlined an important principle: "the wealthier are the people, the stronger is the state." (Mirziyoev 2017). Promoting financial inclusion, that is, providing people with access to payment services, savings accounts, loans, and insurance at a reasonable cost, might be instrumental in achieving this goal. Recent evidence from around the world has shown that financial inclusion can contribute to inclusive growth and economic development (Demirgüç-Kunt and Singer 2017). This chapter therefore aims to assess the state of financial inclusion in Uzbekistan as of 2018 and to identify the obstacles and the opportunities to promote it.

This chapter uses a nationally representative household survey, the Life in Transition Survey Wave III, which the World Bank and the European Bank for Reconstruction and Development administered in 2016. It also uses a firm-level survey called the Business Environment Survey, which the World Bank conducted in 2013. The World Bank also administered the Global Findex Survey among a representative number of individuals in Uzbekistan in 2008 and 2014. The study further uses a range of secondary data from the Central Bank of Uzbekistan (CBU), the World Bank, and the International Monetary Fund (IMF), along with findings from local studies. These are all the most recent sources available on this research topic.

8.2 Overview of Uzbekistan's Financial System

Uzbekistan's financial system is bank-based, with commercial banks playing a key role. The other types of financial intermediaries that

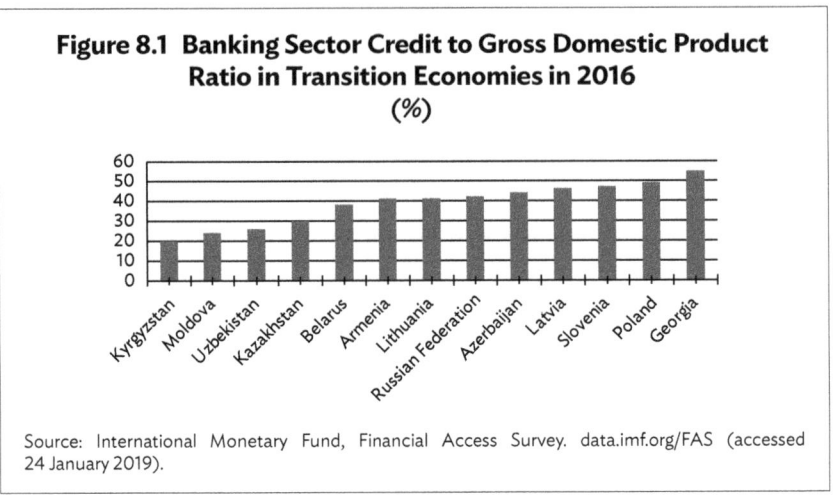

Figure 8.1 Banking Sector Credit to Gross Domestic Product Ratio in Transition Economies in 2016 (%)

Source: International Monetary Fund, Financial Access Survey. data.imf.org/FAS (accessed 24 January 2019).

operate in this market are non-deposit-taking microfinance institutions (MFIs). These play little or no role. Similarly, no formal crowd finance platform exists, and the financial markets are underdeveloped. The level of financial intermediation has traditionally been low, as the relatively low banking sector credit to gross domestic product (GDP) ratio compared with other transition economies shows (Figure 8.1). However, under its new President, the country made significant progress in financial liberalization between 2016 and 2018. As a result, financial intermediation has surged; in 2018, as the CBU reported, the banking sector credit to GDP ratio was 42.2% versus 26% in 2016 and 19.4% in 2012.

Table 8.1 shows that the importance of deposits as a source of funds declined between 2017 and 2018. Thus, the direct borrowing of commercial banks mainly from state funds, and, to a lesser extent, from international credit lines, funded the surge in bank lending reported by the CBU (2018), which observed that the borrowed funds of commercial banks as a share of their total liabilities increased from 36% in 2017 to 50% in 2018. Table 8.1 indicates that deposits as a share of total liabilities decreased from 48% in 2017 to 40% in 2018. As Table 8.1 shows, demand deposits dominated, making up more than half of the total deposits. Only 9.2% of deposits had a maturity of 1 year or more. The funding structure of commercial banks is indicative of two issues: low depositor confidence in banking and the presence of tight constraints on banks' ability to extend loans, especially for long-term periods.

Table 8.2 shows that banks with state ownership dominate. In 2018, 11 out of 28 banks had direct or indirect state ownership.

Table 8.1 Banking Sector Deposits

	2017	2018
All deposits as a percentage of bank liabilities	48	40
Demand deposits	54.0	51.9
Savings deposits with maturity		
1–30 days	5.5	5.5
30–180 days	17.2	17.5
180–365 days	10.4	15.8
1 year and more	12.9	9.2
Foreign currency deposits	27.5	49.1

Note: All numbers are given as of 1 January of the corresponding year.
Source: Central Bank of Uzbekistan. http://www.cbu.uz/en/statistics/bankstats/ (accessed 24 January 2019).

Table 8.2 Uzbekistan's Banking System Ownership and Concentration

	Market Share (% of Banking Assets)			
	2001	2014	2016	2018
Market share of top three banks	86.6	50.6	49.7	59.9
Market share of top five banks	91.3	63.7	62.9	71.8
State-owned banks	82.2	41.2	41.4	48.8
Shareholding banks with indirect state ownership	6.1	35.5	33.7	33.2
Banks with foreign ownership	0.9	8.7	9.9	7.7

Source: Market shares estimated by authors using Central Bank of Uzbekistan data. http://www.cbu.uz/en/statistics/bankstats/ (accessed on 24 January 2019). Data for 2001 and 2014 comes from Ahunov(2015).

All 11 banks jointly controlled over 82% of the total banking sector assets, over 66% of the deposit market share and 88% of the loan market share as of 1 January 2018 (CBU 2018). This is in line with 2012, as the Asian Development Bank (ADB) (2014) noted, declaring that state-owned banks controlled 86.8% of the total loan portfolio and 69.4% of all deposits. The market share of state-owned banks in deposit markets has thus been declining.

As the IMF (2013) reported, state-owned banks mainly finance large government programs and projects. The lending rate in these state-led projects is often below the market rate, which impedes banks' risk management and leads to segmentation of the banking market. For instance, the IMF (2018) stated:

> Uzbekistan's credit market is highly segmented, with SOEs [state-owned enterprises] enjoying preferential access to credit. The FX [foreign exchange] segment of the credit market is dominated by SOEs, which receive FX credit either directly from state banks or through on-lending operations by government entities....These directed FX credits are often granted at highly preferential terms, depressing banks' profitability. By contrast, the private sector is largely confined to the domestic currency segment of the credit market, where loan mark-ups may in part reflect banks' attempt to recoup low margins on concessional lending.

All state banks specialize in a specific sector, and mostly channel state funds. The IMF (2018) declared that 56% of its total loans have been extended to SOEs and joint ventures. Similarly, government deposits and loans constitute 51% of the liabilities of banks. The IMF also reported that SOEs' deposits make up 13% of banking sector liabilities. Thus, banks mainly intermediate between different government-owned enterprises and funds. Each state-owned bank has a specific function. For instance, the National Bank of Uzbekistan for Foreign Economic Activity, the largest bank in the country, specializes, as its name suggests, in financing foreign trade and export facilitation programs. Similarly, the People's Bank, which controlled 3.3% of the banking market share in 2018, is the main state bank for social payments and pensions and for serving public sector payments.

As Table 8.2 also shows, Uzbekistan's banking sector is highly concentrated. The three largest banks jointly controlled 59.9% of the total banking assets in 2018 versus 86.6% in 2001. Thus, concentration has been declining. In 2001, the National Bank alone controlled 76% of the total banking sector assets versus 30.9% as of 1 January 2018. The National Bank is still the largest bank, controlling 19.5% and 18.5% of the deposit and loan market shares in 2018.

Foreign bank penetration remains low. As Table 8.2 shows, banks with foreign ownership jointly controlled 7.7% of the total banking sector assets in 2018. Unlike the situation in other transition economies, like Ukraine, Kazakhstan, and Poland, banks with foreign ownership first entered the country by creating a new institution, that is, through "greenfield investments." The market share of these banks has been small; according to the CBU, it is below 1%, and they have limited their activity to financing businesses from their home countries. The other three banks with foreign ownership resulted from cross-border takeovers, and these control around 9% of the banking sector assets.

Table 8.2 shows that the share of banks with no state ownership increased from 0.8% of the banking sector assets in 2001 to 13% in 2018. Unlike their peers with state ownership, these banks mainly deal with private sector deposits and loans. Note that the number of private banks has been stable, and this is possibly due to the strict licensing regulations for the entry of new private banks (Ruziev and Ghosh 2009).

According to the CBU (2018), almost all the banks in Uzbekistan have a credit ranking from international institutions like Moody's and Fitch, and they are all ranked as stable.[1] This is in line with the IMF (2000, 2008, 2013). The high level of capitalization was due to direct state capital injections into state-owned banks (IMF 2013).

Table 8.3 also reports the key financial performance indicators of the Uzbek banking system. The regulatory bank capital to risk-adjusted asset ratio, profitability indicators such as return on assets, and equity are high and improving, while the level of nonperforming loans is low. Thus, credit rationing seems to be relatively high in Uzbekistan judging from

Table 8.3 Key Performance Indicators of Commercial Banks in Uzbekistan (%)

	2011	2014	2016	2017	2018
Bank capital to risk-adjusted assets	23.4	24.3	14.72	14.73	18.77
Nonperforming loans to total loans	1.0	0.4	1.46	0.74	1.20
Return on assets	1.7	2.0	2.00	2.00	1.87
Return on equity	12.7	17.2	17.47	17.95	17.13
Net interest margin	34.1	36.4	39.90	39.45	32.55
Non-interest margin	70.0	64.0	65.87	64.82	59.30
Liquid assets to total assets	31.2	31.9	23.68	25.36	23.63
Liquid assets to current liabilities	67.3	73.5	43.56	48.36	55.65
Banking capital/assets	13.3	11.2	11.25	10.68	12.41

Source: Data for 2011 and 2012 come from the Centre for Economic Research (2016), and those for 2016 to 2018 come from the Central Bank of Uzbekistan. All figures are as of 1 January of the respective year.

---

[1] Information on credit rankings is available on the CBU website. http://www.cbu.uz/en/kreditnye-organizatsii/kommercheskie-banki/reytingovye-otsenki/ (accessed 24 January 2019).

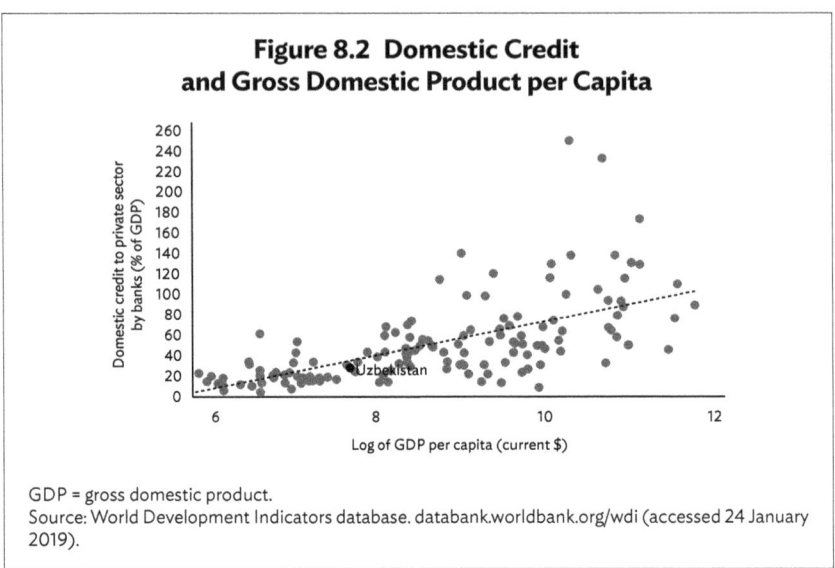

Figure 8.2 Domestic Credit and Gross Domestic Product per Capita

GDP = gross domestic product.
Source: World Development Indicators database. databank.worldbank.org/wdi (accessed 24 January 2019).

the level of domestic credit to the private sector, which is well below the average compared with countries with a similar level of development, as Figure 8.2 shows.

As mentioned earlier, Uzbekistan has no deposit-taking MFIs, such as credit unions, like the Kyrgyz Republic and Tajikistan have. The Credit Union Law came into force in 2002 and led to the rapid entry of new institutions into the financial market—the number of credit unions surged from 20 in 2004 to 163 in 2010 (Table 8.3). However, deposit-taking MFIs disappeared in 2010 with the reversal of the law; they were all turned into non-deposit-taking financial institutions that lend their own funds. The evidence on the quality of credit union services is mixed. Anecdotal evidence suggests that credit unions have been successful in promoting access to finance among micro, small, and medium-sized enterprises (ADB 2009). On the contrary, the Centre for Economic Research (CER) (2011), based on the National Income Mobilization Survey, which claims to be a nationally representative survey, reported that in 2010 50% of respondents complained about a delay in accessing their deposits at credit unions, and 26% of clients declared that the credit union interest rates were high.

Table 8.4 shows that the banking sector outreach surged between 2004 and 2018, as the increase in the number of ATMs per 100,000 adults and per 1,000 square kilometers evidences. In 2004, there were only 0.9 ATMs per 100,000 adults versus 21.6 ATMs in 2016. The banking sector

Table 8.4 Geographic Outreach of Financial Institutions in Uzbekistan

Indicator Name	2004	2006	2008	2010	2012	2014	2016	2018
Number of:								
Commercial banks	31	28	30	31	29	26	27	28
Non-deposit-taking MFIs	1	14	60	93	76	71	76	76
Commercial bank branches/mini banks/units:								
Number	6,701	7,627	7,712	7,900	8,058	8,237	8,263	8,864
Branches per 100,000 adults	39.1	42.3	40.7	39.2	38.0	37.4	36.1	27.7
Branches per 1,000 square kilometers	15.8	18.0	18.2	18.6	19.0	19.4	19.5	19.8
ATMs:								
Number	151	171	318	807	1,417	1,870	4,954	
ATMs per 100,000 adults	0.9	0.9	1.7	4.0	6.7	8.5	21.6	
ATMs per 1,000 square kilometers	0.4	0.4	0.7	1.9	3.3	4.4	11.6	

MFI = microfinance institution.
Source: International Monetary Fund, Financial Access Survey. data.imf.org/FAS (accessed 24 January 2019).

outreach has remained stable in terms of bank branch penetration; for every 100,000 adults, there were 39.1 branches in 2004 versus 36.1 branches in 2016. Table 8.5 shows the banking outreach and indicates that use is uneven across regions. In Tashkent City in 2017, users paid SUM7.6 million per capita terms using point-of-sale terminals, and SME loans issued SUM3.08 million in per capita terms. In the capital city, there was one ATM or unmanned information kiosk per 821 people. The Navoi region has the second-highest bank penetration indicators; however, it has 2.5 times lower per capita payments through point-of-sale terminals, and more than three times fewer SME loans per capita. In the rest of the country's regions, as Table 8.5 shows, banking use is even lower.

The country has made progress in creating infrastructure to support lending. In 2000, the Cabinet of the Minister of Uzbekistan made the decision to create the first credit bureau as part of Uzbekistan's banking

Table 8.5 Banking Outreach and Use in the Regions of Uzbekistan

	Population	Per Capita Payment through POS Terminals, in SUM'000		SME Loans per Capita, in SUM'000		Population per ATM and Informational Kiosk	
	2017	2016	2017	2016	2017	2016	2017
Tashkent City	2,352,300	6,544.9	7,595.3	2,403.1	3,076.0	901.6	821.3
Navoi	913,200	2,276.3	2,240.9	670.1	761.1	7,673.9	6,918.2
Tashkent	2,758,300	1,650.6	1,737.9	390.5	501.5	21,718.9	16,717.0
Bukhara	1,785,400	1,819.5	1,690.3	394.7	467.3	7,170.3	6,156.6
Karakalpak	1,763,100	1,437.6	1,462.8	367.6	488.6	15,465.8	11,832.9
Khorezm	1,715,600	1,253.2	1,347.1	377.5	486.4	15,317.9	11,831.7
Syrdarya	777,100	1,307.0	1,302.5	460.2	498.5	16,534.0	9,251.2
Ferghana	3,444,900	1,267.9	1,129.5	310.2	370.0	8,182.7	6,959.4
Andijan	2,857,300	1,193.8	1,089.8	391.9	446.6	15,118.0	13,737.0
Kashkadarya	2,958,900	1,197.7	1,045.6	309.8	378.6	29,589.0	24,253.3
Djizzak	1,250,100	1,109.0	1,022.4	363.6	427.2	20,493.4	17,124.7
Namangan	2,554,200	1,149.8	1,001.5	260.4	334.9	10,135.7	9,220.9
Samarkand	3,514,800	1,139.2	952.5	346.8	402.2	12,332.6	10,337.6
Surkhandarya	2,358,300	1,027.9	874.8	307.9	364.3	8,766.9	8,188.5

POS = point-of-sale.
Source: The authors based their estimates on Central Bank of Uzbekistan data. http://www.cbu.uz/en/statistics/paysistem/ (accessed 24 January 2019). The population data come from the State Committee on Statistics and include people with permanent residence. https://stat.uz/en/open-data/demografiya (accessed 24 January 2019). For information, readers might use the approximate exchange rate of SUM8,000.00 = $1.00 to convert the figures into United States dollars.

association.[2] In 2004, the bureau was turned into a legally independent unit. In 2012, based on the public credit bureau, the decision was made to create a private credit bureau. As Table 8.6 shows, as of 2016, the private credit bureau covers 27.8% of the adult population. The National Collateral Register commenced operations in 2014.[3]

In Uzbekistan, the Findex 2017 survey reported that 94% of the adult population has a national identity card (passport); this is high

---

[2] The bureau's website describes the history of credit bureau development (in Russian). http://infokredit.uz/ru/o-kompanii/istoriya-byuro (accessed 24 January 2019).

[3] The website of the National Collateral Register states that it was established in 2014. https://garov.uz/ru/about (accessed 24 January 2019).

Table 8.6 Credit Information Sharing

	Private Credit Bureau Coverage (% of Adults)
2008	2.2
2009	2.1
2010	3.3
2011	3.6
2012	15.7
2013	16.5
2014	17.8
2015	19.4
2016	27.8

Source: World Development Indicators database. Available at url: databank.worldbank.org/wdi (accessed on 24 January 2019).

relative to 92% of lower middle-income countries. In addition, in December 2017, the CBU announced that, during 2018, the country will introduce a common national platform for the remote identification of clients. Specifically, this will involve upgrading the National Database of Depositors by creating unique identification numbers for the people registered in the system. As the CBU reported, the introduction of electronic identification numbers will enable people to access remote banking services, which are increasing day by day.[4]

8.3 Status of Financial Inclusion

8.3.1 Financial Inclusion of Households

Uzbekistan, as Yoshino and Morgan (2016) also noted, is among the countries with a low bank account penetration rate; according to the 2014 Findex survey, only 26% of people aged 15 and older held an account with a financial institution. Beck and Brown (2011), based on the nationally representative sample of the Life in Transition Survey II, which the European Bank for Reconstruction and Development and

---

[4] Information on this is available from the CBU website. http://cbu.uz/ru/press-tsentr/obzori/2017/12/96391/ (accessed 19 January 2019).

the World Bank administered in 2010, listed Uzbekistan among the transition countries with a low level of banking service use. However, the 2017 Findex survey reported that 37% of people aged 15 and older had an account; thus, account penetration had increased but remained low. Table 8.7 presents additional evidence on the increase in account penetration, showing that the number of bank cards increased 2.5 times in 2017 relative to 2011. The World Bank World Development Indicators database shows that the account penetration rate in Uzbekistan is higher than in countries with a similar level of GDP per capita. The major driver behind bank card use is the legislation requiring organizations and state-owned companies to pay salaries through a transfer to a bank card. For instance, ADB (2014) reported that the most common method of paying salaries in the formal sector is through direct transfers to employees' bank cards; this is a result of the government policy aimed at reducing money out of bank circulation and deepening non-cash payments. As a result, more than 19 million bank cards were in use as of January 2017 versus only 32,000 in 1999.[5] Similarly, according to the CBU, the total amount of transactions using bank cards increased form SUM0.1 billion in 2004 to SUM53,050 billion ($6.5 billion) in January 2016.

Table 8.7 shows a surge in internet and mobile use in Uzbekistan. The number of internet banking users increased from 0.4% of depositors in 2011 to 2.3% in 2017. The use of mobile banking increased from 0.3% of depositors in 2011 to 32.8% in 2017. The CER (2015) reported that the surge in electronic banking products was a result of the regulatory changes. Table 8.8 shows that most of the laws on the use of information resources and systems, electronic signatures, and commerce have come into force since 2004. An important milestone in the development of electronic payments was the introduction of the mobile payment system by the Common Republican Processing Centre and e-payment company Click. As the CER (2015) stated, the adoption of the law on electronic payments provided a strong impetus for the development of the system. However, mobile banking and internet banking have considerable room to improve. First, the CBU reported that payments for utility services, like the gas and electricity supply, and taxes make up 99% of remote retail banking transactions. The main bottleneck in this development is the low speed of internet in the country; for instance, as of January 2018, out of 129 countries Uzbekistan ranks 122nd for broadband speed and 119th for mobile internet speed, in the Speedtest Global Ranking, which compares internet speed across countries.[6] The countries with

---

[5] Central Bank of Uzbekistan. Available at url: http://www.cbu.uz/ru/platyezhnye-sistemy/29/ (accessed 19 January 2019)

[6] For the country ranks, please visit the website Speedtest Global Index. https://www.speedtest.net/global-index (accessed 19 January 2019).

Table 8.7 Bank Card, Internet, and Mobile Banking Use in Uzbekistan

	2011	2015	2016	2017	Ratio of 2017/2011
Bank cards issued ('000)	7,909	15,215	16,316	19,523	2.50
Transaction volume through bank cards (in SUM billion)	10,192.4	31,324.0	53,050.0		5.20
Payment terminals	85,741	169,581	183,060	208,536	2.40
Information points	491	2012	2,345	4,954	10.10
Number of depositors	1,159,890	143,2849	1,515,004	1,638,673	1.40
Number of deposit accounts	3,926,356	503,0704	5,364,838	5,809,172	1.59
Remote banking users					
Number	24,545	53,4800	1,061,022	2,042,111	83.20
% of depositors	0.6	10.6	19.8	35.2	
Internet banking and bank client network users					
Number	14,241	62,227	81,492	135,629	9.50
% of depositors	0.4	1.2	1.5	2.3	
Mobile and SMS banking users					
Number	10,304	47,2573	979,530	1,906,482	185.00
% of depositors	0.3	9.4	18.3	32.8	

SMS = short messaging service.
Source: Central Bank of Uzbekistan. http://www.cbu.uz/en/statistics/paysistem/ (accessed 24 January 2019).

Table 8.8 Major Events in the Development of Electronic Payment Systems

Timeline	Events
December 2003	Law on the use of informatization
December 2003	Law on electronic signatures
April 2004	Law on electronic documents
May 2004	Law on electronic commerce
December 2005	Law on electronic payments
September 2013	First mobile banking system launched jointly with the Common Republican Processing Centre and the e-payment company Click

Source: Authors' compilation based on the law database lex.uz. available at url: www.lex.uz (accessed 24 January 2019)

the highest rank have high speed and those with a low rank have low speed. Uzbekistan is among the countries with low speed.

Table 8.9 shows the percentage of the adult population with an account at a financial institution, and Table 8.10 shows the percentage of the adult population with a debit card. First, as in the rest of the transition economies in Europe and Central Asia (ECA), account and debit card ownership increased for all groups of adults in Uzbekistan between 2011 and 2017. Five trends are apparent in the table. First, a relatively lower percentage of females than males have a bank account. Second, the gap in account ownership between people within and outside the labor force has narrowed. That is because, in 2015 and 2016, the state started to transfer old age pensions and other social payments to a bank card. Third, young adults are relatively more financially excluded, as evidenced by the relatively low percentage of people in this category who own a bank account. Similarly, this gap is large depending on education and income levels. Table 8.10 suggests that the proportionate increase is greater in account ownership than in debit card ownership. Moreover, account ownership is proportionally higher for males relative

Table 8.9 Formal Account Ownership at a Financial Institution

	Uzbekistan			Europe and Central Asia		
	2011	2014	2017	2011	2014	2017
Have an account:						
All adults	22.5	40.7	37.1	69.3	77.7	81.5
Males	23.8	42.2	38.3	72.6	79.5	83.7
Females	27.0	43.1	38.6	70.5	83.6	88.0
In the labor force	10.5	36.4	34.3	55.5	65.3	71.7
Out of the labor force	21.3	39.3	36.0	66.4	76.1	79.4
Young adults (% aged 15–24)	15.0	24.9	20.9	50.9	59.6	63.8
Older adults (% aged 25+)	26.0	47.9	43.6	73.1	81.0	84.8
Primary education or less	10.3	24.3	20.9	49.0	56.5	67.9
Secondary education or more	28.1	48.2	43.2	75.5	82.4	85.1
Income, poorest 40%	19.3	35.3	29.7	68.1	73.7	76.3
Income, richest 60%	24.6	44.3	42.0	70.3	80.3	84.8
Rural	22.6	42.7	34.4	60.3	76.4	79.2

Note: All numbers are percentages of people aged 15+ in the respective category.
Source: World Bank, Global Findex Database. Available at url: https://globalfindex.worldbank.org/ (accessed on 24 January 2019)

Table 8.10 Debit Card Ownership

	Uzbekistan			Europe and Central Asia		
	2011	2014	2017	2011	2014	2017
Have a debit card						
All adults	20.4	24.6	24.1	54.2	62.5	70.9
Females	19.9	25.8	22.1	51.2	59.2	68.1
Males	21.1	23.3	26.4	57.7	66.2	74.0
Poorest 40%	19.0	17.7	17.6	53.6	55.5	64.4
Young adults (% aged 15–24)	13.8	11.2	12.6	39.8	46.2	55.7
Older adults (% aged 25+)	23.6	30.7	28.8	57.5	65.5	73.8
Primary education or less	9.4	13.9	9.7	30.6	35.5	55.0
Secondary education or more	25.5	29.5	29.6	61.4	68.6	75.2

Note: All numbers are percentages of people aged 15+ in the respective category.
Source: World Bank, Global Findex Database. https://globalfindex.worldbank.org/ (accessed 24 January 2019).

to females; this gap is smaller than in countries in the similar income group. In contrast, 22.1% of females have a debit card versus 26.4% of males. Strikingly, in Uzbekistan, the percentages of adults with an account and a debit card are much lower than those in the rest of the ECA transition economies, as Tables 8.9 and 8.10 show.

Table 8.11 shows that in 2017 only 1.0% of female and 3.3% of male adults had ever borrowed from a formal financial institution. These rates are significantly lower than those in ECA countries. Thus, the degree of financial exclusion is high. The CER (2013) explained that banks' supply of consumer loans is low; in 2012 consumer loans in Uzbekistan constituted only 2.4% of GDP versus 10.2% for the Russian Federation and 6.5% for Azerbaijan. Table 8.11 also reports that relatives and friends are the largest source of borrowed funds relative to formal financial institutions; more than 12.1% of female and 13.8% of male respondents declared that they had borrowed from friends and relatives in 2017. These figures are comparable to the rest of the ECA countries.

In Uzbekistan, unlike in other ECA countries, the proportion of respondents who declared that they saved using a formal financial institution is small (Table 8.12). The Findex survey results show that the proportion of households that save using informal saving clubs or persons outside the households is high relative to ECA economies. This is in line with the CER (2013), which declared that only 5% of the aggregated savings of households is kept in bank deposits. The CER observed that

Table 8.11 Borrowing Behavior in Uzbekistan

	Uzbekistan			Europe and Central Asia		
	2011	2014	2017	2011	2014	2017
Borrowed						
From a financial institution						
Female	1.2	0.7	1.0	9.0	13.1	13.5
Male	1.7	1.9	3.3	11.1	16.4	17.4
From family or friends						
Female	10.4	10.5	12.1	17.7	16.7	18.1
Male	13.0	11.7	13.8	18.4	18.0	18.5

Note: All numbers are percentages of people aged 15+ in the respective category.
Source: World Bank, Global Findex Database. Available at url: https://globalfindex.worldbank.org/ (accessed on 24 January 2019)

Table 8.12 Saving Behavior in Uzbekistan

	Uzbekistan			Europe and Central Asia		
	2011	2014	2017	2011	2014	2017
Saved at a financial institution						
Female	0.5	1.6	1.6	23.2	28.2	31.7
Male	1.1	2.1	3.1	26.3	33.7	37.1
Poorest 40%	0.7	0.8	0.7	24.0	22.9	24.6
Younger adults	0.0	0.6	1.1	19.4	25.0	22.1
Older adults (% aged 25+)	1.2	2.4	2.8	25.9	31.9	36.6
Primary education or less	0.6	0.8	1.2	10.0	13.4	21.9
Secondary education or more	0.9	2.3	2.8	29.2	34.7	37.7

Note: All the numbers are percentages of people aged 15+ in the respective category, unless otherwise indicated.
Source: World Bank, Global Findex Database. https://globalfindex.worldbank.org/ (accessed 24 January 2019).

this limits banks' resource base, explaining the low supply of loans. The CER (2013) claimed that the low levels of saving are partly due to the low supply of attractive saving products at the banks; as a result, people either save informally or invest in real estate. Additionally, Hiwatari (2010) and Kandiyoti (1998) reported that informal rotating savings and credit associations among relatives, people in common neighborhoods, or the professional community are popular in Uzbekistan.

The use of insurance services remains even lower than the use of banking services. The Ministry of Finance of Uzbekistan (MFU) (2017) reported that 26 institutions operate in the insurance market of Uzbekistan, of which 23 are companies that provide general insurance and three provide life insurance. In 2016, the three largest institutions, all of which are state-owned, controlled 47.4% of the insurance market (MFU 2017). The total volume of insurance premiums collected in 2016 constituted SUM629 billion (that is, $77.6 million, based on the exchange rate of SUM8,100.00 = $1.00, or 0.12% of GDP). Of the total insurance premiums, 52.2% were collected in the capital city Tashkent, which has a population of over 3 million people, and the rest came from the regions outside the city (MFU 2017). Thus, the urban–rural gap in access to and use of insurance services is large.

The CER (2015) explained that Uzbekistan's pension system consists of mandatory and accumulated pensions. An extra-budgetary pension fund runs the mandatory pension, whereas the state-owned Halk Bank operates the accumulated pensions. In 2013, according to the CER, 90% of pension funds were with the extra-budgetary pension fund and the rest were with Halk Bank. Like other former Soviet Union transition economies, Uzbekistan has high pension coverage (79% in 2013). The CER (2015) indicated that this is a legacy of the Soviet past, when full employment and thus pension coverage were the norm. However, as other similar countries' coverage declines as a result of the structural transformation of the country, the role of the private sector increases, and employment in the public sector declines, there is a high level of informality (CER 2015). The CER (2015) also reported that the basic-level mandatory monthly pension payments are set at 55% of the monthly average salary and must always be higher than the minimum wage.

8.3.2 Financial Inclusion of Micro, Small, Medium-Sized, and Large Enterprises

Table 8.13 shows the overall increase in the percentage of firms with a bank account: 97.3% of firms declared that they had a bank account in 2013 versus 93.8% in 2008. Bank account ownership is almost universal, independent of the industry, enterprise size, business location, and gender of the business manager.

In 2013, 26.4% of firms declared that they had a bank loan or line of credit versus only 10.5% in 2008; thus, financial inclusion has doubled, but it is still low compared with countries with a similar GDP level (Table 8.13). As Table 8.13 shows, the gaps in having loans and/or lines of credit are significant depending on the establishment size, business

Table 8.13 Financial Inclusion Indicators for Small, Medium, and Large Enterprises in Uzbekistan

Sector	Percentage of Firms with a Checking or Savings Account		Percentage of Firms with a Bank Loan/ Line of Credit		Proportion of Loans Requiring Collateral (Percentage)		Value of Collateral Needed for a Loan (Percentage of the Loan Amount)		Percentage of Firms not Needing a Loan	
	2008	2013	2008	2013	2008	2013	2008	2013	2008	2013
All	93.8	97.3	10.5	26.4	98.7	96.5	129.7	175.7	38.1	74.7
Industry										
Manufacturing	95.6	92.6	9.0	26.8	97.5	98.1	122.2	171.9	28.6	68.0
Services all	93.1	99.8	11.0	26.2	99.0	95.7	131.4	177.9	41.7	78.2
Retail	90.5	99.4	18.2	338.6	99.1	90.8	127.7	199.9	46.9	76.3
Other services	94.9	100.0	6.0	20.5	98.8	99.9	139.6	156.7	38.1	79.1
Size										
Medium (20–99)	99.5	99.5	9.9	24.5	94.6	99.6	146.0	168.6	49.0	66.3
Small (5–19)	92.0	96.5	9.5	26.3	100.0	96.1	125.6	178.2	35.5	78.0
Large (100+)	97.8	98.0	29.3	41.4	97.7	88.9	127.8	162.9	30.4	70.0
Location										
Tashkent	90.8	96.2	9.3	20.8	99.1	90.8	121.6	259.7	47.4	54.6
Outside the capital city	97.9	95.8	12.0	49.3	100.0	99.6	137.5	144.9	29.8	90.6

continued on next page

Table 8.13 continued

Sector	Percentage of Firms with a Checking or Savings Account		Percentage of Firms with a Bank Loan/Line of Credit		Proportion of Loans Requiring Collateral (Percentage)		Value of Collateral Needed for a Loan (Percentage of the Loan Amount)		Percentage of Firms not Needing a Loan	
	2008	2013	2008	2013	2008	2013	2008	2013	2008	2013
Exporter status										
Exporter	97.1	100.0	42.4	42.5		92.7		119.2	28.0	91.4
Non-exporter	93.7	97.3	10.1	26.2	98.6	96.6	129.8	176.8	38.2	74.5
Gender of the top manager										
Female	86.8	100.0	9.2	27.1	100.0	99.4		207.3	42.3	79.4
Male	94.7	96.9	10.7	26.3	98.5	96.1	129.9	170.0	37.4	74.0
Ownership type										
Domestic	93.5	98.4	9.3	26.6	99.1	96.3	129.7	174.8	38.3	76.1
Foreign	100.5	85.8	36.4	24.5	96.2	98.9	130.6	185.9	32.8	59.5

Source: World Bank Enterprise surveys database. www.enterprisesurveys.org (accessed 24 January 2019).

location, and exporter status. The proportion of firms is smaller for small firms, firms located in the capital city, and non-exporters. Strikingly, the proportion of firms with a line of credit and/or loan is independent of the gender of the top manager. Despite these changes, the proportion of businesses that declare that they need no loan has also doubled. The collateral requirements remain high, as evidenced by the high percentage of loans that require collateral and the value of collateral. Businesses managed by women must provide a higher value of collateral than those managed by men.

8.4 Barriers to Financial Inclusion

Column A of Table 8.14 presents the major reasons for not using formal financial services in Uzbekistan. In 2014, the high costs of financial services were reported as the top reason for households not using formal finance. Indeed, as Figure 8.3 shows, the interest rates on commercial loans for individuals (Panel A) and businesses (Panels B and C) are high given that the ADB has published figures of 16% inflation and 4% GDP per capita growth. Blondel (2015) mentioned that the government policy to restrict access to cash and cash transactions translated into additional informal transaction costs that entrepreneurs had to pay to cash their bank loans in 2015.

Table 8.14 Major Reasons for Not Using Formal Financial Services and Reasons for Having No Bank Account

		Major Reason for Not Using Formal Financial Services (a)	Major Reason for Having No Bank Account (b)
1	Insufficient money to use financial institutions	0.4	35.9
2	Lack of necessary documentation	21	17.6
3	Someone else in the family already has an account	30	16.6
4	Financial institutions are too far away	12	11.8
5	Financial services are too expensive	44	11.2
6	Lack of trust in financial institutions	10	9.8
7	Religious reasons	30	2.0

Source: World Bank, Global Findex Database. https://globalfindex.worldbank.org/ (accessed 24 January 2019). Note that in Column (A) we use data for 2014 and Column (B) we report data for 2017. Figures refer to percentage of respondents not using formal financial services (a) or bank accounts (b) who cited that reason.

Importantly, private domestic and foreign banks charge relatively high interest rates. Until 2018, the CBU set the commission fees on the use of bank cards centrally. Anecdotal evidence suggests that the amount of fees charged to private individuals did not enable private banks to offer their services to private individuals. However, in 2018, the CBU started to publish recommended commission fees for the use of bankcards.

Religious reasons are the second most important reason for people not using financial services. The Central Intelligence Agency Factbook reports that 88% of Uzbekistan's population are Muslims; however, the banks offer no Islamic banking products.[7] This is partly a legacy of the former Soviet Union and a cautious approach to reforms in Uzbekistan. In May 2018, a number of news websites announced that, with the support of the Islamic Development Bank, the Ministry of Finance was preparing a presidential decree on creating a legislative base and infrastructure to support Islamic finance.[8]

A lack of documentation and the inability to obtain an account are the next most important reasons for not using formal financial services. A total of 10% of the respondents reported that they do not trust financial institutions. This is in line with the CER (2011), which reported, based on a 2010 Uzbekistan national survey, that 78% of their respondents indicated that they do not save with banks because they cannot withdraw cash when needed.

Findex 2017 asked about the reasons for not having a bank account; this is different from Findex 2014, which asked about the reasons for not using financial services in general. Therefore, Columns A and B in Table 8.14 are not comparable. A lack of money to use an account, a lack of documentation, considerable length of distance to a bank branch, and the high cost of using a bank account are the major reasons for not using formal finance.

Table 8.15 describes the top reasons for firms not using bank loans and/or lines of credit. They ranked high interest rates and complex application procedures as the two major reasons for not applying for a formal loan and/or line of credit. The cost of borrowing from a financial institution increased between 2008 and 2013. Indeed, Blondel (2015) also reported, based on a field study in Uzbekistan, that entrepreneurs declared that the paperwork needed to obtain a loan was among the most difficult barriers to surmount.

---

[7] The website of the US Central Intelligence Agency contains information on the religious composition of the Uzbek population. https://www.cia.gov/library/publications/the-world-factbook/geos/print_uz.html (accessed 24 January 2019).

[8] The news website Gazeta.uz contains information on this. https://www.gazeta.uz/ru/2018/05/16/islamic-banking/ (accessed 24 January 2019).

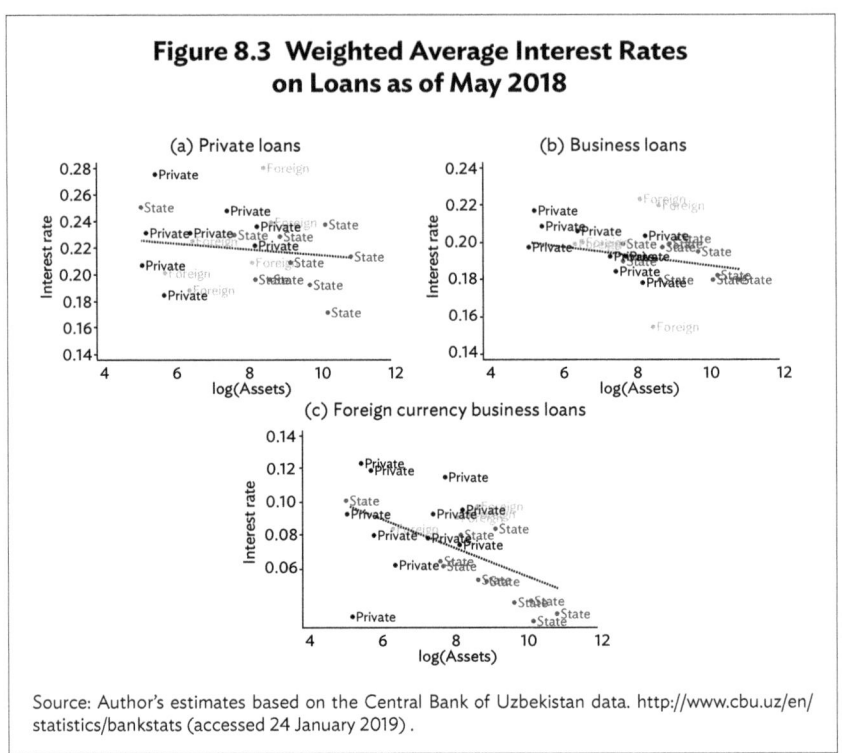

Figure 8.3 Weighted Average Interest Rates on Loans as of May 2018

Source: Author's estimates based on the Central Bank of Uzbekistan data. http://www.cbu.uz/en/statistics/bankstats (accessed 24 January 2019).

Table 8.15 Top Reasons for Not Using Bank Loans or Lines of Credit (%)

	2008	2013
High interest rates	24	42
Complex application process	37	33
High collateral requirements	18	22
Insufficient loan size and maturity	11	3
Won't be approved	8	0

Source: World Bank Enterprise surveys database. www.enterprisesurveys.org (accessed 24 January 2019). Figures refer to percentage of respondents not using bank loans or lines of credit who cited that reason.

The third largest group, containing 22% of firms, reported high collateral requirements as the major reason behind their decision not to use formal finance. Blondel (2015) stated, for the sample of firms that her study covered, that collateral values ranged from 130% to 500% of the loan values, with a median of 175%.

8.5 Financial Regulation and Supervision

The CBU is responsible for regulating and supervising commercial banks and MFIs.[9] The IMF (2008) mentioned that the CBU's on- and off-site supervision is adequate. The IMF (2008, 2013) reported that direct intervention in commercial banks' activity (e.g. through asking banks directly to finance state-owned projects and programs) is widespread, and this hampers competition among banks.

Moreover, banks were burdened with the obligation to report clients' transactions to tax and customs authorities and conduct financial oversight of the cash management of business entities. Commercial banks thus performed non-core functions. The IFC (2006: 38) gives examples of these based on focus group interviews with entrepreneurs; those that are relevant today are as follows:

(i) Each registered export (barter) contract must be monitored by the authorized bank in terms of the operations related to contract enforcement.

(ii) ... in case of failure to receive the export earnings completely or goods within the time frame established by the law (based on the date of border crossing or completion of works), the authorized bank [must] inform the local tax and customs authorities in writing to take measures according to the law.

(iii) ... upon the request of the tax authorities the banks must provide the transaction data of their customers required for monitoring the integrity and completeness of all due tax payments.

All of these non-core functions destroyed the trust in banks and increased their costs. Direct intervention in pricing loans and the presence of direct state loans also damaged banks' risk management practices.

In addition, the CBU maintained a heavily overvalued sum exchange rate by restricting the availability of foreign currency to finance imports. It required exporters of cotton and gold to sell 100% of their foreign currency earnings at this distorted exchange rate, and required other exporters to sell 50% of their foreign currency earnings at a distorted price (IMF 2000, 2008, 2013). Small businesses and private individuals thus had restricted access to international payment instruments and foreign currency, which then created an unofficial black market for foreign currency. Figure 8.4 shows that, until the

---

[9] "Law of the Republic of Uzbekistan on Banks and Banking" #216-I from 25.04.1996 http://lex.uz/pages/getpage.aspx?lact_id=12011 (accessed 24 January 2019).

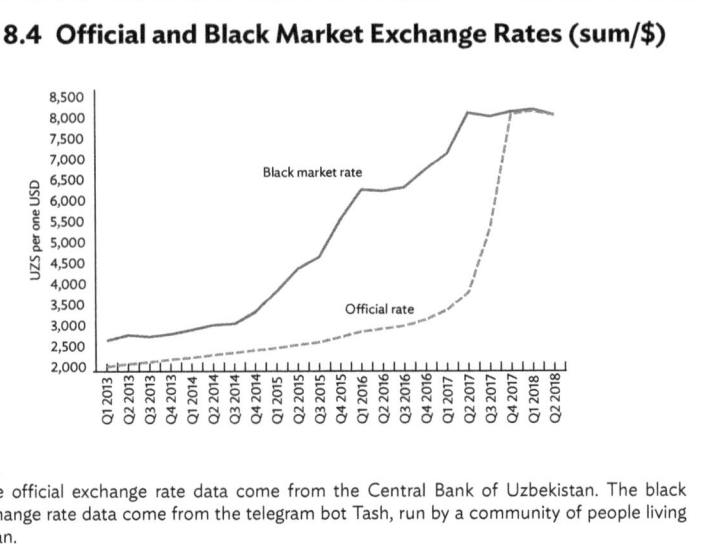

Figure 8.4 Official and Black Market Exchange Rates (sum/$)

Q = quarter.
Source: The official exchange rate data come from the Central Bank of Uzbekistan. The black market exchange rate data come from the telegram bot Tash, run by a community of people living in Uzbekistan.

second quarter of 2017, the gap between the official and the black market exchange rate widened. From September 2017, the government liberalized access to foreign exchange and devalued the Uzbek sum twice, which narrowed this gap.

The Law of the Republic of Uzbekistan on Protection of Consumer Rights has regulated consumer protection since 1996. Article 28 states that all financial service providers need to insure their liabilities in case of bankruptcy or liquidation. This article also requires financial service providers to inform their customers about the existence of insurance. The main organization for implementing this law is the State Committee on Privatization, Demonopolization and Promotion of Competition and Agency Uzbek Standard. In addition, from the start of 2017, the Office of the President of Uzbekistan started to receive direct complaints from individuals on all kinds of issues through hotline and online channels. In one-year period from its first launch, this office received over a million complaints, and the fifth-largest number of objections addressed the CBU and commercial banks.[10] Financial deepening will thus require a more rigorous approach to consumer protection than is necessary now.

---

[10] Information on this is available on the virtual reception website of the President of Uzbekistan's office. https://pm.gov.uz/uz/news/view?id=34 (last accessed 10 January 2018, no longer available).

Uzbekistan has had explicit deposit insurance covering all the banks in the country since 2002. Initially, the deposit insurance was partial. However, on 28 November 2008, a new Presidential Decree announced a blanket guarantee on deposits, and on October 2009 this was replaced by a statutory limit of 250 times the minimum wage (Demirgüç-Kunt, Kane, and Laeven 2014). In December 2017, the minimum wage for 2018 was SUM172,240, approximately $21.00 at the exchange rate of SUM8,000.00 = $1.00. Thus, the statutory limit is $5,382.5.[11] Besides these, there are no regulations protecting depositors or related to FinTech products.

8.6 Financial Literacy and Education

Assessing the level of financial literacy in Uzbekistan is a challenge due to missing micro-data. The only evidence comes from Standard & Poor's 2014 Global Financial Literacy Survey, which only published aggregated results. Interestingly, Uzbekistan has a much lower financial literacy rate than other transition economies, as shown in Figure 8.5.

Uzbekistan has no national strategy for promoting financial literacy. However, the Sparkassen-Finanzgruppe reported that, jointly with the ministries of Uzbekistan, it had developed such a plan, which was pending ratification. On its website, the Sparkassen-Finanzgruppe reported the following:[12]

> Based on an analysis of general financial literacy in Uzbekistan, a gender-specific national strategy was developed to raise the level of basic financial education of the Uzbek population. This 5-year strategy details the objectives, structures, methods and target groups of financial education in Uzbekistan. Furthermore, a two-year action plan was devised, listing specific activities, responsibilities, a timeframe and budget for the strategy's implementation. Sparkassenstiftung completed all of this work by the close of 2016. In all, some 13 Uzbek ministries and institutions helped co-design the action roadmap and the financial and cost plans as well as the monitoring concept. Project

---

[11] Information on minimum wages is available on the information directory website Golden Pages of Uzbekistan. https://www.goldenpages.uz/zarplata/ (accessed 19 January 2019).

[12] Information on this is available from the website of Sparkassen-Finanzgruppe. http://www.sparkassenstiftung.de/index.php?id=34&L=1&tx_ttnews%5Btt_news%5D=1394&cHash=0f8b88b56f943f2f86f02ac167927f2e (accessed 24 January 2019).

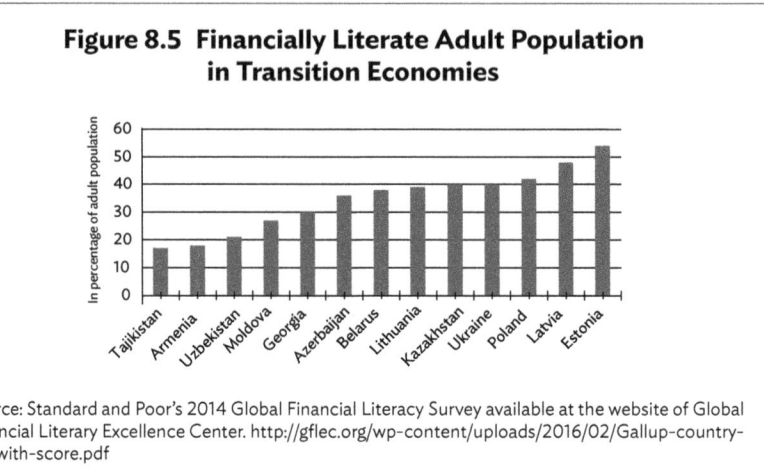

Source: Standard and Poor's 2014 Global Financial Literacy Survey available at the website of Global Financial Literary Excellence Center. http://gflec.org/wp-content/uploads/2016/02/Gallup-country-list-with-score.pdf

activities for the year under review also include several further training inputs for different actors. Courses for local trainers featuring simulations for financial budget planning and the promotion of small-scale enterprises have proven particularly successful in this context. Despite the delay in the adoption of a gender-specific strategy due to the elections of December 2016, the project is continuing to meet the high demand for its further training measures.

In May 2017, the CBU reported that, jointly with the International Finance Corporation (part of the World Bank Group), the Association of Banks of Uzbekistan, and the Chamber of Commerce of Uzbekistan, it had started to implement a new program on financial literacy. The program consists of two parts: the first targets owners of small and medium-sized businesses, and the second aims to educate the general population. It is not clear whether the financial literacy program will be included in the school curriculum. Importantly, this is not the first financial literacy program.[13] A few other programs exist, like the Deutsche Gesellschaft für Internationale Zusammenarbeit project, within which the Sparkassen-Finanzgruppe currently also focuses on financial literacy; for instance, the program operates a "train the trainer" program with a state financial institute. Additionally, the National

---

[13] Information on this is available on the CBU website. http://www.cbu.uz/ru/press-tsentr/press-relizy/2017/11/95839/ (accessed 4 June 2018).

Table 8.16 Who Makes the Decisions about the Savings, Investment, and Borrowing in Your Household?
(%)

	Male	Female	Total
Shared equally between me and my partner	32.39	37.85	34.38
Mostly me	28.87	27.69	28.44
Shared equally between me and someone else in the household	13.91	11.38	12.99
Subtotal for own decision	75.20	76.90	75.80
Mostly my partner	14.08	10.77	12.88
Mostly someone else in the household	10.21	12.00	10.86
Mostly someone else not in the household	0.53	0.31	0.45
Subtotal for decision by others	24.83	23.08	24.19

Source: Author's estimates based on the Life in Transition Survey III. http://litsonline-ebrd.com/ (accessed 24 January 2019).

Association of Microfinance Institutions of Uzbekistan, in partnership with the Microfinance Centre, has implemented a finance literacy program by directly training 633 low-income people and preparing 34 trainers on financial literacy. However, the scale of the current programs is small, and no assessment is available to judge the impact of these programs on financial literacy.

In addition to low financial literacy, the degree of independent decision making with regard to saving and borrowing can affect access to finance in Uzbekistan. Table 8.16 shows that almost one-fourth of adults reported that someone else makes their financial decisions.

8.7 Conclusions and Policy Recommendation

This chapter demonstrates that household and firm financial inclusion in Uzbekistan remains low. First, the majority of households, rather than using formal finance, save and borrow informally. Low-income households have less access to finance than their peers in high-income groups. Although most households are increasingly using a bank account, few borrow and/or save with a formal financial institution. Pension coverage is high, but mainly limited to public sector employment; people employed informally have no pension coverage. The use of insurance services is even lower. Internet and mobile payments have spiked in recent years; however, the usage level remains low relative to that in other countries, like the People's Republic of China, India, and the Russian Federation. Almost all firms use a bank account, but few borrow from a financial institution. Few firms use e-payments. The low banking sector penetration rate in Uzbekistan relative to countries with a similar level of development also suggests that financial inclusion is low. Uzbekistan thus needs to increase the level of financial inclusion for firms and households to achieve equitable and rapid growth in per capita income, which is one of the key goals of all economic reforms.

According to the surveys, both households and firms indicate the high cost of using finance as the top reason for not using it. As the second most important reason for not using formal finance, households declared that religious reasons stop them from using formal finance. Indeed, given that 88% of Uzbekistan's population are Muslims, the fact that no banks offer an Islamic banking product indicates a clear gap in the supply. Unlike households, firms reported that the complex application procedures and high collateral requirements are the second and third most important reasons for not using formal finance. These reasons thus suggest that financial inclusion in Uzbekistan is mainly constrained by supply-side factors.

On the supply side, the financial system is highly concentrated, with five commercial banks controlling more than half of the banking sector assets. This is in line with Beck, Demirgüç-Kunt, and Maksimovic (2004), who, based on a comparison of international evidence, concluded that, in countries with a higher banking concentration, firms face greater obstacles in accessing finance. All large banks are state-owned and mainly focus on financing government-led projects and programs. The lending rate for these state projects is often below the market rate, which undermines the risk management practices of banks and limits the availability of finance to the private sector. The limited supply of finance to the private sector and limited competition in the sector make finance expensive for private-sector players and constrain financial innovation. This is in line with Beck, Demirgüç-Kunt, and Maksimovic (2004), who reported that state ownership of banks and direct intervention in banking activities worsen access to finance.

Strikingly, although the level of financial inclusion is low, the country has no financial inclusion strategy, and, even more surprisingly, we detected no ongoing discussions about such a document. The first policy recommendation, therefore, is that the country needs to formulate a national financial inclusion strategy to enable a strategic approach to the matter. Second, based on international experience, it should promote private and foreign capital participation in banking, insurance, and other segments of the financial markets. Third, financial liberalization, which has accelerated since 2017 through removing most of the restrictions on access to foreign exchange, needs to continue; market-based interest rates and commission fees on financial services are essential to ensure the efficiency and inclusiveness of the system.

The liberalization of the banking system will also require the CBU to move toward the use of market-based instruments to regulate and supervise financial institutions, and the current heavy reliance on the use on non-market-based instruments should cease. The regulator, to foster competition among financial institutions, may also want to license FinTech and telecommunications companies, and promote the legal framework to enable peer-to-peer lending. At the practical level, promoting non-conventional financial institutions and products might not be an easy task. For such cases, countries like Singapore and others have devised clear procedures that financial institutions can apply to create a regulatory sandbox.[14] As the Consultative Group to Assist the Poor explained, a regulatory sandbox is "a framework set up by a regulator that allows FinTech startups and other innovators to conduct live experiments in a controlled environment under a regulator's supervision."[15]

The promotion of financial inclusion might occur through the use of digital finance, including the promotion of mobile and internet banking. To encourage these in addition to financial liberalization and the use of market-based tools of regulation and supervision, the government needs to facilitate infrastructure development, like the creation of remote identification facilities.

The country needs to improve its financial consumer protection. The current institutional structure, which pools together financial and general consumer protection, may not provide adequate safeguards. Rutledge (2010), based on six transition economies, explained that the financial crises of 2008 and 2009 demonstrated that the sustainability of financial systems is highly dependent on the existence of adequate consumer protection. Rutledge further explains that consumer protection must enable consumers to make fully informed decisions when choosing a financial product and service. Moreover, the consumer must have access to low-cost ways of handling their conflicts with financial institutions. Finally, consumers need access to resources that enable them to gain financial education in any form and at the

---

[14] Information on the procedures to apply a Fintech regulatory sandbox in Singapore is available from the website of the Monetary Authority of Singapore. http://www.mas.gov.sg/ Singapore-Financial-Centre/Smart-Financial-Centre/FinTech-Regulatory-Sandbox.aspx (accessed 24 January 2019).

[15] Website of the Consultative Group to Assist the Poor. http://www.cgap.org/ blog/regulatory-sandboxes-potential-financial-inclusion (accessed 24 January 2019).

most convenient time. To achieve this, the government needs to adjust the Law on Consumer Protection to fit the specific needs of financial services. Moreover, the country needs specific institutions that focus on financial consumer protection.

Although evidence remains limited, the available sources imply that the level of financial literacy in Uzbekistan is low. The existing studies, like that by Klapper, Lusardi, and Panos (2013), have suggested, based on the example of the Russian Federation, that financially literate people are more likely than financially illiterate people to use formal finance as opposed to informal finance, and the ability of individuals to avoid negative income shocks and have higher spending capacity increases with their level of financial literacy. Thus, to promote financial inclusion, the country needs to promote financial literacy.

References

Ahunov, M. O. (2015) Uzbek Banking System: Some History and Current State. Available: http://dx.doi.org/10.2139/ssrn.2636002 (last accessed on 24 January 2019)

Asian Development Bank (ADB). 2009. Development Effectiveness Brief Uzbekistan. A Partnership for Growth. Brief. Manila: ADB.

ADB. 2014. Asian Development Outlook. Brief. Manila: ADB.

Beck, T., and M. Brown. 2011. Use of Banking Services in Emerging Markets—Household-Level Evidence. CEPR Discussion Paper No. DP8475.

Beck, T., A. Demirgüç-Kunt, and V. Maksimovic. 2004. Bank Competition and Access to Finance: International Evidence. *Journal of Money, Credit and Banking* 36: 627–648.

Blondel, N. 2015. *Qualitative Impact Study: Uzbekistan Small Business and Entrepreneurship Development Project*. Manila: ADB (unpublished).

Central Bank of Uzbekistan. 2018. *Report on the Performance of the Central Bank of the Republic of Uzbekistan in 2017*. Tashkent: Central Bank of Uzbekistan.

Centre for Economic Research (CER). 2011. *Family Assets Mobilization—2010*. Tashkent: CER.

CER. 2013. Financial Liberalization: Developing the Retail Banking in Uzbekistan. Policy Brief No. 9 (May). Tashkent: CER.

CER. 2015. Electronic Money: Specifics of Circulation and Potential Impact on Economy. Policy Brief. Tashkent: CER (in Russian).

CER. 2016. *Almanac of Uzbekistan 2016*. Tashkent: CER.

Demirgüç-Kunt, A., E. Kane, and L. Laeven. 2014. Deposit Insurance Database. International Monetary Fund (IMF) Working Paper 14/118. Washington, DC: IMF.

Demirgüç-Kunt, A., and D. Singer. 2017. Financial Inclusion and Inclusive Growth: A Review of Recent Empirical Evidence. World Bank Policy Research Working Paper 8040. Washington, DC: World Bank.

Hiwatari, M. 2010. A Network Structure of ROSCAs (Rotating Savings and Credit Associations): ERGMs (Exponential Random Graph Models) Applied to a Leaders' Network in Rural Uzbekistan. Discussion Paper, Series A, 221: 1–24.

International Finance Corporation. 2006. Business Environment in Uzbekistan as Seen by Small and Medium Sized Enterprises: Survey Results Based on 2005. Tashkent: International Finance Corporation.

IMF. 2000. *Republic of Uzbekistan: Recent Economic Developments*. IMF Country Report 00/36. Washington, DC: IMF.

IMF. 2008. *Republic of Uzbekistan: 2008 Article IV Consultation—Staff Report; Public Information Notice on the Executive Board Discussion; and Statement by the Executive Director for the Republic of Uzbekistan.* IMF Country Report 08/235. Washington, DC: IMF.

IMF. 2013. *Republic of Uzbekistan, Staff Report for the 2012 Article IV Consultation.* IMF Country Report 13/278. Washington, DC: IMF.

IMF. 2018. *Republic of Uzbekistan, Article IV Consultation Staff Report; and Statement by the Executive Director for the Republic of Uzbekistan.* IMF Country Report 18/117. Washington, DC: IMF.

Kandiyoti, D. 1998. Rural Livelihoods and Social Networks in Uzbekistan: Perspectives from Andijan. *Central Asian Survey* 17(4): 561–578.

Klapper, L., A. Lusardi, and G. A. Panos. 2013. Financial Literacy and its Consequences: Evidence from Russia during the Financial Crisis. *Journal of Banking and Finance* 37(10): 3,904–3,923.

Ministry of Finance of the Republic of Uzbekistan. 2017. *Report on the Regulation and Supervision of Insurance Activities in the Republic of Uzbekistan for 2016.* Tashkent: Ministry of Finance of the Republic of Uzbekistan.

Mirziyoev, S. 2017. Speech at General Assembly of the United Nations Organization. https://www.gazeta.uz/ru/2017/09/20/un-ga-speech/ (accessed 29 May 2018).

Rutledge, S. 2010. *Consumer Protection and Financial Literacy: Lessons from Nine Country Studies.* World Bank Policy Research Paper 5326. Washington, DC: World Bank.

Ruziev, K., and D. Ghosh. 2009. Banking Sector Development in Uzbekistan: A Case of Mixed Blessings? *Problems of Economic Transition* 52(2): 3–41.

Yoshino, N., and P. Morgan. 2016. Overview of Financial Inclusion, Regulation, and. Education. ADB Institute Working Paper 591. Tokyo: Asian Development Bank Institute.

Index

Figures, notes, and tables are indicated by f, n, and t following page numbers.

A

account ownership
  gender differences in, 55, 268–69
  growth of, 55, 55f, 235
  identification requirements for, 147–48
  international comparisons, 39, 91–92, 91t, 268, 268t
  ratio of per capita GDP to, 8, 9f
  reasons for account nonuse, 94, 172, 274, 274t, 275
  in rural areas, 9, 146, 146n28
  by SMEs, 172
  socioeconomic differences in, 93, 140, 140t, 171, 172t
  in transition countries, 265–66
  by women, 140
ADB. *See* Asian Development Bank
agricultural insurance, 62, 70, 81, 98, 151
Alliance for Financial Inclusion, 3
AMFA. *See* Azerbaijan Microfinance Association
Armenia, 46–81. *See also* Central Bank of Armenia
  account ownership in, 8, 9f, 55, 55f
  ATM distribution in, 7, 53–54, 54f, 79
  bank branch density in, 7, 8f, 53, 53f
  banking card penetration in, 57, 57f, 67
  barriers to financial inclusion in, 19, 48, 61–62, 79
  consumer protection in, 24, 41, 64
  credit databases in, 30, 67
  credit guarantees in, 31
  delivery technologies in, 17
  deposit insurance in, 25, 64, 65f
  electronic identification in, 29, 70
  financial education programs in, 34t, 36–38, 42, 47, 73–78, 74t, 76–77t
  financial literacy in, 33–34, 47, 70–75, 71t, 76–77t, 114, 114t
  financial system in, 47–51, 48–51f, 51–52t
  indicators of financial inclusion in, 5–7, 6–7t, 46, 52–61, 55t
  insurance sector in, 11, 12f, 50–51, 51f, 57, 58f, 65, 70
  loans in, 9, 10f, 15t, 16, 56–57, 56f
  mobile banking in, 58–59, 59t
  pension system in, 12–13, 68
  policy recommendations for, 79–81
  regulatory framework in, 20t, 22–25, 62–65, 63t
  remittances in, 13, 57–58, 59t, 68
  SMEs in, 59–60, 60f, 69, 69t
  strategies for financial inclusion in, 13, 14t, 26–27, 27t, 65–70, 66–67t
  usage of financial services in, 54–55, 55t
ASEAN. *See* Association of Southeast Asian Nations
Asian Development Bank (ADB)
  financial inclusion as defined by, 3, 171
  financial resources from, 29–30, 248
  guarantee funds supported by, 211
  microfinance projects supported by, 1, 193
  promotion of financial education by, 215
  on salary payment methods, 266
  on state-owned banks, 259
  survey research by, 33
Association of Southeast Asian Nations (ASEAN), 1
ATMs
  accessibility to, 29
  banking card penetration and growth of, 232, 232f
  in CASC region, 7, 138, 139f, 198
  policy recommendations for, 121
  population growth and density of, 93
  regional disparities in, 139, 173, 262–63
  regulatory framework for, 18
  in rural vs. urban areas, 53–54, 54f, 61, 79
Azerbaijan, 85–123. *See also* Central Bank of Azerbaijan Republic
  account ownership in, 8–9, 9f, 39, 91–94, 91t
  agriculture-related financing products in, 16
  ATM distribution in, 93
  bank branch density in, 7, 8f, 93

287

288 Index

banking card penetration in, 96–97
bankruptcy laws in, 19, 104
barriers to financial inclusion in, 19, 101–5
consumer protection in, 24–25, 107–8, 122–23
credit databases in, 30, 110–11
credit guarantees and subsidies in, 31, 40, 102, 111
currency devaluation in, 2, 85, 119
delivery technologies in, 17
deposit insurance in, 25, 108–9
financial education programs in, 35t, 36, 37, 42, 118
financial literacy in, 113–19, 114t, 115f, 121–22
financial system in, 86–90, 88t, 89f, 90t, 119–20
indicators of financial inclusion in, 5, 6–7t, 90–101, 92t
insurance sector in, 11–12, 11–12f, 97–98
land registration in, 104–5
loans in, 9–11, 10f, 15t, 16, 39, 94–97, 95–96t, 95f
mobile banking in, 109
pension system in, 13, 99
policy recommendations for, 119–23
regulatory framework in, 20t, 22–26, 105–9
remittances in, 13, 99–100, 100t
saving behavior in, 96, 96t
securities market in, 100–101
SMEs in, 86, 87, 90–91
strategies for financial inclusion in, 13, 14t, 26, 27t, 39, 109–13
Azerbaijan Microfinance Association (AMFA), 89, 106, 113, 116, 118–19

B

bank branch density
account penetration and, 8–9
borrower growth and, 127n4
in CASC region, 7–9, 8f, 93, 138, 138f, 198
evolution of, 53, 53f, 128, 227
population growth and, 7
regional disparities in, 139, 167–68, 169t, 263
banking cards
debit cards, 135–36, 173, 268–69, 269t
declines in use of, 96–97
drivers of usage of, 210, 266
in market infrastructure, 67
penetration of, 57, 57f, 231, 231f, 266, 267t

for pension payments, 171, 231–32
policy recommendations for, 121
in rural vs. urban areas, 96
transaction volume with, 232, 232f
bankruptcy laws, 19, 39, 104, 246
banks and banking services
accounts. See account ownership
branch density. See bank branch density
cards. See banking cards
closure of, 101–2
credits and deposits as percentage of GDP, 49, 49f, 129, 130f, 189, 190f
currency structure of accounts, 236f, 237
deposits as share of liabilities, 258, 259t
dynamics of penetration, 236–37, 236f
financial education by, 37, 38, 217
foreign ownership of, 126n1, 229, 260–61
insurance. See deposit insurance
lending. See loans
lines of credit. See credit lines
liquidity requirements for, 189
mobile. See mobile banking
performance indicators for, 261–62, 261t
privatization of, 86
prudential measures for, 63, 63t
regulation of, 22–23, 63, 105–6, 152, 207, 242–43
sector credit portfolios, 191, 192f, 258, 258f
state ownership of, 86, 189, 258–60, 259t, 282
telephone banking, 17, 25, 61, 135
text message banking, 17, 135
vulnerabilities of, 190–91
barriers to financial inclusion
account nonuse, 274, 274t, 275
autonomy limitations for financial institutions, 241, 252
bankruptcy laws, 19, 39, 104
demand-side. See demand-side barriers to financial inclusion
information asymmetry, 18, 38, 62, 147, 177
institutional, 19, 104, 149
in insurance sector, 62, 233
land registration, 104–5
macroeconomic variables and, 240, 252
in rural vs. urban areas, 18, 19, 48
for SMEs, 205, 219
supply-side. See supply-side barriers to financial inclusion
transparency of financial institutions, 241–42

blockchain technologies, 137
borrowing. *See* loans

C

capital markets. *See* securities markets
cash transfer programs, 4, 38
CBA. *See* Central Bank of Armenia
CBAR. *See* Central Bank of Azerbaijan Republic
CBU. *See* Central Bank of Uzbekistan
Central Asia and South Caucasus (CASC). *See also specific countries*
 banking services in, 7–11, 8–10f
 delivery technologies in, 17
 domestic credit to private sector in, 131, 132f
 financial education programs in, 34–38, 34–36t, 42
 financial literacy in, 33–34, 41
 indicators of financial inclusion in, 5–7, 6–7t
 insurance sector in, 11–12, 11–12f
 loans in, 9–11, 10f, 15t, 16
 pension system in, 12–13
 political and economic instability in, x, 2, 39
 regulatory framework in, 19–26, 20–22t, 41
 remittances in, 13
 strategies for financial inclusion in, 13, 14–15t, 26–32, 27–28t, 39–40
Central Bank of Armenia (CBA)
 consumer protection and, 24, 64
 deposit insurance from, 25, 64
 financial education initiatives from, 36, 47, 75, 77, 78
 financial infrastructure development by, 31, 47
 mediation services from, 64–65
 minimum capital requirements, 51
 regulatory role of, 47, 48, 62
 remittances system from, 68
 strategies for financial inclusion, 65–68
Central Bank of Azerbaijan Republic (CBAR)
 on ATM distribution, 93
 financial education initiatives from, 113, 116–18
 on lending rates, 94–95
 monetary policy from, 99, 105, 111
 regulatory role of, 105, 106
 shortcomings of, 112
 withdrawal of bank licenses by, 101
Central Bank of Uzbekistan (CBU)
 banking card penetration in, 266

bank lending as reported by, 258
 consumer protection and, 278
 financial literacy initiatives from, 280
 on foreign-owned banks, 260–61
 interest rates set by, 275
 on mobile banking services, 266
 policy recommendations for, 283
 regulatory role of, 277
Centre for Economic Research (CER), 262, 266, 269–71, 275
collateral
 gender differences in loan requirements, 274
 moveable registry for, 68, 104
 policy recommendations regarding, 221
 requirements as barriers to financial inclusion, 19, 39, 102, 205, 276
 warehouse receipts as, 213
Consultative Group to Assist the Poor (CGAP), 3
consumer protection
 dispute resolution and, 24–25, 107–8, 123
 hotlines for, 41, 64, 278
 policy recommendations for, 122–23, 283–84
 regulations related to, 153–54, 160, 207–9, 208t
 trust in financial system and, xi, 24
contract financing, 213
corruption, 4, 38, 39, 203, 204, 219
credit databases
 development of, xi, 30–31, 152
 information asymmetry and, 30, 67, 248
 limitations of, 110–11
 policy recommendations for, 120
 in relationship-based banking model, 147
credit guarantees, 31–32, 40, 102, 111, 211–12, 248–49
credit lines, 10, 10f, 172, 271, 274–75, 276t
credit organizations
 agricultural loans held by, 56, 56f
 assets held by, 50, 50f
 consumer protection and, 247
 financial education by, 251
 mobile banking and, 238–39
 nonbank. *See* nonbank credit institutions
 products and services from, 16, 238, 242
 prudential measures for, 63, 63t
 regulatory framework for, 50, 51t, 63, 243
 remittances and, 238
 in rural areas, 79, 242

crowdfunding, 40, 103, 137
cryptocurrencies, 137

D

debit cards, 135–36, 173, 268–69, 269*t*
debt management programs, 118
de-dollarization initiatives, 24, 144, 153–54, 162, 191
default on loans, 142–43, 147
demand-side barriers to financial inclusion
  financial literacy rates, 61–62, 79, 103, 149
  funding issues, 19, 39, 61, 240–41
  knowledge of financial products, 19, 39, 61, 103, 177
  poverty, 61, 79, 148–49, 203
  trust in financial system and, 19, 24, 39, 62, 177, 204
deposit insurance
  bankruptcies and, 25, 247
  financial stability from, 151–52
  guarantee fund programs, 64, 176, 279
  interest and, 108
  public awareness of, 247–48
  revocation of bank licenses and, 109
digital financial services, 7, 17, 109, 120, 283
dispute resolution, 24–25, 107–8, 123

E

EBRD. *See* European Bank for Reconstruction and Development
education. *See* financial education
electronic banking. *See* mobile banking
electronic identification, 29, 70, 265
e-money, 7, 25, 40, 171, 176
Enterprise Georgia, 150–51, 150*n*32
entrepreneurs. *See also* small and medium-sized enterprises
  access to finance for, 90, 102
  barriers to financial inclusion for, 205–6, 274, 275
  development training for, 116
  financial education for, 42, 161
  in shadow economy, 18, 203
  state support for, 31, 111, 211–13
  women as, 26–27, 30, 214, 220
European Bank for Reconstruction and Development (EBRD)
  on account ownership, 172
  financial literacy initiatives from, 118, 215
  financial resources from, 29–30, 248
  Life in Transition Survey, 265–66
  on saving behavior, 135
  expenditures, attitudes toward, 155, 155*f*

F

females. *See* women
FIMSA. *See* Financial Market Supervisory Authority
Financial Capability and Inclusion Survey (FCIS), 62, 91–93, 96–100, 107, 113–14, 136
Financial Capability Barometer (FCB), 47, 72, 73, 78, 79
financial education. *See also* financial literacy
  assessment of effectiveness, 78, 179–81
  by banks, 37, 38, 217
  consultations on, 38
  on debt management, 118
  definitions of, 33, 113*n*6
  elements of, 42
  for entrepreneurs, 42, 161
  institutions involved in promotion of, 36–37, 42, 158, 215, 251
  by MFIs, 37, 38, 217
  quantitative goals for, 73, 74*t*
  rationale for, 4, 32
  in rural areas, 75, 78, 217
  in school curriculum, 38, 75, 77, 122, 159, 217
  for SMEs, 30, 33, 42, 161
  strategies and programs for, 26, 34–36, 34–36*t*, 158
  target groups for, 37, 42, 158–59, 181, 250
  training and workshops on, 37, 250
  for women, 42, 118
financial inclusion
  accessibility issues, 17, 29
  barriers to. *See* barriers to financial inclusion
  definitions of, 3–4, 126, 171
  delivery technologies for, 17
  gender differences in, 92
  as growth and development strategy, 1–2, 46, 257
  income level and, 1, 4, 92, 161
  indicators of, 2, 5–7, 6–7*t*
  institutions involved in, 13, 110, 167, 209
  policies for promotion of, 26–32, 27–28*t*, 120–21
  products and services for, 16–17, 29–30, 120–21
  rationale for, x, 4–5, 38

regulation of. *See* regulatory framework
in rural areas, 40, 249
for SMEs, 26–27, 40, 150–52, 150nn32–33
strategies for. *See* strategies for financial inclusion
financial literacy. *See also* financial education; Global Financial Literacy survey; International Survey of Adult Financial Literacy Competencies
assessment of, 113–19, 154–55, 183, 215, 215t
definitions of, 33, 113n6
gender differences in, 72, 73
heterogeneity of, 70
importance of, x, 32–33, 103, 214, 284
income level and, 161, 215–16
institutions involved in promotion of, 116–17, 215, 251
policy recommendations for, 121–22, 183, 220, 253
product awareness and, 114–15, 115f, 157, 160, 166
program for, 75, 76–77t, 117–18
in rural vs. urban areas, 73, 116
status of, 19, 33–34, 41, 113
target groups for, 117–18, 122
training for, 250, 280–81
in transition economies, 279, 280f
Financial Market Supervisory Authority (FIMSA), 101–2, 105, 109, 110, 112
financial mediation services, 64–65
financial regulation. *See* regulatory framework
financial technology (fintech)
cryptocurrencies, 137
development of, 40
drivers of usage of, 136
e-money, 7, 25, 40, 171, 176
experimentation with, 242
mobile banking. *See* mobile banking
policy recommendations for, 162
regulatory framework for, 25–26, 109
telephone banking, 17, 25, 61, 135
text message banking, 17, 135
Framework on Equitable Economic Development (ASEAN), 1

G
G20. *See* Group of Twenty
GDP. *See* gross domestic product
gender differences. *See also* women
account ownership and, 55, 268–69
collateral requirements and, 274
in decision making, 281, 281t

financial inclusion and, 92
financial literacy and, 72, 73
loan service use and, 269
Georgia, 126–62. *See also* National Bank of Georgia
account ownership in, 8, 9f, 140, 140t
ATM distribution in, 7, 138–39, 139f
bank branch density in, 7, 8f, 127n4, 128, 138–39, 138f
banking card penetration in, 135, 136
barriers to financial inclusion in, 18, 19, 146–49
consumer protection in, 24, 153–54
credit databases in, 30–31, 152
delivery technologies in, 17
deposit insurance in, 25, 151–52
financial education programs in, 35t, 36–38, 42, 158–59
financial literacy in, 34, 154–58, 160–61
financial system in, 127–37, 127n3, 128f, 130–32f
indicators of financial inclusion in, 5, 6–7t, 138–45, 159–60
insurance sector in, 11, 11–12f, 132
loans in, 9, 10f, 15t, 16, 130–31, 131–32f, 141–43, 141–42f
mobile banking in, 135, 148
pension system in, 12, 132–33
policy recommendations for, 161–62
political and economic instability in, 126
poverty rates in, 127, 127n5, 148–49
regulatory framework in, 20t, 22, 24, 25, 150–54
remittances in, 13, 134–35
saving behavior in, 132, 132n12, 149, 156, 157f
securities market in, 133–34, 133nn14–15
SMEs in, 127–29, 143–45, 144t, 145f, 160
strategies for financial inclusion in, 13, 14t, 26, 27t
Global Financial Literacy survey, 33–34, 61–62, 62n6, 72, 279
Global Findex survey
on account ownership, 91, 265, 266, 275
on borrowing behavior, 96, 96t, 197
financial inclusion indicators from, 2, 9, 197, 197t, 234, 234–35t
on national identity cards, 264–65
on saving behavior, 96, 96t, 173, 269
on usage of financial services, 54–55, 55t, 200
Global Partnership for Financial Inclusion, 1, 3
Global Payment Systems Survey, 135, 136

gross domestic product (GDP)
  account ownership and, 8, 9f
  banking sector credit to GDP ratio, 258, 258f
  credits and deposits as percentage of, 49, 49f, 129, 130f, 189, 190f
  domestic credit and, 96, 96t, 262, 262f
  economic structure by sector, 226–27, 226f
  financial sector assets as percentage of, 128–29, 128f
  insurance assets-to-GDP ratio, 50, 50f, 169
  insurance premium volume and, 11–12, 11–12f
  loans and credit lines in relation to, 9–10, 10f
  purchasing power parity adjusted, 148n31
  SME loans as percentage of, 143
Group of 20 (G20), x, 1, 32, 46, 141n25
guarantor protection, 65

H
health insurance
  e-health infrastructure for, 62, 80
  lack of access to, 80
  mandatory, 40–41, 62, 70
  market share of, 132
  underutilization of, 62
High-Level Principles on National Strategies for Financial Education (OECD/INFE), 32

I
IFC. See International Finance Corporation
IMF. See International Monetary Fund
INFE. See International Network on Financial Education)
information asymmetry
  as barrier to financial inclusion, 18, 38, 62, 147, 177
  credit databases and, 30, 67, 248
  e-health infrastructure and, 80
  moveable collateral registry and, 68
insurance and insurance sector
  agricultural, 62, 70, 81, 98, 151
  assets held by, 50, 51f, 65, 132, 169, 195–96
  barriers to financial inclusion in, 62, 233
  contracts signed in, 57, 58f
  deposit. See deposit insurance
  in development process, 97–98
  drivers of growth in, 46, 50–51

health. See health insurance
life, 11, 11f, 98
motor liability, 40, 46, 50–51, 57, 65
ratio of premium volume to GDP, 11–12, 11–12f
regulation of, 105, 153, 153n42, 233, 246
in rural vs. urban areas, 98, 271
underdevelopment of, 167
underutilization of services, 40–41, 80, 98
interest rates
  caps on, 41
  on commercial loans, 94–95, 274–75, 276f
  from MFIs, 188, 194, 230
  as obstacle to borrowing, 40, 60, 102
  in peer-to-peer lending, 136
  regulation of, 153, 207
  for SMEs, 144–45, 145f
  subsidies for, 31–32, 178, 212
International Finance Corporation (IFC)
  collateral registries and, 104
  consumer protection and, 247
  financial education initiatives from, 37, 251
  financial literacy data from, 250
  mobile banking services survey by, 17, 238
  on non-core function of commercial banks, 277
International Financial Reporting Standards, 22, 41, 134, 150, 245
International Monetary Fund (IMF)
  Financial Access Survey, 55
  indicators of financial inclusion from, 5
  methodology for tracking nonperforming loans, 143
  on regulatory framework, 277
  on state-owned banks, 259–60
  structural adjustments by, 187
International Network on Financial Education (INFE), 32, 33, 117
International Survey of Adult Financial Literacy Competencies
  dimensions covered by, 71
  on lending behavior, 149, 157
  participants in, 71n10
  results of, 33–34, 71–72, 71t
  on saving behavior, 79
  sociodemographic background for, 72
internet banking. See mobile banking

K
Kazakhstan, 166–84. See also National Bank of Kazakhstan

accessibility issues in, 29
account ownership in, 8–9, 9f, 39, 171–72, 172t
ATM distribution in, 7, 173
bank branch density in, 7, 8f, 167–68, 169t
banking card penetration in, 173
barriers to financial inclusion in, 19, 177
consumer protection in, 24
credit guarantees and subsidies in, 32
currency devaluation in, 2, 169, 176
deposit insurance in, 25, 176
financial education programs in, 35t, 36, 37, 178–82
financial literacy in, 180, 181
financial system in, 167–71, 168–69t
indicators of financial inclusion in, 5, 6–7t, 171–75, 174t
insurance sector in, 11–12, 11–12f, 167, 169
loans in, 9–11, 10f, 15t, 16, 39, 169–70
mobile banking in, 171
pension system in, 12–13, 170
policy recommendations for, 182–84
regulatory framework in, 21t, 22–25, 175–77
remittances in, 170
saving behavior in, 173
securities market in, 170, 181–82
strategies for financial inclusion in, 13, 14t, 26, 28t, 166–67, 178
Kyrgyz Republic, 187–221. *See also* National Bank of the Kyrgyz Republic
account ownership in, 8, 9f
agricultural sector support in, 212–13
ATM distribution in, 7, 198, 199t
bank branch density in, 7, 8f, 198, 199t
banking card penetration in, 199, 210
barriers to financial inclusion in, 18, 19, 203–6, 204t, 219
consumer protection in, 24, 207–9, 208t
credit databases in, 31
credit guarantees in, 32, 211–12
deposit insurance in, 25
financial education programs in, 35t, 36–38, 42, 216–18, 220
financial literacy in, 34, 214–18, 215t, 218f, 220
financial system in, 188–96, 190f, 192–93f
indicators of financial inclusion in, 5, 6–7t, 196–200, 197t
insurance sector in, 11, 11–12f, 195–96
loans in, 9, 10f, 15t, 16–17, 196
mobile banking in, 199–200, 210, 219
policy recommendations for, 218–21

political and economic instability in, 187–88, 204–5
poverty rates in, 187, 188, 196, 201, 202f
products and services offered in, 16–17, 29, 198, 198f
regulatory framework in, 21t, 22–25, 206–7
remittances in, 13, 201–3, 202f, 220
saving behavior in, 216, 216f
securities market in, 194–95
SMEs in, 200–201, 201f, 211–12
strategies for financial inclusion in, 13, 14t, 26–27, 28t, 39, 209–14

L

land registration, 104–5, 246
lending. *See* loans
life insurance, 11, 11f, 98
Life in Transition Survey, 240, 241, 265–66
line of credit. *See* credit lines
literacy. *See* financial literacy
loans. *See also* credit organizations; microfinance institutions
accessibility to, 17, 39
agricultural, 56, 56f, 212–13
barriers to obtaining, 40, 274–75, 276f
crowdfunding, 40, 103, 137
default on, 142–43, 147
by financial institution, 15t, 16, 95, 95t
GDP and use of, 9–11, 10f
gender differences in, 269
household loans as share of commercial bank loans, 130, 131f
interest rates for. *See* interest rates
mortgages, 56f, 57, 69, 176, 210
nonperforming. *See* nonperforming loans
from pawnshops, 18, 131, 203, 219
peer-to-peer, 40, 136–37, 283
reasons for nonuse of, 241, 275, 276t
refinancing, 134, 176
regulation of, 24, 153
in rural vs. urban areas, 96
sectoral breakdown of, 95–96, 95f, 229–30, 230f
use by income quartile, 97, 97f

M

medium-sized enterprises. *See* small and medium-sized enterprises
men. *See* gender differences
microfinance institutions (MFIs)
assets held by, 128, 129, 193, 193f, 229
barriers to entry for, 18

capital requirements for, 244–45, 244f
consumer protection and, 247
development of, 1, 187, 192–94
financial education by, 37, 38, 217
in financial inclusion policy, 178, 219
group lending by, 16–17, 192, 207
growth of, 16, 39, 89, 128, 169
household and small business lending by, 130
interest rates from, 188, 194, 230
licensing and status of, 23, 106–7, 193, 194
liquidity of, 129n7
operational costs for, 147, 194, 248
product and service offerings of, 90
regulation of, 22–23, 106–7, 170, 206–7, 243–45, 277
repossession of property by, 142, 160
sector trends for, 89–90, 90t
use by income quartile, 97, 97f
mobile banking
 accessibility to, 29, 109, 135, 199–200, 219
 account ownership and, 236
 credit organizations and, 238–39
 electronic payment systems for, 266, 267t
 growth of, 7, 17, 40, 58–59, 59t, 171
 internet usage and, 148, 266, 268
 promotion strategies, 210, 283
 regulatory framework for, 25
 service channels for, 238, 239t
 uses of, 238, 239t, 240f
money laundering, 18, 38, 205
money-transfer operators (MTOs), 13, 100, 135
moral hazard problem, 31, 151
mortgages, 56f, 57, 69, 176, 210
motor liability insurance, 40, 46, 50–51, 57, 65

N

National Bank of Georgia (NBG)
 consumer protection and, 143, 160
 on cryptocurrencies, 137
 financial education initiatives from, 151, 158–59
 methodology for tracking nonperforming loans, 143
 refinance loans from, 134
 regulatory role of, 152–53, 152n40, 156
 on remittance money-transfer units, 135
 structural transformation of banking system by, 126–27
 survey research from, 157–58, 160

National Bank of Kazakhstan (NBK)
 account ownership statistics from, 172
 consumer protection and, 176
 financial education initiatives from, 179–81, 183
 on national payment systems, 168
 regulatory role of, 175
 securities owned by, 170
National Bank of Tajikistan (NBT)
 on account ownership, 235
 autonomy limitations for, 241, 252
 bank licenses revoked by, 229
 consumer protection and, 243, 247
 on credit databases, 248
 financial literacy initiatives from, 249–50
 on foreign currency transactions, 227
 policy recommendations for, 253
 regulatory role of, 233, 242–45
 on remittances, 238
National Bank of the Kyrgyz Republic (NBKR)
 bank licenses issued by, 187
 consumer protection and, 209
 de-dollarization initiatives of, 191
 financial education initiatives from, 217, 220
 financial literacy survey conducted by, 215, 215t
 liquidity requirements for banking sector from, 189
 non-cash payment promotion by, 199
 regulatory role of, 192–94, 196, 206–7
 on remittance spending patterns, 202
 takeover of banks by, 204
National Strategy for Financial Education (NSFE), 47, 66, 73–75, 74t, 77–79
NBCIs. *See* nonbank credit institutions
NBG. *See* National Bank of Georgia
NBK. *See* National Bank of Kazakhstan
NBKR. *See* National Bank of the Kyrgyz Republic
NBT. *See* National Bank of Tajikistan
nonbank credit institutions (NBCIs)
 closure of, 101–2
 credit registry information for, 111
 decline of, 89
 policy recommendations for, 121
 product and service offerings of, 89f, 90
 regulation of, 22–23, 105–7, 126n2
 use by income quartile, 97, 97f
nonperforming loans (NPLs)
 accumulation at commercial banks, 241, 245, 251

credit guarantees and, 31
as financial performance indicator, 261
macroeconomic variables and, 240
methodology for tracking, 143
as share of total loans, 143, 160, 190, 229, 229*f*
NSFE. *See* National Strategy for Financial Education

O

Organisation for Economic Cooperation and Development (OECD)
financial literacy as defined by, 33
High-Level Principles on National Strategies for Financial Education, 32
promotion of financial education by, 215
SME policy index, 60
survey data. *See* International Survey of Adult Financial Literacy Competencies
on unbanked vs. underserved populations, 171

P

pawnshops
assets held by, 129
financial services from, 101, 128
loans from, 18, 131, 203, 219
regulation of, 105, 106, 153
transformation of MFIs into, 194
payment service providers (PSPs), 17, 135, 139, 239, 249
peer-to-peer (P2P) lending, 40, 136–37, 283
pension systems
accumulative, 170
banking cards for, 171, 231–32
defined-contribution, 12, 99
extra-budgetary funds, 271
in formal vs. informal sector, 12–13
governmental, 132
mandatory, 271
multi-pillar, 46, 51, 68
pay-as-you-go, 12
regulation of, 153, 237
self-management of, 32–33
supplementary systems, 133
postal services, 40, 58, 80, 101, 120
poverty
as barrier to financial inclusion, 61, 79, 148–49, 203
economic decline and, 187
financial inclusion in reduction of, 5, 38, 46

international comparisons, 127, 127*n*5
multidimensional, 188
remittances in alleviation of, 134, 201, 202*f*, 203, 220
savings behavior and, 196
Produce in Georgia, 150, 150*n*33
PSPs. *See* payment service providers
P2P. *See* peer-to-peer lending.

R

regulatory framework, 19–26
bankruptcy laws, 19, 39, 104, 246
banks in, 22–23, 63, 105–6, 152, 207, 242–43
as barrier to financial inclusion, 18, 38, 61, 146–48, 177, 242
for consumers. *See* consumer protection
credit organizations in, 50, 51*t*, 63, 243
deposit insurance in. *See* deposit insurance
for e-money, 171, 176
for financial technology, 25–26, 109
for guarantor protection, 65
institutional actors in, 22–23
insurance companies in, 105, 153, 153*n*42, 233, 246
for interest rates, 153, 207
legal basis for, 120, 242–43
for loans, 24, 153
macroeconomic and financial stability within, 107
MFIs in, 22–23, 106–7, 170, 206–7, 243–45, 277
NBCIs in, 22–23, 105–7, 126*n*2
overview of features, 19, 20–22*t*
pawnshops in, 105, 106, 153
for pension systems, 153, 237
risks addressed by, 24
shortcomings of, xi, 41
transparency in, 41
religious considerations, 9, 39, 172, 275, 282
remittances
economic role of, 2, 57, 134, 170, 226
formal vs. informal transfer channels, 58, 59*t*
interbank payment systems for, 99, 100*t*
macroeconomic variables and, 237–38, 240
money-transfer operators and, 13, 100, 135
poverty reduction through, 134, 201, 202*f*, 203, 220
spending patterns and, 202–3

unified system for, 68
repossession of property, 142, 160
retirement savings, 132, 132n12, 156, 157f, 173. *See also* pension systems
RKDF. *See* Russian Kyrgyz Development Fund
rural areas
  account ownership in, 9, 146, 146n28
  ATMs in, 53–54, 54f, 61, 79
  bank penetration in, 9
  barriers to financial inclusion in, 18, 19, 48
  credit organizations in, 79, 242
  financial education in, 75, 78, 217
  financial inclusion strategies for, 40, 249
  financial literacy in, 73, 116
  infrastructure gaps in, 80
  insurance sector in, 98, 271
  loans in, 96
  microfinance in, 17
  policy recommendations for, 120, 121
  remittance income in, 58, 203
  underserved populations in, 160
Russian Kyrgyz Development Fund (RKDF), 32, 211–13, 219

S

savings
  attitudes towards, 70–73, 79
  formal methods for, 96, 96t
  income level and, 149, 173, 196
  passive forms of, 216, 216f
  for retirement, 132, 132n12, 156, 157f, 173
  strategies for promotion of, 68
securities markets, 100–101, 133–34, 133nn14–15, 170, 181–82, 194–95
shadow economies, 18, 195, 203
small and medium-sized enterprises (SMEs). *See also* entrepreneurs
  access to finance for, 60, 60f, 90–91, 102, 160
  account ownership by, 172
  assistance programs for, 69, 69t
  barriers to financial inclusion for, 205, 219
  development of, 200–201, 201f
  employment by, 59–60, 69
  financial education for, 30, 33, 42, 161
  financial inclusion strategies for, 26–27, 40, 150–52, 150nn32–33
  financing options for, 13, 16, 31–32, 86, 87
  indicators of financial inclusion for, 143–45, 144t, 271–74, 272–73t

marginal return to capital in, 4
  policy recommendations for, 161, 220–21
  sources of financial services for, 127–29
  state support for, 211–14, 214t
  subsidies for, 111
  transparency of operations in, 102
South Caucasus. *See* Central Asia and South Caucasus
stock exchange. *See* securities markets
strategies for financial inclusion
  accessibility, 29
  assessment of effectiveness, 111–13
  credit databases. *See* credit databases
  credit guarantees and subsidies, 31–32, 40, 111, 211–12, 248–49
  education. *See* financial education
  electronic identification, 29, 70, 265
  elements of, 13, 14–15t
  innovative products and services, 29–30
  institutional actors in, 110, 167
  market infrastructure development, 65–68
  moveable collateral registry, 68
  national strategies, 26–29, 27–28t, 39, 166–67, 178
  for SMEs, 69, 69t, 211–12
  strategic road maps, 109–10
subsidies, 31–32, 111, 178, 212
supply-side barriers to financial inclusion
  bank and NBCI closures, 101–2
  client trust and, 103
  collateral requirements, 19, 39, 102, 205, 276
  cost of financial services, 17–18, 38, 79, 147
  credit data limitations, 102–3
  infrastructure-related, 18–19, 38–39, 61, 79, 146–48, 242
  in insurance sector, 62, 233
  interest rates, 102, 274–75, 276f
  market-driven factors, 17–18, 61, 146
  regulatory factors, 18, 38, 61, 146–48, 177, 242

T

Tajikistan, 225–53. *See also* National Bank of Tajikistan
  accessibility issues in, 29
  account ownership in, 8, 9f, 235
  ATM distribution in, 232, 232f
  bank branch density in, 7, 8f, 227
  banking card penetration in, 231–33, 231–32f

bankruptcy laws in, 246
barriers to financial inclusion in, 18, 19,
  240–42, 252
consumer protection in, 24, 247
credit databases in, 31, 248
credit guarantees in, 32, 248–49
currency devaluation in, 2, 226, 227,
  240, 251
delivery technologies in, 17
deposit insurance in, 25, 247–48
financial education programs in, 36, 36t,
  37, 250–51
financial literacy in, 249–51
financial system in, 225–33, 226f,
  228–32f
indicators of financial inclusion in, 5,
  6–7t, 234–35t, 234–39
insurance sector in, 11–12f, 12, 233, 246
loans in, 10f, 11, 15t, 16, 39, 227–30,
  228–30f
mobile banking in, 236, 238–39, 239t,
  240f
Moody's credit rating for, 241, 241n1
pension system in, 12, 237
policy recommendations for, 252–53
political and economic instability in,
  226
regulatory framework in, 21t, 22–25, 41,
  242–48, 252
remittances in, 2, 13, 29–30, 226, 237–38,
  240
strategies for financial inclusion in, 13,
  15t, 26, 28t, 248–49
technology, financial. *See* financial
  technology
telephone banking, 17, 25, 61, 135
text message banking, 17, 135
third-party motor liability insurance, 40,
  46, 50–51, 57, 65
transparency
  of borrowers, 241
  of electronic funds transfers, 4
  of financial statements, 167, 241–42, 252
  lack of, 60, 219
  in regulatory framework, 41
  of SME operations, 102
  of technology use, 242
trust in financial system
  account ownership and, 275
  consumer protection and, xi, 24
  financial inclusion and, 46, 149
  guarantee funds and, 212
  index of, 204, 204t
  lack of, x, 19, 39, 62, 177

political instability and, 204–5
strategies for improvement, 41, 47, 176
survey research on, 155–56, 156f

U

United Nations Development Programme,
  248
urban areas
  ATMs in, 53–54, 54f, 79
  barriers to financial inclusion in, 48
  financial literacy in, 73, 116
  insurance sector in, 98, 271
  loans in, 96
  money-transfer operators in, 13, 100
  policy recommendations for, 120, 121
Uzbekistan, 257–84. *See also* Central Bank
  of Uzbekistan
  account ownership in, 8, 9f, 39, 265–66,
    268–69, 268t
  ATM distribution in, 262
  bank branch density in, 7, 8f, 263
  banking card penetration in, 266–69,
    267t, 269t
  barriers to financial inclusion in, 19,
    274–76, 274t, 276t
  consumer protection in, 24, 278,
    283–84
  credit databases in, 30
  decision making in, 281, 281t
  delivery technologies in, 17
  deposit insurance in, 25, 279
  domestic credit and GDP per capita,
    262, 262f
  electronic identification in, 265
  exchange rates in, 277–78, 278f
  financial education programs in, 36, 36t,
    37, 279–80
  financial literacy in, 279–81, 280f, 284
  financial system in, 257–65, 258f, 259t,
    261t, 263–65t
  indicators of financial inclusion in, 5,
    6–7t, 265–74, 267–70t, 272–73t
  insurance sector in, 11, 11–12f, 271
  loans in, 9, 10f, 15t, 16, 269, 270t, 276f
  mobile banking in, 266–68, 267t
  pension system in, 12, 271
  policy recommendations for, 281–84
  regulatory framework in, 22–25, 22t,
    277–79
  saving behavior in, 269–70, 270t
  SMEs and large enterprises in, 271–74,
    272–73t
  strategies for financial inclusion in, 13,
    15t, 26, 28t

W

warehouse receipts, 213
women. *See also* gender differences
  access to finance for, 175, 205, 248
  account ownership by, 140
  as entrepreneurs, 26–27, 30, 214, 220
  financial education for, 42, 118
  as MFI borrowers, 17, 192, 219
World Bank. *See also* Global Findex survey
  on access to financial services, 5
  on bankruptcy laws, 104
  capacity building by, 246
  development data from, 60, 167
  Financial Capability and Inclusion Survey, 62, 91–93, 96–100, 107, 113–14, 136
  financial inclusion as defined by, 3
  financial resources from, 30, 248
  Financial System Assessment Program, 245
  on internet usage, 148
  Life in Transition Survey, 240, 266
  on nonbank credit sector, 16, 89
  PPP adjusted GDP per capita from, 148n31
  promotion of financial education by, 215
  securities market support from, 101
  Universal Financial Access 2020 initiative, 46
  World Development Indicators database, 266
World Trade Organization, 119, 169, 175

Lightning Source UK Ltd.
Milton Keynes UK
UKHW020459090519
342370UK00005B/330/P